JaneKettle
1/96

# CORPORATE CITY? PARTNERSHIP, PARTICIPATION AND PARTITION IN URBAN DEVELOPMENT IN LEEDS

# Corporate City?

Partnership, participation and partition
in urban development in Leeds

*Edited by*
GRAHAM HAUGHTON AND COLIN C. WILLIAMS
*CUDEM, School of the Built Environment, Leeds Metropolitan University*

# Avebury

Aldershot • Brookfield USA • Hong Kong • Singapore • Sydney

Published by
Avebury
Ashgate Publishing Limited
Gower House
Croft Road
Aldershot
Hants GU11 3HR
England

Ashgate Publishing Company
Old Post Road
Brookfield
Vermont 05036
USA

**British Library Cataloguing in Publication Data**

Corporate City?: Partnership,
Participation and Partition in Urban
Development in Leeds. - (Urban & Regional
Planning Development Series)
    I. Haughton, Graham  II.  Williams, Colin C.
    III.  Series
    338.942819

    ISBN 1 85972 265 2

**Library of Congress Catalog Card Number:** 95-81146

Printed in Great Britain by
Antony Rowe Ltd, Chippenham, Wiltshire

# Contents

## I  Introduction

v

## II  The economic machine

## III  The environmental challenge: corporate and community responses

# IV  Local capacity and challenges to social segregation

# List of tables

ix

# List of figures

# List of contributors

**Mike Campbell** is Professor of Policy Studies and Head of the Policy Research Institute at Leeds Metropolitan University.

**Max Farrar** is a Senior Lecturer in Sociology, School of Cultural Studies, Leeds Metropolitan University.

**Claire Freeman** is a Senior Lecturer in Planning and Housing at Leeds Metropolitan University.

**Howard Green** is Professor of Small Business Development in the School of the Environment at Leeds Metropolitan University.

**Graham Haughton** is Professor of Local Economic Development at Leeds Metropolitan University and Head of CUDEM.

**David Hick** is a part-time lecturer in the School of Built Environment, Leeds Metropolitan University.

**Eamon Judge** is Professor of Economics and Spatial Policy in Leeds Business School, Leeds Metropolitan University.

**Jane Kettle** is a Lecturer in Planning and Housing at Leeds Metropolitan University.

**Christine Leigh** is joint director of the Yorkshire and Humberside Regional Observatory and a Senior Lecturer in the School of Geography, University of Leeds.

**Celia Moran** is a Senior Lecturer in Planning and Housing at Leeds Metropolitan University.

**Peter Roberts** is Professor of European Strategic Planning at the University of Dundee, and Emeritus Professor of Urban Planning at Leeds Metropolitan University.

**Leigh Sear** was a post-graduate researcher with CUDEM and is currently a Researcher at Durham Business School, University of Durham.

**Derek Senior** is a Principal Lecturer in Planning and Housing at Leeds Metropolitan University.

**John Shutt** is Professor of Regional Business Development, Leeds Business School, Leeds Metropolitan University.

**Lindsay Smales** is a Senior Lecturer in Planning and Housing at Leeds Metropolitan University.

**John Stillwell** is Senior Lecturer and Head of Department in the School of Geography, University of Leeds, and editor of *The Regional Review*.

**Ian Strange** is an ESRC Research Fellow and Lecturer in Planning and Housing at Leeds Metropolitan University.

**Kevin Thomas** is a Senior Lecturer in Planning and Housing at Leeds Metropolitan University.

**Rhodri Thomas** is a Principal Lecturer in the Centre for the Study of Small Tourism and Hospitality Firms, Leeds Metropolitan University.

**Adam Tickell** is an ESRC Research Fellow and Lecturer in the Department of Geography at the University of Manchester.

**David Whitney** is Head of Planning and Housing in the School of the Built Environment at Leeds Metropolitan University.

**Colin C Williams** is a Senior Lecturer in Urban Development and Planning at Leeds Metropolitan University.

# Preface

> Leeds is usually a dull, spiritless and inert town. It is awanting in social as well as political activity and energy. It is an inert mass always difficult to be moved. It wants the enthusiasm of Manchester, the enterprize of Glasgow, the volatile gaiety of Liverpool, the intense feeling of Birmingham and the power of London.
> (*Leeds Times,* 16th December 1843; cited in Fraser, p.462).

Leeds has often had a poor press, and indeed for much of the post-war period the city got very little press at all, seemingly lacking the glamour or drama of other cities. One of the largest cities in England has managed to generate few lasting images of itself in the national psyche. The feeling that Leeds is in some way less characterful and distinctive than other major British cities persists in many minds: somehow, Leeds for a long time failed to project itself, either positively or negatively, onto the national consciousness. Yet in recent years, a more positive image has begun to seep out, of a city able to withstand national recession rather better than most, with a buoyant services sector and investment in new cultural initiatives, from creating a 24 hour city to building the West Yorkshire Playhouse complex. Added to this, the city's leaders boast of a new spirit of public-private partnership, most visibly signalled in the Leeds Initiative, a partnership vehicle which lies at the heart of the current attempts to create a Corporate City. As political and business leaders have begun to assert a more positive assessment of the city's achievements, the 'grey' image of Leeds has been gradually replaced by some much more positive assessments in the national press too.

This book takes as its starting point, the need to look at the way in which the city of Leeds has undergone a remarkable transformation, particularly over the past decade, from a recession ravaged almost archetypical northern city, to one which has seemingly turned the tide, and is building a strong service sector base to replace some of the many manufacturing jobs which have been lost. The arrival of new businesses and activities, notably in financial services - with the growth of telebanking and legal services especially prominent - has heightened the sense that the city has a claim to be one of the most successful provincial cities in the country. With a strong egalitarian streak still in evidence across the city, the success of some sectors and people within the local economy has nonetheless raised widespread concerns, amongst politicians, business leaders, academics and others, that a two-track city has emerged, with a growing social polarisation between those able to share in the success of the city, and those sidelined, unemployed, under-employed, underpaid or forced to work in exploitative conditions.

This book is the third edited book undertaken by the Centre of Urban Development and Environmental Management (CUDEM), based on the Planning and Housing group at Leeds Metropolitan University. The previous books were *Perspectives towards Sustainable Environmental Development,* edited by Colin Williams and Graham Haughton, and *Reinventing a Region: restructuring in West Yorkshire,* edited by Graham Haughton and David Whitney. Both books were published in 1994 by Avebury. In addition, the Yorkshire and Humberside Regional Research Observatory in 1995 published *Yorkshire and Humberside: monitoring the past, mapping the future,* edited by John Stillwell and Christine Leigh (available from RERO, School of Geography, University of Leeds). The regional context for this book about Leeds has been fairly clearly set out in two of these books, *Reinventing a Region,* and *Monitoring the past, mapping the future,* and the interested reader is referred to these. Given that this regional context setting has already been done, we have sought to avoid duplication here, though inevitably and rightly, local processes of change are set within the context of regional, national and international structures and dynamics.

We are particularly pleased that we have been joined in producing this particular book by colleagues from other parts of the University, and also colleagues from the Universities of Leeds, Manchester, Dundee and Durham, who all bring valuable additional knowledge and insights into the development of Leeds in recent years. In addition, we would like to offer a general expression of thanks to CUDEM researchers Andrea Bottomley, Steve Littlewood, Mark Sage and Aidan While, all of whom helped in various ways in putting together this book.

# I
# INTRODUCTION

# 1 Leeds: A case of second city syndrome?

*Graham Haughton and Colin C. Williams*

## Introduction - Leeds a corporate city?

The city council has worked hard in association with the Leeds Chamber of Commerce to launch the concept of the corporate city - the idea of a partnership between the business sector, national government departments, and the city's major institutions to present and market Leeds to the rest of the country and the world, and to work together in promoting the mutually beneficial improvement of the city as a whole (Burt and Grady, 1994, p.249).

To sell itself effectively in Europe, the City needs a clear, corporate identity. The Initiative sees this as a priority...
    Corporate Identity is often taken to mean a logo and a visual system that goes with it. It is far more than that. It is the means by which the city can express what it is, where it is going and how it intends to get there (Leeds Initiative, Annual Report 1990/91, p.3).

This book sets out to examine in detail the many different factors which have contributed to the distinctive restructuring of one of Britain's leading provincial cities, Leeds, a city of 717,400 people in 1991 (Leeds Development Agency, 1994, p.1: census estimate revision).
    From an archetypal prosperous northern manufacturing centre, once at the heart of the world's textiles and clothing trade, the economy of Leeds has been radically transformed in recent years, entering a period of deindustrialization and attendant recession, possibly culminating in the infamous inner city 'riots' of the early 1980s. Since then, the city's

3

economy overall has assumed a more upward trajectory, with Leeds widely heralded as a national success story (Chapters 3 and 4). But for all the signs of economic success, the city remains a deeply divided one, not least in terms of class, gender and race, as the rich grow richer, and do not necessarily choose to live in the city, and as the poor grow in number, with relatively little choice about where in the city they can live.

The definition of the city of Leeds used here is the metropolitan district of Leeds, created by local government reform in 1974 in a move which saw the city expand to absorb surrounding areas such as Otley, Aireborough, Horsforth, Pudsey, Morley, Rothwell, Garforth, Wetherby and Boston Spa. These additions have added to the sense of Leeds being a collection of villages, and now towns, each with their own distinctive identities. It is fair to say that for different people and for different purposes, Leeds can still be taken as anything from the city centre area to the metropolitan district, and even *in extremis,* a metropolitan region covering much of Yorkshire (Brown, 1967; Hartley, 1980). This latter perspective is now rare, reflecting the municipal imperialist tendencies of earlier generations of civic leaders, some of whom strove hard to extend the city's boundaries outwards in an attempt to consolidate Leeds' position as the regional centre of Yorkshire (Chapter 2). As the expansionary aspirations of the city's leaders have dampened in recent years, our adoption here of a definition of Leeds centred on the existing city boundaries is a reasonable representation of what most people now accept to be the city of Leeds.

The present administrative boundaries of the Leeds metropolitan district were created in the 1974 local government reforms, together with those of the West Yorkshire Metropolitan County Council. This two-tier arrangement was abandoned in 1986 with the abolition of metropolitan county authority, at which time Leeds became a more powerful unitary metropolitan district authority with enhanced resources and powers, notably in planning, transport and economic development (Haughton, Morgan and Whitney, 1994).

As the introductory quotes highlight, in recent years city leaders have set out to create a corporate city, where all the main institutional stakeholders come together to promote the interests of the city, bringing to the same table the public and private sectors in ways not seen in Leeds for some years. Gone, it is hoped, are the days of antagonism between public and private sectors; banished too are the eras of city father paternalism and municipal socialism, supposedly swept away on the tide of growing public-private partnership, with its particular vision of a future for the city of Leeds.

Our intention in this book is to examine the recent development of Leeds, in particular focusing on the ways in which economic and social fortunes are being reshaped, consciously and sub-consciously in pursuit of the city's new growth agenda. The Leeds Initiative currently forms the core of the so-called

4

corporate city, involving an alliance of 'the great and good', the local authority, the chamber of commerce, the chamber of trade, the two universities, Yorkshire Post Newspapers, the Government Office for Yorkshire and Humberside, the Leeds Development Corporation (until it was wound down in April 1995), the Leeds Training and Enterprise Council and the regional trades union congress. In many respects it is already proving an exemplary success: but it is a partial success story, with the main participants of the corporate city still failing to engage with many of the real initiators of change, individual companies and local community groups for instance. Just as some people are incorporated in the mechanisms of the new corporate city, so some are excluded: hence our sub-title, of partnership, participation and partition.

The corporate city notion, as Graham Haughton outlines in greater detail in Chapter Two, centres on ideas of public-private partnership in setting a development agenda for the whole city, which all the main 'stakeholders' of the city can subscribe to, and indeed contribute to. Problems can emerge when certain groups of people who regard themselves as important local stakeholders find themselves either excluded from, or marginalised by, the structures of the corporate city. In Leeds this has involved a tension between the self-declared great and the good, and those working at the grassroots. Awareness of this has begun to impact on the Leeds Initiative, with some slow progress being made towards incorporating community group interests.

So whilst Leeds is in many senses currently pursuing a classic corporate city strategy, it is not without its local specificities, and most importantly perhaps, it is a contested strategy. The various chapters in this book, in different ways, set out to examine the many different processes of decision-making, consensus-building and partnership generation at work in Leeds, for whilst the corporate city agenda is perhaps the most visible, it is far from the only one.

## Second city syndrome?

Leeds proudly proclaims itself as the third largest city in England in population size, after London and Birmingham, and in land area second only to Doncaster amongst the metropolitan districts. It is interesting to reflect that within Britain at the moment, there appears to be a discernible 'second city syndrome,' exemplified by the (selective) upturn in economic fortunes now being experienced in many of Britain's second city economies, notably Leeds, Manchester and Birmingham - all of which would like to be seen as *the* second city for England. Each city has gone its own particular route, but all have been successful in terms of some economic indicators, whilst having

5

a major and continuing residue of acute social and environmental problems. In the case of Leeds, it is difficult to see what has led to such reversals of fortune, whether it is simply a trickle-down effect from global cities, in particular the relocation of back-office activities from London, or whether it has its own dynamic related to the reemergent role of regional centres, whether success comes from specific strategies (land and property flagships, to place marketing and cultural industries promotion), or whether it relates in some way to the emergence of global markets where second cities articulate as administrative centres increasingly at an international level, not least within Europe. As with the global cities debate (cf Sassen, 1991), we also need to examine whether the increasing success of second cities such as Leeds has been at the expense of creating deeper internal social divisions.

It is the internal divisions of the city which are the main focus of this book. In some accounts of the development of western global cities the emergence of dual economies is a central element, where residential and work conditions have tended to polarise, leading to comparisons with the acute social polarisation of some large cities in developing nations (Santos, 1979; Lin, 1995). The existence of major divides in large western cities is generally most evident where enclaves of migrant workers are engaged in low wage, unregulated, exploitative work in a poor work environment, often involving individuals holding multiple jobs, whilst in adjacent areas high wage, specialist office workers work in vastly superior conditions, a juxtaposition particularly evident in New York and Los Angeles (Sassen-Koob, 1984; Sassen, 1991; Mollenkopf and Castells, 1991). The coexistence of these two sectors is far from coincidence: it is argued that the growing cadre of well-paid, high skilled workers in the city *requires* a large body of workers willing to act in low skilled clerical and personal service activities (Sassen, 1991). Similarly, it is argued, high income gentrification and the growing sophistication of consumer demands has fuelled a demand for boutique, specialised goods over mass-production, which in sectors such as clothing, has in some part been met through the increasing use of sweatshop labour. The urban economy also polarises as the very success of some firms raises costs of land and so on, leaving less favoured firms either to seek to cut costs in order to compete still within the city (e.g. through sub-contracting, and use of casualised or illegal labour), or to face the prospect of having to move out (Sassen, 1991, 1994).

In Britain, the continuing flexibilisation of the economy and deregulation of the labour market have seen similar shifts in direction, albeit not yet so accentuated, nor with such clear geographical manifestations of social polarisation. So London is not a mirror image of the New York experience, yet, although parallels are becoming disturbingly evident (see Sassen, 1991; Fainstein, Gordon and Harloe, 1992). Given the emphasis of the global cities literature on the driving role of financial services sector growth over recent years, there is inevitably a concern that the apparent revival of economic fortunes in this sector in Leeds is based on a similar parasitic relationship between a high wage and a no-/low-wage economy.

Social polarisation across the different areas of Leeds appears to be on the increase as gauged by a number of indicators (Leeds Child Poverty Action Group, 1994). John Stillwell and Christine Leigh (Chapter 4) provide a wide ranging review which demonstrates clearly the multi-faceted nature of social polarisation within the city. Although research on the mechanisms at work is still scarce, it is probably safe to assume that there are direct links between the growth sectors of the city and poor work conditions which some are increasingly subject to. Certainly, as Colin Williams and Rhodri Thomas highlight (Chapter 10), there is some evidence of a growing use of casualised labour within a growing informal sector geared to serving the hotel and catering sector, which in turn is primarily meeting the needs of successful city centre businesses.

One consequence of the economic turnaround of Leeds has been a major increase in development pressures, notably for commercial property around the city centre, and also for some strategic locations outside the city centre (Chapter 5). Allied to this, there have been concerted efforts to improve the city centre environment, notably through improved traffic management (Chapter 14), a coordinated approach to city centre management, with a strong design emphasis (Chapter 12), and some attempts at 'greening,' notably with flower displays (Chapter 13). Outlying areas of the city have also been subject to considerable residential building pressures, leading to some denudation of open space in the city (Chapter 13).

Whilst the extremes of nineteenth century air and water pollution associated with rapid industrialisation have long since disappeared, there is still widespread concern about the environment of Leeds, from car congestion to new forms of pollution, such as petrochemical smogs. Responding to such concerns the local authority has been instrumental in creating a strong forum for action in the shape of the Leeds Environment City Initiative. This designation is part of a national scheme, encompassing just four cities which have managed to convince selectors of their 'green credentials.' Operating relatively autonomously, yet very much linked to the Leeds Initiative, this forum and its sub-groups such as the Leeds Business Environment Forum, have begun the process of bringing together the main actors in this field, improving information availability about environmental concerns, and providing a vehicle for some projects to move forward (Chapter 11). One of the key motivations for such policy interventions has been the growing recognition that a high quality of life is a necessary adjunct to achieving success in attracting investment within the city, as part of its shift towards a more service-based economy, competing for investment in this sector at a national and increasingly an international level.

Whilst the academic literature is strongest on the emergent role of global cities, Peter Hall (1995) for one emphasises that there are now a considerable number of sub-global and regional cities which have also experienced a rapid economic resurgence in recent years. This is often based on an ability to attract investment in the producer and consumer service sectors (Chapters 7 and 8). The parallels to Leeds are often strong, and begin to provide some clues as to how the city has managed to ride rather than be submerged by the tide of globalisation, after the initial upsets of deindustrialization from the 1960s to the early 1980s. The growth of successful regional cities, Hall argues, is clearest in countries with a strong federal structure, such as Germany, the United States and Australia, where cities such as Frankfurt, Los Angeles and Melbourne very much carve out their own niche as global cities. Referring to the UK as a more centralised country with a stronger capital, Hall argues that cities such as Birmingham and Manchester (and we would add Leeds) are nonetheless sufficiently vibrant to be counted in this category.

Typically these second tier cities are major administrative and high-order service centres, have a population of 500,000-2,500,000, and in the late twentieth century have been economically successful. To an extent, it can be argued that the loss of large scale or heavy manufacturing, frequently associated with negative environmental impacts and distorting effects on local labour markets, has been essential in allowing cities to shed their former roles in order to re-emerge with a new place in the global economy, occupying a new niche in a reworked international division of labour. At the top end of the second city scale, some cities have succeeded in becoming what Hall calls sub-global cities, poised on the edge of becoming global cities in their own right, part of a core of cities acting as the leading pulses in global financial, innovation, information and cultural flows.

If this is the upside of regional city fortunes in recent years, the downside is that some regional cities are seen to be in some ways remote within their relevant space-economies (national or European for instance) and still dominated by declining industries, a category in which Hall (1995) includes Newcastle-upon-Tyne, Belfast and Glasgow. Leeds would not appear to fall within this category, with the city performing better according to most indicators than similar sized cities in the UK (Chapters 3 and 4). Certainly Leeds' recent resurgence would appear to have been greatly assisted by its good external communications in the shape of excellent rail connections to London (with scheduled journey times of less than two hours possible), superb motorway access via the M1, M62 and A1, and good European access though the regional Leeds-Bradford airport, with Manchester Airport just an hour's drive away, and nearby sea links to Europe from the Humber ports and Trent wharves. Alternatively, as Eamon Judge and David Hick note (Chapter 14), transport access within Leeds is still problematic, particularly city centre congestion. That Leeds has suffered manufacturing decline is undeniable, but dominance by traditional industrial sectors such as coal and clothing has long since waned, which may have contributed to the less than expected decline in the late 1980s-early 1990s recession.

According to Cheshire and Hay (1989), struggling peripheral regional cities may also typically: have highly organised labour forces which are resistant to change, often based in large firms; have not attracted back-office type functions; lack a tradition of small firm entrepreneurship and be challenged by nearby regional cities for service functions. Again, Leeds appears to have been reasonably positioned in respect of such factors: there are very few large companies in the local economy, particularly in manufacturing (see Chapter 5), considerable back-office and similar types of activity have emerged in Leeds (Chapter 6), whilst the economy has long been dominated by small and medium sized firms (see Chapter 8). Although Leeds has faced competition from its regional neighbours, such as York, Bradford, Wakefield and Sheffield, it has successfully carved out a renewed regional role over the past twenty years, most notably through the ascendancy of its financial services sector, and its role as an administrative centre for government offices.

Hall's (1995) analysis is an intriguing one, albeit one which leaves as many questions as it answers: all the best analyses do. In particular, though Hall outlines the role of restructuring processes such as globalisation, place marketing, privatisation and deregulation, the rise of the information economy, technical change, the growth of environmental awareness, demographics and migration patterns, and the putative rise of an urban underclass, these are not combined together in a way which permits a deeper understanding of how they interact and map out in different ways in different places. Particularly notable is a lack of emphasis on urban and regional governance, that is the ways in which change is facilitated, negotiated, accommodated, engendered, mediated and implemented, both by individual players and by various networks, partnerships and other mechanisms. This acts as a prompt for reflection on what combination of circumstances it is which has brought about the change of economic fortunes for the Leeds economy as a whole, and whether this might link into a specifically British example of second city syndrome. These are themes which the various chapters in this book begin to contribute to in the particular case of Leeds.

9

**Moving into the fast lane...**

The recent history of Leeds is most remarkable for the turnaround in the city's economic fortunes, as job losses in traditional industries, such as clothing, engineering and coal, have in some part been compensated for by job creation in services (see Chapter 3). In particular, Leeds has emerged as a buoyant regional centre, with a considerable growth in consumer services, such as retailing (Chapter 7), whilst also attracting considerable inward investment in producer services, most notably in the increasingly vibrant financial services sector, one of the strongest concentrations outside London (Chapter 6). The city's leaders have also sought to promote a 'Europeanisation' and 'cultural renaissance,' attempting to lift the sights of the city to those of continental competitors, with major initiatives including the waterfront regeneration, the city centre design initiative, and attempts to promote tourism in the city, with the development of the Royal Armouries and Brewery Wharf museum complexes (Chapter 8). The city council and others in the city also make much of the fact that Leeds is relatively economically buoyant, surviving the recession of the late 1980s and early 1990s much better than any other large city in England (Chapters 3 and 4).

The hyperbole which has grown up around this apparent success is telling in its own right. A *Daily Telegraph* (25th May 1994) special on 'Business Investment in Leeds' tells us that the city has experienced a "'rags to riches' transformation" (p.33).

> The region continues to generate successful entrepreneurs... This has led wealth chasers like Coutts, the private bankers, to home in on the area and brokers like Panmure Gordon's Pat O'Reilly to call Leeds "the Texas of England" (p.33).

Naturally, the city's boosterists have similar stories to tell, of a city at the heart of Europe (aren't they all?), displaying a notable attractiveness to business investors, and with a buoyant cultural life.

> Leeds is not just another northern city. Its our proud boast that we are now the Capital of the North...
> Leeds' success as the major business, financial and administrative centre of the North is based on the natural advantage of its location, first-class communications and the business acumen, skills and motivation of its people. The City's green environmental setting coupled with its reputation as being second to none (outside London) for arts and entertainment has also helped. But, above all, the secret is the City's belief in partnership and cooperation to achieve what is best for the people of Leeds (*Looking*

*at Leeds - a better place to live, work and enjoy,* Leeds Planning
Department, n.d., circa 1990, p.2).

The notion of 'working together' is an unusual centrepiece for this kind of
promotional publication, which more usually simply proclaim the advantages
of location and a pliable workforce, sometimes with a leading high
technology industry of some sort. The sense of purposeful and harmonious
working together towards a vision for the city is in fact one which is
frequently met, indicating a particular desire in Leeds to sell itself as a very
distinct political entity to the so-called 'loony left,' conflict-prone
administrations which the national media was so keen to 'expose' in the
1980s, notably in Liverpool and Sheffield. This is combined with a very
long-standing attention to keeping local authority spending under control and
what a Financial Times reporter refers to as "ruthless pragmatism" (Gowers,
1995, p.16), a term which is rather confusing, though it manages to convey
the sense of 'getting things done.'

With the changing fortunes of the Leeds economy very much centred on
a growth in services and a decline in manufacturing, Max Farrar (Chapter
17) notes that some groups within the city have been more disadvantaged
than others. He argues that one of the outcomes of these uneven processes
of change has been that jobs typically held by inner city residents, and in
particular by males from ethnic minority communities, have disappeared and
not been replaced by other jobs. Jane Kettle (Chapter 15) similarly notes that
the restructuring of work has been highly gendered, and whilst many more
women have entered the job market in Leeds, major inequalities in access
to the best jobs remain, something which in Leeds is being addressed with
some success by Opp2K, a sub-group of the Leeds Initiative.

Of the new jobs created in Leeds, it is those associated with inward
investment which are most visible and which attract most attention. Recent
arrivals in Leeds have included First Direct, the telebanking arm of the
Midland Bank, the administrative head offices of the Department of Social
Security, and a major office of Direct Line Insurance. In trying to illustrate
why Leeds was attracting investment in financial services, a *Financial Times*
1993 survey of the city used the example of British Telecom's relocation
two years earlier of its mobile communications business, which involved 767
full-time equivalent jobs, from Euston Tower in London. According to the
company, the move removed the need to pay London weightings on salaries,
reduced labour turnover and reduced office rents from £53 to £11 per square
foot. Added to this, Leeds was seen as offering good communications not
only to the regional market, but also to the rest of the country, a refrain
which is taken up by other company managers cited in the article. Another
often quoted factor in enticing telephone-based operations (such as tele-

banking and insurance) was a report for First Direct which argued that the accent of Leeds people could be readily understood by people from all parts of the country. Although ready labour availability was also a factor for many firms, in recent years there has been growing concern that a labour scarcity in this sector may be imminent.

In Leeds, the financial services sector has benefited from what might be termed 'back office' development, but tellingly this has been accompanied by a more subtle form of change, an improvement in the breadth and level of services provided by some existing companies. This has included the emergence of much stronger regional offices for some of the major accountancy and legal firms, plus the development of new relatively autonomous operating divisions for new market activities, as with First Direct. As such, Leeds has benefited from growth across a range of office occupations, from the relatively lowly to the relatively highly placed.

Alternatively, as Kevin Thomas and John Shutt illustrate (Chapter 5), manufacturing employment continues to decline in Leeds, with very little inward investment. The reason for this failure to attract mobile manufacturing capital is in part linked to land and labour costs which are high relative to some neighbouring areas (engineering wages for instance, can be up to 20% higher in Leeds than Wakefield, Haughton and Thomas, 1990). But perhaps most importantly, central government policies appear to have contributed to the deindustrialization of Leeds since the 1960s. Rainnie and Wilkinson (1967), for instance, argued that as Leeds was perceived to be relatively prosperous, factories there appeared to have difficulties getting the Industrial Development Certificates (IDCs) necessary to allow factory expansions of over 5,000 square feet at that period, as part of a national effort to redirect industrial investment to less prosperous regions. Although IDCs have long since been abandoned, there remains a considerable regional shadow effect, with Leeds deemed ineligible for British regional assistance and European regional funding, whilst nearby areas such as Wakefield and Humberside are funded, and are therefore able to offer considerable incentives to entice manufacturers in particular to locate there (see Chapter 5). As Leeds is still relatively prosperous, it remains difficult to justify the case for regional assistance being granted to the city, although more targeted urban assistance is clearly desirable.

The point being made here is that the restructuring of the Leeds economy is far from a simple outcome of the interplay of global restructuring forces, but rather it reflects the intersection of global trends with national policy regimes, in this case regional policy, and local conditions, from policy interventions to, apparently, the flat vowels of the Leeds accent.

### ... and staying on the hard shoulder

It is a hallmark of the Leeds political scene that evidence about the growing social polarisation within the city provokes considerable concern, a feeling which the 1993 *Financial Times* survey of Leeds picks up on.

> Sharp differences between the haves and have-nots of modern urban society have become increasingly obvious in Leeds...
>
> The new jobs [in financial services] give the impression of widespread economic regeneration, but they have been largely confined to the city centre. In some areas, local unemployment has risen in the wake of the decline in old manufacturing concerns.
>
> The trappings and symbols of city centre investment - such as new office buildings, expensive clothes shops and good quality wine bars and restaurants - have highlighted social differences. This is much to the concern of the city council's Labour Party leadership (Dalby, 1993, p.32).

Later in the same article, the leader of the council, Jon Trickett, is quoted as saying that "Increasingly, people in these areas are being left out of the economy. A priority is to provide training and incentives so they can get jobs and be part of the city's development. It is difficult." Two and a half years later, in a new *Financial Times* supplement on 'Leeds and the North' (*Financial Times*, 20.6.1995, pp. 14-17), Jon Trickett is again quoted about the concerns which social polarisation within the city are causing

> We cannot continue like this, with fast growing influxes of prosperous commuters driving past deprived inner-city areas, without risking some kind of social explosion (Cllr Jon Trickett, Leader of Leeds City Council, quoted in the *Financial Times*, 20.6.95, p.16).

Sadly, just a few weeks later this prophecy proved all too accurate, with the Yorkshire Post (12.7.1995, p.6) reporting that "Drivers were pelted with missiles as they travelled along one of the main commuter routes out of Leeds during the rush hour... police in the area confirmed that young men... had been picking on executive type cars."

Not surprisingly then, competing with "Celebration City" and "European City" are the less savory titles sometimes used in local and national newspapers. With the headline "A city in peril" the *Yorkshire Evening Post*, (12.7.1995, p.1) tells its readers that "An evil tide of drugs is defiling our city streets, bringing shootings, beatings and arson in its wake;" and, in an article on Chapeltown, the inner city of Leeds was said to possess "the meanest streets in Britain" (*The Guardian*, 1.11.1994). Sensationalist

13

perhaps, but indicative of another perspective altogether on the recent development of Leeds, one where problems such as drug dealing and street violence dominate. In effect, Leeds has two sets of dominant discourse, discourses which both compete with and complement each other. The discourse of the successful city, of coordination and partnership, is necessary to counter the more negative images of the city which abound, whilst selectively using these same negative images to back up its bids for government regeneration grants. In a similar vein, the discourses of a deeply divided, heavily contested city necessarily rely for effect on the co-existence of an increasingly prosperous city centre based on a successful integration into the national and global economy, whilst in adjacent areas of acute deprivation people are increasingly tied to dependency on state benefits or to an expanding informal economy of unregulated work and illegal work, most high profile in the case of drug dealing.

The tension here is clear, jobs are being created in Leeds, but they appear not to be percolating through to people living in areas of acute deprivation. Most indicators of disadvantage demonstrate that problems in the inner areas remain stubbornly above those of the rest of Leeds. Whilst the housing stock of the inner city still leaves much to be desired, there have been considerable advances on this front (Chapter 16). It is in the arena of getting people into jobs that the inner city areas are still most clearly failing. Even though 20,000 jobs were created between 1981 and 1991, the overall impact on unemployment in the city has been negligible, owing to an increase in the overall size of the workforce and the increase in the number of jobs being taken-up by commuters from outside the city.

To the extent that job creation has most benefited those living outside the inner city areas, it is as well to remember that labour and housing market dynamics are such that it is not possible to read off people's job prospects simply by where they live and changes in commuting patterns. Many people from the inner city who do get jobs will decide to join the outflow to more prosperous areas, with their places filled by others unable to find secure reasonably paid work. Nonetheless, the persistence of unemployment in the inner city wards of Leeds at a time of overall improvement in economic prosperity must raise questions of who is getting access to jobs in the city, and who appears to be being denied access. Politicians and officials prefer to talk about a skills mismatch, where inner city residents lack the skills to take up the new jobs on offer in the services sector. Though there is a strong element of truth in this, it is far from the only explanation. Racial and sexual discrimination remain rife in Leeds, as in most other cities, whilst those living in the most stigmatised inner city areas claim that 'post code prejudice' is prevalent amongst employers in the city, many of whom are said to prefer not to recruit people who live in certain neighbourhoods

14

(Chaudhary, 1994). This is not simply a supply side problem.

The Chapeltown area in north Leeds, with its high concentrations of unemployment and ethnic minorities, is perhaps the best known inner city 'problem' area in the city. It is an area which gained a national reputation for social malaise, racial unrest and street violence, with the inner city 'uprisings' or 'riots' of July 1981 part of the folkloric mythology which now surround the area. In an archetypal article on the area, by-lined "The other side of hell," *Guardian* newspaper writer Vivek Chaudhary writes of the "frontline," "besieged" streets of Chapeltown, where "urban warriors" have reportedly turned to drug dealing and mugging as a way of life (Chaudhary, 1994). This "pariah area" we are told, is "often called 'the most unpoliceable area in Britain.'" As Max Farrar (Chapter 17) seeks to demonstrate, Chapeltown is part of a particular discourse within the city, and more generally amongst those concerned with the welfare of British cities, which necessarily demonises some areas, often racially defined, as "unpoliceable" or in some other way different from the aspirations of the "ordinary people," serving to provide a salutary warning of the dangers of societal breakdown which would allow the 'Others' to threaten the well-being of the rest of the city.

It is worth emphasising here that the existence of rich-poor area divides within cities such as Leeds is part of a unity, representing the logic of the neo-liberal economic policies being pursued at national level, with their emphasis on labour market deregulation, and conservative social policies, with their emphasis on reducing the state welfare net, as a spur to accepting severely eroded working conditions and as a means of reducing the tax burden, primarily for businesses and individuals with high incomes. Assisting the well-off at the expense of the less well-off has been an implicit national strategy for over fifteen years. Whilst Leeds' civic leaders may deplore this tendency, virtually the only game which they *can* play in this new competitive environment is the corporate city game, hoping against hope that it will succeed in its own terms, and that some benefits will percolate through to the less well-off in the city (Cochrane, Peck and Tickell, 1995).

For the purposes of this chapter, it is perhaps sufficient to conclude this section by noting that like many other cities of its size in England, Leeds is suffering from a continuing social and economic polarisation, with long-standing class, race and gender divides being reworked across the city, sometimes in the same areas of deprivation which have been evident since the nineteenth century, sometimes in new areas, such as Seacroft and other outer estates.

## Corporate city - cul-de-sac or vital link?

In setting out to examine the many facets of recent urban development in Leeds, the various chapters in this book examine both its positive and its less positive outcomes. In the process we hope to contribute an understanding of how growth has come about, including something of the social and cultural construction of the main visible strategies and institutions for change. In addition, some chapters set out to examine the less tangible ways in which the urban economy, built environment, physical environment and social infrastructure of the city have been altered as part of this. The argument is not that the 'corporate city' has created such invisible divides within the city, but rather that it has not yet set out to address them with the vigour which they merit. This said, as the following chapters frequently highlight, on many fronts the recent restructuring of Leeds has to be regarded as a success story, in which the corporate city approach can be seen as a necessary stepping stone towards future success, including a more participatory approach to managing and instigating processes of change which necessarily affect all sections of the city, not just its 'major stakeholders'.

## Acknowledgement

Many thanks to Adam Tickell for comments. The usual disclaimer applies.

## References

Brown, A.J. (1967), 'What is the Leeds region?' in Beresford, M.W. and Jones, G.R.J. (eds) *Leeds and its Region,* Leeds Local Executive Committee of the British Association for the Advancement of Science, Leeds, 200-214.

Burt, S. and Grady, K. (1994), *The Illustrated History of Leeds,* Breedon Books, Derby,

Chaudhary, V. (1994), 'The other side of hell,' *The Guardian,* pp.2-3.

Cheshire, P. and Hay, D. (1989), *Urban Problems in Western Europe: an economic analysis,* Unwin Hyman, London.

Cochrane, A., Peck, J.A., and Tickell, A. (1995), 'Manchester plays games: exploring the local politics of globalisation,' presented to the Tenth Urban Change and Conflict Conference, University of London, September.

Dalby, S. (1993), 'City of rich and poor' *Financial Times,* FT Survey

Leeds, January 23rd, p.32.

Fainstein, S. Gordon, I. and Harloe, M. (eds) (1992), *Divided Cities: New York and London in the contemporary world,* Blackwell, Oxford.

Gower, A. (1995) 'Service industries transform the city,' *Financial Times,* 20th June, 14-16.

Hall, P. (1995), 'Towards a general urban theory,' in Brotchie, J. et al (eds) *Cities in Competition: productive and sustainable cities for the 21st century,* Longman Australia, Melbourne, 3-31.

Hartley, O. (1980), 'The second world war and after, 1939-74,' in Fraser, D. (ed) *A Modern History of Leeds,* Manchester University Press, Manchester, 437-61.

Haughton, G., Morgan, J. and Whitney, D. (1994), 'Economic, social and political transition in a pioneer industrial region' in Haughton, G. and Whitney D. (eds) *Reinventing a Region: restructuring and policy response in West Yorkshire,* 3-33.

Haughton, G. and Thomas, K. (1990), 'Local sector studies, skills shortages and supply chains' *CUDEM Working Paper,* 8, Leeds Polytechnic.

Leeds Child Poverty Action Group (1994), *Always Struggling: child poverty in Leeds 1981-1991,* LPAG, Leeds.

Leeds Development Agency (1994), 'The economically active in Leeds,' July, LDA, Civic Hall, Leeds.

Leeds Initiative (1991), *Annual Report 1990/91,* LDA, Civic Hall, Leeds.

Leeds Planning Department (n.d., circa 1990), *Looking at Leeds - a better place to live, work and enjoy,* Leeds City Council, Leeds.

Lin, J. (1995), 'Polarised development and urban change in New York's Chinatown,' *Urban Affairs Review,* 30 (3), 332-354.

Mollenkopf, J. and Castells, M. (eds) (1991), *Dual City: restructuring New York,* Russell Sage Foundation, New York.

Pennington, S. (1995), 'Debt, the old-fashioned way' *Independent on Sunday,* p.19.

Santos, M. (1979), *The Shared Space: the two circuits of the urban economy in underdeveloped countries,* Methuen, London. Trans. C. Gerry; original, 1975.

Sassen, S. (1991), *The Global City: New York, London, Tokyo,* Princeton University Press, New Jersey.

Sassen, S. (1994), *Cities in a World Economy,* Pine Forge Press, Thousand Oaks, California.

Rainnie and Wilkinson (1967), 'The economic structure,' in Beresford, M.W. and Jones, G.R.J. (eds) *Leeds and its Region,* Leeds Local Executive Committee of the British Association for the Advancement of Science, Leeds, 215-38.

# 2 Local leadership and economic regeneration in Leeds

*Graham Haughton*

## Re-building an economy: the rise of the entrepreneurial city

The recent economic resurgence of Leeds owes much to its developing role in the international economy, and more specifically to its changing role as a regional centre in the UK and European space economies. The Leeds economy is not a simple passive receptor of external competitive pressures and other restructuring impulses: in a variety of ways the civic leaders of the city have set out to attract, maintain and promote economic development in Leeds. In doing this they have in part sought to react to changing external economic conditions and to the policy directives of the national state in particular, but they have also sought to follow their own course, in response to more localised needs, histories and contestations over preferred policy approaches. Leadership in this policy area in Leeds has primarily rested with local government, although in recent years the emphasis has shifted towards the corporate city alliance of major institutional players across the public and private sectors. It is important in this respect that whilst attempts to regulate economic growth occur at various spatial levels, supra-national, national and local, in recent years it has been widely argued that as part of the after-Fordist search for a new sustainable regime of capitalist accumulation the local state has become an increasingly important site of action for economic regeneration policy (Mayer, 1992; Peck and Tickell, 1994; Tickell and Peck, 1995).

This section introduces aspects of the policy and academic background to the distinctive 'Corporate City' approach to local economic development adopted in Leeds. Later sections provide a brief introduction to the dominant position of the local authority through to 1980, followed by a more focused

19

examination of attempts to create an economic development strategy for the city since then. In particular, the chapter focuses on the work of the Leeds Initiative, which since 1990 has been central to attempts to pursue a corporate city model of public-private partnership action, building a consensus around a strategy for Leeds, and beginning to effect some change.

In the British local government literature of the 1970s, a new corporate approach was advocated as a means of bringing about a shift within local government from relatively unstrategic responses to duties and powers, to a more generalised, strategic responsibility for the well-being of people within an area (Bains, 1972; Stewart, 1973; Keith-Lucas and Richardson, 1978; Cochrane, 1993). This was seen to involve improved high level executive powers within the local authority, and improved working with other local agencies concerned with the overall development of an area, in particular those engaged in the delivery of 'welfare state services.'

Successive central government policy interventions since 1979 have combined to make this style of inter-corporate working a central element of local authority work, as local authorities have lost responsibilities (such as opted-out schools, further education colleges and the former polytechnics), been forced to comply with Compulsory Competitive Tendering, and experienced resource cutbacks which have hit discretionary spending. In addition, their local external operating environment has altered dramatically, with the re-distribution of powers and resources to a wide range of non-elected local bodies, such as health trusts, Urban Development Corporations (UDCs) and Training and Enterprise Councils (TECs). The combination of increasing resource and legislative constraints on local authorities and an increasingly complex array of edge-of-state bodies, has generated a general shift in policy emphasis from local govern*ment* to local govern*ance*.

In this process of the fracturing and dispersal of powers and resources to a wide range of new bodies operating at the local level, the role of local government has altered dramatically. In particular, it has shifted from being predominantly a frontline provider of services towards being a facilitator and enabler, working with other local bodies to ensure that services are provided within a strategic context for the area as a whole, in a cost-effective and equitable fashion. Local governance then represents a more porous system of power sharing and resource coordination than in the days when many more services were delivered directly by local authorities themselves. Within the still emergent system of UK local governance, accountability has become a major concern: only local government has a direct electoral link, which gives it a unique position. However, it is not an unassailable position, as local councils struggle to improve upon the rigidities of representative democracy, notably through experimentation with various forms of participatory democracy (Clarke and Stewart, 1991).

In looking at how the corporate city works, it is also helpful to refer to some of the approaches to urban development which have come out of the United States in recent years. Of particular note are two highly influential bodies of work have grown up around notions of growth machines/growth coalitions, and urban regimes. *Growth machines* are usually created by coordinated business interests concerned to promote local growth, through permissive land use policies. These "place entrepreneurs" (Logan and Molotoch, 1987, p.3) usually coalesce around property interests, whilst seeking to mobilise others behind their strategies, such as local utilities and universities, and even in some cases successfully coopting neighbourhood organisations in pursuit of their agenda (Goetz and Sidney, 1994).

Typically growth machines seek to put their case as a 'value-free' one at the political level, whilst mobilising local media interests, which also have a place-bound local interest in growth, in backing pro-growth politicians and strategies (Logan and Molotoch, 1987). Attempts to 'depoliticise' economic development represent an attempt to construct it as an arena where growth is regarded as a self-evident good, amenable only to public consensus (Peterson, 1981). This can be related to the contentious logic which has seen economic development powers in the UK increasingly placed with quasi-autonomous development bodies, such as TECs and UDCs. In practice, however, development policies are often highly politicised and divisive at the local level, and in some instances it may well have been precisely because of local friction that independent bodies or partnerships have been formed (Judd and Ready, 1986). Indeed, it is in part this politicisation of local economic development, and also in part the need to address issues raised by international restructuring processes (Leitner, 1990), which have contributed to the continuing so-called rise of the entrepreneurial state (Eisinger, 1988). Responding to increasing inter-locality competition, the entrepreneurial (local) state seeks to encourage private investment, incorporating both supply side interventions to subsidise mobile capital (e.g. subsidised taxes, land, buildings and training), and more recently demand side interventions, working with firms in pursuit of opportunities to develop new or expanding markets. Where there is a strongly mobilised entrepreneurial state, private sector-led growth coalitions, formed primarily to overcome 'state' barriers to development, may be less appropriate than attempts to create productive public-private sector relationships.

It is in this area that *urban regime* analysis is particularly helpful, with its emphasis on different models of private and public cooperation. As most influentially articulated by Stone (1989), urban regimes emerge from a political or financial incapacity of local government, and are structured around attempts to mobilise private-public sector actions through informal mechanisms. In this argument, the emphasis is less on the coercive powers and countervailing strategies of public and private sectors, and more on the processes of working together on common strategies. Regimes as such do not exercise power, but instead use "civic cooperation" (p.5) between those who are able to mobilise significant institutional resources in support of development within a city. Typically, members of a regime will benefit from both material and symbolic gains; they will also tend to mobilise around areas of mutual interest, with an emphasis on small manageable tasks, rather than holistic grand visions (DiGaetano and Klemanski, 1993). As with growth machines, the business sector finds itself in a privileged position within these regimes, in large part as a consequence of their considerable resources (Harding, 1994). Community interests are typically marginalised, except where they are sufficiently able to mobilize protests and articulate alternative strategies such that the main players can no longer ignore them.

It is possible to identify a number of different types of regime (see for instance: Stone, 1989; DiGaetano and Klemanski, 1993; Harding, 1994). Most notable in the present context are the various form of pro-growth *corporate regimes,* which seek to bring public and private sector activists together around a vision of economic development for the city, which is typically focused on creating and meeting city centre development opportunities. These may be *market-led,* focused on reducing the role of local government regulation, or *government-led,* with an emphasis on subsidising the private sector to invest through grants, loans, site provision and so on (DiGaetano and Klemanski, 1993). *Caretaker regimes* tend to be service delivery-oriented, rather than seeking to transform a city's economic prospects (Stone, 1989). *Progressive regimes* typically adopt a far greater concern with equity issues, and can manifest themselves as either *social reform* oriented, centred on community rather than business development, or *anti-growth/growth management*-oriented (DiGaetano and Klemanski, 1993). Progressive regimes then, provide an alternative vision of what economic development means and how it takes place, with an emphasis on whole community participation, growth which incorporates explicit redistributive mechanisms, and possibly alternative local mechanisms for engaging with local residents (Clavel, 1986).

The corporate-centred approach, with its central emphasis on public-private partnership, has arguably been the dominant form of urban governance in the USA since the 1980s, leading to considerable concern about the policy scope for more 'progressive' strategies (Clavel, 1986; Nickell, 1995). As with growth machines, corporate-centred approaches typically concentrate on land use issues, especially city centre property developments (Stone, 1989). In emphasising these concerns, the corporate city typically privileges the government and private sectors, with the community sector again often able to exercise only marginal influence (Stone, 1989; Harding, 1994).

It is when the notion of the corporate city is juxta-positioned with ideas of a progressive city agenda, that the shortcomings of the corporate city model are most clearly highlighted. Reacting to the perceived near hegemony of the corporate city approach in US cities during the 1980s, Clavel (1986) set out to try to identify alternative strategies, which he labelled as progressive, where community development needs were placed centre stage rather than economic development. In progressive strategies, economic redistribution issues were accorded primacy along with, or instead of, economic growth. In addition, mechanisms were in place to mobilise a wide section of community interest groups to help shape a city's development agenda. Although in a minority, significant numbers and variants of the progressive city were identified, not least those where environmental concerns are to the fore (Judd and Ready, 1986).

There are substantial difficulties in translating these models to the British context (DiGaetano and Klemanski, 1993; Harding, 1994; Peck and Tickell, 1995), not least because British local authorities have, until recent years, had sizeable financial resources and greater powers in the development field relative to their US counterparts, notably in land use planning. Alternatively, urban governments in the US have generally enjoyed greater political autonomy than in the UK (Levy, 1992), and have been less prone to central government prescription over their activities. Accepting the importance of local democracy, British business leaders have generally been less ready to articulate a coherent development strategy in opposition to the perceived political legitimacy of local government. Added to these differences, British local authorities also hold a considerable degree of political legitimacy in seeking to represent community groups and interests themselves, albeit not unproblematically. For all these differences, it is possible still to see that the US models have a degree of salience for British cities (DiGaetano and Klemanski, 1993).

Harding (1994, p.375) refers to the late 1980s development of partnerships in British cities "as something of a compromise model - a growth machine or corporate/entrepreneurial regime with a muted social agenda," a description which describes the Leeds model reasonably accurately. Leeds appears to incorporate elements of both the corporate city and progressive city models, with added ingredients of its own. In the shape of the Leeds Initiative, the main public-private partnership vehicle in the city, there is an almost classic example of a corporate city approach. For instance, in its early years there was a strong emphasis on city centre flagship development, meriting a separate section and full page in Leeds Initiative Annual Report of 1990/91. This, however, had disappeared as a separate section by the 1993-94 and 1994-95 reports, reflecting a growing public concern that city centre development was not percolating through to other parts of the city. For the most part, the Leeds Initiative has to date acted as an economic development forum, with only marginal engagement with social issues. It appears to have been generally accepted by the main players that extending consensus building through the Leeds Initiative into the community development area would be difficult, at least in the early years. Allied to this was the view that the city council was the legitimate major player in bringing about community development, and that the Leeds Initiative as an organisation would be well advised not to challenge this aspect of the local status quo. It is at this level that it is possible to see elements of progressive city movements within Leeds, in which the city council is the lead player, but with local groups sometimes struggling to make their voice heard by both the city council and the Leeds Initiative.

The emergence of British-style regimes, and they are so different in style that a new term may be preferable, is centred less on the accommodation of local business and state interests, and much more on the political machinations of central and local government. Looking back on the 1980s, Government minister John Gummer (1995) justified attempts to curtail local government powers by referring to the growing politicisation of some local authorities and their attempts to engage in the arena of national politics rather than concentrating on local needs. It was this alleged tendency which led central government to set up ways of disempowering local authorities, in order to bring them to heel. In consequence, in Britain local regimes have often sought to co-opt local business interests either to help overcome central government hostility, particularly important in funding bids, or to provide much needed financial resources in pursuit of narrow development opportunities. Given the rapid growth of new locally created and centrally imposed bodies in regeneration there has been a need to shift from narrowly constructed, action-oriented development partnerships, towards area-wide bodies seeking to provide a strategic agenda centred on economic development (Haughton and Whitney, 1994). So following a very different evolutionary path, some British cities have found themselves at a stage where their dominant vehicle for economic development strategy often appears remarkably similar to those of their US counterparts a decade earlier.

In this chapter, the emphasis is on the emergence of different styles of leadership in local economic development activities in Leeds, with a brief historical sketch followed by a more detailed consideration of events since 1980. In undertaking the research, personal interviews were undertaken with 35 local leaders in the public, private and voluntary sectors.

## Changing styles of governance: from "I am Leeds" to "corporate city"

A number of very good histories highlight the distinctive municipal politics of Leeds in the Victorian era, a period when civic leaders very much set out to influence the development of the city overall, in particular seeking to build a regional supremacy within Yorkshire (Hennock, 1973; Fraser, 1980; Burt and Grady, 1994). It is worth recalling Bateman's (1986) view, that Leeds' regional ascendancy within Yorkshire was far from a natural one, and that its leaders very much had to compete with other towns and cities in the region for this role: Wakefield not Leeds was the administrative centre for the West Riding County and subsequently for the West Yorkshire Metropolitan County Council, whilst Bradford retained strong regional leadership ambitions, as part of its historical rivalry with Leeds.

For most of the twentieth century a consensus existed that leadership in Leeds was to be in the hands of the local authority. Party political control has been fairly volatile, so that the form of more or less constant Labour leadership experienced in cities such as Sheffield was not replicated in the city. This may have contributed to the politics of pragmatism which has been pervasive in Leeds for much of this period: certainly the policy differences between local parties appeared to be negligible for considerable periods of time. According to Hartley (1980, p.438), so weak was party political ideology in the immediate decades following the second world war that changes in political control led to little policy change. Indeed, much of the business of policy formation and implementation was said to have been left to council officers. In place of ideological conflict, Hartley argues that party politics was dominated by charismatic personality politics, centred on who could claim the glory for any policy successes, with Sir Charles Wilson providing the model which later politicians in part sought to emulate. It is worth looking in a little more detail at the larger than life Sir Charles and his vision for the development of Leeds.

In the 1926 *Leeds Tercentenary Official Handbook* (Hirst, 1926), the frontispiece talks of the book as "a brief account of the origin of Leeds, the growth of its Vast Industries and the Romance of its Great Municipal Services." According to a chapter titled "The 'Do-it-all' Corporation"

The Leeds Corporation does more than purvey water, gas and electricity, run the tramcars and dispose of the sewage. *It nurses and shields the inhabitants from the cradle to the grave...*

By the Corporation the citizens are protected from the adulterator who would poison us with bad food, from the short-weight cheat, from the mischance of fire and the attentions of the thief that walks by night or picks pockets during the day (p. 65).

Following a list of responsibilities which covers two pages, the text resumes

> These are a few of the many little known duties attended to unostentatiously by our fatherly Corporation so that the health, education, livelihood and personal safety and comfort of the citizens can be promoted (p. 67).

The paternalism of the "fatherly" corporation of this period was clearly embodied in the approach of Sir Charles Wilson, who joined the council in 1890, became its leader from 1907-28 (with a short break), and was also elected as a local member of parliament from 1923-30. As a 'municipal imperialist' it was Sir Charles' stated ambition to expand the boundaries of the city, aiming to control everything from the Pennines to the sea (Meadowcroft, 1980, p.416). When questioned about improving local government at one inquiry he famously went on record as saying "I am Leeds" (ibid). A self-styled wheeler dealer, Sir Charles set out to expand the city's municipal sphere of influence through boundary extensions which saw the city absorb outlying areas such as Shadwell, Roundhay, Seacroft and Crossgates (1912), Middleton (1919), and Adel (1927) (see Hartley, 1980).

In jocular fashion, Sir Charles is teased in the city's Tercentenary Handbook, as being "a man of dignity if not of humility," with the view expressed that if he were to ever have a statue erected to his memory it would have to be manufactured out of brass. The tone of this piece, presumably sanctioned by him, is impish in itself, not least as it assesses Sir Charles' municipal ambitions

> If he has a weakness it is his ambition to see Leeds surpass in size and population any other city in Yorkshire. In seeking to extend the city no man has schemed with such pugnacity (Hirst, 1926, *Leeds Official Tercentenary Handbook,* p. 70)

Other charismatic leaders were to follow, most notably the Reverend Charles Jenkinson, whose efforts in the 1930s towards slum clearance are still remembered many years later (Bateman, 1986). Seventy years on, the very basis of much of the municipal pride evident in the Tercentenary Handbook has disappeared, with nationalisation, privatisation and compulsory competitive tendering, amounting over the years to a wholesale dismantling of activities previously undertaken by the local authority. The basic utilities, water, sewage, gas, electricity and sewage, have all been transferred to other forms of ownership and are now organised at a broader geographical scale, with the effect that the city council is no longer in control over these services, nor is it necessarily the major stakeholder for the new providers of services to the city's people and businesses. This said, with an annual budget of around £1 billion in 1995, assets of £3 billion and a workforce of 34,000, the city council remains the single largest employer in the city.

## Testing the waters: early efforts towards local economic development

Whilst it is possible to portray the immediate post-war decades as relatively free of political dogma and with policies largely led by powerful council officers (see Hartley, 1980), the policy outcomes were not always well-regarded locally, as conflicts over housing policy illustrate (Gibson and Langstaff, 1982; Burt and Grady, 1994). In the area of planning and economic development too, business leaders frequently railed against what they perceived as restrictive planning policies. This was a period when planning officers around the country engaged in similar policies to remove 'non-conforming' and noxious industries where possible away from residential areas, a process often facilitated by road building and housing renewal programmes (City of Leeds, 1972). Not surprisingly perhaps, business people felt under pressure from such interventions, which together with the annual arguments following statutory consultation over the business rate (since abandoned), often led to both public and private acrimony, as one of today's elder statesmen in the business community recalls. He moved his factory out of Leeds because

> I had increasing frustration with the local authority in Leeds, who would not give permission for this, that and the other... [so] eventually we moved out... One of the reasons Leeds has become a financial centre is because there was such a lot of bureaucracy in the '50s, '60s and '70s, I think a lot of companies moved away... The planning office was very strong. The smaller towns, Dewsbury, Batley, even Bradford, Pudsey, they were a bit more responsive, encouraged people to create jobs. So you tended to keep away from the local government.

By the early 1970s, talk of compulsory purchase of industrial premises was already being seen as problematic, as costs rose and the availability of finance declined (City of Leeds, 1972). Instead, a gradual shift began to emerge which favoured a more strategic approach to local economic development, although initial efforts to bring this about during the 1970s were blocked by senior councillors and officers who felt that local economic circumstances did not merit such an active approach (Mawson, 1983). Attempts to engage in productive relationships with the private sector were also set in train, most notably the launching of *Project Leeds,* a joint venture between the Chamber of Commerce and the local authority, and the concept of Leeds as the "Motorway City of the Seventies" (Burt and Grady, 1994). By the late 1970s industrial development officers had been appointed and action on providing industrial land development was being pursued more vigorously than hitherto (Mawson, 1983).

Politically, the council had been hung or Conservative dominated for much of the 1970s. Following the return of a Labour-dominated council at the end of this period (Labour have been in control ever since), the economic development activities of Leeds began to alter dramatically, both in scale and in leadership. Development issues were still mainly addressed through the Planning and Property Department of the city council, with no separate economic development body either within or outside the council. The in-coming Labour administration brought about a radical shift in emphasis, focusing on analyzing the local economy and seeking to intervene where appropriate to improve local job prospects.

> They used to talk about planning giving jobs and things like that, but not in terms of attempting to influence the local economy through training, through grants and all those mechanisms... I think that its fair to say that when George Mudie became the leader in Leeds, that was one of his platforms - that the economic base had not been looked at, not been thought about. Market forces got it wrong, and he began to wonder what we could do about it (business leader).

Historically, it was argued, Leeds had benefited from having a large number of small and medium sized firms, without a single dominant employer or dominant sector, and from firms which had strong local roots. By the 1970s, with multinational takeovers, these roots were seen to be weakening with a series of takeovers and rationalisations bringing about local job losses.

The mechanism used in the early 1980s to instigate a more active era of local economic development was to take on responsibility for the council's land holdings

> There was a small body at that time called the Land Sub-Committee and its job was to buy and sell land in Leeds; it had millions of pounds but nobody knew it existed... So we took over the Land Sub-Committee... and then started to use the land sales strategically. Yes we sold land, but we sold one piece of land to fund ten people in the industrial development unit, to go round and start the action. And that's how we started building up local employment development strategies. It got parodied a bit as exclusively co-ops, it wasn't - a lot of it was quite commercial activity (local politician).

The analytical base was strongly sectoral, with local politicians and officers for the first time starting to set up a database on local firms, using the City Library to obtain information about them in the first instance. As the emergent industrial development unit began to expand its activities, in particular seeking to assist small firm start-ups at the neighbourhood level, the external political environment in the city became increasingly fraught.

> I can show you the press cuttings from when [we were] doing the strategy: 'Red Ruin: extreme marxist... says people can run their own lives'. And we got hammered: mention gay and lesbian - I was taken to court by [the local paper] for giving them a nightline, and plastered with shit through my letter box and my windows ripped in... It was a very violent time because it was seen as a 'left' strategy, and the left were under very heavy attack for doing it. And as George was leading that [strategy] it became convenient for them to say George Mudie's a Chicago City boss... The trouble was, the [local paper] and others colluded all the time to just hammer us (local politician).

Certainly, for this local politician, the early 1980s had been politically heated, a view which stands in some contrast to the more usual local view that Leeds has always avoided the intensely politicised battles which were experienced in some other cities. From this perspective, recent attempts to view Leeds as a city without major political tensions represents either a form of collective amnesia or a form of retrospective whitewashing.

The other ingredient in economic development at the time was the West Yorkshire Metropolitan Council. The main advantages associated with the metropolitan county were the wider strategic perspective of the West Yorkshire sub-region, and the greater resources it was able to bring, most notably with the formation of the Yorkshire Enterprises, which set out to help fund small firms (see Gunnell, 1990).

By the mid-1980s, the neighbourhood emphasis of local economic development activities became subject to criticism within the council leadership, primarily on the grounds that visible signs of progress were slow in manifesting themselves. For a period in the mid-1980s, economic development activities lost their ascendancy, re-emerging with a property focus with the creation of the Leeds City Development Company (LCDC) in 1988. This was in fact an existing company which was revived as a public-private development venture by council leaders in an abortive attempt to see off the imposition of an Urban Development Corporation on Leeds (see Whitney and Haughton, 1990; Haughton and Whitney, 1994). For a brief period in the late 1980s, the LCDC was a major player in promoting development in the city centre, drawing in private sector partners to work on sites owned by the city council. The advent of the property recession in the late 1980s, and the growing dominance of the much better funded Leeds Development Corporation (LDC), the local urban development corporation, however, meant that by the early 1990s its role became greatly diminished.

By the late 1980s, as the vacuum left by abolition of the county council became apparent, and as a new local leadership took control of the Labour Party, a more active approach to economic development in the council once more emerged, centred on the Leeds Development Agency. This embraced the property dealing arm of the council, the Leeds City Development Corporation, and a wide-ranging economic development unit remit, including a strong analytical capacity, a sectoral support strategy, and an inward investment team. Keen to stress a pragmatic approach, the new developments became more centralised within the Civic Hall, and explicitly eschewed some of the less-conventional approaches to community-based economic intervention in the early 1980s

> There was a realisation, perhaps, that a lot of effort was being put into forming co-operatives but very few long-term jobs were being generated through that route. If you look at what happened in the 1980s in small business start-ups and self-employment there were a huge number of people who went in to that part of the economy, very few in co-ops. On an objective assessment of how best to use officer time to maximise the benefit to the Leeds economy, co-ops dropped off the agenda (council officer).

This was an important staging post to the events of the early 1990s, as the city council learnt to work with the private sector and with private sector-led quangos, such as the LDC. Certainly, the private sector welcomed the change in political leadership, with the new leader, Jon Trickett, generally seen as more consultative than his predecessor. Alternatively, the council were seen by many in the voluntary sector as uncomfortable in working with them, as the next section illustrates.

### The Leeds Initiative: corporate city embodied?

*The main stakeholders*

Launched in June 1990, the Leeds Initiative has come to be a major part of the institutional landscape of Leeds as far as economic development is concerned. Very much construed as a rapprochement between the public and private sectors after a period of some tension, the new body was set up as

30

a joint exercise, chaired by the leader of the council, with the President of the Chamber of Commerce as the vice-chair. It is one of its trademarks that the main participants believe that they were central to the creation of the Leeds Initiative concept: this sense of shared ownership has helped to keep the main partners as solid supporters.

The Leeds Initiative does not have a formal constitution, being instead a loose federation of the main institutional stakeholders in the city, notably the city council, the chambers of commerce and trade, the major local newspaper group, the regional trade union congress, both universities, the UDC and the TEC. These form the main 'board' of the Initiative, with the senior executive of each organisation expected to attend the regular meetings. One consequence of this high level attendance based on institutional affiliation was that the members of the board were all men for the first four years, after which Jude Kelly, director of the West Yorkshire Playhouse was invited to join. There is still no representative of the voluntary sector at this level. The loose federation structure of the Leeds Initiative is very much underpinned by a sub-structure of working groups, which exist with varying degrees of formality. As Kevin Thomas and John Shutt (Chapter 5) illustrate for engineering and Adam Tickell (Chapter 6) for financial services, these can emerge with a strong separate identity and a formal constitution, in both these cases employing executive officers. In some cases, local groups which are strongly linked into national initiatives, such as the Environment City (see Chapter 11) and Opp2K (see Chapter 15) groups, have been placed under the Leeds Initiative umbrella. Other sub-groups are less formally constituted, such as the Gateways and Corridors group (aiming to improve the aesthetics of the main approaches into the city). Membership of the sub-groups can be drawn from a much broader base than the main board, usefully widening the net of participants. The structure of the Leeds Initiative is undoubtedly one of its main assets

It's a very loose association. All of its different arms are separate entities in a sense. That's its strength. I suspect that had it been the more normal type of organisation with a central committee and subcommittees it would probably not have got off the ground (trade union leader).

The loose association model works because of the flexibility it allows to enable sub-groups to develop at their own pace, as they learn ways of operating and begin to clarify their objectives and priorities for action. In the early days it also had the advantage of being politically expedient, in that it could have been fairly readily dismantled if the partnership had not worked. A common version of events leading up to its formation, told here by a leading player in the city, is that the city council heard that the

Chamber of Commerce had commissioned a consultancy firm to provide a strategy for Leeds, using a City Action Team grant. This evidently set some alarm bells ringing

> And because relationships between the Chamber and the council had not been so good, I mean they just sat in different rooms and shouted at each other, I rang the chamber people and said "Look, if you produce this' without consulting the city council, you're just going to pull things further apart. Why don't we make an effort to get together?"... Bluntly it took me a long time to persuade [council leadership]... to sit around the table. And we eventually did it surreptitiously one night in the Merrion Hotel... There was a lot of fencing and sparring, before the thing got off the ground. And it was a reaction to *that,* i.e. we can always break it up easily if things go wrong [which dictated the shape of the Leeds Initiative].

Very quickly, such fears of partnership disintegrating receded into the background, and the Leeds Initiative became a widely respected vehicle for pulling together the public and private sectors around local economic regeneration initiatives. Its six objectives remain to:

- Promote the city as a major European centre.
- Ensure the economic vitality of the city.
- Create an integrated transport system for the city.
- Enhance the environment of the entire city.
- Improve the quality and visual appeal of the city.
- Develop the city as an attractive centre for visitors.

Something of the flavour of what the Initiative was setting out to achieve and its modus operandi is further revealed in its first annual report (Leeds Initiative, 1991, p. 1), which trumpets achievements in terms of acting:

- as an agent for creating a city-wide consensus on the future of Leeds, drawing in ideas and views from a wide range of agencies and institutions and from the people of Leeds;
- as an important advocacy and lobbying agent for Leeds presenting the City's needs and assets in Government and increasingly in Europe;
- as a focus for the development of City networks bringing together the resources of the Initiative members and, just as important helping other organisations find project partners and giving advice and assistance to existing schemes; and
- as a catalyst for its own special projects.

Using these same four key ingredients, the position five years later can now be reassessed. In drawing together stakeholders to form a vision for Leeds, progress is now evident. The Leeds Initiative has become the vehicle for a wide-ranging review of the economy of the city by a broad group of local groups and individuals. As part of the information sharing process, the city council and TEC both work closely on economic analysis, to prevent duplication and strengthen overall capacity.

In terms of advocacy and lobbying, the Leeds Initiative was the successful vehicle for providing a united front to external bodies, resulting in the attraction of investment of £42.5m in the Royal Armouries museum, and a successful first round bid for Single Regeneration Fund (SRB), bringing in £17m. The symbolic importance of both these should not be under-estimated. The Royal Armouries bid was very much led by the Leeds Development Corporation, with strong support from the city council, with the Initiative providing the necessary evidence of a united front between the public and private sectors. In the process of working through such bids, some of the sharp antagonisms between the LDC and the local authority did diminish, a situation helped by the fact that three influential local councillors sat on the LDC board, whilst the LDC was on the Leeds Initiative main board. The SRB bid was important in that it followed an earlier unsuccessful bid for City Challenge funding, which had evidently failed to portray that it was backed by a 'deep' local partnership. The SRB grant is administered through a sub-group of the Leeds Initiative, a group which for the first time has allowed a greater representation from local voluntary and grassroots groups (see below).

The downside of having to focus on the pursuit of government grants has been that this has tended to work against attempts to bring about a broader strategic framework for local regeneration activities. Forced by central government to make funding bids in partnership, at times this has led to the adoption of what one partner referred to as "lowest common denominator" project proposals.

The third key ingredient, building stronger networks across Leeds, remains a powerful beneficial influence for those involved

It has opened doors and has been very useful. It does mean that I can pick up the phone and speak to anyone in the city without them saying 'who?,' and that's terribly helpful (Leeds Initiative board member).

Without the Leeds Initiative we would all have remained in splendid isolation (business leader).

Certainly for the private sector, the Leeds Initiative is seen as a powerful voice for the city, a role which is enhanced by the strong involvement within it of the Chamber of Commerce. The Leeds Initiative has also served as a vehicle for greater engagement with the regeneration quangos created by central government for Leeds, the UDC and TEC, both of which had some early problems in establishing local credibility and legitimacy. Alternatively, for those not directly engaged in the Leeds Initiative network, there has been a sense of growing isolation from local decision-making, a prospect which has most hit community and voluntary sector groups

> ... people like the Chamber of Commerce and the universities feel at least they can sit round a table with the Council... The impression I've got is that it has enabled a very important conduit of information to be opened up... in theory people with a stake in the city, at that level, can have their voice heard. My problem is that sooner or later you've got to filter that down to the communities that make up Leeds and not just the vested interests of the powerful places in the city (community leader).

> ... the Leeds Initiative is very much about business, it is very much about industry, commerce and the local authority. It is not about smaller organisations or people who perhaps have needs and want to put these forward (voluntary sector).

The final ingredient for reassessment is the work of the individual sub-groups in bringing forward innovative projects. Again, the overall assessment has to be a positive one, in so far as new projects have been instigated, and the spending priorities and timescales of individual partnership organisations have sometimes been successfully 'bent' or coordinated in pursuit of the collective regeneration goals (a number of chapters in this book look at the work of such groups in greater detail). Although there is some criticism locally that "What the Leeds Initiative has developed into now, is largely a department of the city council" (business leader), most players accept the inevitability and even the legitimacy of the local authority's dominant role. In part this reflects the democratic legitimacy of the local authority, and its own internal requirement to be seen to be accountable for those of its activities which are conducted through the Leeds Initiative. It is also fair to say that the local authority is the main provider of financial resources and staffing support for the Leeds Initiative.

> It's inevitably a local authority-led partnership, but that's not a bad thing: someone's got to drive it, and in a sense what it's doing (quite bravely in a way) is inviting all the other people who are part of the Leeds Initiative to have an input into the decision-making (business leader).

34

There have been a considerable number and range of 'progressive city'-type alliances formed in Leeds over the past decade. These include the community development initiatives around housing management and community enterprise entered into by the residents of Belle Isle, the business sector-inspired interest in fostering community economic development in Ebor Gardens (Business in the Community, 1994), and the community activism of the Kirkstall Valley Campaign in responding to development threats in their area (Chapter 13; People of the Valley, 1990).

At the local level, the richness of this vein of community activity is remarkable. However, this activism has yet to be incorporated into meaningful engagement at the strategic level for the city as a whole, whilst many local activists still regard the city council as antipathetic to local activism. At the same time as civic leaders publicly agonize about the need to ensure that local people get more of the jobs being created in the city, the organised groups at local level too often feel that they face incomprehension about their potential to contribute to the development of the city as a whole, at times veering towards outright hostility.

In the 1970s and the 1980s much valuable work at the neighbourhood level in Leeds had been funded through the local authority under two central government schemes, the Community Programme and the Urban Programme. As these were wound down, the city council's will and resources to maintain a high profile community base were seen by community activists to have receded for a period, as it refocused on city centre development and working with the private sector. That the local authority was unsuccessful in its bid for City Challenge was possibly a consequence of the poorly developed community base. One related consequence of failing to obtain City Challenge funding, was that as other local authorities were rediscovering and remaking links into local community groups as a part of the regeneration process, the local authority in Leeds went down a different route, courting the major institutional players of the city through the Leeds Initiative. Given the traumas of the first half of the 1980s, attempts to rebuild positive links with the private sector were both important and necessary: the problem is that community groups feel they have been neglected in the process of providing a strategic vision for Leeds.

The relationship between the economic development focus of the Leeds Initiative and the broader community development desires of grassroots groups has become increasingly uncomfortable. The continuing centrality accorded by the major Leeds Initiative players to the local authority in leading on community development work reflects both a degree of contentment that it should continue with its 'traditional' role in this area and a disinclination to challenge how it sets about doing this. In addition, it has to be said, there is a lack of a common interest in intervening in this sphere. In other words, though many of the city's leaders want to see community development initiatives taken forward, they do not see this as part of the role of the Leeds Initiative, but something which is done separately through individual organisations or left to the local authority to get on with. As one business leader forthrightly expressed it

> the city council can concentrate on the community issue. They're not actually of interest to a lot of people on the Leeds Initiative.

For those excluded from, or on the margins, of the corporate city, there has been a growing concern about the development agenda which is being set for the city, and the role which community groups have been accorded within it. The lack of grassroots involvement is clearly seen to be warping the priorities of the Leeds Initiative. So whilst it is acknowledged to have

> a very impressive track record in some respects, in dealing with the big questions of bringing the Royal Armouries together and in partnerships and so on, it would be nice to feel that that magisterial power of different interests in the city could actually be brought to bear on some of its more intractable problems (community leader).

Many community groups feel they have a legitimacy in their own right, and whilst accepting the role of political leadership from the council, they are increasingly keen to open up alternative mechanisms for influencing local development decisions. That the Leeds Initiative still has no voluntary sector representation at board level five years after its inception is widely seen as an indication of a council leadership more at ease with the private sector than with the grass roots. From such perspectives "It [the Leeds Initiative] has become something that is very detached and has moved another level up: it has lost contact with the roots" (voluntary sector).

Already, a process of evolutionary change is underway. As noted earlier, the new SRB sub-group of the Leeds Initiative is for the first time bringing a limited number of community groups into the ambit of the corporate city, albeit at a second tier level. Within months of its designation, some community sector members of the new group found themselves confronted by a style of corporate working already so embedded that it appeared as if their incorporation was in danger of becoming largely symbolic. Community leaders complained bitterly about the opacity of processes of bidding for funding in particular, and the seemingly secret mechanisms for soliciting and deciding on which bids should go forward. These tensions are still being struggled over (June 1995), but it does appear as if, bit by bit, in a process of gradual and mutual learning, some form of acceptable accommodation is being worked towards, which provides community groups with more than a symbolic role, whilst decision-making processes have been opened-up. Given the unsatisfactory speed with which central government expected the new arrangements for SRB to be put in place, and the tendency of the local authority still to assume it has an unchallengeable sole right to decide on local community development priorities, some initial feelings of local disquiet were perhaps to be expected. What is important is that a first step towards incorporation of community interests has begun. Whether it will be sufficient to stabilise and maintain the corporate city approach against alternative pro-growth regimes, or progressive city alliances, remains to be seen.

## Conclusion

> Jon [Trickett, the council leader] has understood the PR of corporate image for Leeds. He has done very, very well. The press image of Leeds is very high, we get no flak. [Previously it was] very highly politically contested... Not now. It seems stable, visionary: 24 hour city, 'Cafe Leeds,' the images are getting across. There is a very, very strong corporate dimension to Leeds and that is a good thing... what is sometimes glossed over, are the conflicts and the tensions and the divisions that are still within the city that are not being addressed by that corporate city (local politician).

For all its corporate city resemblances, it would be misleading to regard the Leeds Initiative as having yet evolved as the umbrella group for the overall strategic development of the city, even though its leaders sometimes choose to cast it in this role. Instead, it is possible to see the Leeds Initiative as a vehicle for mobilising public and private sector interests behind a broad economic development vision for the city, with a growing number of areas of policy development, mobilised through the sub-groups. It has also developed a useful informal coordination role, and most importantly a central role in presenting a public image of harmonious public-private relationships when wooing inward investors or seeking central government or European Union grants. However, in seeking to build consensus around economic development issues, the Leeds Initiative for its first four years in effect side-lined community development issues, albeit with occasional hand-wringing about the need to make sure that some of the new jobs being created went to local people. The problem with this initial focus on the

37

views of the major institutional stakeholders of the city is that it has perhaps unwittingly sidelined some powerful grassroots voices, voices which are already clamouring to be heard not just at the neighbourhood level, but on a city-wide stage. The more successfully the Leeds Initiative is able to project itself as the 'corporate' voice of the city, the louder the calls will become for inclusion from those on the margins. The next step for the Leeds Initiative has to be to engage with such groups in as productive a fashion as possible, at all levels, from setting the grand strategic visions, to making it work on the ground. The dangers of doing anything else are all too apparent

> It's one thing to project the city as an exciting, innovative, forward-looking, prosperous place, which it is in part, but that should not be at the expense of actually covering up some of the rottenness and severe deprivation that is actually around in parts of Leeds. Underneath there may be a great deal of frustration and anger, and unused energy, from people who want to have their voice heard (community leader).

## Acknowledgements

Particular thanks to Aidan While of CUDEM, who undertook a good number of the interviews for this project. In addition I would like to thank the 35 people who gave us their valuable time. The interviewees included chief officers and board members of bodies such as the Leeds Development Corporation, the Leeds Initiative, the Chamber of Commerce and Leeds TEC, plus local politicians (two MPs, two councillors), local authority officers, the Government Office for Yorkshire and Humberside and voluntary sector representatives. Thanks also to Kevin Thomas, Adam Tickell and Aidan While for comments on an earlier draft. Naturally, I alone am responsible for the analysis here.

## References

Bains Report (1972), *The New Local Authorities: management and structure. Report of the study group on local authority management structures,* London, HMSO.

Bateman, M. (1986), 'Leeds: a study in regional supremacy,' in Gordon, G. (ed) *Regional Cities in the UK, 1890-1980,* Harper and Row, London, 98-115.

Burt, S. and Grady, K. (1994), *The Illustrated History of Leeds,* Breedon Books, Derby.

Business in the Community (1994), *Seeing is Believing Programme 1994,* December, Business in the Community, London.

City of Leeds (1972), 'Industrial renewal and rehabilitation 1972-91,' City of Leeds, Leeds.

Clarke, M. and Stewart, J. (1991), *Choices for Local Government for the 1990s and Beyond,* Longman, London.

Clavel, P. (1986), *The Progressive City: planning and participation, 1969-1984,* Rutgers University Press, New Brunswick, New Jersey.

Cochrane, A. (1993), *Whatever Happened to Local Government?,* Open University Press, Milton Keynes.

DiGaetano, A. and Klemanski, J. (1993), 'Urban regimes in comparative perspective,' *Urban Review Quarterly,* 29 (19), 54-83.

Eisinger, P.K. (1988), *The Rise of the Entrepreneurial State: state and local economic development policy in the United States,* Wisconsin University Press, Madison, Wisconsin.

Fraser, D. (ed) (1980), *A Modern History of Leeds,* Manchester University Press, Manchester.

Gibson, M. and Langstaff, M. (1982), *An Introduction to Urban Renewal,* Hutchinson, London.

Goetz, E.G. and Sidney, M. (1994), 'Revenge of the property owners: community development and the politics of property,' *Journal of Urban Affairs,* 16 (4), 319-334.

Gummer, J. (1995), 'Working relations,' *The Guardian,* 28th June, 6-7.

Gunnell, J. (1990), 'Enterprise boards: an inside view,' in Campbell, M. (ed) *Local Economic Policy,* Cassell, London, 128-155.

Harding, A. (1994), 'Urban regimes and growth machines: towards a cross-national research agenda,' *Urban Affairs Quarterly,* 29 (3), 356-382.

Hartley, O. (1980), 'The second world war and after, 1939-74,' in Fraser, D. (ed) *A Modern History of Leeds,* Manchester University Press, Manchester, 437-61.

Haughton, G. and Whitney, D. (1994), 'Dancing to different tunes: the growth of urban development partnerships in West Yorkshire' in Haughton, G. and Whitney D. (eds) *Reinventing a Region: restructuring and policy response in West Yorkshire,* 107-126.

Hennock, E.P. (1973) *Fit and Proper Persons: ideal and reality in nineteenth century government,* Edward Arnold, London.

Hirst, S. (ed) (1926), *The Leeds Tercentenary Official Handbook,* second edition, Tercentenary Executive, Leeds.

Judd, D.R. and Ready, R.L (1986), 'Entrepreneurial cities and the new politics of economic development,' in Peterson, P.E. and Lewis, C.W. (eds) *Reagan and the Cities,* The Urban Institute Press, Washington.

Leeds Initiative (1991), *Annual Report 1990/91,* Leeds Initiative, Civic Hall,

Leeds.

Leitner, H. (1990), 'Cities in pursuit of growth: the local state as entrepreneur,' *Political Geography Quarterly,* 9 (2), 146-70.

Levy, J.M. (1992), 'The US experience with local economic development,' *Environment and Planning C,* 10, 51-60.

Logan, J. and Molotoch, H. (1987), *Urban Fortunes: the political economy of place,* University of California Press, Berkeley.

Mawson, J. (1983), 'Organising for economic development: the formulation of local authority economic development policies in West Yorkshire,' in Young K. and Mason, C. (eds) *Urban Economic Development: new roles and relationships,* Macmillan, London, 79-105.

Mayer, M. (1992), 'The shifting local political system in European cities,' in Dunford, M. and Kafkalas (eds) *Cities and Regions in the New Europe: the global-local interplay and spatial development strategies,* Belhaven, London, 255-78.

Meadowcroft, M. (1980), 'The years of political transition, 1914-39,' in Fraser, D. (ed) *A Modern History of Leeds,* Manchester University Press, Manchester, 410-436.

Nickel, D.R. (1995), 'The progressive city? Urban Redevelopment in Minneapolis,' *Urban Affairs Review,* 30 (3), 355-77.

Peck, J.A. and Tickell, A. (1994), 'Jungle law breaks out: neo-liberalism and global-local disorder,' *Area,* 26 (4), 317-26.

Peck, J.A. and Tickell, A. (1995), 'Business goes local: dissecting the 'business agenda' in Manchester,' *International Journal of Urban and Regional Research,* 19 (1), 55-78.

People of the Valley (1990), *Kirkstall Valley Development Plan,* March, Kirkstall Valley Campaign, Leeds.

Peterson, P. (1981), *City Limits,* Chicago, Chicago University Press.

Stewart, J. (1973), 'Developments in corporate planning in British local government,' *Local Government Studies,* 5 (first series), 13-29.

Stone, C.L. (1989), *Regime Politics: governing Atlanta 1946-1988,* University Press of Kansas, Lawrence.

Taylor, A.J. (1980), 'Victorian Leeds: an overview,' in Fraser, D. (ed) *A Modern History of Leeds,* Manchester University Press, Manchester, 389-407.

Tickell, A. and Peck, J. (1995), 'Social regulation after Fordism: regulation theory, neo-liberalism and global-local nexus,' *Economy and Society,* 24 (3), 357-386.

Whitney, D. and Haughton, G. (1990), 'Structures for development partnerships in the 1990s' *The Planner,* June 1st, 15-19.

# 3 The Leeds economy: Trends, prospects and challenges

*Mike Campbell*

## Introduction

This chapter examines both recent trends in the Leeds economy and its prospects for the future. The analysis begins with an outline of the broader economic context within which the Leeds economy operates. This is followed by a review of the current economic situation in the city; the pattern of economic change since 1981; and the likely pattern of change up to the year 2000. The chapter also includes a comparison of the performance of the Leeds economy with other major cities in the UK over recent years. In the final section some of the key economic issues facing the city are discussed. It is argued that Leeds is currently undergoing profound economic changes and that whilst the prospects of capitalising on this to bring about improved economic fortunes for the future are considerable, there remains considerable concern about how equitably the benefits of growth are spread.

## The economic context

Leeds, like all major cities, is deeply dependent on economic conditions external to it. Changes in the volume and structure of international and national demand; changing patterns of trade; international and national policies on interest rates, exchange rates and economic integration; these are all crucial in shaping the city's economy. As the world economy becomes increasingly integrated through the free flow of goods, services, capital, technology and information, economic impulses are transmitted with ever greater speed and intensity. There is seemingly no escape from the competitive forces shaping contemporary cities. Cities must adapt to the changes taking place and seek positions of competitive advantage in relation to such changes. It is through this process of adapting local economic structures that employers, workers and development agencies can influence the prospects for the city's economic fortunes.

At the global scale, current prospects in this external economic environment are the most favourable for many years. World trade is growing rapidly and both OECD and EU economic forecasts (OECD, 1994a; European Commission, 1994) predict steady growth in the years up to 2000. This growth will be export and investment-led, with the growth in consumer and government expenditure being much more limited. Similarly in the UK, the growth prospects are better than for many years, though unemployment is likely to fall only slowly and perhaps remain above two million right through to the millennium despite continuous economic growth (Cambridge Econometrics, 1995). The reasons for these high levels of structural unemployment are the source of considerable political and academic debate, with each explanation having very different implications for policy at the local as well as national and international levels (OECD, 1994b; ILO, 1995).

A number of major changes in this external competitive environment can be anticipated, not least:

- The development of further economic integration in the European Union including the continuing competitive effects of the single European market, the implementation of the Maastricht Treaty (in particular the pursuit of the 'convergence' criteria), the outcomes of the 1996 intergovernmental conference ('Maastricht II') and the possible adoption of a single currency in 1999, including or excluding the UK.

- The continuing rapid development of information and communication technologies. Their integration, reduction in cost and widening of access will have a considerable impact on local economic development prospects.

- The further development of the Newly Industrialising Countries, including the South East Asian Tiger and 'Cub' economies, as well as China and Indonesia. These economies are experiencing rapid economic and export growth, whilst securing significant improvements in their education and training levels. As new markets they offer considerable opportunities, but also enormous competitive threats.

- Increased trade liberalisation as a result of the completion of the

42

Uruguay round of the General Agreement on Tariffs and Trade (GATT) and the formation of competitor free trade areas to the European Union, like the Association of Pacific Exporting Countries (APEC) which accounts for 50 per cent of world GNP; and the Association of South East Asian Nations (ASEAN) which will develop a full free trade area by 2002 - these too will intensify the extent and nature of global competition.

- Foreign Direct Investment, offering the opportunity of access to it, to assist in local economic transformation, but also the threat of 'outward' investment from localities in the UK in pursuit of more attractive local conditions elsewhere.

- Government policy on a range of issues which will directly impact on localities' economic prospects, for example public expenditure, taxation, industrial policy and education and training policies.

In seeking to adapt to changing external competitive pressures, adapting the local 'supply side' is vital. Three main elements in this supply side are crucial to enhanced local competitiveness. Firstly, infrastructure - both the 'hard' infrastructure of telecommunications and transport and the 'soft' infrastructure of the cultural and physical environment. Secondly, human resource endowments - the quantity and quality of the labour force, in particular the availability of skills and qualifications appropriate to the trajectory of the local economy. The development of managerial skills is an ingredient which should not be neglected in pursuing this theme. Thirdly, there is the critical area of research and technology development - the development of, and investment in, processes and products at, or close to, the leading edge in order to provide competitive advantage and activities/employment at the front end of the 'product life cycle.'

**The Leeds economy: yesterday, today and tomorrow**

Leeds is, in population terms, the third largest city in the UK with a population of around 680,000 in 1991, with subsequent revisions based on estimates of census non-returns providing a figure of 717,400. As we shall see the Leeds economy has recently developed into one of the most successful local economies in England.

Contrary to much received wisdom, Leeds is not a manufacturing city and does not possess a particularly diverse industrial structure. Table 3.1 reveals that manufacturing accounts currently for just over 20 per cent of employment in the city, whilst the three dominant sectors are distribution (22 per cent), public services (22 per cent) and banking, insurance and business services (15 per cent). No other sector accounts for more than 10 per cent employment. Thus, nearly six jobs in ten are in just three sectors of the local economy, all in services. This is nearly three times the number of jobs in manufacturing.

Of course, this distribution of employment is highly gendered. For example, engineering employs over 21,000 men but less than 4,000 women. On the other hand public services employ twice as many women as men and both distribution and banking, insurance and business services employ more women than men.

Furthermore, more than one job in four is now part-time with over two thirds of these being in just two sectors - public services and distribution.

## Table 3.1 1991 Industrial structure of Leeds

|  | Total | | Male | | Female | | Part-Time | | Full-Time | |
|---|---|---|---|---|---|---|---|---|---|---|
|  | Nos | % | Nos | % | Nos | % | Nos | % | Nos | % |
| Agriculture | 1000 | 0.3 | 700 | 0.4 | 300 | 0.2 | 300 | 0.3 | 800 | 0.3 |
| Mining | 1600 | 0.5 | 1400 | 0.8 | 200 | 0.1 | 100 | 0.1 | 1500 | 0.7 |
| Utilities | 5800 | 1.9 | 3900 | 2.4 | 1900 | 1.3 | 500 | 0.6 | 5300 | 2.3 |
| Metals, minerals | 5200 | 1.7 | 4500 | 2.7 | 700 | 0.5 | 200 | 0.2 | 5100 | 2.2 |
| Chemicals | 4200 | 1.4 | 2700 | 1.7 | 1500 | 1.0 | 600 | 0.7 | 3700 | 1.6 |
| Engineering | 25400 | 8.1 | 21500 | 13.1 | 3900 | 2.6 | 1100 | 1.3 | 24300 | 10.5 |
| Food, drink, tobacco | 4100 | 1.3 | 2800 | 1.7 | 1200 | 0.8 | 400 | 0.5 | 2600 | 1.6 |
| Textiles, clothing | 7300 | 2.3 | 3100 | 1.9 | 4200 | 2.8 | 800 | 1.0 | 6500 | 2.8 |
| Other manu-facturing | 18000 | 5.7 | 12200 | 7.5 | 5700 | 3.8 | 2000 | 2.4 | 16000 | 6.9 |
| Construction | 13300 | 4.3 | 11500 | 7.0 | 1900 | 1.2 | 1000 | 1.2 | 12400 | 5.4 |
| Distribution | 69600 | 22.2 | 33900 | 20.6 | 35800 | 23.9 | 26100 | 31.5 | 43500 | 18.8 |
| Transport, commun-ications | 18100 | 5.8 | 13800 | 8.4 | 4300 | 2.9 | 1300 | 1.5 | 16800 | 7.3 |
| Banking, insurance | 45700 | 14.6 | 21800 | 13.3 | 24000 | 16.0 | 8300 | 10.0 | 37500 | 16.2 |
| Public Admin | 70900 | 22.6 | 23400 | 14.3 | 47500 | 31.7 | 30000 | 36.2 | 40900 | 17.7 |
| Miscellaneous services | 23300 | 7.4 | 6800 | 4.2 | 16500 | 11.00 | 10400 | 12.5 | 12900 | 5.6 |
| Total | 313700 | 100.0 | 164000 | 100.0 | 149700 | 100.0 | 82900 | 100.0 | 230800 | 100.0 |

*Source: Census of Employment (1991)*

## Recent economic change and performance

How has this industrial structure changed over time? Table 3.2 summarises the main recent changes based on an analysis of 15 industrial sectors. There has been considerable growth in recent years in banking, insurance and business services by more than 16,000 jobs or nearly 55 per cent. Other major growth sectors are miscellaneous services (21 per cent) and public services (16 per cent). On the other hand textiles and clothing (-35 per cent) and mining (-66 per cent) have experienced dramatic reductions in employment. Most manufacturing sectors experienced job loss except chemicals and metals/minerals.

### Table 3.2 Employment change 1984-1991

|                      | Absolute | %     |
|----------------------|----------|-------|
| Agriculture          | -100     | -9.3  |
| Mining               | -3,000   | -65.6 |
| Utilities            | -700     | -10.4 |
| Metals, minerals     | 300      | 6.9   |
| Chemicals            | 100      | 2.4   |
| Engineering          | -2,100   | -7.5  |
| Food, drink          | -700     | -14.3 |
| Textiles, clothing   | -3,900   | -34.9 |
| Other manuf'g        | -1,300   | -6.7  |
| Construction         | -1,200   | -8.4  |
| Distribution         | 2,000    | 3.0   |
| Transport            | -400     | -2.1  |
| Banking etc.         | 16,200   | 54.6  |
| Public Admin.        | 9,600    | 15.7  |
| Miscellaneous services | 4,100  | 21.1  |

*Source: Census of Employment, 1984, 1991.*

At a more detailed level we can identify those sectors which made the largest gain in employment terms (see Table 3.3); business services, medical services, education, social welfare and community services along with banking and finance and retailing, are the main contributors.

This strong economic performance is even clearer when we compare trends in employment over recent years across major British cities (see Table 3.4).

## Table 3.3 Employment change in Leeds (TTWA), 1981-1991: the largest gains

| | |
|---|---|
| Business Services | 11,100 |
| Medical Services | 7,600 |
| Education | 5,800 |
| Social welfare/ community services | 5,200 |
| Banking and finance | 5,100 |
| Retail Distribution | 5,000 |
| Sanitary Services | 2,800 |
| Wholesale Distribution | 1,700 |
| Insurance | 1,100 |

*Source: NOMIS*


## Table 3.4 Comparative economic change in major British cities

| LAD | % Change in Employment[1] (1981 -1991) | | | Unemployment[2] | |
|---|---|---|---|---|---|
| | Total | Male | Female | % Feb 1995 | % change 1983-94 |
| Leeds | 4.0 | -6.6 | 8.7 | 7.7 | -22.9 |
| Birmingham | -8.5 | -17.0 | 3.7 | 10.0 | -27.0 |
| Cardiff | 4.3 | -5.4 | 16.0 | 8.9 | -16.2 |
| Glasgow | -10.9 | -16.7 | -4.1 | 9.6 | -39.6 |
| Bristol | 3.6 | -6.8 | 17.7 | 7.9 | -2.5 |
| Manchester | -10.5 | -18.2 | -0.7 | 8.7 | -21.4 |
| Newcastle | 1.0 | -13.7 | 8.7 | 10.7 | -23.9 |
| Sheffield | -12.4 | -22.0 | 0.9 | 10.5 | -22.4 |
| Liverpool | -23.3 | -31.0 | -14.5 | 12.8 | -33.2 |
| Edinburgh | 4.1 | -1.8 | 10.8 | 6.9 | -20.6 |
| Nottingham | -0.1 | -4.5 | 4.9 | 9.8 | -3.5 |
| Leicester | -5.3 | -14.3 | 4.6 | 7.4 | -17.4 |

*Source: Census of Employment (NOMIS)*

Notes:
1. These figures are based on Local Authority Districts (LADs)
2. These figures are based on the 1984 travel-to-work areas (TTWAs)

The absolute growth of employment in Leeds between 1981-1991 was greater than in any other major city in Britain and, relative to comparable large cities like Manchester, Birmingham, Glasgow and Liverpool, which all lost large numbers of jobs in the same period, the performance is outstanding. It is important to note, however, that all the cities lost 'male, jobs' and all (except Manchester, Glasgow, and especially, Liverpool) gained 'female jobs'. Nonetheless Leeds lost a smaller proportion of 'male' jobs than, inter alia, Birmingham, Glasgow, Manchester and, especially Liverpool which lost nearly one-third of all men's jobs over the period.

As one would expect from this superior employment performance, current unemployment in Leeds is lower now than in any other major city in Britain, except Edinburgh. In fact, unemployment fell by nearly a quarter between 1983-1994. Interestingly, this fall was not very different from those cities with much inferior job generation and was, in fact, a much smaller fall than in Liverpool and Glasgow which have a poor job generation record. Whilst in Liverpool and Glasgow this is associated with heavy out-migration this is not the case in Leeds. The reason for the limited impact of new jobs in reducing unemployment in the city is a theme which is returned to later.

**Key features of the Leeds economy**

*Occupational structure*

The occupational structure of the Leeds economy is very similar to that of Britain as a whole, and is highly gendered (Table 3.5). Women are strongly concentrated in clerical and secretarial occupations (nearly one in three women work in these jobs), personal and protective services, and sales. Indeed more than half of all women work in these three groups of jobs. On the other hand, women are significantly under-represented in managerial, craft and plant and machine operative occupations.

*Employment status*

Nearly three quarters of all jobs in the city (73 per cent) are full-time and over a quarter are part-time (27 per cent). Whilst part-time jobs are overwhelmingly held by women (83 per cent), nonetheless 54 per cent of women work full-time. Overall, 48 per cent of all jobs are now held by women. In recent years, there has been a dramatic growth in part-time employment. For example, between 1984 and 1991, the number of jobs in the city increased by nearly 19,000, of which part-time jobs accounted for 17,000, whilst full-time jobs increased by less than 2,000.

## Table 3.5 Occupational structure of Leeds, 1991: % by major SOC group

|  | Total (%) | Male | Female | Total Numbers |
|---|---|---|---|---|
| Managers-Admin | 14.3 | 18.0 | 10.7 | 42,000 |
| Professional | 8.9 | 8.7 | 8.7 | 26,000 |
| Assoc. Prof'l | 8.2 | 8.0 | 9.1 | 24,000 |
| Clerical-Secretarial | 17.5 | 7.5 | 30.6 | 51,000 |
| Craft and Related | 15.4 | 24.4 | 3.8 | 45,000 |
| Personal | | | | |
| -Protective | 8.9 | 5.0 | 13.8 | 26,000 |
| Sales | 7.5 | 5.6 | 10.7 | 22,000 |
| Plant & Machine | | | | |
| Operatives | 10.3 | 15.6 | 3.8 | 30,000 |
| Other | 8.9 | 7.5 | 10.0 | 26,000 |

*Source: Census of Population (1991)*

## Table 3.6 Net capital expenditure per worker in Leeds manufacturing

|  | % of Leeds Manufacturing Average | % of GB Sector Average |
|---|---|---|
| Mechanical Engineering | 62 | 76 |
| Printing and Publishing | 152 | 94 |
| Chemicals | 270 | 71 |
| Food and Drink | 200 | 111 |
| Electrical and electronic engineering | 47 | 48 |
| Metal Goods | 73 | 96 |
| Timber and Furniture | 62 | 107 |
| Mineral Products | 6 | 70 |
| Textiles | 51 | 86 |
| Motor Vehicles/parts | 56 | 16 |
| Clothing | 21 | 79 |
| Manufacturing Sector | 100 | 72 |

*Source: Census of Production 1991*

Although manufacturing industry only accounts for 20 per cent of employment in Leeds, its value to the economy is significantly greater than this suggests. Not only does the sector have a high export intensity but many 'service sector' activities depend on it for their survival and growth. Moreover, as a share of the city's GDP, manufacturing will account for significantly more than its employment share, given its high output per worker relative to the service sector. In 1991 net manufacturing output in the city amounted to £1,700 million.

Output per worker (productivity) in manufacturing is 17 per cent above the regional average but 9 per cent below the average for British manufacturing as a whole. This relatively weak competitive position reflects both the structure of manufacturing in the city and its poor, compared to the national level, productivity performance. Nonetheless, since 1983 output per worker has grown by 33 per cent in Leeds compared to just 20 per cent in the region and 27 per cent in Britain as a whole. Thus, the 'productivity gap' is being narrowed. Indeed the output of the manufacturing sector in Leeds over the same period grew by 27 per cent - more than *double* the national rate.

The main growth sectors in this period were mineral products, where real output increased by over 140 per cent, chemicals, where the real value of output nearly doubled (95 per cent), metal goods (82 per cent), electrical and electronic engineering (64 per cent) and printing and publishing (54 per cent). All of these grew faster than their national counterparts. On the other hand, the value of net clothing output fell by nearly 40 per cent and food and drink grew by only 8 per cent.

The productivity, and therefore, all else being equal, the competitive, performance of industries in the city differs widely. Whilst metal goods, mechanical engineering and timber/furniture have productivity levels superior to the British average for their sector all too many have levels of productivity less than the average. In particular, motor vehicle parts, electrical and electronic engineering and printing and publishing have productivity levels at least 15 per cent below the national average for their sector.

One of the major reasons for the overall lower productivity levels in Leeds manufacturing is the low level of capital expenditure in Leeds companies. Table 3.6 summarises the position. On average, net capital expenditure per worker in Leeds manufacturing is more than a quarter below the national average. Even two of the three 'big spenders' have investment levels below their national sector average.

## Small firms

The small firm sector in Leeds is dealt with in greater depth in Chapter 9. For the purposes of this chapter, it is possible therefore to be brief. There are around 17,500 VAT registered companies in Leeds, between them employing around 312,000 people. Around 87 per cent of these companies employ less than 25 people, 12 per cent employ between 25-200 people and only one per cent employ more than 200 people (Census of Employment 1991). In this sense, the local economy is dominated by 'small firms.' However, whilst 87 per cent of all companies employ less than 25 people they account together for only 29 per cent of all employment in the city. The 12 per cent of companies which employ between 25-200 people account for 39 per cent of employment, and the one per cent of companies employing more than 200 people, account for nearly one-third (32 per cent) of total employment. In this sense the local economy depends on the economic well-being of all sizes of company.

## Self-employment

Around 9.5 per cent of the labour force in Leeds are now self-employed, well below the national average of 11.5 per cent and indeed one of the lowest of any locality in the country. Furthermore whilst the numbers in self employment grew by 39 per cent between 1981-1991, this was well below the national rate of 61 per cent. Some 30 per cent of all the self employed in Leeds work in the distribution, hotels and repairs sector with a further 23 per cent work in the construction sector.

## Skill shortages

As local economies undergo restructuring the scope for mismatches between the skills required by employers in the 'new' jobs and those possessed by former employees in the 'old' jobs increases (Campbell and Baldwin 1993). In 1994 nearly one company in four in Leeds was experiencing difficulty in filling vacancies. Nearly a half of these recruitment difficulties related to skill shortages.

## Workforce qualifications

Education and training have a central role to play in local economic development (Campbell 1994, 1995). The National Targets for Education and Training set targets for assessing localities' positions and the progress required to meet the skill challenges for the rest of the decade. The key measurable targets, and where Leeds is positioned on them are outlined in Table 3.7. These targets are stretching but probably represent the minimum the city needs to achieve to compete effectively in high value-added, high wage, sectors of the economy given increasing competitive pressures.

### Table 3.7 Leeds and the national training targets

|  | Current Position (1994) | Target |  |
|---|---|---|---|
| Foundation Target 1 | 60% | 80% | (1997) |
| Foundation Target 3 | 34% | 50% | (2000) |
| Lifetime Target 1 | 44% | 100% | (1996) |
| Lifetime Target 3 | 39% | 50% | (2000) |

Foundation Target 1:   80% of young people to reach NVQ 2 or equivalent
Foundation Target 3:   50% of young people to reach NVQ 3 or equivalent
Lifetime Target 1:     all employees to take part in training or development
Lifetime Target 3:   50% of the workforce qualified to NVQ 3 or equivalent


*Unemployment*

The unemployment rate in Leeds in February 1995 was 7.7 per cent, a rate which has fallen from 9.0 per cent, or by 13 per cent, over the previous year. This means that around 30,000 people are currently registered as unemployed. Of these, around 39 per cent have been unemployed for more than one year, a slightly higher proportion than the national average, and one which shows no sign of falling. The highest rates of unemployment are amongst those aged under 24 and the lowest amongst those aged above 45. Whilst older people experience relatively low rates of unemployment, they do however suffer disproportionately from high levels of long term unemployment.

Most importantly, unemployment is concentrated amongst certain ethnic minority groups and in particular parts of the city. Table 3.8 shows the large variation in rates across different ethnic groups. We can see that unemployment is extremely high amongst Caribbean, Pakistani and Bangladeshi men and amongst Pakistani and Bangladeshi women. We can also see that for both men and women the 'non-white' unemployment rate is more than double the white rate.

51

## Table 3.8 Unemployment rates (%) amongst selected ethnic groups

|  | Male | Female |
|---|---|---|
| White | 11 | 6 |
| Caribbean | 26 | 11 |
| Indian | 12 | 11 |
| Pakistani | 31 | 28 |
| Bangladeshi | 42 | 29 |
| All non-white | 23 | 14 |

*Source: Census of Population (1991)*

Unemployment is heavily concentrated in a number of localities within the city. The 'inner area' of Leeds, comprising 12 of the city's 33 wards has an unemployment rate more than two and a half times the average in the rest of the city, 16.8 per cent compared to 6.3 per cent. The variation is even greater for men alone, 22.9 per cent compared to 8.3 per cent. In University ward, the overall unemployment rate is around 24 per cent, in Harehills 20 per cent, in Seacroft 18 per cent and in Burmantoffs 17 per cent. On the other hand it is 4 per cent in Wetherby and 3 per cent in Otley and Wharfedale.

More generally, the 'Index of Local Conditions' (Department of the Environment 1994) shows that eight of these inner wards in Leeds are amongst the 10 per cent most deprived wards in England.

## The future

It has been estimated that over the next three years (1994-1997) the Leeds economy will generate an additional 5,600 jobs, of which 5,000 will be taken by women, and of which 3,800 will be part-time (Policy Research Unit, 1995). This increase in employment of 1.7 per cent is associated with a growth of the local economy, in terms of output, by 9.9 per cent. This is a low employment intensity of growth.

The industries expected to grow most strongly in employment terms in the period up to the year 2000 are public administration, health and education, banking, insurance and business services (largely in the latter category) and the heterogeneous 'miscellaneous services' sector covering cleaning services, radio and television, theatres, nurseries and even dating agencies. There will be only small job losses across manufacturing and utilities, but transport and communications may suffer large losses associated with deregulation and privatisation, for example in postal services, the railways and telecommunications. Just as importantly, there will continue to be significant changes in many sectors as a result of the changing patterns of exports, imports, investment and consumer expenditure which will drive industrial change in the city over the next few years. Table 3.9 identifies the main industries that are likely to undergo significant change up to the year 2000.

In occupational terms, the jobs which are most likely to grow are managers, professionals and associate professionals, with slower growth in personal services and sales. On the other hand clerical/secretarial, semi-skilled manual, skilled manual and unskilled occupations are likely to continue their decline.

In terms of changes in the nature of labour supply up to the year 2000 there are three important points to make. First, the female labour force will continue to grow, by perhaps five per cent, but the numbers of men will actually fall. Second, 80 per cent of new labour market entrants will be women. In consequence, by the year 2000, women will constitute the majority of the labour force in the city. Third, the workforce is getting older. The number of 20-34 year olds in the labour force is likely to fall by 13,000 and the number of 35-54 year olds will increase by the same amount in the period up to the year 2000. Indeed the only growing sections of the labour force are men aged 45-59 and women aged 35-59. All other age/sex groupings will decline in size.

**Key issues**

Following from this brief examination of the changing nature of the Leeds economy, there are a wide range of important issues that need to be identified and addressed in terms of policies to secure a competitive and prosperous future for the city.

At the most general level, it is important for development agencies in the city, most notably the Government Office, Leeds Development Agency, Leeds Training and Enterprise Council, as well as employers and individuals, to secure both a greater knowledge of, and willingness to adapt to, the changes taking place in the city's economy.

This involves, at a minimum, a commitment to the collection and collation of appropriate economic, corporate and labour market information; the development of a range of research projects to turn information into usable intelligence; and the development of the technical capacity of all those engaged in the economic development process in the city. The city is fortunate to have development agencies who take such information and research seriously. It also involves ensuring that this intelligence is used to

## Table 3.9 Key sectors 1995-2000

| | |
|---|---|
| Output Growth[1]: | Engineering, electrical equipment, optical equipment, transport equipment, hotels/ restaurants, telecommunications, business services. |
| Employment Growth[2] | Retailing, distribution, hotels/catering, other business services, education, health/social welfare, miscellaneous services, professional services |
| Output per Head[3] | Pharmaceutical, metals, mechanical engineering, electronics, vehicles, aerospace, transport equipment, gas supply, rail transport, communications. |
| Exports[4] | Paper, printing and publishing, drinks, pharmaceutical, chemicals, rubber/plastics, electronics, instruments, vehicles, aerospace, air transport, professional services, computing services. |
| Imports[5] | Oil/gas, drinks, textiles, wood/wood products, paper/printing/publishing, pharmaceutical, chemicals, rubber/plastics, metal goods, electronics, instruments, hotels/catering. |
| Consumer Expenditure[6] | DIY goods, furniture, carpets, major appliances, textiles, hardware, travel, telecommunications, sports goods, betting, pharmaceuticals, NHS, catering, expenditure overseas. |
| Investment in Plant Machinery[7] | Electrical and optical equipment, vehicles, hotels/restaurants, air transport, telecommunications, roads |
| Investment in Building Works[8] | Metals, electrical/optical equipment, transport equipment, paper, printing and publishing, other manufacturing, retailing, hotels/restaurants, rail transport, air transport, telecommunications, financial and business services. |

Notes
1 More than 4% per annum      5 More than 4% per annum
2 More than 10.000 per annum  6 More than 4% per annum
3 More than 3% per annum      7 More than 5% per annum
4 More than 5% per annum      8 More than 5% per annum

*Source: Adapted from Cambridge Econometrics (1995).*

inform strategy, policy and planning and to make decisions about priorities and subsequent resource allocation. Both these are necessary, but not sufficient, conditions for success. In addition organisations must be committed to responding to the changing economic landscape in a proactive way.

More specifically, there are a range of issues that require attention. Perhaps the most pressing of these is to ensure that the benefits of economic success reach as wide a range of citizens as possible. The growing polarisation of the labour market associated with recent economic change, has created a range of well-paid, relatively interesting, reasonably secure full-time jobs taken largely by those who live in outer Leeds, largely by men and largely by 'whites.' But it has also created a range of poorly paid, dull, insecure, often part-time jobs taken largely by those who live in inner Leeds, done largely by women and often by young people. It has also created a large pool of long-term unemployed people who are increasingly detached from the labour market. The risk of increasing economic and social exclusion which is generated by the segmented nature of the labour market, is serious indeed. A 'two speed' city, with little chance to change gear, is an unstable city. The city council and the Leeds Initiative are both committed as one of their principal objectives to see "that all the citizens of Leeds must benefit from improvements to the city." Key to securing this objective is much wider access to enhanced skills and qualifications as well as action by employers and development agencies to link access to jobs to those groups and communities most in need. There is an enormous mismatch between the skills and experience of job seekers and the skills and experience required by many of the new jobs being created. There is also a mismatch between, broadly speaking, men losing jobs and women gaining them. The prospects for men, especially those with low levels of qualification and specific job experience in declining industries and occupations, are poor unless they can adapt to new labour market requirements.

Another important issue can be expressed as a tension between 'jobs *in* Leeds and jobs *for* the people of Leeds.' Who is getting, and who will get, the new jobs that are being created? Whilst nearly 12,000 (net) new jobs were created between 1981-1991, unemployment in the city fell by only about 1,000. Whilst many of those jobs were taken by those previously not registered as unemployed, mostly women returners to the labour market and new labour market entrants, it is likely that most of the remainder were taken by commuters, that is those living outside the city. There were at least 20,000 more in-commuters to the city in 1991 than there were in 1981. Moreover, net in-commuting has increased over the same period by 18,000. As many as a quarter of the jobs in Leeds are held by residents from outside

55

Leeds. This reflects the increasing inter-penetration of local labour markets and the growth of Leeds as a major employment centre as well as increasing travel to work distances and population dispersal. However, it also shows, rather graphically, that many of the benefits of local economic success in recent years have by-passed some local residents to the benefit of those living in neighbouring localities.

It is also vital to raise overall skills and qualifications levels to those that can compete with other major cities elsewhere in the UK, the rest of the European Union, and increasingly the World. If Leeds is to really become a major European city it will need a highly qualified labour force to focus on the knowledge and information intensive jobs of the next millennium.

The city will also need to ensure that its economy becomes more diverse. By 2001, six jobs in every ten are likely to be in just three sectors: Distribution, Hotels and Catering; Public Services, Health and Education; and Banking, Insurance, Finance and Business Services. The danger is that if any of these sectors undergo major restructuring or decline as a result of increasing competitive pressure domestically or internationally, the Leeds economy may find itself vulnerable. A greater focus on high technology organisations; on organisations undertaking 'Head Office' and Research and Development functions; on activities at the front end of the product life cycle would be beneficial, particularly in finance, insurance and manufacturing. A clear focus on the development of growth industries around leisure and the coming together of information and communication technologies in telecommunications and the media, would also be beneficial.

These are just some of the key challenges facing Leeds in the next few years. The Leeds Development Agency (LDA), the economic development arm of the City Council, and the Leeds Training and Enterprise Council (TEC) will need to work together with other key partners in economic development like the Chamber of Commerce and the Universities, probably through the Leeds Initiative, in tackling these challenges. The Single Regeneration Budget, any future rounds of City and Regional Challenge, as well as the LDA's and TEC's economic development strategy, will play a key role in developing a shared view of problems, their causes and their policy solutions in the years ahead. For Leeds to remain one of the most successful local economies in the UK, it will need to continually adapt to the opportunities and threats it faces. But perhaps the most pressing challenge, for all of us, is to find the determination, resources and policies to ensure that many more of Leeds' citizens benefit from its continuing economic success.

# Further reading

Leeds TEC's Annual Labour Market/Economic Assessment provides considerable detail on the Leeds economy, especially in relation to labour market and training issues. The Leeds Economic Development Strategy Draft Economic Assessment (1994), produced through the Leeds Initiative, provides a more analytical but shorter review. The Policy Research Unit (Leeds Metropolitan University) has produced a wide range of studies on the Leeds economy including those on women; the media; health; clothing and the cultural industries.

The Leeds Economic Bulletin, produced jointly by the LDA and the TEC, provides a monthly update on local economic trends.


# References

Campbell, M. (1994), 'Education, training and economic performance,' Policy Research Unit, Leeds Metropolitan University, Leeds.

Campbell, M. (1995), 'Learning pays: individual commitment, learning and local economic development,' Employment Department, Sheffield.

Campbell, M. and Baldwin, S. (1993), 'Recruitment difficulties and skill shortages in Yorkshire and Humberside,' *Regional Studies*, 27 (3).

Cambridge Econometrics (1995), *Industry and the British Economy*, Cambridge Econometrics, Cambridge.

Department of Environment (1994), *Index of Local Conditions* HMSO, Department of Environment, London.

European Commission (1994), *Economic Outlook*, European Commission, Brussels.

ILO (1995), *World Employment Report 1995*, ILO, Geneva.

OECD (1994a), *Employment Outlook*, OECD, Paris.

OECD (1994b), *The Jobs Report Volumes I/II*, OECD Paris.

Policy Research Unit (1995), 'Leeds local labour market forecasts: Policy Research Unit forecasting model,' Policy Research Unit, Leeds Metropolitan University, Leeds.

# 4 Exploring the geographies of social polarisation in Leeds

*John Stillwell and Christine Leigh*

## Introduction

In common with most large cities in north western Europe, Leeds is comprised of neighbourhoods or localities whose socio-economic characteristics vary considerably across the social spectrum and whose physical fabric bears witness to past eras of industrial development and residential planning. Current opinions of city prosperity tend to be divided between those who identify with Leeds as the 'capital of the north of England,' riding on the crest of a wave of service sector employment growth in which financial and legal services are predominant, and those who regard the civil disturbances during the summer of 1995 as indicative of the social malaise that exists in some of the inner city areas where unemployment levels are well above regional norms and where the quality of the housing stock is low.

It is inevitable in a complex, cosmopolitan city, with a population of nearly 715 thousand people in 1991, that social inequalities will be reflected in spatial patterns of relative affluence or poverty. This was the case 100 years ago when Leeds was considered to be a vibrant commercial and industrial centre with coal, engineering and leather tanning as its core industries and with its clothing trade in expansion. In reality, many of its working residents were living in squalid residential areas packed together in an atmosphere heavily polluted from nearby factory emissions. The worst slum conditions were to be found in areas such as the Leylands and Quarry Hill where the immigrant communities of Irish and east European Jews congregated (Caunce and Honeyman, 1993) whilst the wealthy bourgeoisie lived in suburban splendour, particularly to the north of the city. In the

1990s, although the social inequalities are much less extreme, significant geographical variations occur across the city that now reflect only in small part the historical legacy of nineteenth century industrial development. Whilst economic restructuring and diversification in the last 25 years have transformed the Leeds skyline as well as the employment structure, and whilst Leeds has tried to promote itself as a European city of culture, entertainment and consumption, parts of inner city Leeds have suffered the socio-economic problems familiar in other large cities. These are the problems of unemployment, poverty and crime which are popularly associated with an urban 'underclass' and which have been the focus of attention for central and local government policymakers during the last fifteen years.

In this chapter, the primary aim is to present a factual account of spatial inequality across the whole of Leeds district by exploring the geographies of selected social indicators using the results of the 1991 Census of Population. One of the most difficult problems confronting geographical research is that of choosing an appropriate level of spatial resolution in order to interpret statistical information effectively. In this case, pragmatic reasons suggest that the ward scale is most suitable; enumeration districts are too small and there are too many of them for exploring city-wide patterns. Thus, the wards that make up the metropolitan district of Leeds (Figure 4.1) are used as the spatial units for the analysis reported in the third section of this chapter. These wards are comprised of some 1,400 enumeration districts and the fourth section aims to provide a brief presentation of the extent of variation in the incidence of one indicator, ethnic minority populations, within the inner city wards. We begin, however, in the next section, with a comparison of Leeds against five other principal cities in England using a selection of social indicators. This comparison attempts to establish a context for the intra-urban analysis which follows thereafter.

**Leeds as a principal city**

Leeds is classified as a principal city by the Office of Population Censuses and Surveys (OPCS). Other provincial cities in this district category are Birmingham, Manchester, Liverpool, Sheffield and Newcastle-upon-Tyne. Population estimates for mid-1991 which take into account the results of the 1991 Census have been produced for these metropolitan districts by the OPCS (1993), allowing some comparison of overall demographic size. Birmingham has the largest provincial metropolitan district population whilst the population of Leeds is greater than any of the other principal city districts (Table 4.1). In terms of population dynamics, all the big cities

experienced decline during the 1980s as people moved down the urban
hierarchy and towards the more rural areas (Stillwell et al., 1993). The
relative population decline in Leeds was less severe than from the other
principal cities and in particular in Liverpool where the population dropped
by over -10.4 per cent between 1991 and 1981.

**Figure 4.1 Ward boundaries of the Leeds district, 1991**

**Table 4.1 Population statistics, principal cities**

| Principal city | Population mid-1991 | Change 1981-91 Number | Change 1981-91 % | Area (Ha) | Density 1991 (Pers/ha) |
|---|---|---|---|---|---|
| Birmingham | 1,002,900 | -59,600 | -5.6 | 26,547 | 37.8 |
| *Leeds* | *714,800* | *-28,000* | *-3.8* | *56,172* | *12.7* |
| Sheffield | 527,400 | -36,600 | -6.5 | 36,734 | 14.4 |
| Liverpool | 479,000 | -55,700 | -10.4 | 11,282 | 42.5 |
| Manchester | 436,900 | -41,900 | -8.8 | 11,612 | 37.6 |
| Newcastle | 277,100 | -16,200 | -5.5 | 11,178 | 24.8 |

*Source: OPCS (1993); 1981 and 1991 Censuses*

It is necessary, however, to recognise that this type of broad comparison ignores the fact that districts vary substantially in area and that population statistics are partly a function of the way in which the administrative boundaries have been drawn. The boundary of Leeds metropolitan district (Figure 4.1), for example, encloses over 56,000 hectares and includes several peri-urban and rural communities beyond the extent of the built-up area of the city itself.

Despite the problems inherent in comparative analysis, three sets of indicators selected from the 1991 Census Local Base Statistics (LBS) are used to provide some contextual insights into how Leeds compares with its main competitor cities. The sets of indicators are focused on measures of socio-economic disadvantage, affluence and ethnic composition.

Seven variables have been chosen as indicators of disadvantage in 1991 (Table 4.2). Unemployment rates are a common yardstick for measuring economic disadvantage and the percentages of the male and female economically active population aged between 16 and retirement age that are unemployed are lower in Leeds than in other principal cities. Female unemployment rates in Leeds are lower than the average for the whole of England, with 37 per cent of economically active women in the city working full-time and 24 per cent work part-time; in Manchester, the comparable statistics are 30 per cent and 15 per cent. The 'unskilled' socio-economic group is defined by OPCS to include unskilled manual workers, farmers and agricultural workers and 6.2 per cent of the economically active residents of Leeds are defined in this category, a lower proportion than in other principal cities apart from Birmingham.

Three other social indicators are presented in Table 4.2. The first of these is the percentage of all households that contain a single parent with dependent children. There are around 275,000 households in Leeds according to the 10 per cent sample data on family type, of which 5.5 per cent are lone parents with dependent children. Although this proportion is higher than in Sheffield, the picture in Leeds is much brighter than in Liverpool and Manchester where single parent families are 9.7 per cent and 11.5 per cent respectively. The second variable, the percentage of households that have no access to a private car, indicates that Leeds is in a better position than the other principal cities; although the no car proportion is well below the national average, the proportion is some 15 percentage points lower than the Manchester proportion. It is not surprising, therefore, to discover that 52 per cent of persons economically active drive to work in Leeds whereas only 42 per cent do so in Manchester. The third indicator is a measure of housing tenure, the percentage of households that rent from the local authority. Leeds has a similar proportion to Birmingham and Liverpool in this respect, with 76,500 council house tenants.

**Table 4.2 Selected indicators of disadvantage, principal cities, 1991**

| Principal city district | Unemployment rate (%) Male | Female | Unskilled (%) | Lone parent + dep children (%) | No car (%) | LA renting (%) |
|---|---|---|---|---|---|---|
| Birmingham | 14.6 | 6.7 | 5.9 | 7.2 | 45.1 | 26.4 |
| *Leeds* | *10.4* | *4.4* | *6.2* | *5.5* | *41.3* | *27.3* |
| Sheffield | 13.8 | 5.6 | 7.4 | 5.0 | 44.9 | 33.4 |
| Liverpool | 20.3 | 9.2 | 9.2 | 9.7 | 56.9 | 28.6 |
| Manchester | 17.4 | 7.4 | 9.3 | 11.5 | 56.6 | 38.4 |
| Newcastle | 15.7 | 6.5 | 8.5 | 7.4 | 54.4 | 34.6 |
| England | 9.6 | 4.6 | 6.9 | 5.2 | 32.4 | 19.9 |

*Source: LBS, 1991 Census*

There exists a wide literature on urban deprivation analysis using census data (for example, Hirschfield, 1993) and recent work for the Department of the Environment by Robson et al. (1995) reports a new approach to the construction of a composite index of deprivation. However, the set of variables identified here provides sufficient evidence to suggest that the problems of disadvantage are less pronounced in Leeds than in the other principal cities. This is not to say, however, that Leeds does not have its problem areas where conditions are adverse; these variables are re-examined at the ward scale later in the chapter.

The flip side of this approach is to consider a second set of variables that measure some of the dimensions of urban affluence or prosperity. In this case, five variables have been selected (Table 4.3). The first two are measures of male and female self-employment which, in both cases, show that Leeds performs better than the other principal cities. Leeds also shows up well when we consider the proportion of the economically active population classified as professional or managerial and when we compare the proportion of households with access to two or more cars. The final variable is owner occupation which indicates that one in five households in Leeds own their own properties; a proportion which compares favourably with the other principal cities apart from Birmingham.

The third dimension used in this comparison is that of ethnic composition of the residential population. The statistics presented in Table 4.4 indicate that minority ethnic groups are a much larger proportion of the population in Birmingham and in Manchester than they are in Leeds where there are approximately twice as many Indians, Pakistanis and Bangladeshis as there are Blacks from the Caribbean, Africa and elsewhere. Thus, Leeds has a non-White ethnic minority percentage that is similar to that in the country as a whole.

The variables discussed is this section suggest that social conditions in Leeds as a whole at the beginning of the 1990s were not as negative as in several of the other principal cities of England. An assessment of the profile of Leeds relative to other districts in Yorkshire and Humberside is available in Duke-Williams et al. (1994).

**Table 4.3  Selected indicators of prosperity, principal cities, 1991**

| Principal city district | Self employed (%) Male | Female | Professional & managerial (%) | 2 or more cars (%) | Outright owner occupier (%) |
|---|---|---|---|---|---|
| Birmingham | 9.0 | 2.4 | 16.2 | 15.8 | 22.3 |
| *Leeds* | *11.2* | *3.4* | *19.0* | *18.3* | *20.5* |
| Sheffield | 10.1 | 2.9 | 17.5 | 15.3 | 19.3 |
| Liverpool | 7.2 | 1.8 | 12.5 | 9.4 | 17.0 |
| Manchester | 8.2 | 2.1 | 15.6 | 9.6 | 14.8 |
| Newcastle | 7.8 | 2.6 | 17.6 | 10.5 | 16.2 |
| England | 13.4 | 4.0 | 20.0 | 23.9 | 24.1 |

**Table 4.4  Population by broad ethnic group, principal cities, 1991**

| Principal city district | White (%) | Black Caribean, African, Other (%) | Indian, Pakistani Bangladeshi (%) |
|---|---|---|---|
| Birmingham | 78.5 | 5.9 | 13.5 |
| *Leeds* | *94.2* | *1.6* | *3.2* |
| Sheffield | 95.0 | 1.6 | 2.3 |
| Liverpool | 96.2 | 1.6 | 0.5 |
| Manchester | 87.4 | 4.7 | 5.4 |
| Newcastle | 95.9 | 0.4 | 2.5 |
| England | 94.1 | 1.8 | 2.9 |

*Source for both tables: LBS, 1991 Census*

## Social polarisation: a spatial analysis

The metropolitan district of Leeds is divided into 33 wards and in this section of the chapter, we consider the extent of geographical disparity across the district by examining a number of social indicators at this spatial scale. The first of these variables is the main indicator of socioeconomic disadvantage, the rate of unemployment computed by dividing the number of persons recorded at the time of the 1991 Census of Population by the economically active population (Figure 4.2).

**Figure 4.2 Male and female unemployment rates by ward, 1991**

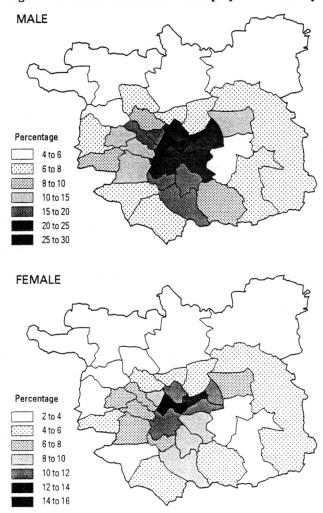

65

The patterns suggest a significant concentration of unemployment in some of the central areas of the city including the wards of University and Harehills in particular, where 20 per cent of the economically active population are unemployed. There is a wedge of higher unemployment that extends southwards to Middleton whilst the wards across the north of Leeds (Aireborough, Otley and Wharfedale, North and Wetherby) together with Halton, all have relatively low rates of male and female unemployment. There is, of course, a distinct gender differential in the unemployment rate. In 1991, the mean male unemployment rate for the city was 12.2 per cent compared with a mean rate for females of 6.6 per cent. Although the range of rates is much narrower for females and the coefficients of variation, which provide a standardised measure of variation around the mean, are higher for males, the spatial patterns are similar: unemployment is higher in the inner city wards. The statistical relationship between unemployment and distance from the city centre can be determined by taking measurements of the distance of each ward centroid from the centre of the city and computing correlation coefficients. The correlation coefficient (R) for total unemployment rates against distance is -0.75 and is statistically significant.

The availability of data from the 1981 Census on the number of males and females seeking work allows some comparison between unemployment rates at the beginning of the 1990s with corresponding rates a decade previously. It is fortunate that there were no major revisions of the ward boundaries in Leeds between the two Censuses. Both Census dates fell during periods of recession and consequently the mean rate of unemployment by ward in 1991 is almost exactly the same as in 1981. The evidence from this comparison is that the range of person unemployment rates widened during the 1980s. In 1981, the range was from 4.1 per cent to 19 per cent whilst in 1991, the minimum was 3.8 per cent and the maximum was 21 per cent. However, those areas experiencing high rates of unemployment in 1991 were much the same as those in 1981; i.e. University, Harehills, Seacroft, Chapel Allerton, City and Holbeck, Richmond Hill and Burmantofts all had rates of total unemployment over 15 per cent at both Census dates. At the extreme, rates of unemployment increased in both University and Harehills wards. At the other end of the spectrum, several wards, including Otley and Wharfedale, Aireborough and Pudsey North in particular, recorded lower rates of unemployment in 1991 than in 1981.

The spatial patterns of four other indicators selected from the Census are illustrated in Figure 4.3. The first two of these variables are indicators of disadvantage, the second two are car ownership and housing tenure variables; they are not gender-specific. The 1991 Census provides counts from a 10 per cent sample for persons in different social classes based on occupation. The unemployed are included in this classification according to their occupation in their most recent job in the last 10 years. Figure 4.3a illustrates the spatial pattern of those residents aged 16 and over in households who were classified in social class 5, unskilled occupations, as a proportion of all residents over 16 in households. The counts have been multiplied by 10 to compensate for their sample nature and the values range from 12.6 per cent in Burmantofts to 2.3 per cent in Roundhay. The inner city wards of Hunslet, University and Richmond Hill, in addition to Burmantofts, have proportions of unskilled that are above 11 per cent of the population aged 16 and over.

**Figure 4.3 Selected indicators of social disadvantage by ward, 1991**

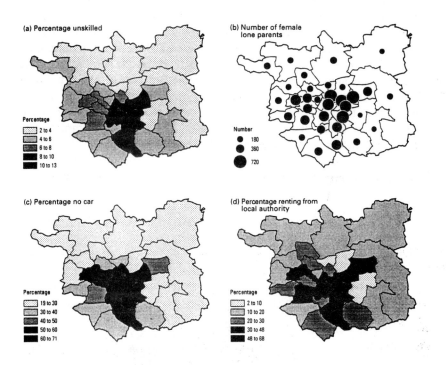

The second variable is a measure of lone parents aged 16 and over in households with a child or children aged 0-15. The lone parent is not necessarily the parent of the child and the count excludes lone parent families living in a household with other adults. The Census indicates that a very high percentage of these parents are female; for example, in Chapel Allerton, which has the highest absolute number of lone parents, there were

67

719 females and 38 males in this category in 1991. In relative terms, 8 per cent of the female resident population aged 16 and over were lone parents and 95 per cent of all the lone parents in Chapel Allerton were female. Figure 4.3b uses proportional symbols to depict the absolute number of female lone parents.

Overall, 41 per cent of the households of Leeds contain residents that do not have access to a car. At ward level, this proportion (Figure 4.3c) varies widely between the extremes of University ward, where 70.5 per cent of the household do not have a car, and Wetherby, where the corresponding proportion is 19.1 per cent. Clearly, the importance of car availability will differ according to residential location and therefore this particular variable is perhaps of less value than others as a measure of social disadvantage.

The fourth indicator is from the housing section of the LBS and is a count of the number of households that rent from the local authority expressed as a percentage of the number of households across all tenure groups (Figure 4.3d). The geographical pattern of council house renting reflects the previous state housing programmes and there are clearly parts of Leeds where a high proportion of properties are council-owned. In particular, Seacroft was the focus of new housing construction in the late 1960s and early 1970s, as areas of back-to-back housing close to the city centre were redeveloped and as 'Coronation Street moved out of town'.

**Figure 4.4 Council house stock unfit or in need of repair by ward, 1991**

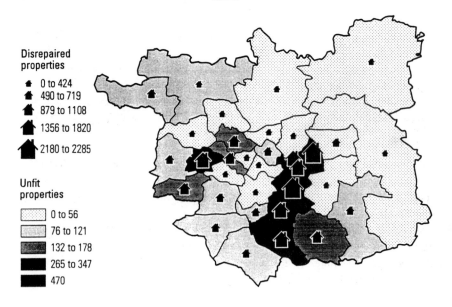

Disrepaired properties

- 0 to 424
- 490 to 719
- 879 to 1108
- 1356 to 1820
- 2180 to 2285

Unfit properties

- 0 to 56
- 76 to 121
- 132 to 178
- 265 to 347
- 470

Seacroft now has 67 per cent of its households classified as renting from the local authority in comparison with Halton or Roundhay where the proportion of households renting from the council is under three per cent. The quality of the council housing stock is an important consideration and data from the city's housing department for 1991 indicates the distribution of council properties that were unfit or in a state of disrepair (Figure 4.4).

Burmantofts, Harehills, Hunslet, Richmond Hill and Seacroft are the wards where physical problems of the housing stock are greatest and it is therefore not surprising to discover that Burmantofts, Hunslet and Richmond Hill are the wards which received most expenditure through the various housing programmes.

The indicators that have been presented so far have been selected to provide a series of measures of relative disadvantage. Four further variables are now used to explore the geographical distribution of those sections of the population who are potentially more affluent. Whilst high unemployment rates are associated with disadvantage, high rates of self-employment do not necessarily represent greater advantage but they do indicate the entrepreneurial characteristics of local populations which are likely to translate into greater wealth. Figure 4.5 illustrates male and female self-employment expressed as a percentage of economically active residents aged over 16. The counts include self-employed people both with and without employees. The rates are considerably lower for females than males but the spatial patterns are similar. Wards in the north of Leeds tend to have the highest self-employment rates notably North, Roundhay and Otley and Wharfedale, whereas inner city wards in general have much lower rates.

Social classes 1 and 2 are defined in the Census to include professional occupations and managerial and technical occupations respectively. The spatial patterns of these variables together with the distributions of households with two or more cars and of households who own their properties outright are presented in Figure 4.6.

The distribution of professionals (Figure 4.6a) is interesting in that the ward with the highest proportion in this category is Headingley. Proximity to the University of Leeds is likely to be one explanation for this ward having nearly 13 per cent of residents aged 16 and over recorded as professional. Seacroft and Burmantofts, in complete contrast, have less than 1 per cent of their populations classified in social class 1. The geographical pattern of those residents in managerial and technical occupations (Figure 4.6b) tends to follow the north-south, inner city-outer suburbs division that several of these maps depict. In this case, the proportions of the population represented are much greater. In Roundhay and Wetherby, for example, 40 per cent of residents are classified as managerial and technical compared with 13 per cent in Seacroft, Hunslet, Richmond Hill and Burmantofts.

## Figure 4.5 Self-employment rates by ward, 1991

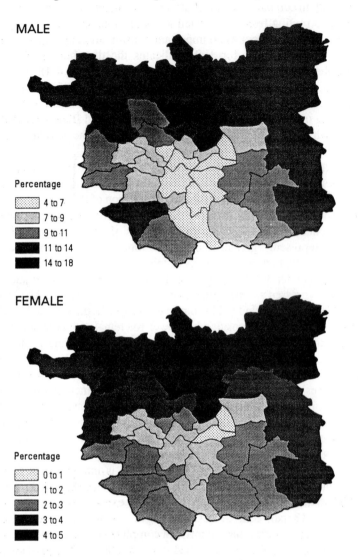

MALE

Percentage
- 4 to 7
- 7 to 9
- 9 to 11
- 11 to 14
- 14 to 18

FEMALE

Percentage
- 0 to 1
- 1 to 2
- 2 to 3
- 3 to 4
- 4 to 5

A relatively significant proportion of households in Leeds have access to two or more cars. The average across the wards is 18 per cent, the percentage varying from 42.5 per cent in Wetherby to 5 per cent in University and City and Holbeck wards. The inner city-outer areas contrast is again evident in Figure 4.6c. On the other hand, the distribution of those households which own their properties outright is rather different (Figure 4.6d). Just over 35 per cent of households in Halton are owned in this way and wards like Moortown, Pudsey North and Morley North also have over 25 per cent of owner occupiers who have bought outright.

**Figure 4.6 Selected indicators of social advantage by ward, 1991**

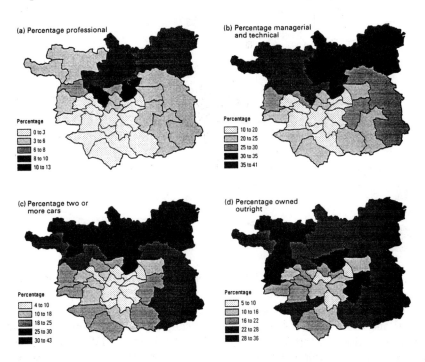

The 1991 Census was the first to include a question about ethnicity. Although it has been shown earlier that the proportion of the population of Leeds which is recorded as being in an ethnic minority group in 1991 is not as high as in other principal cities, these groups are nevertheless important components of particular localities within the city. Figure 4.7 shows that the non-white population is concentrated predominantly in inner city wards where on average they constitute over 5 per cent of the population. In Chapel Allerton, this proportion rises to 33.8 per cent, and in Harehills and University wards the proportions are 30 per cent and 20 per cent respectively. In contrast, wards on the periphery such as Barwick and Kippax, Rothwell, Otley and Wharfedale, Garforth and Swillington and Wetherby all have non-White ethnic minority populations that constitute less than one per cent of their total populations.

**Figure 4.7 Non-white population by ward, 1991**

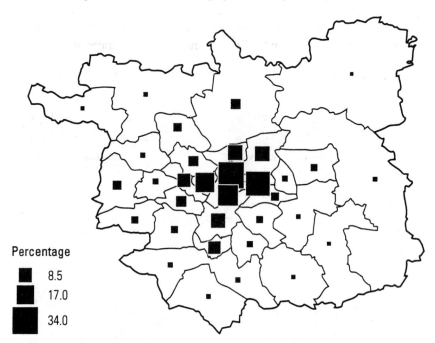

Percentage

■ 8.5

■ 17.0

■ 34.0

There is little doubt that the locations of ethnic minority groups within the inner city of Leeds coincide with the incidence of high unemployment rates. Correlation coefficients measuring the relationship for males and females are 0.59 and 0.64, both of which are statistically significant given the sample size. It is also clear from previous analysis (Rees et al., 1993) that it is not appropriate to consider the non-White population of Leeds as a homogenous group. Rees et al. have conducted an analysis which distinguishes between Blacks, Indians, Pakistanis and Others, which examines the geographical distribution of these groups at the ward scale, and which discusses some of the socioeconomic characteristics of these particular groups. In the next section of this chapter, the ethnic variable is used as an example to illustrate spatial variations within the wards of central Leeds.

**The distribution of ethnic groups in inner city Leeds**

Data from the 1991 Census for enumeration districts in Leeds is available from the Small Area Statistics (SAS) computer files. In the case of ethnicity, the standard ten ethnic group classification used in the LBS is condensed to four groups: White; Black; Indian, Pakistani and Bangladeshi; and Chinese and Other. The distributions of two groups are used here to illustrate how the residential locations of minority populations vary between enumeration districts in the wards of inner Leeds. Figure 4.8 illustrates the relatively concentrated distribution of Leeds' Black population. The data for each enumeration district is the count of the ethnic group expressed as a proportion of the total population. It is clear from the map that the focus of the Black residential community is in the south of the Chapel Allerton ward where Black proportions of the total population are in excess of 50 per cent and reach 73 per cent in one enumeration district. University ward also contains enumeration districts where Blacks comprise between 10 per cent and 20 per cent of the total population.

**Figure 4.8 Distribution of the Black population by enumeration district, 1991**

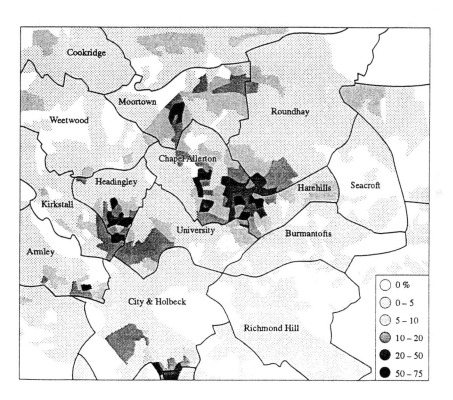

The distribution of Indians, Pakistanis and Bangladeshis in inner Leeds is much more widely scattered with centres of relatively high concentration in Harehills, Chapel Allerton, Moortown, Headingley, Kirkstall, Armley, University and City and Holbeck (Figure 4.9). It is unfortunate that the Census data at this scale is not sufficiently disaggregated to be able to examine the distribution of these three ethnic minority populations separately since one suspects the existence of three distinct geographies.

What these two maps do clearly illustrate is that there are considerable spatial variations occurring within wards. In Chapel Allerton ward alone there are areas in the north and west with relatively low penetration of ethnic minority populations, whereas in the central, south and eastern areas, there are enumeration districts where Blacks and Asians concentrate in high proportions. As the spatial scale becomes refined, the more detailed geographical characteristics of the residential population begin to emerge. It would be informative to use the ethnic data to measure indices of segregation or dissimilarity at this level, for example.

**Figure 4.9 Distribution of the Indian, Pakistani and Bangladeshi population by enumeration district, 1991**

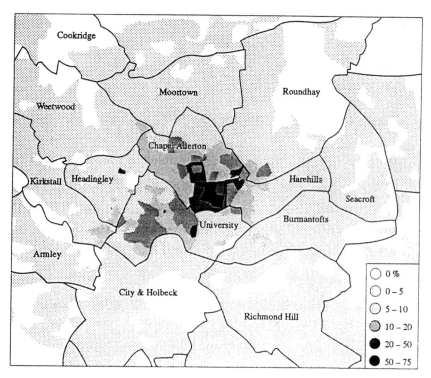

## Conclusions

This chapter has addressed three questions: How does Leeds compare with other principal cities in terms of certain social indicators? What are the geographical patterns of variation in social indicators across the city as a whole? Are there significant variations in ethnic minority populations within central Leeds?

The comparison of Leeds with other cities is complicated by the way in which the Boundary Commission has defined the boundaries of the large metropolitan districts that are used for the publication of Census data by OPCS. Given this limitation, the evidence suggests that social conditions in Leeds metropolitan district, as measured by rates of unemployment, proportions of unskilled, lone parents, households with no car and households renting from the local authority, are better than in most of the other principal city districts. Moreover, Leeds has higher percentages of males and females self-employed, professional and managerial and with two or more cars than the other cities. Leeds also has much lower proportions of Black and Asian ethnic minority populations than Birmingham or Manchester.

The ward maps presented have demonstrated that variations across the city as a whole are quite dramatic when particular indicators are utilised. Geographical patterns are dominated by the differences between inner city and outer suburban areas and the relative affluence of the northern wards of the district. In order to summarise the distinctive characteristics of different parts of Leeds, profiles of two wards are included from a set of profiles produced by Duke-Williams and Williamson (1993). These profiles contain an age pyramid, a tenure categorisation, the ratio of single males to single females and the proportions in occupational and ethnic groups. They also show the unemployment rate, the proportion of students, the proportion of households with central heating and the proportion of households with dependent children. The first profile is for the inner city ward of Harehills (Figure 4.10) which suffers from many of the problems of urban disadvantage, whilst the second is for the northern ward of Otley and Wharfedale (Figure 4.11), a relatively prosperous and suburban outer area. A comparison of these two profiles is sufficient to demonstrate the extent of the contrast which exists between some of the inner and outer wards of the metropolitan district.

Data from the 1991 Census SAS have been used to produce detailed maps of the distributions of ethnic minority populations within the wards of inner Leeds which demonstrate the value of using the enumeration district scale and which indicate that Blacks are concentrated in the south of Chapel Allerton whereas concentrations of Indians, Pakistanis and Bangladeshis are more widely distributed.

Whilst the analysis of geographies of social polarisation reported in this chapter at ward scale has indicated that Leeds is a city of widely contrasting communities, there is good reason to further utilise the rich resource of the Census of Population to explore social contrasts in more detail at the enumeration district scale - the preparation of an atlas of the demographic and socioeconomic structure of Leeds would be a good starting point.

**Figure 4.10 Census profile of Harehills ward, 1991**

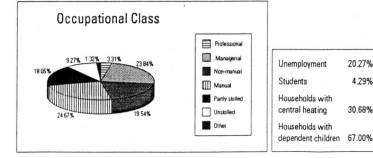

Source: Adapted from Duke-Williams and Williamson (1993)
Census data courtesy of the OPCS, funding from the ESRC

**Figure 4.11 Census profile of Otley and Wharfedale ward, 1991**

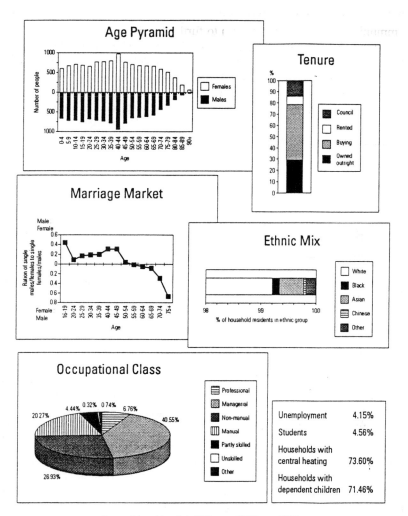

Source: Adapted from Duke-Williams and Williamson (1993)
Census data courtesy of the OPCS, funding from the ESRC

Another important and productive line of research might involve a comparison of the geography of need in Leeds against the provision of services or the incidence of public expenditure available through the various local and central goverment initiatives that have been or are now in operation.

**Acknowledgements**

Files containing enumeration district boundaries in digital form were obtained from the 1991 Census Digitised Boundary data at the University of Edinburgh. The authors are grateful to Alistair Towers at Edinburgh for his assistance in facilitating the process of digital data acquisition, and to Ian Kyles, Leeds City Council Department of Housing Services, for providing data on council house stock for Figure 4.4. All Census data have been provided courtesy of the OPCS and are subject to Crown Copyright. Finally, thanks to the Graphics Unit, School of Geography, University of Leeds, for producing the figures.

**References**

Caunce, S. and Honeyman, K. (1993), 'The city of Leeds and its business 1893-1993,' in Chartres, J. and Honeyman, K. (eds) *Leeds City Business 1983-1993*, Leeds University Press, pp. 1-23.

Duke-Williams, O. and Williamson, P. (1993), 'A 1991 Census profile of Leeds wards,' *Working Paper 93/15,* School of Geography, University of Leeds.

Duke-Williams, O., Stillwell, J.C.H and Williamson, P. (1994), 'Yorkshire and Humberside: a regional profile,' *Working Paper 94/12,* The Yorkshire and Humberside Regional Research Observatory, Leeds.

Hirschfield, A. (1993), 'Using the population census to study deprivation,' Paper presented at the joint IBG, RSA, BSPS Conference on 'Research on the 1991 Census' University of Newcastle-upon-Tyne, September.

OPCS (1993), 'Revised final mid-1991 population estimates for England and Wales and constituent local and health authorities based on the 1991 Census results,' *OPCS Monitor PP1 93/1,* HMSO, London.

Rees, P.H., Phillips, D. and Medway, D. (1993), 'The socioeconomic position of ethnic minorities in two northern cities,' *Working paper 93/20,* School of Geography, University of Leeds.

Robson, B.T. et al. (1995) *Assessing the Impact of Urban Policy, Inner Cities Research Programme,* HMSO, London.

Stillwell, J.C.H., Rees, P.H. and Boden, P. (eds) (1993), *Migration Patterns and Processes Volume 2: Population Redistribution in the United Kingdom,* Belhaven, London.

# II
# THE ECONOMIC MACHINE

# 5 World Class Leeds: Sectoral policy and manufacturing alliances in the 1990s

*Kevin Thomas and John Shutt*

Our aim is to ensure that Leeds stays at the top of the tree in Britain and is recognised world-wide for the skills of its workforce and the quality of the products it produces (Andrews, 1994, p.2)

## Introduction

'World class,' 'European city,' 'the Intelligent city' are all phrases recently coined to represent Leeds' economic development ambitions. Such phrases embody notions about the competitive advantage of the city relative to other cities, and the need for Leeds to improve its competitiveness. They show awareness of the much broader geographical scale at which current, as opposed to traditional, industrial competitiveness is played out; and they demonstrate participation in the global arena of 'place marketing' in which external perceptions of local economic dynamism and growth potential are seen as critical in attracting new investment to established cities. As we shall show, the key to achieving such ambitions is thought by key stakeholders in the Leeds economy to lie in collaborating to develop sectoral initiatives. This outlook is most clearly demonstrated by the approach taken to economic development strategy elaboration by the most significant active stakeholder agencies: the Leeds Training and Enterprise Council (Leeds TEC), and the Leeds Development Agency (LDA), the department of Leeds City Council responsible for economic development.

The way that corporatist partnership arrangements have evolved in relation to the manufacturing sectors of the Leeds economy forms the main theme of this chapter. A range of partnership-based sectoral projects have been undertaken in the city, with varying degrees of success. In looking for explanations we argue that the difficulties encountered in mounting a coherent and effective sectoral intervention strategy lie less within the sectoral mechanisms, where there is some evidence of coalitions of interest and effort, than in broader influences and processes. Further, we argue that the constraints faced by city-based sectoral partnership strategies are likely to be encountered in any similar British city, not just Leeds. More positively, we consider whether opportunities for galvanising manufacturing sector revival in Leeds are likely to improve in the near future.

**Rationales for a sectoral coalition approach**

The main reason why the development of successful sectoral coalitions has not proved easy, even in an avowedly corporate city, is that the sectoral strategies and mechanisms are modest and partial responses to broad, deep and powerful economic processes. Leeds, which has fared better than most other British cities from the uneven development of the national economy, nevertheless provides examples of what Massey identifies as the three main explanations for shifts in the spatial arrangement of the UK economy: "the international division of labour, the (related) changing sectoral structure of the economy, and the dominant modes of technological organisation" (Massey, 1988, p.273). The first of these elements is probably the most powerful, resulting in an increasingly international restructuring of manufacturing production. A 'global shift' of manufacturing results as capital pursues economies in the factors of production, particularly labour costs, in a 'new international division of labour.' And the evidence of the local impacts of such global processes can be seen quite clearly in the decline of the clothing industry in Leeds, an industrial sector which in many ways characterises the new global economic order (Dicken, 1992). The impact of globalisation varies with the sectoral mix of local economies and with local economic, social and cultural traditions. Indeed, it can be argued that "Increasingly the pressure posed by globalisation is to divide and fragment cities and regions, to turn them into arenas of disconnected economic and social processes and groupings" (Amin and Thrift, 1995, p.97). As has recently been shown in neighbouring Bradford, the impacts of such broad processes on specific groups in the labour market can vary dramatically (Haughton et al., 1993). Amongst the 'winners' in the Leeds labour market have been women seeking part-time jobs, who account for all of the net job gains in the city. Amongst the losers must be counted disadvantaged groups such as males seeking full-time jobs and ethnic minorities, for whom the unemployment rate, at 20 per cent in 1994, was over twice the rate for whites, with sub-groups suffering much more - e.g.

82

Bangladeshi males at 42 per cent, or over four times the white unemployment rate (Leeds City Council, 1994a).

Many of the manufacturing sectors in Leeds are players in international markets and, increasingly, owned by international companies. The implications of dispersed ownership for local control and influence over investment and employment decisions in the city are evident in the recent history of manufacturing jobs loss from Leeds. International comparative studies have pointed to regional production centres like Leeds sharing a similar pattern of de-industrialisation, new inward investment, service sector and regional consumption and administration growth. This has resulted in a common pattern of internally fractured city economies, with the component parts absorbed into wider webs of capital accumulation (Amin and Thrift, 1995).

The commitment of the 'corporate city' to establish or reclaim Leeds' position as a 'world city' represents, in part, a recognition that Leeds, as a place, is competing internationally with other cities, in ways analogous to the competition between different firms in their respective product markets. This interest is reflected in the way the city promotes itself to potential investors, although the Leeds approach to place marketing was anticipated by other towns in the region (Smales, 1994). Claims to be the 'capital of Yorkshire' and, more controversially, 'capital of the North' represent the city's collective perception of its role in the national space economy, and may be a necessary precursor to more international claims of eminence. Such claims may also form an important element of social bonding between the partners in the growth coalition for the city and a motivation for the competitive pursuit of city growth. That motivation is needed to engage in corporatist strategies is shown by the problems found in Leeds of establishing and maintaining private sector involvement in sectoral partnerships. Constraints on stakeholder engagement can include: most obviously, the shrinkage of manufacturing sectors in the city, reducing the pool of potential partners; the difficulty business people can have in finding time for partnership activities; and the effect of non-local ownership of 'local' companies, for whom the development of the Leeds economy may be of marginal concern. This issue of the 'business leadership resource' has been problematic for a number of Leeds' manufacturing sector projects.

Before surveying the economic condition of manufacturing industries in the city and the sectoral institutional arrangements, some account is needed of the conceptual basis for the sectoral partnership approach which so dominates the local economic development agenda. The sectoral approach has been a key feature of local economic development strategies in UK local government, particularly since the mid-1980s (Haughton and Thomas, 1992). The origins of the approach lay in an assumption that local government interventions, such as local enterprise boards, could significantly influence the direction and rate of change of local economies, so as to increase local control of the means of production and create an advantage for local labour, whilst becoming less dependent on (largely non-local) capital (Boddy, 1984). This 'local state' response was quickly tempered by, first, a realisation that the politically opposed central government would not allow such 'alternative' economic strategies to be pursued on any scale, along with a reduction in resources for spending on such strategies; second, new legislation which circumscribed more adventurous local economic policies; and third, the abolition of the metropolitan counties and the Greater London Council, which had been important supporters of local economic strategies (Eisenschitz and Gough, 1993). By the 1990s the 'new realism' of local economic development strategies often included an element of focusing on industrial sectors as a means both of targeting scarce council resources and of developing networks of private sector partners for collaborative initiatives within those sectors (Haughton and Thomas, 1992).

An important part of the conceptual underpinnings for sector-based strategies was provided by accounts of the development of 'new industrial districts' in parts of Europe, particularly in 'the third Italy' (Best 1990; Murray, 1991; Pyke et al., 1990; Scott, 1988). These accounts held out the prospect that modestly resourced local and regional development agencies might intervene to assist the development of mutually supportive networks of small and medium enterprises which, by organising production in a system of 'flexible specialisation' might produce local economic regeneration to help counteract the local job losses from the restructuring of large, multinational 'Fordist' companies. The new industrial districts were based on small scale craft production, although often with a high-tech, or high fashion product content, and appeared to challenge the notion of the inevitability of manufacturing jobs decline in European cities. If such conditions could be created or re-created in cities such as Leeds, manufacturing jobs might revive, and local authorities, in partnership with the private sector, might have a real influence on city economies. The appeal of such an approach to local policy makers included:

- the apparent scope for local small and medium enterprises to provide an alternative to dependence on external large firms for economic and jobs growth;

- the importance of proximity and of local cultural and community influences in fostering formal and informal sectoral inter-firm linkages;

- the apparent applicability of well-understood mechanisms from UK local economic development practice to the development of inter-firm networks of SMEs.

Our discussions with actors in the Leeds Initiative sectoral projects indicated that such a conceptualisation of the basis for sectoral strategies had had some influence in the city, particularly in the LDA, although mostly implicitly, rather than explicitly. There is no LDA policy document which explains the conceptual basis for sectoral policies, but much documentation which implicitly relies on the logic of local inter-firm coalitions as the basis for local economic growth (e.g. LDA, 1993, 1994a, 1994b). There have been other accounts of local economic development which locate particular local strategies within a sectoral coalition framework (e.g. Geddes and Bennington, 1992). The most comprehensive attempt to effect such an approach was the (now abolished) Greater London Council's London Industrial Strategy (GLC, 1985).

However, caution needs to be used in promoting industrial district-derived revival strategies. Amin and Thrift (1995) point out that cities are not necessarily the natural location for modern industrial district development. Few such districts studied have been located in major cities, and, of course, many traditional manufacturing districts in cities have declined significantly. Additionally any success created may be confined to the focus sectors, which remain as "self-contained islands in a disarticulate city economy" (ibid, p.92). Thus the sectoral specificity of industrial district/ sector project strategies may provide limited spillover benefits for broader urban regeneration. There is also the danger that the 'new localist' analysis of local regeneration potential is being absorbed too uncritically by the participants in local coalitions who harbour 'transition fantasies' in which the emerging forms of local governance effortlessly transform local economies by dint of purely local collaborative institutional adjustments (Lovering, 1995). There are thus good grounds for scepticism about the power of local coalitions to deliver substantial economic, political and social recovery in the teeth of hitherto overwhelming global processes.

Whatever the conceptual origins of the Leeds Development Agency's approach to economic development, any success from its strategy would need to be balanced against the demonstrated and long-term effects of de-industrialisation in the Leeds economy. The continuing globalisation of its manufacturing sectors indicates probable further competitive disadvantage for manufacturing in Leeds. In addition the success of the institutional mechanisms being used to attempt sectoral recovery depends on drawing from a limited supply of the key business stakeholder inputs, as pressure on their time grows in a competitive economic situation.

In the following sections we trace the recent history of the development of key manufacturing sectors in the Leeds economy, and outline the policy mechanisms adopted to pursue sectoral growth through coalitions. Finally we draw conclusions about the direction and impact of manufacturing sectoral initiatives in Leeds and their potential.

## The Leeds manufacturing economy

*Leeds as an industrial district*

Leeds had developed into one of the major industrial centres in the UK by the time of its incorporation as a city in 1893. At that time coal mining, engineering and tanning were dominant industries, followed by clothing and printing. However Leeds, even then, was a notably adaptable and flexible local economy:

> The organic industrial structure of Leeds was a powerful source of development and key factors in the long-term regional pre-eminence of Leeds were its ability to shift investment into new fields; the interaction between many diverse industries and firms; the support they provided for each other, and the flexibility of the economy as a whole (Caunce and Honeyman, 1993, p.14).

Bateman (1986) records how the flax and dying manufacturing industries of the nineteenth century gave way to the growing engineering and ready-made clothing industry of the twentieth century and how the "industrial structure of Leeds was resilient in the face of change, always producing new entrepreneurs and industry to fill any growing gaps." Rather than any particular geographical advantage, such as raw material availability, it has been entrepreneurial expertise and adaptability in a mutually supportive business culture which seems to explain the relative economic buoyancy of the city.

Local specialisms - niche markets and 'flexible specialisation' - were key features of nineteenth century Leeds. Thus the printing industry developed early specialisations in colour printing and packaging and in educational printing. The clothing industry benefited from the local capacity for engineering innovations. The Leeds-invented 'band knife' enabled precision cutting of cloth which transformed the economics of mass tailoring. It was adapted by all the major retailer-producer tailoring chains which concentrated in the city (including John Collier, Hepworth and Montague Burton), developing Leeds as the largest tailoring centre in Europe by the inter-war years. Local engineering industries also developed rapidly in

86

response to the demands of Leeds businesses, establishing sectoral diversity in instrument, electrical and mechanical engineering, in vehicle production and metal manufacturing.

As the twentieth century progressed, the local engineering sector's innovative capacity declined as locally owned companies began to be swept up into the subsidiaries of United Kingdom companies based outside Leeds. By 1967, half the engineering workers in Leeds were employed in the 20 per cent of engineering firms owned by UK multinational companies - GKN, British Leyland, Hawker Siddeley, Tube Investments and ICI, which began the task of rationalisation and restructuring in response to the competitive pressures of the 1960s and 1970s (Weiner, 1976).

Clothing and tailoring declined dramatically after the Second World War as the clothing industries failed to respond to the post-war trend away from mass-produced suits and tailored coats. Leeds clothing producers had to adapt not only to the loss of UK demand and the 'retailing revolution', which led to the closure of Leeds-based multiple chains such as Hepworth and John Collier, but they also had to respond to the new international division of labour in clothing manufacture in which, at the lower end of the market, expensive UK labour was displaced by cheaper overseas labour and, in traditional suiting, with more stylish European products made with high labour costs, but with the aid of high technology equipment. Thus the once globally eminent Leeds clothing district was out-competed partly by the kind of advances in production technology which had earlier led to its growth. Also the features of the Leeds economy which had once made it resemble a classic Marshallian industrial district, at least in the clothing sector - high output levels making specialised contracting using expensive specialised machinery viable, high levels of local inter-firm networking, permitting external economies of scale for small companies and making it possible for the city to be 'collectively entrepreneurial' - had diminished substantially. It is an irony of the city's present sectoral coalition strategy that it is seeking to achieve economic growth initially created, but not sustained, by historic industrial district conditions.

In the late twentieth century Leeds has a much reduced manufacturing employment base, like all British cities. Manufacturing employment now accounts for just over 20 per cent of employment in the city, though the city is still an important base for many manufacturing firms (Chapter 3). In 1991 the engineering sector employed 24,300; textiles 6,500; chemicals 3,200 and 'other manufacturing' 16,000 people, all manufacturing sectors having experienced dramatic employee reductions throughout the 1980s, except the chemicals and metals/minerals sectors. Closely allied to the wider changes occurring in the British economy, the Leeds manufacturing base has been diminished and restructured. Local control of industry has passed into external multinational control. Increasingly, the city's top manufacturing companies are either American or European-owned as control moves away from a local and even a national base.

## The key firms in manufacturing

As a basis for manufacturing growth, it would be helpful if Leeds had either a concentration of major 'global player' companies headquartered or with important decision-making centres located in the city. In that case Leeds would have the level of access to influence over the investment decision processes in the internationalised economy that is an essential component of 'world city' status (see Chapter 1). Alternatively, taking an industrial district hypothesis, it would be helpful if Leeds had substantial clusters of small and medium size companies in sectors with growth potential, around which appropriate institutional mechanisms could be built to encourage mutually supportive inter-firm networks for collaborative innovative within and across sectors. Little evidence is available in the city about the size structure, technical capacity, or collaborative inclination, against which to test the latter hypothesis. An overall enterprise size league table for Leeds would show (excluding the public sector) privatised utilities at the top of the table, employing over 1,500 each, followed by financial services companies and retailing. The absence of dominant private sector employers in services is echoed in manufacturing.

Few manufacturing establishments in Leeds now employ more than 1,000 people - just four in 1995. The largest companies now typically employ 200-1,000 people in Leeds plants. Many Leeds-based and Leeds-founded firms have continued to be absorbed into larger, international holding companies, a process which has accelerated in recent years. The internationalisation of production and the inter-connections between the different sectors of Leeds Manufacturing are symbolised by the strategy of John Waddington Plc, a company regarded by Chartres (1993) as 'almost synonymous with Leeds' and famous for its games division manufacturing Monopoly, Cluedo and Subbuteo. In December 1994 Waddington sold its games division to Hasbro of the United States for $50 million. The cash generated by the company was used in the paper and board division to fund the acquisition of Inca, a Dutch company. This has given the Waddington paper and board packaging business an opening in Europe and helped to double its turnover. The John Waddington printing business provides specialised products for the building societies and financial institutions based in Leeds, at a time when the building society mergers and acquisition process is providing new demands for the Leeds printing industry.

## Spatial impacts of manufacturing investment decisions

Before the LDA recently focused on sectoral initiatives, land and premises initiatives, including spatial planning strategies, dominated the local economic policy agenda in the city, and they still remain important. To understand this historic policy position it is necessary to consider the spatial implications of manufacturing investment decisions over time in Leeds. The spatial and the sectoral interact one with another, increasingly so as globalisation of capital provides investors with ever-growing freedom to pursue their own company's economic advantage. Each investment decision has a spatial impact, most obviously where a new factory is built or expanded, or where plant is renewed; but also where plants are closed down or 'rationalised' - i.e. disinvestment. The origin of local economic development strategy in UK local authorities can be traced to local and regional industrial development policy, whose primary focus was on land and premises supply to enable and encourage investors to locate new plant in receptive, needy areas.

Even after the dramatic expansion of non-land and premises policies during the 1980s local economic development strategies may well still be dominated, at least in spending terms, by land and premises provision initiatives designed to attract new companies or to enable local companies to expand or remain in the locality. In Leeds the provision of infrastructure accounted for over half of economic development spending in 1993/4 and 1994/5 (Leeds City Council, 1994b). Leeds City Council is a major owner of industrial land in the city, and external financial support from the UK government and from the European Union has subsidised and encouraged land-based initiatives. It should also be noted that the Leeds Development Agency is essentially an expanded version of the City Estates Department, whose primary function was to manage the Council's estate of industrial and other land and to deal with land sales and acquisitions.

The City Council's land-based initiatives, based on its land holding, its access to funds for infrastructure projects such as access roads, and its powers of compulsory purchase for land assembly, are major tools in pursuing the Council's overall economic strategy, alongside the other main policy plank, sectoral initiatives. Land-based initiatives have been critical both in attracting and retaining manufacturing employment (with an emphasis on retention) and in trying to address the spatial shifts of manufacturing employment to, from and within Leeds. There are three main dimensions to the spatial redistribution of industry affecting the city: the suburbanisation of industry; regional redistribution of industry; and global redistributions.

The *suburbanisation* of industry is a long-established process in most countries of the developed world. Automated mass-production systems have required large acreages of level land on which to build, with much lower space densities per production worker. Old multi-storey mills and older factories dependent on fixed power sources are no longer viable for many production functions, particularly those in inner city areas which suffer from poor road access, inefficient layout and traffic congestion. Newer factories have been built in suburban locations, where large plots of land were available and relatively cheap, particularly where there was good access to major roads. The spatially liberating effect of road haulage over rail and canal-based transport has reinforced suburban advantages. Shortage of industrial development land in Leeds has frequently led to suburbanising moves by Leeds manufacturers, and the shortage is exacerbated by high land costs. Industrial land in the city in March 1994 was costing in excess of £200,000 an acre, compared with £150,000 in Wakefield and Bradford, £125,000 in Sheffield and £100,000 in Hull/South Humberside.

The land cost 'push factor' has been reinforced by the attraction of cashing in land assets in high-priced Leeds, at least central Leeds, and moving outwards. The financial services boom in Leeds has fuelled this process, making it feasible and attractive for owners to abandon their centrally located factories, driving the manufacturing restructuring process forward. As an example of this process the printing and packaging company John Waddington plc's former production site at Wakefield Road, Stourton, Leeds, was redeveloped in 1994/95 as a new office building for the First Direct Bank. Reinvestment in Leeds by Waddingtons Cartons included a new £17m factory in a cheaper suburban location off Dewsbury Road, containing £5m of 'state of the art' packaging and printing equipment. Throughout the 1980s Leeds manufacturing firms were rationalising their old inner city locations, establishing property development arms and building new plants either in suburban Leeds locations or elsewhere in the region.

Once the decision to relocate a factory has been made, the outcome may be suburbanisation or it may be a much further move, and there are some examples of moves from Leeds to elsewhere in Yorkshire and Humberside, producing *regional restructuring*. The interplay of the Leeds industrial land market with the internal restructuring processes of these major firms and their engagement with regional policy produces a familiar story throughout the 1980s and early 1990s. Often the decision to relocate regionally is influenced by regional assistance grant-aid. In 1994 the last remaining large Leeds-based tailoring company, Centaur Clothing, moved its production to Goole, Humberside, switching 490 jobs out of the City. A similar decision was taken by Yorkshire Chemicals plc, which has re-invested in a new £10m plant, not at their Leeds base but in Selby, North Yorkshire where a cheaper greenfield site was available.

Against the trend for outward movement, it was possible for Leeds to 'win' in the *global redistribution* of manufacturing industry capital, sttracting some limited inward investment. Exsa, a subsidiary of a privately owned Turkish business active in textiles, car manufacturing, banking and hotels built its new £15m polyester yarn textualising plant in Garforth, Leeds, in 1991. Employing 150 people, this is the most modern factory of its type in Europe. The Exsa decision shows how the technological and skills base of Leeds, and access to the city's know-how in clothing and textiles markets can attract investment of a sectorally-specific kind, suggesting potential for the LDA's sectoral approach. The ability of LDA and the YHDA to find an appropriate site quickly was critical in attracting Exsa.

The predominant flow of manufacturing investments affecting the city has been outwards, less in the form of decisions by Leeds based firms to close down local factories and invest elsewhere, than in the indirect effects of the broad flow of investment decisions globally. The Leeds main firms that were once global players, such as Montague Burton in tailoring, are no longer so powerfully positioned. That particular firm has retreated into retailing products frequently made in Hong Kong, China and Eastern Europe. In effect, Leeds products have been replaced by sub-contracted imports, even in a Leeds-based retail chain. There is no sign yet of a reversal of the process of globalisation by Leeds firms, and no reason to suspect that the relative attractiveness of China and Yorkshire for factory locations is changing. Returning to the example of Yorkshire Chemicals, a genuine global player in dyestuffs production, the main growth in its markets is in the Far East, where textile production is booming and it is unlikely that Leeds, as opposed to the Far East, would be the favoured location for a new plant to exploit the expanding market for the company. Even though industrial restructuring and the growth of manufacturing world-wide is being conducted and masterminded from a Leeds base, increasingly and inevitably locality ties are being reduced.

## Spatial policies for manufacturing jobs

As a location for new manufacturing investment, Leeds is hampered by the city's lack of access to regional assistance funds and to funding for infrastructure provision through European Structural funds. In addition (and partly explaining the high land costs problem) there is a shortage of industrial land, aggravated by the need to restructure and reclaim derelict land and invest in new road infrastructure in brownfield locations. South-East Leeds, which has itself suffered from twenty years of deindustrialisation, is seen by the City Council as the major location for future new industrial development in the city, and is allocated for such growth in the draft Unitary Development Plan (UDP), the statutory land-use plan for Leeds. The Aire Valley Employment Target Area identified in the UDP assumes the completion of the M1/A1 motorway link road, together with the East Leeds Radial trunk road. It is hoped that these proposed improvements in road access, adjacent to the Stourton rail freight terminal, together with reclamation and servicing work, will enable the development of 188 hectares of industrial development land, and lead to the creation of 12,000 to 15,000 jobs (Leeds Initiative, 1995).

### Sectoral alliances and manufacturing

The City Council cannot and does not wish to control the local economy, but by working in partnership with others it can help to bring the resources and talents of many organisations in Leeds together for the common good (Leeds City Council, 1994b, p.3).

Like many British cities Leeds still harbours hopes that somehow manufacturing can be 'regenerated' in the twenty-first century. Manufacturing regeneration and sectoral policy initiatives in manufacturing were not held up in the 1980s as a solution to the problems of the changing local economy. Leeds did not join Sheffield, Bradford and Hull in the early 1980's in elaborating a vision of a 'Left' economic strategy to prevent deindustrialisation, as an alternative to central Conservative economic policies (e.g. Blunkett and Jackson, 1987; Boddy, 1984). Its ruling Labour Party elite was forced to recognise the need to retain the confidence of capital and adjust to the realities of a new global economy. For much of the post-war period, Leeds was Conservative Party-controlled unlike its rival in Sheffield which has had over seventy years of stable Labour Party control. It has always had a pragmatic approach to local economic policy, based on the city's considerable 'regional potential' and the need for a strong alliance with the private sector. Leeds in the 1990s has developed an 'industry sector approach,' shared by the city council and the Leeds TEC. These players have set out to foster a greater awareness in the early 1990s of the broader geographical scale at which current, as opposed to previous, industrial competitiveness is now played out.

In the 1970s the City Council had relied mainly on its land use plans and on its participation in the regional forums which produced regional strategies, both economic and land-use (Mawson, 1983). It was not until the aftermath of the abolition of West Yorkshire County Council (1986) and the introduction of legislation in 1989 requiring local authorities to produce an annual economic development strategy that Leeds City Council began to organise for the production of a more localised version of an economic strategy. The relative complacency about local economic strategies in Leeds, compared with similar-size UK cities can be explained by a combination of the less dramatic decline in manufacturing jobs in the city (compared with, for instance Birmingham and Sheffield), the more balanced and diverse local industrial structure, including high levels of growth in service sector jobs, long periods of non-interventionist Conservative political control, the lead taken by West Yorkshire County Council (until its abolition) in local economic strategies for the whole sub-region, and diminishing City Council resources for interventionist measures.

The Leeds City Council approach to economic strategy during the 1990s has been dominated by the sectoral partnership idea. This approach is clearly underpinned by a strong belief at the highest political level in the principle of public-private partnerships for local regeneration. The ways in which the council has developed, promoted and maintained this commitment has been relatively flexible, un-bureaucratic and responsive to the emerging analysis of the threats to and opportunities for the Leeds economy. Under the umbrella of the Leeds Development Agency (LDA), the Council has exhibited "tremendous organisational and constitutional flexibility" (Haughton and Whitney, 1994, p.122) in responding to issues in the city economy. Two prominent features of the Council's response concern us here: the development of partnerships with business interests and the focusing of economic development activity around industrial sectors.

The clearest expression of the City Council's commitment to a partnership style of working can be seen in the overarching partnership supported by the LDA, the Leeds Initiative launched in 1990 (see Chapter 2). Beneath the formidable policy coalition of public sector and business interests which is the Leeds Initiative, a series of industrial sector-focused initiatives has been fostered along similar partnership lines.

The origins of the sector initiative approach can be traced to the early 1990s, with its first published expression in the Local Economic Development Strategy of 1992. Until that time, Leeds' economic strategy had been mainly confined to issues of land and property and the major formal expression of the strategy had been through land-use development plans. The LDA was responsible for the City Council's land and property portfolio, through which the council could directly participate in realising those policies. During 1992, when demand for industrial and commercial land and property was in decline, the limitations of a land and property-led strategy led to recognition of the need for a better understanding of the underlying processes in the city's economy and for a more direct engagement with sectors. However, the style of engagement was unlike earlier more interventionist local strategies such as local enterprise boards (Haughton and Thomas, 1992). The recent Leeds-style has been based around dialogue, encouraging rather than directing or requiring responses from business interests. As one LDA officer puts it:

A lot of our [economic development] work is targeted through sector analysis and the formation of sector groups. Our philosophy is that we are an enabler, a facilitator, a catalyst, and that the leadership in the sector has to come from the primary actors in the sector. It's up to [the sector groups] to tell us what the issues are affecting their sector, to identify what action can be taken locally to address these issues and to come up with a programme of events - seminars, training etc..

The first sector initiative to be formally launched, and the most successful and self-sustaining, was the Leeds Financial Services Initiative (LFSI) (see Chapter 6). On the manufacturing side, the Leeds Engineering Initiative (LEI) has been the most substantial sector initiative, involving most of the major engineering employers in the city and operating largely independently of the LDA. The Leeds Printing Initiative was established in 1993. Other manufacturing sectoral dialogue has focused on clothing and textiles, medical instruments and health care. Initiatives being considered or developed at the time of writing included construction, wood products (including furniture) and cultural industries (see Chapter 8).

Although each sector project has its unique features, it is possible to generalise a typical process leading up to the culminating adoption of the sector project as a sector initiative of the Leeds Initiative. A typical sector project development process would include the following stages:

1. Analysis of the local economy by LDA or its consultants identifies a growing or promising local sector;

2. Canvass the sector proposal amongst Leeds Initiative members, LDA contacts, relevant industry bodies and local firms in the sector;

3. From the initial trawl of potential sector group members, identify about six key, keen members and form a sector steering group;

4. Commence a series of regular meetings (about every two months) to identify key issues, analyse and discuss issues and develop strategies for the sector in Leeds;

5. Once established and accepted into the Leeds Initiative fold, gaining the

status of 'the Leeds X Initiative,' giving membership of the Leeds Initiative committee;

6. Develop into a self-sustaining industry organisation, not needing the support of LDA officers.

The timescale for developing sector initiatives varies, but typically a year can elapse between stage 1 and the completion of stage 3. Once stage 4 is reached, and the programme for the steering group looks to be well supported and vigorous, granting of Initiative status rapidly follows. To date four sector projects had reached that stage: the Leeds Financial Services Initiative, Leeds Engineering Initiative, the Leeds Printing Initiative and the Leeds Media Initiative. Initiative status amounts to achieving credibility with the 'upper echelon' of the Leeds Initiative, formal recognition by the Council and the Chamber, and an invitation to be directly represented at Leeds Initiative meetings.

A critical stage in the process seems to be the translation from stage 3, assuming enough key people can be engaged from the target sector, to stage 4. At stage 4 the workload for the LDA becomes more intense, as regular meetings are organised and outcomes noted and circulated, interest and enthusiasm of steering groups maintained, issues for further work identified and requested information supplied. LDA officers encourage groups to define vision or mission statements at the initial meetings, from which issues for further meetings and initiatives can be identified.

Only one of the sector initiatives, the LFSI, had so far achieved the ultimate status of self-sustaining sector initiative, although the LEI is moving towards that goal. Once established the sector initiatives typically engage in a range of sectoral networking, promotion and awareness raising activities, including: research into sector needs; building links with education; business information exchange and awareness raising, including technology transfer; plugging into broader sectoral support networks; identifying approaching industry challenges; and, in a few cases, development of resource centres for technical support and demonstration e.g. the Clothing and Textiles Centre and the manufacturing centre of excellence proposal.

This list of activities shows that LDA pursues through the sectoral projects a broader agenda than is implied by the rhetoric about responding to business needs and demands, although the agenda is much more modest than the grand claims of earlier local state strategists seeking to restructure local industry in the interests of labour. Nevertheless, some of the more progressive, welfare-oriented elements of the City Council's local LED strategy, involving "tackling discrimination and disadvantage" in the labour market (LDA, 1994b, p.25), are being pursued to a limited extent, through the sector projects. Thus LDA officers will raise issues of under-representation of women and ethnic minorities in sector labour forces where appropriate. However, given the policy of "putting the business leaders in the driving seat" of the sector projects, as one respondent expressed it, gentle reminders and persuasion, rather than any stronger measures, are the characteristic means of pursuing sector aims. The following outline of progress on the Engineering Initiative, the most advanced of the manufacturing sector initiatives, illustrates the potential and pitfalls of the sectoral approach.

*Profile of the Leeds Engineering Sector Initiative*

The Leeds Engineering Initiative (LEI), the most advanced of the manufacturing sectoral initiatives in the city, made rapid progress from its initiation in 1991. The idea for the LEI went rapidly through all six stages of the typical sector initiative model outlined above, but faltered after appearing to achieve self-sustaining momentum and initiating some bold and innovative schemes.

There was genuine interest within the city to develop the Engineering Initiative, particularly from the larger engineering companies, notably AE Turbines, Vickers, Sulzer Pumps, Cooper Oil, DePuy, Optare, and West Yorkshire Foundries, supported by the related utility companies, Yorkshire Electricity and National Power. The 1991 Census of Employment showed 25,372 people (85 per cent male) were employed in engineering in Leeds, making the city the sixth largest engineering centre in the UK. Eight hundred engineering companies were identified during the research phase of the LEI, suggesting plenty of scope for the initiative (LDA, n.d.). A dynamic, well-respected chairman was recruited on a voluntary basis from one of the major companies, and a chief executive appointed to manage LEI. One of the first initiatives was the proposal for a 'regional manufacturing centre of excellence.' The centre was to promote the adoption by small and medium engineering companies of advanced equipment and techniques, to improve their efficiency and competitiveness. The advanced equipment was to be accessible in a new facility, supported by the Universities, and training and advisory services were to complement the facility. The centre initiative was led by Leeds TEC, in cooperation with the other West Yorkshire TECs, and the national Engineering Council and the Department of Trade and Industry had promised financial support. However, by mid-1995 the project was stalled by a combination of: locational disputes about the best location for the centre; lack of financial backing (as opposed to 'support in kind') from engineering companies, and because of an inability to find a dynamic person to front the project.

Most progress within LEI has been made on the education front. There was a perception that the engineering industry was unattractive as a career direction to school leavers, particularly in view of the growth of more glamorous and 'cleaner' service sector jobs in Leeds competing for recruits. The LEI Schools Project, combining a PR consultant's promotion of the industry with visits by senior engineers to schools to spread the message, was an early initiative which still continues. The more ambitious City Apprenticeship Scheme, to provide an advanced training programme for the city through collaboration between companies and Leeds TEC, and compensate for large scale abandonment of apprenticeships in the city, has so far failed to take-off. However, the apprenticeship idea is due to be revived as part of the re-launch of LEI being planned in mid-1995.

The reasons for the loss of momentum of the LEI as a whole and its disappointing achievements so far are mainly given by participants in terms of loss of leadership. The original chairman was redeployed by his company to duties which precluded his continuing to lead the LEI, and about the same time the chief executive left. In the absence of the former dynamic leadership the LEI was unable to maintain its coherence and influence, and apparently lost its ability to harness the collective motivation of the partners, especially in terms of securing commitments of continuing financial support. A new chair was recruited in 1995, in an attempt to re-enegise the LEI. Education and training initiatives are expected to form the focus of the reformed LEI. In the hiatus of leadership it was necessary for the LDA to 'nurse' the LEI through a period of uncertainty, illustrating the vulnerability of voluntary collaborative sectoral initiatives to changes of key personnel.

## The developing context for sectoral coalitions

The Leeds TEC and the Leeds Development Agency and the Leeds Chamber of Commerce have developed a series of alliances in the 1990s, all of which are designed to regenerate Leeds and build on the local success and to increase the competitiveness of the local economy. These alliances themselves have been achieved in a situation of fragmented local governance where not all the partners can agree on the precise role of each agency in economic development. Leeds Chamber of Commerce, for example, shared a nationally common suspicion by Chambers of the burgeoning presence of TECs as key stakeholders in local economic development and enterprise support programmes.

Into this fragmented alliance another new player has now been inserted by central government. The Leeds Business Link is a new company formed as part of the national Business Link network to promote small firms (see

Chapter 9). The Business Links initiative sits within a broader government-sponsored analysis of the explanations for the success of top manufacturing companies: if the lessons learned from those companies were adopted widely, then the UK would be 'manufacturing winners' (DTI/TECNC/EDG, 1995). The prescription offered to manufacture winners avoids structural issues and the impacts of global capital restructuring, focusing instead on the softer areas of good practice in production processes, the advantages of visionary leadership, communication, labour flexibility, and good market intelligence. In this exhortatory framework, the function of Business Links is seen, in part, as the formation of local mutually supportive partnerships between support agencies and local firms "helping to create new local networks of [small and medium sized manufacturing] companies" (DTI et al., 1995, p.9).

Business Links, as so far described in this preliminary phase, appears to offer an opportunity to build on strategies for regenerating manufacturing at city level. To this extent the ministerial rhetoric chimes with elements of the local sectoral coalition approach. However Business Links is inadequately resourced and is being inserted as another agency into a weak and fragmented array of players in most areas. It remains to be seen whether, once in position, the Personal Business Advisors, the key resource of Business Links, will be able to do much more than promote one or two key growth sectors and assist small groups of companies. Their ability to address the major structural problems involved with manufacturing decline and pro-active revival strategies would appear very limited.


**Conclusions**

A critical issue for Leeds in the mid 1990s is whether or not manufacturing sector strategies can now be realistically pursued at city level in the age of globalisation, flexible automation and specialisation. A second issue is whether the globally competitive American and European multinationals represented in the city will, in fact, stay into the twenty-first century and allow Leeds to continue to portray an image as a mainstream European manufacturing city. A third issue is the potential of indigenous small and medium-sized manufacturing firms to regain their innovative capacity and resume growth. West Yorkshire, including Leeds, is the largest base for new firm formation in the Yorkshire and Humberside region but the evidence provided by VAT data reveals aggregate growth dominated by financial services, transport and wholesaling, with production firms growing faster elsewhere in the region than in West Yorkshire during the 1980-93 period (see Shutt, Robertson and Sear, 1995).

Reservations remain about the ability of city-based institutional initiatives to revive local economies by themselves. Sectorally targeted policies are by definition partial in their impact. To make a substantial impact a number of parallel sectoral projects would need to succeed, but so far only one has 'taken off' under the Leeds Initiative, and that in the service sector, not in manufacturing. The manufacturing project which has made most progress, in engineering, has been badly hampered by changes of personnel and uncertainty about the depth and length of commitment by leading companies to the project. This problem may be read as a side-effect of the need for major manufacturing companies to compete in a global market place. The need for this broad commitment limits the availability of executives' time to participate in sector coalitions. The concentration of the LDA on the engagement of major players, whilst effective in targeting key decision-makers in city companies, may be problematic in that successful industrial district coalitions elsewhere have been mainly based on networks of small and medium enterprises.

There are few examples to be found of success in creating or reviving urban industrial districts on the basis of local public sector initiatives (and, despite the rhetoric about business leadership they are all initially, and most still, driven by local government and quangos, not by industry). It seems that the influence of global economic processes will continue to dominate developments in the Leeds manufacturing economy, and that, even if what Amin and Thrift (1995) describe as 'institutional thickness' were to be achieved in the city, broader economic strategies and supply-side measures such as infrastructure improvements, coordinated at least regionally, will continue to be needed.

Institutional thickness implies a successful achievement of the kind of coalition that Leeds' efforts have only fitfully begun to approach. It is difficult to see how the ideal type industrial district prescription could be achieved within prevailing UK economic, cultural and political conditions. Institutional stability, sharing of knowledge communally in an environment of trust and reciprocity, local institutional flexibility and learning, high innovation capacity and a widely shared commitment to mobilising the local economic system towards mutually agreed development goals, are not a set of qualities that spring to mind as epitomising local growth coalitions in UK cities. Recent changes in the institutional map of local governance in cities may hinder progress in these directions. It is also important not to oversell the 'new localist' prescription within which local coalition-building is often bundled, and, in Lovering's (1995) phrase, to avoid creating discourses rather than jobs. More positively, the steps taken by the LDA in sector projects may be seen as useful initial steps towards creating conditions for improvements in local innovative capacity amongst local enterprises through encouraging inter-firm networking, counteracting the isolating tendencies encouraged by globally-oriented competition.

In the global arena of place marketing in which external perceptions of local economic dynamism and growth potential are seen as critical in attracting new investment to established cities, Leeds is trying in the 1990s to explore manufacturing opportunities, including the potential for indigenous growth. A promising avenue to achieving such ambitions may lie in the sectoral coalition approach. This approach is harder to pursue in manufacturing than in the service sector, because remaining manufacturing firms are less tied to locality - less 'embedded' in local economic institutions, and the question must be asked, 'will they deliver new manufacturing investment at city level?' The formation of the new Leeds Business Link as part of a national network aimed at stimulating 'world class' manufacturing may assist the city in developing a new strategy for growth for the 21st century. But agency fragmentation could well prevent city sectoral initiatives from achieving their full potential. Sectoral initiatives and local strategies will not be enough to produce substantial manufacturing growth; traditional measures to address relative regional disadvantage in the European and global economies, such as regional policy measures and infrastructure support will continue to be needed.

## References

Amin, A. and Thrift, N (1995), 'Globalisation, institutional "thickness" and the local economy,' in Healey, P. et al. (eds) *Managing Cities: the new urban context,* Wiley, Chichester, pp.91-108.

Andrews, R. (1994), 'What we mean by world class Leeds,' *Yorkshire Evening Post, 26/9/1995, World Class Leeds Special Supplement.*

Bateman, M. (1986), 'Leeds: a study in regional supremacy,' in Cherry, G. (ed) *Regional Cities in the UK,* Harper and Row, pp.99-115.

Best, M. (1990), *The New Competition: institutions of industrial restructuring,* Polity Press, Cambridge.

Blunkett, D. and Jackson, H. (1987), *Democracy in Crisis: the town halls respond,* Hogarth, London.

Boddy, M. (1984), 'Local economic and employment strategies,' in Boddy, M. and Fudge, C. (eds) *Local Socialism? labour councils and new left alternatives,* Macmillan, London, pp.160-191.

Chartres, J. (1993), 'John Waddington plc, 1890s-1990s: a strategy of quality and innovation,' in Chartres, J. and Honeyman, K. (eds), *Leeds City Business 1893-1993,* Leeds University Press, Leeds, pp.145-180.

Caunce, S. and Honeyman, K. (1993), 'The city of Leeds and its business

1893-1993,' in Chartres, J. and Honeyman, K. (eds), *Leeds City Business 1893-1993,* Leeds University Press, Leeds, pp.1-23.

Department of Trade and Industry (1995), *Competitiveness: forging ahead,* HMSO, London, Cm. 2876.

Department of Trade and Industry, TEC National Council, and the Employment Department Group (1995), *Manufacturing Winners: creating a world-class manufacturing base in the UK,* DTI, London.

Dicken, P. (1992), *Global Shift: The internationalisation of economic activity,* second edition, Paul Chapman Publishing, London.

Eisenschitz, A. and Gough, J. (1993), *The Politics of Local Economic Policy,* Macmillan, London.

Greater London Council (1985), *The London Industrial Strategy,* GLC, London.

Haughton, G., Johnson, S., Murphy, L. and Thomas, K. (1993), *Local Geographies of Unemployment,* Avebury, Aldershot.

Haughton, G. and Thomas, K. (1992), 'The role of local sector studies: the development of sector studies in the UK,' *Local Economy,* 7, 2, 100-113.

Haughton, G. and Whitney, D. (1994) 'Dancing to different tunes: the growth of urban development partnerships in West Yorkshire,' in Haughton, G. and Whitney, D. (1994), *Reinventing a Region: restructuring in West Yorkshire,* Avebury, Aldershot, pp.79-105

Honeyman, K. (1993), 'Montague Burton Ltd: the creators of well-dressed men,' in Chartres, J. and Honeyman, K. (eds), pp. 186-216.

Leeds Development Agency (no date), *The Leeds Engineering Initiative,* Leeds City Council.

Leeds Development Agency (1993), *Ten Years of Employment Change in Leeds,* Leeds City Council, Leeds.

Leeds Development Agency (1994a), *The Leeds Economic Development Strategy: An Economic Assessment,* Leeds City Council, Leeds.

Leeds Development Agency (1994b), *Economic Development Annual Statement 1994/95,* Leeds City Council.

Leeds Initiative (1995), *Removing Barriers-Creating Opportunities: the Leeds Initiative bid to the Single Regeneration Budget 1995/6,* Leeds City Council, Leeds.

Leigh, C., Stillwell, J. and Tickell, A. (1994), 'The West Yorkshire economy: breaking with tradition,' in Haughton, G. and Whitney, D. (1994a), 61-90.

Lovering, J. (1995), 'Creating discourses rather than jobs: the crisis in the cities and the transition fantasies of intellectuals and policy makers,' in Healey, P. et al. (eds) *Managing Cities: the new urban context,* Wiley, Chichester, pp.109-126.

Massey, D. (1988), 'Uneven development: social change and the spatial divisions of labour,' in Massey, D. and Allen, J. (eds) *Uneven Redevelopment: cities and regions in transition,* Hodder and Stoughton, Sevenoaks, pp.250-276.

Mawson, J. (1983), 'Organising for economic development: the formulation of local authority economic development policies in West Yorkshire,' in Young, K. and Mason, C. (eds) *Urban Economic Development,* Macmillan, London, pp.79-105.

Murray, R. (1991), *Local Space: Europe and the new regionalism,* Centre for Local Economic Strategies, Manchester.

Pyke, F., Becattini, G., and Sengenberger, W. (1990), *Industrial Districts and Inter-Firm Cooperation in Italy,* International Labour Office, Geneva.

Scott, A.J. (1988), *New Industrial Spaces,* Pion, London.

Smales, L. (1994), 'Desperate pragmatism or shrewd optimism? The image and selling of West Yorkshire,' in Haughton, G. and Whitney, D. (eds) *Reinventing a Region: restructuring in West Yorkshire,* Avebury, Aldershot, pp. 35-60.

Wiener, R. (1976), 'The economic base of Leeds,' Workers' Education Association, Leeds.

# 6 Taking the initiative: The Leeds financial centre

*Adam Tickell*

## Introduction

During the past fifteen years, Leeds has emerged as one of the most rapidly growing financial centres in the United Kingdom, a process which has accelerated particularly since 1989. Employment in financial services in Leeds grew by 68 per cent between 1981 and 1991 and, latterly making Leeds the fastest growing regional financial centre, by 19 per cent between 1989 and 1991 alone.[1] This recent growth has taken place against a national backdrop of falling employment in key elements of the financial sector, particularly in banking which, after strong growth during the 1980s, is suffering significant national job losses and in 1993 employment in banking fell to its lowest point since 1986. It is not simply in employment terms that Leeds has emerged as a significant regional financial centre: the number of financial service companies registered for VAT more than doubled between 1981 and 1991 (Tickell, 1993); Leeds has become home to some of the highest profile telephone-based consumer financial service companies (such as First Direct Bank and Direct Line insurance); and the city has developed a financial community with both self-confidence and 'voice', exemplified by the successful launch of the Leeds Financial Services Initiative (LFSI) in 1993 and its influential membership role within the Association of European Regional Financial Centres.

In many respects, Leeds is on the way to becoming as powerful a financial centre as is possible in the context of a national financial system that remains highly centralised and centred on London. Leeds has a wide range of banks, building societies and insurance companies with regional offices (and to a very limited extent national headquarters) in the city; it is reported to be the most important legal centre in England outside London (and some of the larger local firms compete effectively against City law firms); it has a developing venture capital market; and the 1980s saw the number of people working in accountancy and management consultancy grow faster than in any comparable city. Taken together, the importance of these institutions is greater than the sum of the parts. Leeds has developed a constellation of financial service firms that can, according to their representatives at least, cope with any but the most complicated of financial transactions from conception to completion.

And yet. But. However. Leeds is not London. Although the growth of employment in finance is impressive, the total still stands at less than 3 per cent of employment in financial services in London and most non-partisan observers believe that while employment may be growing faster in Leeds, Manchester remains a more developed and sophisticated financial centre (see, for a recent example, Gowers, 1995). Beyond the bald figures, the picture is similarly confused. While Leeds *has* undoubtedly become relatively more powerful on a regional scale, some firms in the city have seen their power wane as control has passed elsewhere. The merger of the Leeds Permanent and Halifax Building Societies in 1995, for example, meant that Leeds lost the headquarters of a major British financial institution (although it is true that employment is likely to *increase* as a result, as the new Halifax concentrates its telephone banking operations in Leeds). This chapter seeks to explore the paradoxical growth of the Leeds financial centre at a time of falling employment in the sector overall by, first, exploring the development of the city and, second, outlining the emergence of the Leeds Financial Services Initiative.


## The growth of Leeds financial sector

Leeds' development as a financial centre has been both recent and rapid. On both quantitative and qualitative measures, the city has emerged as one of the UK's fastest growing and most self-confident financial centres over the past decade. On most indicators, Leeds has grown both absolutely and - perhaps more importantly in terms of the intense but often unstated inter-city competitive games - relative to its national and regional competitors. For example, in 1981 employment in financial services in Leeds stood at 57.6 per cent of the total in Manchester - by 1991 it stood at 86.4 per cent and the differential is continuing to narrow. Similarly, in 1981, Leeds accounted for 46.4 per cent of employment in the three main Yorkshire financial centres (Leeds, Bradford and Sheffield) while ten years later this had grown to 54.8 per cent of a cake that had grown by a third. The developing strength of the Leeds financial community has recently been awarded that ultimate accolade: the advertising supplement (see, for example, *Financial Times*, 1988; 1991; 1993; 1995; *Daily Telegraph* 1994; *Investors Chronicle*, 1994), while a report in *The Economist* dubbed Leeds as "Pinstripe City" in recognition of its depth of professional expertise (June 19th 1993, p. 93). Nevertheless, as intimated in the introduction this needs qualification: the developing strength of the Leeds financial sector has coincided with the loss of key locally-headquartered institutions such as the Leeds Permanent Building Society and the Yorkshire Bank, although the Yorkshire Bank continues to operate relatively independently of the other UK institutions owned by the National Australia Bank. This section explores the contradictory dimensions of the 'new' Leeds financial sector and argues that although it *is* true that the city has developed considerable expertise, it is important to recognise that this has happened within a wider context of restructuring in the financial sector as a whole.

Table 6.1 shows that between 1981 and 1991 there was a net increase of nearly 11,000 people working in the financial services sector in Leeds. Although regional financial centres as a whole continued to experience employment growth during a period when the financial sector was contracting, at 19 per cent, growth in Leeds between 1989 and 1991 was higher than any comparable city within the UK. This sustained employment growth means that financial service companies employed 9.7 per cent of the city's workforce in 1991 (compared to 5.7 per cent in 1981). Furthermore, although data are only available until 1991, employment in major employers has increased since then, as companies such as First Direct and Direct Line have expanded their telephone-based operations. Overall employment change in financial services is, however, a crude measure which tends to undervalue the depth and breadth of a regional financial centre which conflates functionally different aspects of financial services. How then can we best understand the role and development of a financial centre such as Leeds? There are two stages necessary in answering this question. First, the city needs to be situated within its national context and, second, there is a need to explore the recent development of the British regional financial system.

London is dominant within the British financial system. London is not only the location for the largest concentration of foreign banks in the world, it is the headquarters location for the vast majority of British-owned financial institutions. With the exception of the Scottish banks, all of the main clearing banks are headquartered in London following successive rounds of bank consolidation (Kindleberger, 1974), although some headquarters *functions* have been decentralised: for instance Barclays' mortgage centre in Leeds. Less high-profile elements of bank capital are also predominantly based in the City. Wholesale banking institutions, which rely

## Table 6.1 Financial service employment change, Leeds 1981-1991

|  | 1981 | 1984 | 1987 | 1989 | 1991 | Change 1981-1991 | % change 1981-1991 |
|---|---|---|---|---|---|---|---|
| Banking employment | 4,700 | 5,200 | 5,600 | 5,900 | 7,600 | 3,000 | 61.7 |
| Other financial institutions | 2,300 | 2,400 | 3,100 | 3,400 | 4,500 | 2,200 | 95.7 |
| Insurance | 5,300 | 5,600 | 5,900 | 6,500 | 7,300 | 2,000 | 37.7 |
| Legal services | 1,700 | 1,800 | 2,600 | 3,300 | 3,600 | 1,800 | 111.8 |
| Accountants, auditors, tax experts | 2,000 | 2,200 | 2,800 | 3,400 | 3,700 | 1,800 | 85.0 |
| **All financial services** | **15,900** | **17,200** | **20,000** | **22,400** | **26,700** | **10,800** | 67.9 |

Note: Row and columns totals may not add up due to rounding.

*Source: Census of Employment, 1981, 1984, 1987, 1989, 1991*

on face-to-face interaction, are overwhelmingly centred in London (McKillop and Hutchinson, 1991), while nearly 75 per cent of venture capital institutions are located within the 'London area' (Mason, 1987; Martin, 1989b).[2] Only the building societies, with their localised histories and mutual ownership arrangements which, until 1987, afforded some significant protection against take-overs, have managed to evade the metropolitan magnet (Marshall et al., 1992), although the current wave of mergers and conversions to banks may lead to geographical centralisation. For example, the take-over of the Bradford-based National and Provincial Building Society by Abbey National bank will result in the transfer of head office functions to Milton Keynes. Output and employment in the financial sector also tend to concentrate in London. Using the entire financial services sector (SIC Division 8), McKillop and Hutchinson (1991) demonstrate that, despite the fact that financial institutions are represented throughout the country, over one-half of the sector's output in 1989 was generated in London and the South East. Similarly one third of financial sector employment in 1991 was based in London, predominantly centred in the banking industry (Marshall et al., 1992).

London's overwhelming dominance over the British financial system should not, however, blind us to changes. Much of London's strength reflects the City's position as one of the 'triple pillars' of the international financial system and a developing body of work on financial services has argued that it is too simplistic to stress that London is the centre of all financial activity. In particular, Leyshon et al. (1989) have argued that during the 1970s and 1980s there was the development of a series of provincial financial centres within the UK. These authors argue that the significance of a provincial financial centre should be evaluated according to the following criteria:

- the number of 'key financial functions' performed. These include corporate headquarters, institutional investors, insurance companies, investment and unit trust companies, pension fund managers and self-investing pension funds;
- the demand for office space in the centre;
- the volume of floor space given over to commercial floor space;
- the relative importance of finance-related occupations within the overall labour market; and
- total employment within financial and producer service industries.

In a conscious attempt to mirror Reed's (1981) classification of international financial centres, this definition uses a broad-ranging set of criteria in order to identify the growth of provincial financial centres. In a further echo of Reed's work, Leyshon et al. use employment figures to classify the 25 largest centres of financial and producer services into pre-eminent, regional and sub-national financial centres.

Table 6.2 draws upon and extends Leyshon et al.'s categorisation, attempting to consider processes in addition to employment levels. As shown in Table 6.2, the City of London is defined as the British pre-eminent financial centre on the basis of employment, while regional financial centres exist in Scotland, the North West, Yorkshire and Humberside, the West Midlands and the South West. The pre-eminence of London is underscored by the fact that all of the major financial markets are located in the City.

Although London is clearly pre-eminent in the British financial system, Leyshon et al. argue that as a centre of financial and producer service employment... its relative dominance in Britain has in fact been in decline in recent years. This has not resulted from employment decline in the capital but from rapid employment growth in certain regional and sub-regional financial centres (1989: 168-169).

## Table 6.2 The hierarchy of British financial centres

| Characteristics | Articulation with national financial system | Examples |
|---|---|---|
| *Pre-eminent financial centre* | | |
| Headquarters location for national institutions and large number of large industrial corporations. Active use of telecommunications and management of large amount of assets and liabilities. Large number of foreign institutions. financial service employment: 709,000 | Source of critical information and critical contacts with international financial centres | London |
| *Regional financial centre* | | |
| May be headquarters location for small number of locally active institutions. Enhance financial infrastructure by attracting foreign institutions. Financial service employment range: 20,000-35,000 | Largely responsive to action from higher order financial centre, although some capacity for autonomous information generation/use may exist | Birmingham, Edinburgh, Glasgow, Leeds, Manchester, Liverpool, Bristol |
| *Sub-regional financial centre* | | |
| May be data processing. No headquarters. Enhance infrastructure by attracting domestic financial institutions. Financial service employment range: 7,770-19,999 | Little local autonomy. Dependent upon other financial centres for critical information. | Aberdeen, Newcastle, Bootle, Bradford, Sheffield, Nottingham, Norwich, Leicester, Coventry, Northampton, Oxford, Reading, Cardiff, Southend, Bournemouth, Southampton, Brighton |

*Source: derived from Leyshon et al., 1989, and author's own analysis.*

However, within this broad pattern there has been considerable variation, with provincial financial centres in the South of England growing more strongly during the early 1980s than was the norm elsewhere. The level of local consumer and business demand is held by Leyshon et al. to account for 65.2 per cent of the variation in financial service employment outside London.[3] In explaining the residual variation, Leyshon et al. identify three major inter-related sets of changes. First is the growth of local firms which are said to have benefited from the vertical disintegration of production and contracting out of certain managerial services (Atkinson, 1984; Marshall, 1985); the poor quality of service that domestic companies have received from London-based financial service companies; and, more contentiously, technological change which had undermined "the functional importance of location for certain financial service activities" (Leyshon et al., 1989, p.187). In their analysis of the ways in which the 'deregulation' of personal financial services has affected the building societies, Marshall et al. (1992) show that there has been a concentration of activity in the largest societies. As West Yorkshire has the largest concentration of building societies in the UK such changes have contributed to the growth of provincial financial activity (Tickell et al., 1992).

Second, Leyshon et al. document the expansion of large financial service firms into provincial centres. This is argued to have the same underlying rationale as the growth of local firms, although - as Allen (1992) has argued - this is 'transmitted growth' rather than an autonomous development. Research on foreign banks conducted during the mid-1980s supports this argument:

In most cases the decision to establish [offices outside London] may reflect a desire to improve client services or the colonization of new markets after becoming firmly established in the initial location (Daniels, 1986, p.278).

Third, the decentralisation of offices from London has also contributed to the growth of provincial financial centres. During the 1980s such decentralisations tended to occur over relatively short distances. For example between 1979 and 1985, 78.1 per cent of 'decentralising' offices relocated within the South East and a further 9.1 per cent went to the South West (predominantly to Bristol) (Leyshon et al., 1989: Table 29). Although Leyshon et al. (see also McKillop and Hutchinson, 1991) recognise that the increasing complexity of data processing activities precludes much decentralisation, technological change and the growth of telephone banking is leading to more substantial decentralisation. For example, in 1982 Chemical Bank moved its data processing centre to Cardiff (Morris, 1987) while in 1989 Midland Bank decided to locate its telephone banking subsidiary in Leeds. Although commonly associated with data processing activities, some financial service decentralisations have involved head office functions, such as the partial movement of Lloyds Bank management to Bristol.

In addition to identifying the possible emergence of provincial financial centres, Leyshon et al. argue that the growth of regional financial activities has had a series of potentially beneficial effects on local economies. First, the growth of financial services in provincial cities has had two effects on employment structure: (a) the absolute number of people employed in financial services has increased in most provincial financial centres; and (b) as the growth of financial services occurred at the same time as the decline of other employment sectors the *relative* importance of financial activities increased. Second, provincial financial activity has spawned both direct and indirect multiplier effects. Directly, there has been a boost to the demand for ancillary services and a stimulus to local office building. Furthermore, the spending power of the financial community may be contributing to local economies (although it must be recognised that senior financial sector employees rarely live in the cities within which they work). Indirectly, Leyshon et al. argue that financial and producer service companies "may be encouraging economic growth for the agency services they perform for capital" (1989: 216; although see Brunskill and Minns, 1989). A strong banking community may, for example, increase the level of local funding on management buy-outs and, thus, increase the level of local decision-making. The presence of overseas banks may help to attract overseas manufacturing plants to a region (on which see Tickell, 1992), while some anecdotal evidence from interviews in Leeds suggests that during the early 1990s recession firms that had their principal bankers in Leeds were less likely to be put into administration than firms whose bankers were based in London. Although it has been argued that a large and competitive local financial community may lead to the development of cheaper finance for local industry (Gertler, 1984; Dow, 1987; Hutchinson and McKillop, 1990), the UK's centralised financial structure means that this effect is likely to be of marginal impact. Third, Leyshon et al. argue that the development of provincial financial centres *may* affect the spatial polarisation of control within the UK. On the one hand it is possible to interpret the growth of branch offices as the extension of control held by the City of London, in much the same way as Black (1989) theorises the Bank of England's activities in the nineteenth century. On the other hand, branches may have a significant degree of autonomy and may afford a financial centre business which contributes to the success of local firms.

As competitive pressures have intensified during the 1990s, the financial services sector as a whole has seen a steady and progressive reduction in employment. However, the available data suggest that some provincial financial centres have continued to experience growth. In Leeds, for example, financial sector employment rose by 4,000 between 1989 and 1991, at a time when there was a fall of 11,000 in the whole of Britain. This overall pattern, of course, hides a more complex set of changes within the individual component elements of the financial sector, which are now briefly considered. As at the macro-level, contradictory developments are at work: growth is co-existing with decline.

The most rapidly expanding element of the Leeds financial sector is clerical employment, particularly in banking. At just over 30 per cent, banking employment grew between 1989 and 1991 at nearly three times the rate of any other provincial financial centre in the UK (Tickell, 1993) and all of Leeds' regional rivals experienced a contraction of employment in banking during the same period. This reflects the emergence of Leeds as a major centre for telephone-based banking operations, which has a much lower cost base than traditional branch-based banking.[4] Not only does Leeds have the headquarters of First Direct and will be the location of the Halifax's new banking operation, but it is also the headquarters for Next's 'Club 24', which sub-contracts operations to financial and non-financial companies, including the Co-operative Bank which also operates a centralised telephone banking operation. Alongside other telephone-based firms, such as Green Flag National Breakdown and the regional headquarters of Direct Line insurance, these firms are increasingly drawing upon part-time, female labour. When First Direct opened in the city they explained that they chose Leeds because of its relatively low-cost, large labour pool among other factors such as accent (see, for example, *Yorkshire Evening Post*, 30th October 1989; *Financial Times*, 28 January 1993). Table 6.3 shows the extent to which part-time work has increased in financial and producer services in Leeds, particularly for women. These growth rates are significantly higher than in any other regional financial centre in the UK. There is, however, some emerging evidence that the burgeoning demand for this labour force may lead to recruitment problems unless firms employ and train people from those areas of Leeds with high unemployment rates and relatively low skill levels. Leeds TEC and the city council are developing training and recruitment strategies both to help the more disadvantaged of Leeds to get jobs and to overcome any potential skills shortage.

**Table 6.3 Employment in Leeds in SIC Division 8 (1980), 1989-91**

|                   | 1989   | 1991   | Change | % change |
|-------------------|--------|--------|--------|----------|
| Male full-time    | 19,400 | 20,100 | 800    | 4.0      |
| Male part-time    | 1,200  | 1,600  | 400    | 37.5     |
| Female full-time  | 15,400 | 17,300 | 1,900  | 12.6     |
| Female part-time  | 4,200  | 6,600  | 2,400  | 56.5     |
| All employment    | 40,000 | 45,700 | 5,600  | 13.8     |

*Source: Census of Employment, 1989, 1991*

If Leeds has emerged as a major location for data-processing and telephone-based banking employment, this is not evidence that it has emerged as a major regional financial centre. A recent article in the *Financial Times* (June 20 1995, p.14) acerbically commented that "In their more excited moments, local business leaders and politicians talk of Leeds already ranking second to London as a financial centre. This is - to put it kindly - a bit ahead of the game." However, although Leeds is not Britain's 'Second City,' its emergence as a regional financial centre is not solely based on the growth of clerical employment. The city has developed a critical mass of banks, building societies, corporate lawyers, venture capitalists, insurance companies, stockbrokers, accountants and merchant banks which have, over the past decade, progressively developed the capacity to substitute local expertise for advisors previously 'imported' from London. While in 1985, deals worth over £5 million would have been handled in the City, two recent management buy-outs worth over £25 million each were executed exclusively by Leeds-based professionals.[5]

The development of this local capacity has been a process echoed in a few other regional financial centres, including Manchester, Birmingham, Bristol and Edinburgh, often at the expense of sub-regional financial centres. Leeds is, however, unusual in the strength and depth of its legal services and some law firms, such as Dibb Lupton Broomhead exploit the low cost base in Leeds by partially treating their London branch as a sales office and undercutting City law firms. However, the maintenance of the full regional financial centre requires that the critical mass is maintained. The long-term presence in West Yorkshire of the largest building society (The Halifax) and five others in the top 20 (the Leeds Permanent, National and Provincial, Bradford and Bingley, Leeds and Holbeck and the Yorkshire) has provided a major stimulus to the development of a range of financial services. For example, whenever possible, the Leeds Permanent used Leeds-based advisors rather than professionals in London.[6] The merger of the Leeds and the Halifax and the take-over of the National and Provincial by the Abbey National will reduce the demand for professional services in the region, irrespective of the capacity of Leeds to provide them. This does not, of course, mean that decline is inevitable. As the unrivalled centre for Yorkshire and Humberside, and the (rivalled) centre for parts of the North East, Leeds has a large number of companies within its hinterland; indeed the region accounts for approximately 8 per cent of the UK gross domestic product and has more PLCs than any other region outside the South East.

## Corporate city? The Leeds Financial Services Initiative

The growing *profile* of Leeds' financial community owes much to the Leeds Financial Services Initiative (LFSI). LFSI was formally launched under the auspices of the Leeds Initiative in November 1993, although this only occurred after an earlier attempt by the city council to galvanise the sector failed. The subsequent launch of LFSI provides a telling commentary on the restructuring of urban politics in the 1990s. Leeds City Council first became concerned that the financial services sector needed a forum after analysing the results of the 1989 Census of Employment which revealed that the sector was becoming a major employer in the city. The council's initial response was to invite financiers and lawyers to a dinner and meeting at the Town Hall to discuss areas of common interest between the financial community and the local authority. The reaction to this event was, to say the least, muted. Few senior members of the financial community attended, preferring either to ignore the event altogether or to send relatively junior and powerless deputies. Those people that did attend were hostile to the council and made it clear that they felt that the local authority could best help the financial sector to thrive by leaving it well alone. If anything, they argued, the city council should concentrate on providing an attractive environment for, rather than attempting to intervene in, the world of business.

Although the council's attempt to galvanise the financial community was stillborn, partly because it was poorly marketed and because it failed to attract sufficiently powerful or well-networked individuals, it did perform one useful function. It served to alert a small group of people from *within* the financial sector that Leeds could benefit from a financial services representative body. While Leeds was antipathetic to the local-authority initiative, other regional financial centres were developing a significant national and international profile as a result of the activities of local representative bodies. The Manchester Financial and Professional Forum (MFPF), for example, launched an audacious (and largely promotional) bid to become the site for the European Central Bank which generated a large amount of free publicity for the city and underscored its claim to be the financial capital of the north of England, and while Edinburgh became a founder member and strong supporter of the Association of European Regional Financial Centres (AERFC), which aimed to represent the interests of secondary financial centres across the European Union at a time when the financial system was centralising, MFPF joined shortly after.

In early 1993 a small group of individuals from within the financial sector decided that the council's earlier initiative should be resurrected. While this group acknowledged the important role of the local authority, and included the council's director of economic development, it was private sector dominated and included representatives from some of the largest firms in the city, as well as key members of the Leeds Chamber of Commerce. LFSI was formally incorporated as a joint company owned by the City Council and the Chamber, although its exclusively private sector members vote on the policy and direction of the organisation, and it exists to foster co-operation between financial companies in the city, to promote the city as a financial centre and to represent the interests of the financial sector within the city. To this end, it organises seminars and, to encourage informal co-operation, lunches; it acts as a conduit for journalists; and it has close relationships with the city council and has joined the Association of European Regional Financial Centres. When Leeds/Bradford airport was lobbying for planning permission for night flights, prior to the formal launch of LFSI, the launch committee wrote to the City Council, the Secretary of State and the region's Conservative MPs in strong support of the proposal, arguing that it would benefit the business community in Yorkshire and Humberside as a whole.

The *motivations* of the individuals involved in constructing the LFSI were primarily to market the city as a multifunctional, high order financial centre (although, as one informant put it, "it doesn't do your career any harm either") and - where that marketing hype exceeded the reality - to develop the range of expertise in the city. On a more abstract level, however, the LFSI's successes have been indicative of the changing nature of British local politics during the 1990s. Local politics are currently undergoing something of a transformation, shifting from local govern*ment* to local govern*ance*, from hierarchical and bureaucratic forms of decision-making to new forms based on local self-organisation, networking and negotiation (Cochrane, 1993). Although the traditional conduits for local politics and policy implementation - the local authorities - remain important, increasingly they are having to co-exist, collaborate *and compete* with a plethora of new agencies, networks and organisations, all jostling for local resources, power and influence. One of the defining characteristics of these new structures of governance is that in different ways and to different degrees they are *business-led*. This new complex of governance institutions range from comparatively 'autonomous' business organisations and partnerships such as LFSI, usually governed by a self-selected elite and which have their own 'roving' agendas, through to local 'quangos' such as the TECs, those unelected, arm's-length agencies which typically have a business majority at board level and which have been charged with the more 'efficient' delivery of services previously the responsibility of government (Peck and Tickell, 1995). The local quangos - the urban development corporations, training and enterprise councils, housing action trusts, regional and district health authorities and National Health Service Trusts - already spend more money than the whole of local government put together, yet their government-appointed boards have little responsibility to account for their actions to local people (Davis and Stewart, 1993). This is not, of course, to argue that LFSI have a conscious political programme or intend to displace the local authority - relations between the two organisations are very good and much better than comparable organisations in other cities. However, the changes in local politics *do* provide the space for LFSI's voice to be heard and influential, for instance with the Leeds TEC and the city council.


**Conclusion**

This chapter has detailed the rise of Leeds as one of Britain's major regional financial centres. The Leeds economy has, undoubtedly, been a beneficiary of the current round of technological change in the financial sector, as banks and insurance companies are replacing branches and brokers with telephone-based direct selling operations. However, in one of the most technologically dynamic industries in Britain, the maintenance of such success can never be assured. The increasingly widespread diffusion of personal computers and cable television networks may undermine even the most recent innovations such as telephone banking. Already, the Co-operative Bank, a pioneer in *telephone* banking, and BSkyB Television are conducting trials of 'interactive banking', where customers can dial a telephone number and see their statements on screen. Yet, it is important not to become too driven by the technological *possibilities* in assessing the medium-term future of banking and finance. While full home banking may become the norm for a small segment of the market, on-line banking is likely to be restricted for the foreseeable future because it remains reliant upon expensive equipment and a technological literacy that is far from being the norm.

It is worth remembering, however, that Leeds' recent success as a financial centre - whether in terms of employment, profile or number of institutions in the city - is part and parcel of the restructuring of the financial sector and implies failure elsewhere. But it is a quiet failure, associated with the incremental closure of branches and reduction of employment in the remaining branches (see Leyshon and Thrift, 1995) and Leeds is itself not immune from branch closure in some neighbourhoods just as the city is booming as a centre for processing. As the city becomes a major regional financial centre, it remains a city with pockets of extreme poverty, increasingly excluded from the financial centre, and where the poor rely on extortionate loan companies to access credit (Pennington, 1995).

**Notes**

1. Accurate data for employment in the financial sector for individual cities are obtained from the (usually) bi-annual Census of Employment. The latest available data refer to September 1991. It is a requirement that data extracted from the Census of Employment are rounded to the nearest 100 and this convention is followed here.
2. In the case of venture capital firms the 'London area' is used here to refer to the "area within 100 mile radius of the City, and includes locations such as Cambridge" (Martin, 1989b, p.394).
3. London was excluded because of its pre-eminent world position. In addition, Bootle was excluded following problems in specifying local demand for financial services there.
4. For example, *The Economist* estimates that First Direct has a cost-to-income ratio of approximately 25 per cent, compared to ratios in the high 60s for traditional banks.
5. Interview with Michael Gagen, Chairman of LFSI. Furthermore, a Leeds-based law firms were the principal legal advisors in the £402 million management buy-out of Gardner Merchant from Forte (Daily Telegraph, 1995, 25th May, p.33).
6. Source: Roger Boyes, acting Chief Executive, November 1993.

**Acknowledgements**

I would like to thank members of the Leeds financial community for their time in assisting me with my research for the ESRC research fellowship 'Regulating finance: the political geography of financial services' (award number H52427001394) on which this paper is based. Particular thanks are due to John Howley for comments on an earlier draft. Some of the empirical detail draws upon research completed for the Leeds Financial Service Initiative in 1993 and thanks are also due to them.

**References**

Allen, J. (1992), 'Services and the UK space economy: regionalization and economic dislocation,' *Transactions, Institute of British Geographers,* 17 (3), 292-305.

Atkinson, J. (1984), *Flexibility, uncertainty and manpower management,* University of Sussex, Institute of Manpower Studies, Report 89.

Black, I. (1989), 'Geography, political economy and the circulation of finance capital in early industrial England,' *Journal of Historical Geography,* 15, 366-384.

Brunskill, I. and Minns, R. (1989), 'Local financial markets,' *Local Economy,* 3, 295-302.

Cochrane A (1993) *Whatever happened to local government?,* Open University Press, Milton Keynes.

*Daily Telegraph* (1994), 'Business investment in Leeds,' *Daily Telegraph,* 25th May 1994, pp. 33-35.

Daniels, P.W. (1986), 'Foreign banks and metropolitan development: a comparison of London and New York,' *Tijdschrift voor Economische en Sociale Geografie,* 77, 269-287.

Davis, H. and Stewart, J. (1993), 'The growth of government by appointment,' *mimeo,* INLOGOV, University of Birmingham, Birmingham.

Dow, S. (1987), 'The treatment of money in regional economics,' *Journal of Regional Science,* 27, 13-24.

*Financial Times* (1988), 'Survey: Yorkshire and Humberside financial and professional services,' *Financial Times,* 7th December, Section IV, pp.1-8.

*Financial Times* (1991), 'Survey: West Yorkshire,' *Financial Times* 27th November, pp.31-33.

*Financial Times* (1993), 'Survey: Leeds,' *Financial Times,* 28th January, pp.31-33.

*Financial Times* (1995), 'Survey: Leeds and the north,' *Financial Times,* 20th June, pp 14-17.

Gertler, M. (1984), 'Regional capital theory,' *Progress in Human Geography,* 8, 50-81.

Gowers, A. (1995), 'Service industries transform the city,' *Financial Times,* 20 June 1995, p. 14.

Hutchinson, R.W. and McKillop, D.G. (1990), 'Regional financial sector models: an application to the Northern Ireland financial sector,' *Regional Studies,* 24, 421-431.

Kindleberger, C.P. (1974), *The formation of financial centers: a study in comparative economic history,* University of Princeton, Princeton Studies in International Finance, 36.

Leyshon, A. and Thrift, N. (1995), 'Geographies of financial exclusion: financial abandonment in Britain and the US,' *Transactions, an international journal of geography,* 20, 312-341.

Leyshon, A., Thrift, N. and Tommey, C. (1989), 'The rise of the British provincial financial centre,' *Progress in Planning,* 31, 151-229.

Marshall, J.N. (1985), 'Services in a post-industrial economy,' *Environment and Planning A* 17, 1155-1167.

117

Marshall, J.N., Gentle, C.J.S., Raybould, S. and Coombes, M. (1992), 'Regulatory change, corporate restructuring and the spatial development of the British financial sector,' *Regional Studies,* 26, 453-468.

Martin, R. (1989), 'The growth and geographical anatomy of venture capital in Great Britain,' *Regional Studies,* 23, 389-403.

Mason, C. (1987), 'Venture capital in the United Kingdom: a geographical perspective,' *National Westminster Bank Quarterly Review,* May, 47-59.

McKillop D.G. and Hutchinson, R. W. (1991), 'Financial intermediaries and financial markets: a United Kingdom perspective,' *Regional Studies,* 25, 543-554.

Morris, J. (1987), 'The internationalisation of banking, technological change and spatial change: a case study of South Wales,' *Geoforum,* 18, 257-267.

Peck, J.A. and Tickell, A. (1995), 'Business goes local: dissecting the "business agenda" in Manchester,' *International Journal of Urban and Regional Research,* 19, 56-78.

Pennington S (1995), 'Debt the old-fashioned way,' *Independent on Sunday,* 22nd January, p. 19.

Reed, H.C. (1981), *The pre-eminence of international financial centers,* Praeger, New York.

Tickell, A. (1992), 'The social regulation of banking: restructuring foreign banks in Manchester and London,' Unpublished PhD thesis, University of Manchester.

Tickell, A. (1993), *The role of Leeds in the regional financial system.* Report prepared for the Leeds Financial Services Initiative and available from ReRo, School of Geography, University of Leeds, Leeds LS2 9JT.

Tickell, A., Robbins, P. and Hart, T. (1992), 'Financial services in West Yorkshire,' *The Regional Review,* 2 (2), 4-6.

# 7 Consumer services and the competitive city

*Colin C. Williams*

## Introduction

For many involved in formulating local economic policy, the notion that consumer services could be used to help regenerate a local economy is anathema. The aim of this chapter, however, is to show that for cities such as Leeds, consumer services can and do play a central role in economic development. First, therefore, the theory underlying popular prejudices about the function of consumer services in local economic development will be critically evaluated and, in doing so, the potential contributions of the consumer services sector to economic growth is reconsidered. Following on from this, the extent to which the consumer services sector fulfils these functions in practice is investigated through an empirical study of the Leeds economy. This will reveal that the creation of a competitive city is as much dependent upon a competitive consumer services sector as it is upon competitive manufacturing and producer service sectors.

## The growth of the service sector

Service sector growth is a principal feature of contemporary economic restructuring in Britain (see Table 7.1). Between 1981 and 1991, the number employed in services rose from 12.9 million to 14.9 million whilst the proportion of all employees working in the service sector rose from 61.0 per cent to 69.1 per cent. By 1991, therefore, the service sector employed three times as many people as the extractive and manufacturing sectors together. This absolute and relative increase in service employment, moreover, is

119

mirrored in measures of the contribution of service industries to Gross Domestic Product (*Regional Trends*, 1994).

**Table 7.1 Employment change in Great Britain: by sector[1]**

|  | 1981 | 1991 | % Change |
|---|---|---|---|
| Production activities | 8,338 | 6,704 | -19.6 |
| Extractive & manuf'g inds | 6,652 | 5,026 | -24.4 |
| Utilities | 1,686 | 1,678 | -0.5 |
|  |  |  |  |
| Services | 12,911 | 14,901 | +13.4 |
| Producer Services | 1,819 | 2,336 | +28.4 |
| Consumer Services | 6,869 | 8,113 | +18.1 |
| Mixed Prod./Cons. Services | 2,718 | 3,090 | +13.7 |
| Public Services | 1,505 | 1,362 | -9.5 |
|  |  |  |  |
| All employees | 21,148 | 21,569 | +2.0 |

Note
1.     The definition used to categorise service sector activity into producer, consumer and mixed producer/consumer services is that developed by Marshall (1988: Table 2.4).

*Source: Marshall (1988, Table 2.4) and Census of Employment, 1991*

Given that manufacturing industries are rapidly declining in both absolute and relative terms whilst service industries are growing, it is little surprise to find that attention in local economic development has quite correctly started to shift towards the service sector. Running alongside this expansion, therefore, has been a reconsideration of the role that the service sector can play in local economic development. To this end, much attention has been paid to the producer services sector (Daniels and Moulaert, 1992; Illeris and Phillipe, 1993; Marshall, 1988; Marshall and Wood, 1992; Michalak and Fairbairn, 1993), which encompasses those services supplying business and government organisations, and grew by 28.4 per cent between 1981 and 1991. Rather less effort has been spent on explaining the role of consumer services, that is services which supply private individuals, in revitalising local economies. Given that well over one in three (37.6 per cent) of all employees in employment worked in consumer service industries in 1991 and that jobs in this sector expanded by 18.1 per cent between 1981 and

120

1991, this neglect is perhaps surprising. After all, more people are employed in consumer services than in the primary and secondary sectors combined, yet they receive relatively little attention in the economic development literature.

## Theorizing the role of consumer services in local economic development

Conventionally, consumer services have been seen as 'parasitic' activities living off the enterprise of other sectors and contributing little, if anything, to the growth of local economies (Kaldor, 1966). The rationale for such a perception lies in 'economic base' theory (Glickman, 1977; Haggett, Cliff and Frey, 1977; Wilson, 1974). Assuming that an area needs to attract external income in order to grow, economic base theory divides any economy into two sectors: 'basic' industries which bring external income into the economy and are seen as the 'engines of growth' and 'dependent' industries which serve the local market and are perceived as 'parasitic' activities, contributing little if anything to the economy since they merely circulate money within the local area.

Traditionally, the dominant approach was to regard basic industries as being composed of primary and manufacturing sector firms whilst service sector activities were seen as dependent industries, reliant upon the primary and manufacturing sectors which attract external income (Bachtler and Davies, 1989; Williams, 1994a). However, during the past decade, an abundance of literature has displayed that producer services export not only on an inter-urban and inter-regional basis (Daniels and Mallard, 1992; Marshall, 1988) but also internationally (Bhagwati,, 1987; Daniels, 1991; Riddle, 1986; Segebarth, 1990). The outcome is that producer services have now become widely accepted as 'basic' sector activities.

Indeed, the basic sector is now recognised as being composed not only of industries which export but of all industries which generate external income. Hence, one can identify two types of 'basic' sector activity: export industries which sell their products outside the local area and industries which draw consumers into a locality in order to spend their money (Farness, 1989; Hefner, 1990). Since both earn external income for a locality, both are accepted as basic activities. Much of the focus in local economic policy, nevertheless, has been on developing and attracting export-oriented activity. Less effort has been put into cultivating basic activities which attract consumers into the area in order to spend their money. By definition, those activities which draw consumer spending into a locality, whether it is a regional shopping centre, sports stadium, tourist facility or higher education establishment, are primarily consumer services and henceforth, will be referred to as 'basic consumer services' (Williams, forthcoming).

Few local authorities, however, promote basic consumer services. The tourist industry is one notable exception (Eadington and Redman 1991; Law, 1991; Nilsson, 1993). Even this, nevertheless, is viewed as being different from 'mainstream' economic development activities by local authorities. Tourism strategies, for instance, are usually separate from, rather than a part of, economic development strategies and the responsibility for this function is frequently distinct from economic development. Even so, at least it receives some consideration. Local economic policy has paid much less attention to many other basic consumer services, such as sports facilities (Bale, 1992; Hefner, 1990), higher education establishments (Armstrong, Darral and Grove-White, 1994; Lewis, 1988) and regional shopping centres (Williams, 1993). The result is that most development agencies pursue inward investment in the shape of manufacturing and many chase producer services, but few try to attract the full range of basic consumer services.

To understand the role of consumer services in local economic development, however, one has to move beyond merely an evaluation of their basic sector characteristics. To look solely at the basic sector would be to assume that economic growth is simply a product of the level of external income generating activity in an area, when research reveals that economic growth is not so strongly correlated with external income generation as many previously assumed (Giaratani and McNelis, 1980; Mandelbaum and Chicoine, 1986; McNulty, 1977). This is because what is needed for an economy to grow is not a rise in external income *per se* but, rather, an increase in net income. Net income, to explain, is determined by total external income, times a multiplier (which is larger the more self-reliant the economy), minus total external spending (Williams, 1994a). Local economic growth is thus dependent on not only attracting external income but also preventing the leakage of money out of the area (Persky, Ranney and Wiewel, 1993). Consumer services can prevent money from draining out of a locality either by supplying facilities which thwart the need and desire of the local population to travel outside the area to procure that service or by changing the expenditure patterns of the local population by increasing the share of total local expenditure on consumer services. Where such seepage of personal income is successfully prevented, this not only creates the additional benefit of higher local multipliers but also reduces the requirement for so much external income generation. Without so many imports into a locality, less external income generation is required to pay for them.

The difficulty at present is that the positive role that locally-oriented activities play in economic growth as leakage preventers is frequently under-emphasised. As Persky et al. (1993) assert, most development agencies pursue export-led development policies by cultivating the basic sector of their economy with little regard for the extent to which seepage of income is taking place. The consequence is that many local economies leak like a sieve. Consumer services, therefore, perform two functions in local economies. First, they can act as 'basic activities', drawing income into the economy from outside and, second, they can operate as 'leakage preventers' serving the local market and thus retaining and circulating money within the locality. Both are equally important since both are required to increase net income. Indeed, a consumer service can perform both a basic sector function of inducing income into a locality whilst, at the same time, retaining income within the area which would otherwise seep out. Regional shopping centres, for example, not only keep income within the locality but also attract external income (Williams, 1993).

## Consumer services in Leeds

To understand the current contribution of consumer services to Leeds, it is necessary to know whether this sector is a net loser or gainer of income for the locality. More particularly, those specific consumer service industries which currently generate income for the area and which prevent leakage of income out of the area require identification. The problem, however, is the poverty of the data available. There are no official surveys of expenditure habits of either businesses or individuals which identify the local or regional source of the goods and services consumed in Britain. As such, one cannot accurately state whether consumer services are currently net losers or gainers of income for a locality. To overcome this problem, two indirect measures can be used which utilize the data available to provide a 'rule of thumb' assessment of whether consumer services are net losers or gainers of income for Leeds. These are the 'location quotients technique' and the 'minimum requirements method', both of which have long been used to make such appraisals.

The location quotient (LQ) technique examines the degree to which a sector is under- or over-represented in a locality relative to the national level in terms of the jobs it provides. This is used as a crude indicator of whether the sector is a net exporter or net importer. To calculate a sector's location quotient, the percentage of all employees employed in a sector in the local economy is divided by the percentage employed in that sector nationally. Expressed as a formula, the location quotient (LQ) for a given activity in any area j is:

$$LQ_j = \frac{X_j}{Y_j}$$

where     $X_j$ = % of employees in employment in activity in area.

            $Y_j$ = % of employees in employment in activity in nation.

A value of 1.0 signifies that the sector is represented in the area to the same proportion as nationally, whilst an LQ of under 1.0 reveals that this sector is under-represented in the area. So, those industries with LQs greater than 1.0 can be interpreted as 'income generating' industries for the locality, whilst those with LQs less than 1.0 can be viewed as sectors which are of insufficient size to meet local demand, meaning that demand has to be satisfied from outside the local economy.

The second technique employed here is the 'minimum requirements method' (Ullman and Dacey, 1962). This allows one to calculate the extent to which sectors are net losers or gainers of jobs. Any locality is declared to have a minimum requirement for every industry, which is the number of jobs required to meet local demand. So, in terms of jobs, a proportion of the workforce in each industry in a local economy is seen to be meeting local needs and any employment in excess of this is equated with producing for export. The minimum requirement is thus found by calculating the number of workers in each industry who are surplus to those required to produce for local consumption. The latter ratio is assumed to be the share of the sector in the total employment of the nation. The formula used to identify the number of surplus workers in a sector or in a local economy is:

$$S = ei - \frac{et}{Et} \times Ei$$

where   S   = minimum requirement

        ei   = employment in sector i in the area

        et   = total employment in the area

        Ei   = employment in industry in the nation

        Et   = total national employment

A shortfall in the number of workers required to satisfy even local demand suggests that local demand is being met by external firms. A surplus, in contrast, implies that a proportion of production is being sold to customers from outside the locality. The difference between the location quotients method and this minimum requirements (MR) method is that the latter allows one to measure in terms of jobs the extent of the shortfall or surplus in each sector.

## Table 7.2 Employment in Leeds: by sector

| | | % of all employees | LQ | MR |
|---|---|---|---|---|
| **Production activities** | | 29.7 | 0.96 | -4,391 |
| **Services** | | 70.3 | 1.01 | +3,867 |
| | *Producer Services* | | | |
| 61-3 | Wholesale, distribution/ scrap dealing, etc | 5.8 | 1.34 | +5,651 |
| 723 | Road haulage | 1.0 | 0.98 | +71 |
| 831-2 | Auxiliary services to banking/insurance | 0.7 | 1.06 | +125 |
| 837-8 | Professional/technical services;advertising | 1.3 | 1.02 | +258 |
| 839 | Business services | 2.6 | 0.97 | -153 |
| 841-3 | Hiring out machinery etc | 0.3 | 1.00 | -66 |
| 849 | | 0.2 | 0.50 | |
| 94 | Research and development | neg | - | -1,177 |
| 963 | Trade unions, business & prof'l assoc.s | 0.1 | 0.63 | -121 |
| | Sub-total | 12.0 | 1.11 | +5,334 |
| | *Consumer Services* | | | |
| 64-65 | Retail distribution | 10.7 | 1.00 | +2 |
| 661 | Restaurants, cafes etc | 1.2 | 0.92 | -351 |
| 662 | Public houses and bars | 1.7 | 1.08 | +317 |
| 663 | Night clubs, licensed clubs | 0.8 | 1.23 | +456 |
| 665 | Hotel trade | 0.5 | 0.39 | -2,469 |
| 667 | Other tourist/short- stay accommodation | neg | - | -527 |
| 672 | Footwear/leather repairs | neg | - | +2 |
| 673 | Repair of other consumer goods | 0.1 | 1.00 | +21 |
| 721-2 | Road passenger transport/ urban railways | 0.9 | 1.09 | +208 |
| 846 | Hiring out consumer goods | 0.2 | 1.00 | -5 |
| 931 | Higher education | 1.4 | 1.33 | +1,117 |
| 932 | School education | 4.9 | 0.88 | -2,029 |
| 936 | Driving and flying schools | neg | - | -10 |
| 95 | Medical/health/veterinary | 7.2 | 1.03 | +405 |

| | | | | |
|---|---|---|---|---|
| 96 | Welfare/religious/community services | 4.2 | 1.01 | +83 |
| 97 | Recreational/cultural | 2.5 | 1.05 | +519 |
| 982-9 | Personal services | 0.5 | 0.78 | -473 |
| | Sub-total | 36.8 | 0.98 | -2,732 |
| | *Mixed Prod./Cons. Services* | | | |
| 664 | Canteens | 0.3 | 0.56 | -605 |
| 671 | Repair/servicing of motor vehicles | 0.7 | 0.89 | -270 |
| 71 | Railways | 0.7 | 1.13 | +245 |
| 726 | Transport nes | neg | - | |
| 74-5 | Sea/Air Transport | neg | - | |
| 76 | Trans support services | 0.2 | 0.59 | -427 |
| 77 | Miscellaneous transport services nes | 0.6 | 0.70 | -927 |
| 7901 | Postal services | 0.7 | 0.73 | -669 |
| 7902 | Telecommunications | 1.6 | 1.55 | -916 |
| 814 | Banking | 2.4 | 1.22 | +1,268 |
| 815 | Other financial institutions | 1.4 | 1.69 | +1,848 |
| 82 | Insurance | 1.7 | 1.35 | +1,339 |
| 834 | House and estate agents | 0.4 | 0.87 | -315 |
| 835 | Legal services | 1.1 | 1.28 | +855 |
| 836 | Accountants, auditors, tax experts | 1.2 | 1.56 | +1,324 |
| 848 | Hiring out transport equipment | 0.1 | 1.00 | +186 |
| 85 | Owning and dealing in real estate | 0.9 | 1.22 | +303 |
| 933 | Education nes and vocational training | 1.8 | 1.28 | +1,076 |
| 981 | Laundries, dry cleaners, etc | 0.3 | 1.30 | +986 |
| | Sub-total: | 16.1 | 1.12 | +6,552 |
| 91 | *Public Services* | 4.6 | 0.73 | -5,393 |

Note

1.  The definition used to categorise service sector activity into producer, consumer and mixed producer/consumer services is that developed by Marshall (1988, Table 2.4).

*Source: Census of Employment, 1991*

Table 7.2 examines the location quotients and number of surplus workers for each sector of the Leeds economy. This reveals that the service sector as a whole is over-represented in Leeds since it has a location quotient (LQ) greater than 1.0 and employs 3,867 surplus workers. The primary and manufacturing sectors, meanwhile, are under-represented relative to the national level.

Within the service sector, the Leeds economy is over-represented by producer services and mixed producer/consumer services. Noteworthy sub-sectors in which Leeds particularly prospers include wholesale distribution, banking and other financial institutions, insurance, accountants, auditors and tax experts, and education.

Somewhat surprisingly, however, given its role as the regional capital, Leeds is a net importer not only of public services but also of consumer services. Although over one in three of all employees in employment in Leeds work in consumer services, this sector still shows a shortfall of -2,731 jobs compared with the national average. This is surprising because popular wisdom would suggest that Leeds might show a net income in both of these sub-sectors due to function as a regional capital. To examine why this is not the case with regard to consumer services, and which sub-sectors are net losers and gainers of jobs for Leeds, attention turns towards an analysis of some of the prominent sub-sectors.

*Retail distribution*

In 1991, 10.7 per cent of all employees in employment worked in retail distribution. This is exactly the same as the national average. One would expect, however, that as the principal shopping centre for the region, Leeds would be over-represented in retail employment. The fact that it is not is even more surprising when it is recognised that Leeds now has a greater proportion of the region's retail trade and employment than a decade ago (Williams, 1994a). The question, therefore, is why this intra-regional success is not manifested in terms of jobs. Here, it is suggested that the reason may be that the retail sector, similar to other industrial sectors, benefits from economies of scale with regard to both individual retail units in particular, and shopping centres more generally, which means that as retail floorspace increases, retail job numbers do not witness a parallel linear increase.

Nevertheless, Leeds city centre is one of the principal regional shopping centres in the North of England. As such, it acts as an external income generator by bringing people into Leeds from outside in order to spend their money. This, in turn, creates multiplier effects which produce yet further jobs in the local economy beyond retail distribution itself. In an era of competitive advantage where cities are competing with each other across all industrial sectors, no sector can escape from having to compete with its equivalent in other towns and cities. Leeds, although having a competitive advantage over many of its rivals at present so far as retail distribution is concerned, in part due to its size, must continue to improve the quality of the facilities it offers the consumer if it is not to lose its customers. This competition comes from two sources: established city and town centres such as York, Manchester, Sheffield, Wakefield, Bradford and Harrogate, and a host of out-of-town regional shopping centres. To the South of Leeds, there is Meadowhall in Sheffield, to the North the MetroCentre, and to the West, there is the proposed Trafford Centre in Manchester. Many established shopping centres, have in recent years, as in Leeds, established town centre management teams to attempt to organise a more co-ordinated approach to making their town centres more competitive (see Chapter 12). If Leeds is to retain its place as a first-order centre in the North, it will need to improve its shopping environment continuously from the viewpoint of consumers. The construction of the White Rose Centre at Millshaw, Morley, seen within the context of inter-city competition, may be a blessing. If Leeds had not captured such a complex, it is likely that one of the other neighbouring cities would have done so, which would have had harmful impacts on the continuing position of Leeds as the main regional shopping centre.

*Higher education*

In recent years, it has been increasingly recognised that universities provide a major fillip to the economic well-being of any city (Goddard et al., 1994). The consequence is that all major towns and cities are attempting to develop Universities if they do not already possess one, including Lincoln, Inverness, Telford and Milton Keynes.

Some two decades ago, Brownrigg (1973) provided one of the first assessments of the economic benefits of a university by examining the local economic impact of the new University of Stirling. This stimulated a good deal of work on the nature of the local multiplier and the input-output models which would be appropriate for analysing the impact of Universities on local economies. With the expansion of student numbers in the University system in the late 1980s and early 1990s, there has been a renewed interest in the local economic impacts of Universities (Armstrong, Darrall and Grove-White, 1994; Florax, 1993; Goddard et al., 1994; Lewis, 1988).

The nine Universities in Yorkshire and Humberside create 24,000 jobs, have a combined income of £728 million and spend £417 million on wages, making them one of the region's biggest employers. Although a detailed calculation of the full economic impact of Leeds University and Leeds Metropolitan University on the city of Leeds is beyond the scope of this paper, there is little doubt that these two institutions represent two of the largest employers in the city of Leeds. As such, they not only bring into the local economy a large amount of money, both in the form of student income and University fees, but also introduce an 'innovation' and 'research and development' capacity into the city which would otherwise be much less prevalent. In so doing, they are key 'engines of growth' for the city of Leeds. Campbell (1993), for example, estimates that the number of indirect jobs sustained by Leeds Metropolitan University amounts to 3,500. This is in addition to the 1,500 full-time equivalent jobs directly created by the University. In total, therefore, Leeds Metropolitan University maintains some 5,000 jobs in Leeds. Indeed, the figure for indirect job creation will be somewhat higher than for most manufacturing companies in the locality, due to the higher levels of local sourcing. One can assume that at least the same number of jobs, and probably more, are also created by the University of Leeds, meaning that well over 10,000 jobs are maintained by the two Universities. Given their relatively stable incomes and jobs compared with manufacturing, one can understand why so many towns and cities are currently competing for market share in the higher education industry by seeking to establish their own University.

*Nightclubs and licensed clubs*

During the past decade or so, inter-city competition for customers has intensified in this sector. The competitive city of the 1990s has to be alive and aware of the economic impacts of neglecting the 'clubbing' phenomenon. However, little if any evidence has been collected so far in Britain on the nature and extent of this inter-urban trade. Table 7.2, however, reveals that there are 2,507 jobs in this sub-sector of consumer services, which is 456 jobs greater than the national average. Of course, some of these additional jobs will be due to the fact that Leeds, as a major city, attracts people into its environs from surrounding smaller towns and cities, such as Wakefield, Barnsley and Bradford. However, a further proportion of these extra-jobs will have been created by Leeds competing effectively with other major cities in the North, such as Manchester and Sheffield, for customers in clubs such as Vague and Back to Basics. However, this is an increasingly competitive market-place and many of the social groups who form its customer base have a finely attuned perception of whether a city is meeting its desires.

Many cities, moreover, have begun to recognise the economic benefits of this sub-sector. Sheffield, for instance, has recently had a major and ongoing debate in its local media about the contributions of this consumer service to local economic development. This arose as a result of the licensing magistrates refusing a liquor license and extension to a nightclub which would have stopped some of the exodus of Sheffield people to alternative cities, such as Leeds and Manchester. Leeds itself has responded with the 24-hour city initiative (see Chapter 12).

The development of such activity, moreover, has many 'knock on' effects for the growth of other economic sectors. A principal reason for many students deciding to come to Leeds to study, for example, has been due to its 'clubbing' reputation, revealing the way in which the various sub-sectors of consumer services are closely inter-connected.

*Restaurants, snack bars and cafes*

There has been much talk by Leeds City Council in recent years about making Leeds into a '24-hour city' and creating a more 'European' character in its city centre. To achieve this, however, the private sector services need to be present. Currently, they are not. Employment in restaurants, snack bars and cafes is under-represented compared with the national level in the sense that there are 3,837 jobs in such premises, which is 351 jobs fewer than the national average, according to the minimum requirements technique. Again, one would think that as a regional capital, which acts as a magnet for night-life and a focus for business, this sector would be over-represented in Leeds. It is not. How, therefore, can this be explained? One reason may be that compared with neighbouring cities such as Bradford, there has been little development of a 'cultural identity' for its restaurant sector in a bid to entice people into Leeds to spend their money. Thus, whilst Bradford has managed to entice people from Leeds to visit its restaurants, with its marketing appeal as 'curry capital of the North', there has been little coordinated and managed response from Leeds itself. If progress is to be made towards the 'European 24-hour city', then a more co-ordinated approach to this sub-sector of consumer services will be required.

*Hotel trade*

Another peculiar finding is that the hotel trade is under-represented in the Leeds economy. In 1991, the 1,501 jobs in the hotel trade fell short of the national average by 2,469 jobs, leaving Leeds very badly under-represented in this sub-sector of consumer services. Recent writing has referred to the fact that jobs in the hotel trade in the Leeds economy are very much characterised by 'cash-in-hand' payments (Thomas and Thomas, 1994). However, there is no reason to believe that the manifestation of the black economy is any greater in the Leeds hotel sector than elsewhere.

These two techniques for evaluating the current contribution of consumer services to the Leeds economy provide some idea of the extent to which particular consumer service industries are under- or over-represented in Leeds and, in consequence, whether they are net exporters or importers. There are, however, problems with these techniques which mean that they can be poor measures of the level of exports and imports in a sector (Williams, 1994b). What is required, therefore, is more detailed information on the source of customers and suppliers in Leeds, on a sub-sector by sub-sector basis. Only then can a more detailed understanding of the contribution of a particular sector to the Leeds economy be gained and an action plan developed for the future development of consumer services in Leeds.

## Conclusions

Through a critical review of economic base theory, this chapter has asserted that the ability of locally-oriented activities to prevent income from leaking out of an area is as important to local economic development as the external income generating function of export-oriented industries. In consequence, consumer services have been argued to contribute to local economic development not only in their much neglected role as basic activities which bring in external income but also in their non-basic locally-oriented role of preventing the leakage of income out of an area.

To investigate the extent to which the consumer services sector fulfils these functions in practice, this case study of Leeds has revealed that although Leeds is the regional capital, consumer services are under-represented relative to the national average. As such, there is considerable leakage of money out of the Leeds area. Preventing this seepage would produce a major boost for the Leeds economy. The competitive city, as we approach the end of the millennium, is as dependent upon retaining money within its boundaries as it is upon generating additional external income. Leeds, it appears, has a long way to go in mending some of these cracks so as to prevent the trickle outwards turning into a flood.

## References

Armstrong, H.W., Darral, J. and Grove-White, R. (1994), *Building Lancaster's Future: economic and environmental implications of Lancaster University's expansion to 2001,* Department of Economics and Centre for the Study of Environmental Change, Lancaster University, Lancaster.

Bachtler, J. and Davies, P.L. (1989), 'Economic restructuring and services policy', in Gibbs, D. (ed) *Government Policy and Industrial Change*, Routledge, London.

Bale, J. (1992), *Sport, Space and the City*, Routledge, London.

Bhagwati, J. (1987), 'International trade in services and its relevance for economic development' in Giarini, O. (ed) *The Emerging Service Economy*, Pergamon, Oxford.

Brownrigg, J. (1973), 'The economic impact of a new university,' *Scottish Journal of Political Economy*, 20, 123-39.

Campbell, M. (1993), 'Leeds Metropolitan University: the economic impact,' *Leeds Direct*, 4, p.3.

Daniels, P.W. and Moulaert, F. (1992), *The Changing Geography of Producer Services in the United Kingdom*, Belhaven, London.

Eadington, W.R. and Redman, W. (1991), 'Economics and tourism' *Annals of Tourism Research*, 18, 41-56.

Farness, D.H. (1989), 'Detecting the economic base: new challenges,' *International Regional Science Review*, 12, 319-28.

Florax, R. (1993), *The University: a regional booster*, Avebury, Aldershot.

Giaratani, F. and McNelis, P. (1980), 'Time series evidence bearing on crude theories of regional growth,' *Land Economics*, 6, 238-248.

Glickman, N.J. (1977), *Econometric analysis of regional systems: explorations in model building and policy analysis*, Academic Press, London.

Goddard, J., Charles, D., Pike, A., Poots, G. and Bradley, D. (1994), *Universities and Communities*, CVCP, London.

Haggett, P., Cliff, A.D. and Frey, A.E. (1977), *Locational analysis in human geography*, Edward Arnold, London.

Hefner, F.L. (1990), 'Using economic models to measure the impact of sports on local economies,' *Journal of Sport and Social Issues*, 14, 1-13.

Illeris, S. and Phillipe, J. (1993), 'The role of services in regional economic growth,' *Service Industries Journal*, 13, 3-10.

Kaldor, N. (1966), *Causes of the slow rate of growth in the United Kingdom*, Cambridge University Press, Cambridge.

Law, C.M. (1991), 'Tourism and urban revitalisation,' *East Midlands Geographer*, 14, 49-60.

Lewis, J. (1988), 'Assessing the effect of the Polytechnic, Wolverhampton on the local community,' *Urban Studies*, 25, 53-61.

Mandelbaum, T.B. and Chicoine, D.L. (1986), 'The effect of timeframe in the estimation of employment multipliers,' *Regional Science Perspectives*, 12, 37-50

Marshall, J.N. (1988), *Services and uneven development*, Oxford University

Press, Oxford.

Marshall, J.N. and Wood, P.A. (1992), 'The role of services in urban and regional development: recent debates and new directions,' *Environment and Planning A*, 24, 1255-1270.

McNulty, J.E. (1977), 'A test of the time dimension in economic base analysis', *Land Economics*, 7, 358-368.

Michalak, W.Z. and Fairbairn, K.J. (1993), 'The producer service complex of Edmonton: the role and organisation of producer services firms in a peripheral city,' *Environment and Planning A*, 25, 761-777.

Nilsson, P.A. (1993), 'Tourism in peripheral regions: a Swedish policy perspective,' *Entrepreneurship and Regional Development*, 5, 39-44.

Persky, J., Ranney, D. and Wiewel, W. (1993), 'Import substitution and local economic development,' *Economic Development Quarterly*, 7, 18-29.

Riddle, D.I. (1986), *Service-led Growth: the role of the service sector in world development*, Praeger, New York.

Sayer, A. and Walker, R. (1992), *The New Social Economy: reworking the division of labour*, Blackwell, Oxford.

Segebarth, K. (1990), 'Some aspects of international trade in services: an empirical approach', *Service Industries Journal*, 10, 266-83.

Stabler, J.C. and Howe, E.C. (1993), 'Services, trade and regional structural change in Canada, 1974-1984,' *Review of Urban and Regional Development Studies*, 5 (1), 29-50.

Thomas, R. and Thomas, H. (1994), 'The informal economy and local economic development policy,' *Local Government Studies*, 20 (3), 486-501.

Williams, C.C. (1993), 'The implications of regional shopping centre development', *Local Government Policy-Making*, 20, pp.50-55.

Williams, C.C. (1994a), 'Changing attitudes of government towards retail development: the end of the road out-of-town?' *Regional Review*, 4 (2), 6-7.

Williams, C.C. (1994b), 'The role of the service sector in the economic revitalisation of West Yorkshire' in Haughton, G. and Whitney, D. (eds) *Reinventing a Region: the West Yorkshire experience*, Avebury, Aldershot.

Williams, C.C. (forthcoming), 'Understanding the role of consumer services in local economic development: some evidence from the Fens', *Environment and Planning A*.

Wilson, A.G. (1974), *Urban and Regional Models in Geography and Planning*, John Wiley, Chichester.

# 8 Pragmatism, opportunity and entertainment: The arts, culture and urban economic regeneration in Leeds

*Ian Strange*

## Introduction

In recent years, many British cities have turned to the arts and cultural industries in their search for solutions to the problems of deindustrialization and economic restructuring. Arts and cultural policy has become an integral part of the renewal strategies of cities seeking to rebuild their economic and social structures. More fortunate than some cities in its recent ability to weather economic recession, Leeds has not enjoyed high profile campaigns such as those pursued in Glasgow or Bradford. However, Leeds is still faced with economic and social problems and challenges, not least in terms of inner city unemployment, social polarisation, physical dereliction, and an increasingly competitive inter-urban environment for mobile capital and inward investment. As part of the city's economic strategy to address some of these issues, the arts and cultural industries have emerged as an important constituent element. This chapter examines the developing role of the arts and cultural industries in the economic and social regeneration of the city.[1] Before moving on to analyze Leeds in detail, the general contribution of the arts and cultural industries to urban economic regeneration is considered.

## Arts, culture and urban economic regeneration

Across the country local authorities, often in partnership with private and voluntary sector groups, have seized upon the notion that the arts and cultural industries can contribute to economic regeneration in a variety of ways including job creation; income generation; cultural tourism;

environmental improvement; community development; and place marketing (Griffiths, 1993; Williams et al., 1995).

The creation of jobs and the generation of income is assumed to flow from a developed arts and cultural sector. Estimates of employment generation vary, but the most comprehensive survey of the relationship between the arts and the economy suggests that by the mid-1980s 486,000 people were employed in the arts and cultural industries, with an employment growth rate of 23 per cent between 1981 and 1986 (Myerscough, 1988). Other assessments of employment activity in the arts stress the importance of indirect job creation in the form of services such as catering, transportation, and accommodation (Mulcahy, 1988; McNulty, 1988). Locally, the picture is less clear as few economic impact studies have been undertaken. However, one study of Manchester indicates that heritage-tourism has generated 2,500 jobs (Shaw, 1992a), whilst in Birmingham it was estimated that 7000 people were employed in the cultural industries at the end of the 1980s (BAAA, 1989). In terms of income generation, national estimates suggest that in 1984 the arts and cultural industries accounted for three per cent of all export earnings and four per cent of invisibles (Myerscough, 1988). Again, at the local level, evidence of income generation is limited. In the most extensive study undertaken, Shaw (1992a) valued the output of Manchester's cultural industries at £343 million by the end of the 1980s.

Arts and culturally-based tourism is also becoming a key element in the regeneration of urban economies (Bianchini, 1988; Law, 1992; Urry, 1990). As the nature of leisure activity shifts from the mass consumption of homogenised services towards the production and consumption of more differentiated leisure forms, cities have been presented with opportunities to rebuild and recreate themselves through cultural tourism (Urry, 1995). For example, Birmingham has focused on performing arts in its attempt to raise the city's international profile. The rebirth of the Birmingham Symphony Orchestra and the construction of a £30 million symphony hall housed in the International Conference Centre, were at the heart of its cultural strategy. In Liverpool, the Tate Gallery 'of the north' was a significant element in the package of developments designed to regenerate the Albert Dock (Griffiths, 1993). Arts-based tourism is perhaps at its most heightened in Glasgow, where under the promotional banner of its 'Miles Better' campaign, together with its European City of Culture designation in 1990, the city demonstrated the economic benefits of manipulating urban imagery and local cultural heritage (Boyle, 1990; Shaw, 1992b).

Improvements to the environment have also been associated with development in the arts and cultural industries. Shaw (1992a) argues that cultural projects contribute to environmental improvement through the renovation of derelict buildings used to house new arts and cultural amenities, and through the spread effects of refurbishment on existing cultural and leisure facilities. For example, the redevelopment of Dean Clough in Halifax from a nineteenth century textile mill to an industrial heritage complex incorporating theatre companies, a design centre, a gallery and sculpture workshops, has led to environmental improvements, better facilities, and has acted as a catalyst to other regeneration projects in Halifax (Bianchini et al., 1990). Such artistic and cultural developments have also been used as a tool for enabling community development. Again, the Dean Clough enterprise has been seen as an environment which "elevates the view people have of themselves and what they can achieve" (Pearman, 1990, p.3 quoted in Williams et al., 1995, p.75). Similarly, community arts projects have emerged as one way to regenerate localities ravaged by economic restructuring. The Fishquay Festival in North Shields has used its local fishing heritage to establish a new civic ritual, regenerate the area, and reinvigorate local tradition (Landry and Bianchini, 1995, p.37). On a larger scale, the creation of specific cultural industry quarters, such as that developed in Sheffield, have sought to increase community participation in artistic endeavours with "the provision of subsidised studio spaces for local musicians; venture capital and business and technology advice for local designers and crafts people; and strategies to link local designers and art colleges with local manufacturers" (Griffiths, 1993. pp.44-45).

In addition to the potential benefits of job creation, income generation, cultural tourism, environmental improvement, and community development, the arts and cultural industries are also perceived to be important urban regenerators through their ability to transform the image of a place. In an increasingly contested inter-urban market for mobile capital, where the rise of a culturally dominant and influential 'service class' is significant (Urry, 1990), the promotion of place through a strong artistic and cultural profile is viewed by all cities as a necessity rather than an option. Cities which are portrayed as culturally dynamic, diversified, and sophisticated places are perceived to accrue a 'cultural capital', which, when combined with other resources they may have, makes them significantly more marketable than other places (Kearns and Philo, 1993). Glasgow, Leeds, Manchester, and Sheffield have all sought to re-image themselves in ways which challenge their traditional or stereotyped images. In their search for a new urban imagery these cities have played on cultural tourism, cultural activity, and their overall 'quality of life'. In so doing, they have reconceptualised themselves as places of consumption rather than places of production (Shaw, 1992a, 1992b; Strange, 1993; Smales, 1994).

Without doubt the vast range of cultural and artistic events embraced by cities' strategies for renewal are about promoting places to attract investment. However, as Griffiths (1993) points out, urban cultural policy

137

can be used in other ways. For example, the work of authors within the Comedia organisation (Bianchini, 1989, 1990; Montgomery, 1990; Mulgan and Worpole, 1986; Worpole, 1992) has argued for the use of cultural policy as a way of tackling contemporary urban problems such as:

> the fear of walking alone on the streets, the deep mistrust of strangers, the collapse of civility and social cohesion, the decline of conviviality, the sameness of city centres, the disappearance of vibrant public spaces, [and] the squalor of the public realm (Griffiths, 1993, p.44).

These commentators have also challenged prevailing notions of what constitutes art, and what has cultural value. For them the cultural life of a city refers as much to the experiences of people's day to day lives, including a range of domestic and work related activities, and the social relations they establish, as to received notions of art and culture (Griffiths, 1993). In policy terms, alternative approaches to culture can be found in Sheffield's cultural industries quarter with its focus on a range of cultural activity rather than so-called 'high art', and its attempt to bring together people involved in various facets of creative life in new creative spaces. Such spaces can also be found in Liverpool's Duke Street area and Little Germany in Bradford. Similarly, attempts by cities such as Leeds and Manchester to reclaim the public realm by improving street furniture, public information systems, street lighting and night-time public transport, as well as trying to lengthen the amount of time in which people stay in the city centre, are all part of a movement to extend the view of what constitutes artistic and cultural planning (see Chapter 12).

Whether promotional in approach or alternative in style, or, which is probably more common, by a combination of the two, the arts and cultural industries are now commonplace elements in the regeneration strategies of cities. Despite what is still patchy evidence for the use of culture as a tool in economic development, there are few cities which do not see value in using culture and the arts in their search for jobs, investment, stronger communities, and a feeling of urban well-being. The remainder of this chapter moves on to consider the role of the arts and cultural industries in the process of urban regeneration in Leeds .

## Promoting the arts, promoting the Leeds economy

Establishing Leeds as a major social and cultural centre is a key objective in the city council's economic strategy (Leeds City Council,1992). Despite the fact that the sector employs some 14,000 people in 500 companies, it is the contribution that the arts and cultural industries can make to improving the profile of the city on which Leeds' economic strategy places its greatest stress. The strategy document makes clear that it is through the careful nurturing and promotion of the arts and cultural sector that cities such as Birmingham, Manchester and Glasgow have emerged as centres of cultural excellence. However, in contrast to other cities which have focused on promotion of one aspect of the arts, Leeds has chosen to concentrate on three areas: property initiatives to encourage and develop cultural activities; promotional activities to encourage awareness of local facilities, opportunities and networks with other agencies; and the continued development of established events.

It is fair to say that whilst Leeds has not chosen to sell itself as the 'city of culture' in the manner of Glasgow, the promotion of the arts and cultural tourism are now emerging as key strands in the package to market the city. The task that Leeds has set itself is to improve the promotion of its artistic endeavours and develop its existing cultural base. The performing arts are particularly well represented with Opera North, the West Yorkshire Playhouse (a local, regional and national theatre of renown), the Phoenix dance company, and the northern school of contemporary dance located in the city. Leeds also hosts an International Piano competition, and has an annual concert season including brass bands, string quartets and chamber music. In terms of the visual arts and media Leeds can lay claim to a successful international film and music festival, the Henry Moore Institute, Yorkshire Television, BBC North East, two radio stations, and more than twenty independent film, television or video producers, and ten recording studios (Leeds City Council, 1992).

The city council has also promoted a number of populist arts and cultural events which have become regular features in Leeds' cultural calendar. Such 'street-level' entertainments include Opera in the Park at Temple Newsam; Party in the Park (an open air popular music concert), also at Temple Newsam; Jazz on the Waterfront at the Granary Wharf development; Rhythms in the City, a five week summer festival of music and performance on 'the streets of Leeds'; and the Leeds West Indian Carnival. Leeds has also embarked on a campaign to become a 24 hour city, further attempting to expand its cultural base and reclaim 'lost' public space. Using its week-long St Valentine's Fair in February the City Council has sought to create a carnival atmosphere in the town hall square using fairground cafes, restaurants and bars (Landry and Bianchini, 1995).

To build on this artistic and cultural platform, Leeds has established a Tourism Development Strategy which is seeking to encourage the growth of new and existing tourism facilities; expand its visitor information services; encourage tourism development partnerships (such as the Tourism Industry

Group); develop Leeds as a visitor destination; and create tourism training initiatives to expand the range and quality of employment opportunities for the people of Leeds (Leeds City Council, 1992). Leeds has not been behind in the race to market its cultural attractions, particularly those with a national and international dimension such as Opera North, the West Yorkshire Playhouse and the film and music festival. Promoting these cultural gems, and developing new flagship projects such as the Royal Armouries and the proposed Leeds arena and exhibition hall, are part of the process of maintaining and enhancing the city's 'rich cultural life'. It is through the promotion of cultural tourism that Leeds is seeking to market itself as a major cultural centre on a regional, national and international scale. It is widely perceived that the promotion of Leeds' cultural life has already been responsible for the relocation of new organisations and businesses to the city:

> Top business people will tell you how important the arts are in their decision making. The DSS made the decision to relocate to Leeds because of the arts and cultural life of Leeds. They said there were lots of places with nice country just outside... The thing that distinguished Leeds from other places was the cultural life of Leeds. They couldn't believe that the cultural life was so rich. We've found that with a number of major organisations which have moved here (local councillor).

However, the economic benefit of arts and cultural activity is difficult to measure. Positive images of place are assumed to be important factors in relocation, but there is only limited empirical evidence to support this (Crocker and Lawless, 1994). Equally, the multiplier effects of culturally related tourism are hard to calculate (Meethan, 1994). The difficulty in connecting the arts with economic regeneration in these instrumental ways is acknowledged in Leeds. However, although no impact studies have been carried out it is clear that developing the economic potential of the arts and cultural industries is important. For example, the Royal Armouries development is intended to be the catalyst to the regeneration of South Central Leeds. Moreover, the decision to relocate the Armouries to Leeds has been used to demonstrate the city's vibrancy as a major tourist centre. References to the £45 million project are littered throughout the city's promotional material in an attempt to combat the regionally competitive visitor attractions of the Museum of Photography, Film and Television in Bradford, and Halifax's Piece Hall. The city's major public-private sector partnership, the Leeds Initiative (see below), has also identified the cultural industries as a key sector of the Leeds economy, and one which needs to be developed. Work has already begun on a media and cultural industries sector study to outline the economic potential of the industry. The regenerative potential of new cultural spaces has similarly been recognised. Plans to develop a cultural industries quarter, bringing together a number of the city's cultural activities at the Quarry Hill site in South Leeds, are being formulated by the local authority in partnership with other local cultural institutions.

## Performing players and performing partners

The movement to raise the cultural profile of Leeds is being driven by a range of institutional and individual players. At the institutional level, Leeds City Council, through its Leisure Services department, is at the forefront of the race to make Leeds a cultural centre of significance. The department has a £19 million budget for cultural services, which is spent on libraries, art galleries, museums, halls and venues, and arts development, promotion and tourism. The department also grant-aids local community arts groups, and provides financial support for arts companies such as Opera North, the West Yorkshire Playhouse and the Grand Theatre. Additionally, it promotes a wide range of events such as Opera in the Park, and the film and music festival. Indeed, the city council is widely perceived to be the key player in arts provision and promotion, and certainly its funding and co-ordinating role make it a major stakeholder in the local cultural arena:

Leisure Services run the entertainment in this city (community arts worker)

In terms of putting on events and artistic activity, it's very much the city council as promoter (local councillor).

Another institutional actor is the Leeds Initiative, the city's strategic level public-private sector partnership organisation (Haughton and Whitney, 1994; Smales, 1994). As 'the official image setter for Leeds', the Initiative has engaged in a number of projects such as the 'gateways and corridors' campaigns designed to market and improve the image of the city (Smales, 1994, p.48). It has also pressed hard for new culturally-based tourism in searching for the economic benefits of tourist-related activity. Indeed, the relocation of the Royal Armouries to Clarence Dock in South Central Leeds, is popularly attributed to the marketing pressure placed on the Armouries Board by the Initiative (Haughton and Whitney, 1994, p.122). The Initiative has also promoted the media and cultural industries sector in the city, and has been involved in city-wide discussions to develop a cultural strategy for

Leeds (see below). It is also participating in a media sector study currently being carried out by Leeds TEC and Leeds Metropolitan University (Leeds City Council, 1994).

Other important institutional players on the cultural scene include the West Yorkshire Playhouse, Opera North, and the Henry Moore Institute. The West Yorkshire Playhouse is perhaps the most significant of these both in terms of its national and international standing, and because of its role in developing arts and culture in Leeds. The Playhouse lays great store in its community and educational work, which is very high profile within Leeds and surrounding areas. Both on its own, and in conjunction with other organisations, the Playhouse is quickly moving the city towards a situation where it has achieved a major critical effect, which in turn attracts further arts and cultural activities to the city.

It is also important not to lose sight of the role played by Yorkshire and Humberside Arts Board (YHA). As one of the ten Regional Arts Boards in England, YHA has a key role to play as both a source of funding for the arts, and an arts development agency. In 1993-94, YHA received £5.3 million to support a range of arts and cultural activities in partnership with local authorities. The Arts Council also spent £6.8 million in the region, mainly in grant-aid to Opera North and regional theatres including the West Yorkshire Playhouse (Harrison, 1994). However, the cultural remit of the YHA is regionally rather than specifically Leeds focused. As such, direct input into fostering the cultural development of Leeds is tempered by the need to consider the demands and interests of Yorkshire and Humberside's other local authorities.

As far as individuals involved in the cultural regeneration process are concerned two figures currently stand-out: Bernard Atha, chair of Leeds City Council Cultural Services Committee; and Jude Kelly, artistic director of the West Yorkshire Playhouse. Both are widely seen as movers and shakers in the cultural life of Leeds. Bernard Atha, in particular, is considered as the guiding spirit of the council's cultural policy driving its development forward. Similarly, the high profile of Jude Kelly within the national and international arts community has allowed her to engage in initiatives related to the performing arts which have sought to develop the cultural life of the city, and which have built on the partnership framework provided by the Leeds Initiative. Despite the existence of this network of individuals and institutions it is not possible to speak of a clearly defined coalition of arts interests in Leeds. Instead, what tends to characterise collaborative arts relationships in Leeds is 'pragmatic partnership' between institutions, agencies and private sector companies. Such partnerships relate more to specific events and initiatives than to attempts at strategic-level co-operation and co-ordination. The local authority, in particular, has engaged in numerous partnership and sponsorship arrangements and deals with the private sector, in which both have benefited:

Partnerships with the private sector are important... We have a lot of sponsorship deals with the private sector. So our brass band concerts are always sponsored by Tetleys, because it fits their image and it suits us... They've [Tetleys] opened a brewery museum and we've been very supportive of that right from the beginning. We've given conceptual advice, and advertising in our brochures (local councillor).

However, the dominance of this approach has not prevented attempts to create a city-wide forum for the arts. The department of Leisure Services has been seeking to establish such a forum for the visual arts, although intra-departmental conflict and a poor response from potential members of this group have prevented the development of the project. At the same time, the West Yorkshire Playhouse, in conjunction with the Leeds Initiative, has been working towards a city-wide body for the performing arts, although this is still at an early stage of development. Recently, there have also been moves by the city's cultural partners to begin thinking about the development of a cultural strategy for Leeds. Such an approach has not been without its problems (see below), but it demonstrates an initial stirring to establish a city-wide vision for the arts and cultural industries. In spite of these moves towards co-ordination, there are at present no forums which represent either the diversity of arts interests in the city, or which articulate the demands of the industry in a coherent and co-ordinated way.

So far, Leeds' pragmatism has served it relatively well in its search for a higher artistic and cultural profile. However, the presence of a strategic-level co-ordinating body dedicated to arts development is likely to become increasingly necessary. New urban regeneration funding regimes such as the Single Regeneration Budget, and the financial opportunities offered by the National Lottery and the Millennium Fund, require the close co-operation of local partners in order to access available resources. If the arts are to play a significant part in the economic and social regeneration of Leeds, the city's cultural and artistic players will need to establish a partnership which goes beyond short-term opportunism for it to make a case for funding arts and cultural projects as part of an overall package for regeneration. As one key local authority official expressed it at present:

There isn't any organised structure. There isn't any map that says this is what we want. I think that we're getting there, because we have things in embryonic form that we're looking to develop... thinking about opportunities coming through the Lottery and the Millennium Fund...

organisations are already beginning the debate... doing a simple SWOT analysis and finding out what we need to complete the package... looking at new relationships which might be able to put things together in more productive ways (local authority officer).

## Arts and cultural policy in Leeds

Despite a wide range of cultural and artistic events, and the attempts by the city council in partnership with the private sector to promote Leeds through aspects of culturally related tourism, it is difficult to find anything which equates to a clearly identified and articulated cultural policy for the city. Leeds City Council's Leisure Services Department has produced numerous documents concerned with the arts and cultural activity, identifying important areas for development (such as community arts initiatives), or the promotion of specific events, but they do not amount to an integrated set of policies which encapsulate the city's overall view of the arts. Rather, what characterises the approach in Leeds, is an enterprising, but ad hoc, search for new cultural opportunities:

We have one of the most rich and vibrant cultural lives of any city in the UK, and we are one of the few without any written policy... it's what you do that counts, not what you write. There'll be some who say that if it's not written down, how do you know where you are going? Well, it's very easy, an opportunity occurs, and in artistic life if an opportunity occurs and you want to take it, you take it (local councillor).

Not-withstanding this pragmatic modus operandi, it is possible to identify a number of strands in the arts and cultural documents published by the City Council which together constitute an 'unarticulated' approach to cultural planning in Leeds. The provision of entertainment and facilities *accessible* for all sections of the community is one discernible feature. For example, Opera in the Park and Party in the Park are free, as are a majority of the concerts in the City Council's Concert Season. Concessionary prices are also available at the local authority-subsidised West Yorkshire Playhouse, and at the City Varieties and Civic theatres. The philosophy is that no one should be prohibited by expense from going to an event of their choice. Another feature is the attempt to provide *quality* arts and cultural provision irrespective of the nature of the event. Equally important is the notion of widespread *participation* in cultural and artistic endeavours. Much of the local authority's community arts activity in grant-aiding community arts and drama groups, and ethnic, youth and disabled arts initiatives, is designed to increase the involvement of local people in art and cultural activities. Similarly, street-level entertainment such as Rhythms in the City, is about drawing together artists, entertainers and local people in the public realm.

The notion of *universality* is also a key element in Leeds' unarticulated cultural policy. Despite the concentration of major arts and cultural developments in the city centre, there are attempts to widen the spatial distribution of cultural activity. For example, many community arts projects are designed to find new audiences across the city, particularly in the ethnic minority communities. There are plans to develop a media and cultural quarter in South Leeds, while the Northern School of Contemporary Dance is located in Chapeltown. As well as the movement to increase the geographical coverage of the arts, the split between what constitutes art and popular culture is also being challenged by initiatives such as Opera in the Park and Ballet in the Park which have attracted mass audiences. Similarly, both the music and film festivals produce programmes which cater for all artistic and cultural tastes. The final strand is *opportunism*. As has already been mentioned, Leeds has been opportunistic in its search for new cultural activity, and it is the main trait which has underpinned past developments:

Leeds' successes are not structured successes... it's very opportunistic, and in many cases that's worked (local authority officer).

As opportunities arise we want to be poised and equipped to grasp them. You can see it in all the theatres in Leeds. We have an opera company and a ballet company, as well as a contemporary dance company - bingo! If it was possible for us to get the Central Ballet School in Leeds next year, we'd take it, but it wasn't in our minds two years ago... We take the view that we know what we want - the richest and widest range of events (local councillor).

*Towards a cultural strategy for Leeds?*

Leeds' opportunistic and pragmatic approach has been relatively successful in producing a range of cultural activities and events which cater for a culturally diverse audience. Nevertheless, this success appears to have been achieved more by luck than by judgement, with little in the way of communication between different actors and institutions in the city's arts community:

Leeds was successful in spite of itself. It [sic] didn't sit down and say this is what we measure success by, and this is where we want to go to... There was a lack of communication amongst all the people who were part of that success... that things suddenly erupted, that somebody had an idea and it either happened or it didn't happen (local authority officer).

Recently however, there have been attempts to move towards a more co-ordinated approach to arts provision in the city. Much of the drive to pull together the various strands which make-up cultural policy in Leeds has come from the Leisure Services department and the Leeds Initiative. Both agencies have engaged in work across the city to sharpen Leeds' cultural and artistic focus, as well as beginning the task of producing an integrated cultural package which relates to the overall vision for the city. This process has not been without its problems. Competition between these agencies over who should lead the development of a cultural strategy does not lie far beneath the smooth surface portrayed by the public face of partnership. The following comments are illustrative of these tensions:

> The Leeds Initiative has made noises about the need for a cultural policy for the city... and it's been pushing quite hard for that... They keep talking about it, but I'm not aware of any work on the ground... they [the Leeds Initiative] come in and say they want to be an equal partner in the discussions that go on... in the end it is the council that delivers (local authority officer).

> I suppose that we feel that we are demonstrating more energy in these things, and that we could start to have even more initiative, and be even more of a catalyst (member, Leeds Initiative).

Such institutional bickering is perhaps inevitable in what is a new and tentative partnership dialogue. However, it indicates the problems associated with establishing institutional co-operation in a policy area which has long been characterised by local authority leadership and pragmatic opportunism. At a different level, the internal structure of the Leisure Services department has also handicapped its contribution to wider cultural debate in the city:

> We as a department need to define our own ideas before we get into wider debates. If you go to the West Yorkshire Playhouse they've got very clear views. For a department like this with such diverse range, it's more difficult for us to define what we're trying to do (local authority officer).

Similarly, vacillation by local politicians has, until recently, prevented attempts to reform the city's traditional opportunistic approach:

The City Fathers said at one time, yes we do want a policy document, but we're not quite sure the way it will be slanted, but I think now we're at the stage where we have political support for it ... Arts and culture have come up the agenda in the last 2 to 3 years... Suddenly the political leadership in the city have begun to acknowledge the role that arts can play in the image of a city (local authority officer).

Institutional competition, local authority departmental concerns, and local political rigidity, have not helped in the process of establishing a strategy. Indeed, as yet, it appears that there is no detailed cultural blueprint for the city. Leeds is still playing largely with its promotional approach to the arts, which points towards the direction of continued opportunism and the search for 'the big event'. Within the city's cultural network, organisations and institutions are continuing to 'sound each other out' in their attempt to produce a more structured stance towards arts policy. It is likely that the ground may now be more fertile for the development of a coherent and integrated approach; one which is the product of city wide discussion and inter-agency negotiation. However, the impression is still very much one of pragmatic opportunism and only a limited view of how a cultural strategy might relate to wider regeneration plans for the city:

It's nice having a cultural strategy, but somebody has to deliver it, and the pragmatic approach is very important. I think we've got to get to that stage of having some kind of policy on culture and the arts for the city, but it also comes back to the question of the overall strategy for the city. Where does that want to be in 2010, and where will the arts fit in? There are very strong visions about where the city wants to go from an awful lot of people... but I don't think there is a common articulated vision, and that's one great disadvantage in Leeds (local authority officer).

*'Corporate hospitality is not the same as culture'*

One of the assumptions behind the use of arts and cultural policy pursued by cities is that local people will benefit from the events and initiatives being promoted. However, as Griffiths (1993, p.44) argues, there is a wide variety of potential beneficiaries whose interests may not always be compatible. These interests range from local hoteliers and traders, to property developers and large businesses, and from the professional artistic community to those who consume artistic and cultural products. The opportunistic approach to cultural policy in Leeds has not helped to reconcile the different constituencies to which it is seeking to address itself. Indeed, there are clear tensions in the way that cultural policy in Leeds has tried to reconcile some of these varied interests.

Clearly, the notions of access and participation feature within Leeds' approach to arts and culture. Events such as Opera in the Park and Ballet in the Park demonstrate the commitment of the city council to widen the base of popular support for what are often seen as elite forms of entertainment. Local authority funding of community arts groups also illustrates an attempt to use the arts as a way of linking cultural activity and social regeneration. Similarly, the West Yorkshire Playhouse is engaged in community development through its work with local ethnic minority and disadvantaged groups. However, these endeavours do not please everybody in the arts community, with some viewing such institutionalised community work and local authority promoted events as top-down, commercially-imposed forms of entertainment:

> Leeds doesn't have an arts policy and it doesn't have a funding structure for community arts development... except in the ethnic community... The whole thing needs overhauling badly (local performance artist).

> There used to be community festivals and these used to be inspired by the local authority, but they've all gone... they gave the community a chance to experience itself in a positive way... it made people think it was worth while living where they lived... now everything has become centralised and commercialised, so events happen in the city centre, in the parks, they're all large-scale. They're all very well run, but they've managed to alienate the feeling of community celebration in people's minds. People don't relate to things in the same way (community arts worker).

Other projects demonstrate a face of cultural policy which relates more to the needs of the tourist industry than to community regeneration. For example, the Gateway Yorkshire Initiative is a campaign designed to create a forum in which the city's major entertainment providers and hoteliers can debate ways of increasing local tourism potential. Moreover, the Royal Armouries development is as much about marketing the city on a national and international scale as it is about being a catalyst for the regeneration of South Central Leeds. Flagship developments such as this raise important questions about the balance of cultural activity being pursued in the city, and the potential marginalisation of less high profile projects. Equally, the often critical and questioning role of the arts is not furthered by building cultural policy around large-scale development projects and cultural tourism. For some involved in arts-based community work in Leeds, the arts as a voice for the marginalised has diminished as its economic and image-building potential has been exploited:

The Armouries is a £42.5 million development and its taken years to get into place. They've had to move heaven and earth to make it happen... it's the major tourism initiative in the city, and I think its unbalanced (community arts worker).

A lot of the city fathers are philistines when it comes to events. There's a lot of 'I don't know if its art, but I know if I like it' thinking. If you're in the arts its about provoking thought and debate, and having a role in affecting social change (local performance artist).

The issue of local democracy and accountability is also important. To be fair, some of the city's cultural institutions have made progress in opening themselves up to greater community participation in their work. However, the opportunistic and pragmatic stance adopted to the development of art and culture to date has only been possible by reacting quickly as opportunities arise. This has meant that wider community debates on the merits of the projects or events which the larger institutional actors are seeking to attract has not always taken place. Similarly, moves towards a more co-ordinated policy based on a partnership between the city's largest cultural players, may result in an approach characterised by a policy of least resistance in the search for a broad consensus. The result is likely to be the continuation of high profile initiatives, and of major image-enhancing events. This trend can be seen in the development of the putative cultural strategy for the city. What can be gleaned from its visible elements suggests a greater emphasis on cultural tourism and the pursuit of large-scale initiatives, than on community-oriented arts development. An approach which is led by a policy of least resistance is likely to produce strategies which push to the margins more critical and community-based cultural activity:

We're going into a five year celebration culture up to the Millennium, and I think if they [the city's major cultural institutions] are going to spend money, they should go and speak to people who understand what celebration is. Corporate hospitality is not the same as culture (local performance artist).

**Leeds, 'a centre of culture for the North': artistic license or artistic reality?**

To call Leeds the cultural centre of the North would be to exaggerate its standing within the national arts community, and underplay the significant challenge to the statement which could be made by cities such as

Manchester, Liverpool, and Newcastle. However, it is fair to say that in terms of the number and range of arts and cultural events which take place, Leeds has a variety of experience which compares favourably with other cities in Britain. Leeds' opportunistic and pragmatic approach to the arts has served its people relatively well. However, there are signs that a more structured and coherent view of art and cultural policy is being taken, although this is still at an early stage of development. Many current initiatives and events are subsidised and promoted by the local authority, but as public funds continue to diminish, new partnership arrangements to fund and develop projects will have to emerge. This means more than simple sponsorship deals for one-off events between the local authority and private sector companies, and requires the development of arts-based partnerships at a more strategic level. However, the movement towards establishing greater coherence and co-ordination will not be easy given the diversity and range of interests involved.

The current approach to cultural policy in Leeds is largely, although by no means exclusively, promotional. Any new arrangements will have to tread a delicate path between the need to promote the city in an increasingly competitive inter-urban market for mobile capital, and the need to allow for the development of more community-based or esoteric cultural activity. Again, this is an inherently difficult process given the need for partnerships to establish common goals and objectives and engage in consensus building. The problem with partnership working is that in order to establish such consensus, policies of the lowest common denominator tend to prevail. The challenge to Leeds' cultural players and partners is to develop greater coherence without losing sight of the positive aspects of an opportunistic and pragmatic style, such as dynamism and flexibility, and without producing a policy which limits and circumscribes the available range of cultural activity. The task, then, for the city's cultural players as we move towards the next millennium, is to develop a strategy which relates to the broader regeneration of the city, but which also connects with the lives and cultural experiences of as wide a cross-section of the community as possible.

## Acknowledgements

The research for this study included discussions with a range of individuals involved in Leeds' arts and cultural community. All interviews were conducted with an agreement to confidentiality. Consequently, in the text, where quotes have been used the source has been anonymised. Thanks must go to them for the time and information they gave. I would also like to thank Andrea Bottomley and Mark Sage for their research assistance.

## Note

1. The phrase 'arts and cultural industries' is used throughout this chapter to include the performing and visual arts, film, broadcasting, photography, fashion and the heritage industry. See Williams, A., Shaw, G. and Huber, M. (1994), for a justification of this interpretation.

## References

Boyle, R. (1990), 'Regeneration in Glasgow: stability, collaboration and inequality', in Judd, D., and Parkinson, M. (eds) *Leadership in Urban Regeneration. Cities in North America and Europe*, Sage, California.

British American Arts Association (1989), *Arts and the Changing City. An agenda for urban regeneration*, British American Arts Association, London.

Bianchini, F. (1989), 'Cultural policy and urban social movements: the response of the new left in Rome (1976-85) and London (1981-86)', in Bramham, P. et al. (eds) *Leisure and urban processes*, Routledge, London.

Bianchini, F. (1990), 'The crisis of urban public life in Britain: origins of the problem and possible responses', *Planning Practice and Research*, 5, (3), pp.4-7.

Bianchini, F., Fisher, M., Montgomery, J., and Worpole, K. (1988), *City Centres, City Cultures*, Centre for Local Economic Strategies, Manchester.

Bianchini, F., Dawson, J., and Evans, R. (1990), 'Flagship projects in urban regeneration', working paper No.6, Centre for Urban Studies, University of Liverpool.

Crocker, S., and Lawless, P. (1994), 'Image and place marketing in Sheffield', *The Regional Review*, 4, (3), p.10.

Griffiths, R. (1993), 'The politics of cultural policy in urban regeneration strategies', *Policy and Politics*, 21, (1), pp.39-46.

Harrison, S. (1994), 'Arts funding in Yorkshire and Humberside, *The Regional Review*, 4, (3), pp.5-7.

Haughton, G., and Whitney, D. (1994), 'Dancing to different tunes: the growth of urban development partnerships in West Yorkshire', in Haughton, G., and Whitney, D. (eds) *Reinventing a Region: Restructuring in West Yorkshire*, Avebury, Aldershot.

Kearns, G., and Philo, C. (eds) (1993), *Selling Places: The City as Cultural Capital, Past and Present*, Pergamon Press, Oxford.

Landry, C., and Bianchini, F. (1995), *The Creative City*, Demos, London.

Law, C. (1992), 'Urban tourism and its contribution to economic regeneration', *Urban Studies*, 29, pp.597-616.

Leeds City Council (1992), *Leeds: Economic Development Strategy*, Leeds City Council, Leeds.

Leeds City Council (1994), *Economic Development Annual Statement, 1994-1995*, Leeds City Council, Leeds.

Meethan, K. (1994), 'Arts, culture and tourism on Humberside', *The Regional Review*, 4, (3), p.9.

McNulty, R. (1988), 'What are the arts worth?', *Town and Country Planning*, 57, (10), pp.266-268.

Montgomery, J. (1990), 'Cities and the art of cultural planning', *Planning Practice and Research*, 5, (3), pp.17-24.

Mulcahy, K. (1988), 'The arts and the urban economy', Town and Country Planning, 57, (10), pp.268-270.

Mulgan, G., and Worpole, K. (1986) *Saturday Night or Sunday Morning?*, Comedia, London.

Myerscough, J. (1988), *The Economic Importance of the Arts in Britain*, Policy Studies Institute, London.

Pearman, H. (1990), 'Riding high in the North: the West Riding culture trail', *Sunday Times,* 25th February, pp.2-3.

Shaw, G. (1992a), 'Culture and tourism: the economics of nostalgia', *World Futures*, 33, pp.199-212.

Shaw, G. (1992b), Growth and employment in the UK's culture industry', *World Futures*, 33, pp.165-180.

Smales, L. (1994), 'Desperate pragmatism or shrewd optimism? The image and selling of West Yorkshire', in Haughton, G., and Whitney, D. (eds) *Reinventing a Region: Restructuring in West Yorkshire*, Avebury, Aldershot.

Strange, I.R. (1993), *Public-Private Partnership and the Politics of Economic Regeneration Policy in Sheffield, 1985-1991*, unpublished Ph.D, University of Sheffield, Sheffield.

Urry, J. (1990), *The Tourist Gaze: leisure and travel in contemporary societies*, Sage, London.

Urry, J. (1995), *Consuming Places*, Routledge, London.

Williams, A., Shaw, G., and Huber, M. (1995), 'The arts and economic development: regional and urban-rural contrasts in UK local authority policies for the arts', *Regional Studies*, 29, (1), pp.73-80.

Worpole, K. (1992), *Towns for People: transforming urban life*, Open University Press, Buckingham.

# 9 Small business development and enterprise support

*Leigh Sear and Howard Green*

## Introduction

Since 1979 and the election of the Conservatives to office, the enterprise culture, however defined, has played a central role in government policy towards both regions and cities, such as West Yorkshire and Leeds (Storey, 1994a). The political project of Thatcherism was presented as a painful but unavoidable cure to the ills that emerged from the 'big is beautiful' era of the 1960s. Various commentators, such as Jessop et al. (1988), have suggested that the enterprise culture was intended to lead to industriousness, regeneration and hence, national recovery. Small businesses have become fashionable once again.

Over the last 15 years or so, it is true that small businesses have become a major contributor to private sector employment and output and they now constitute the vast bulk of enterprises. For example, in the United Kingdom almost three million businesses have less than 10 employees and these account for approximately 90 per cent of all enterprises (Daly and McCann, 1992). In 1979, one million businesses had less than 10 employees. This resurgence in the numbers of small businesses, at a national level, has been paralleled by a resurgence of interest in the small business sector by academics and politicians. The small business policy community have seized upon such statistics to justify spending considerable amounts of public money to stimulate the development of the small business sector, in order to solve the economic and social ills of both cities and regions (Bennett et al., 1994). For example, the work of David Birch (1979) was highly influential in shaping the early form of national small business policy. Despite methodological weaknesses, Storey (1994a, p.161-162) notes that,

Birch was widely interpreted as showing that two-thirds of new [net] jobs in the United States between 1969 and 1976 were in new firms with less than twenty workers. His work was cited extensively in the UK to justify the benefits which could be obtained by the creation of a more enterprising society... the inference was clear: that small firms could be a massively important source of job creation, provided an appropriate environment for them was created.

Accordingly, policy makers and support agencies have increasingly focused their economic development efforts on the mobilisation of indigenous potential and this has led to a focus on small businesses as a possible source of jobs and wealth. This has coincided with increasing recognition that competing for, and attracting, inward investment from overseas multi national companies is something of a zero sum game (Dicken, 1992). Not only are small businesses seen as a source of jobs and wealth, they are also seen to contribute to innovation and industrial diversification and to create fundamentally different jobs to those created within larger businesses (Mason, 1987). This focus on the positive attributes of small businesses and the need for a conducive environment to foster enterprise has led to a great variety and number of policy initiatives being targeted to the small business sector. For example, Beesley and Wilson (1984) documented that 100 initiatives were introduced between 1979 and 1983 by the Conservative government, to assist the small business sector. Training and Enterprise Councils (TECs),[1] on average, have between £3 million and £7 million to spend on enterprise (Bennett et al., 1994) and the majority of local authorities, throughout the United Kingdom, support a variety of types of small businesses in one way or another.

Developments within other countries such as Germany and Italy have also provided a rationale for supporting, and developing, small businesses within cities and regions. Several commentators, such as Piore and Sabel (1984) believed that they had located the beginnings of a 'second industrial divide', based on flexible specialisation, in regions such as Emilia Romagna. In this new industrial form, small independent enterprises which specialised in one activity combined with other small enterprises to become highly competitive thus forming industrial districts centred on products such as textiles, food processing and engineering. Within the United Kingdom, the so-called 'Cambridge Phenomenon' of high-technology small businesses has been regarded as an emerging industrial district and the industrial district thesis has been used to underpin a political strategy that sees such districts "as a way of harnessing the dynamics of small firms and local economic strengths for Britain's economic future" (Curran and Blackburn, 1994, p.8; see also Chapter 5).

The literature investigating enterprise support structures and assistance for small businesses has mushroomed alongside the increasing number of initiatives which have been provided for the small business and a review of this literature highlights a number of issues:

- First, there is no overall objective underpinning the policy of the Government, apart from the claims made with regards to the job and wealth creation potential of small businesses (Storey, 1994b);

- Second, an un-coordinated rag bag of initiatives targeted at different types of business in different sectors and regions has emerged (Johnson, 1990);

- Third, and associated to this lack of strategic vision, there are a large number of service providers creating a great deal of confusion within the client market (Haughton, 1993). This lack of inter agency co-operation can be explained with reference to the competition that has emerged between the various enterprise support agencies for the money of the small business owner manager;

- Fourth, assistance has tended to have been provided on a reactive rather than proactive basis, in that small businesses have to find the assistance before making use of that support;

- Fifth, there are considerable variations in the quality of enterprise support at a variety of geographical scales. As Green and Cruttenden (1990) highlighted in a review of enterprise support structures in Leeds, support agencies vary in their levels of funding and staffing and the adoption of quality systems such as Investors in People (IIP);

- Finally, and of great concern to the present government, there is the low take-up rates of enterprise support schemes. Curran and Blackburn (1994) found that within a survey of small service sector businesses, in five different localities, that approximately one in ten businesses used their local TEC as a source of advice or support. In the DTI One Stop Shop prospectus, it was recognised that "the take up of services is much lower than it should be and we probably do not reach many of those who most need assistance" (DTI, 1992, p.5). But, within this prospectus, a suitable level of uptake is not specified. Is it 25 per cent, 60 per cent or 90 per cent?

Bennett and McCoshan (1993) suggest that such criticisms are indicative of a 'systems failure' and it was in response to such criticisms that Michael Heseltine (ex-President of the Board of Trade and Industry) announced a new direction in government policy for small businesses, through the establishment of a number of One Stop Shops, now renamed Business Links.[2] Further importance has been attached to such local partnerships between service providers with the announcement of a number of pilot mergers between TECs and local Chambers of Commerce (Clement, 1994). This new direction in government policy is grounded in the idea of planning assistance more geared towards meeting the needs of small businesses at the local level. This change in direction is part and parcel of the twin trends of localisation (i.e. the devolution of responsibility to local agents) and quasi-markets (i.e. the replacement of administrative structures by contractual relationships) (Bartlett, 1991; Green and Johnson, 1992). A range of public policy areas have been subject to these two trends - including health, education and housing - in which the responsibility for the development, management, delivery, monitoring and evaluation of initiatives is devolved to locally based agencies. As well as pervading the thinking behind the TEC system (Bennett et al., 1994), this rationale clearly underpins the Business Link model.

This chapter focuses on such concerns by examining the small business sector of Leeds. The first part of the chapter considers small business development in Leeds by examining Census of Employment statistics and VAT data. The second part of the chapter focuses on enterprise support structures in Leeds by investigating the form that national trends, such as localisation of support structures, has taken in Leeds. The findings from a research project investigating the support needs of small businesses in Leeds[3] and a telephone survey of a sample of the small business policy community[4] within Leeds will be drawn on to highlight how such national concerns have manifested themselves in Leeds. Finally, a number of policy implications are presented.

## Small business development in Leeds

This section reviews the major aspects of small business development in Leeds in order to provide a context for the examination of business support policy. The analysis is based on two data sets, VAT registrations and de-registrations and the Census of Employment. Unfortunately, these two data sets are neither compatible in terms of data collected nor in time series, and hence any analysis has major limitations. Additionally, the data is limited by the different policies which individual companies have towards the reporting of information. For the purposes of this analysis, VAT data will be used to report of the dynamics of the business sector, whilst the Census of Employment will provide information on the unit size structure of individual businesses.

*Business size*

The Census of Employment permits us to make comments on the pattern of unit size over the period 1981 to 1991. This data source highlights that over 93 per cent of all business units within Leeds employ less than 50 people; over 46 per cent employ less than four people. The distribution of size of units in Leeds is broadly similar to that which obtains nationally; only in the larger size bands does Leeds have more units than nationally.

There are some variations in the size distribution of units across sectors, reflecting both the operational and organisational characteristics of the sectors. At the very small micro unit level, the construction sector has a particularly large number of units of less than five employees (63.48 per cent) and the production sector a low number (32.14 per cent). These figures compare with the Leeds average for all sectors of 46.62 per cent.

What can we learn from these figures? For the support services, perhaps the most important observation is that the vast majority of business units are small or very small. Consequently, other than those which are part of multi-unit organisations, it is unlikely that complex management structures will be in place with time available to consult and reflect. Equally, for those which are part of multi-unit organisations with specialist management, it is likely that this function will in many cases be outside Leeds. For a large proportion of the companies, their requirements for support will be limited.

*VAT statistics*

The analysis of VAT registrations and de-registrations gives us an excellent view of the dynamics of the business sector in Leeds. Although the data does not refer specifically to small firms, however defined, we know from Census of Employment data that the majority of units are small. Probably around 95 per cent of the VAT registered business have an annual turnover of less than £1 million (Daly, 1990). If we assume that those firms which are registering for VAT are new businesses and those deregistering are business failures, then we can begin to unpack the key elements of business dynamics in the city.

Although there was considerable growth in the number of businesses in the 1980s, VAT registrations over the period 1980-1993 in Leeds were proportionately less than for the UK as a whole. Figure 9.1 shows the stock of businesses registered in the period 1979-1993. At the start of the period

# Figure 9.1 Businesses registered for VAT in Leeds, 1979-1993

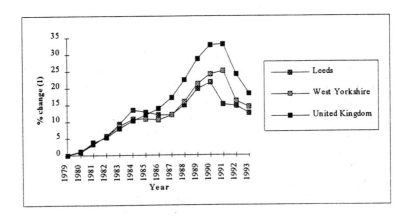

Note

1. % change from a base of 100. 1979 = 100.

# Figure 9.2 VAT registrations in Leeds, 1980-1993

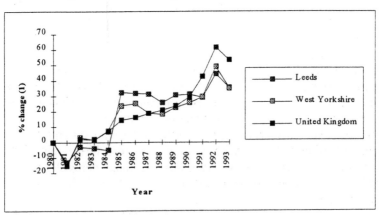

Note

1. % change from a base of 100. 1980 = 100.

**Figure 9.3 VAT de-registrations in Leeds, 1980-1993**

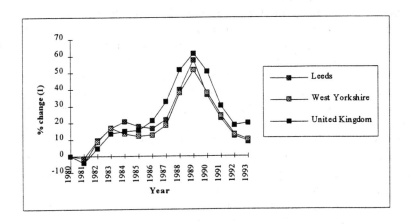

Note
1. % change from a base of 100. 1980 = 100.

there were 14,541 businesses in Leeds; by the end this had risen to 16,361. This increase of 12.5 per cent conceals the significant pattern of change during the period, with stock peaking at a figure of 17,694 in 1990. The percentage figures reveal that Leeds businesses developed in a similar way to those in West Yorkshire and in the UK as a whole where overall changes of 14.4 per cent and 18.4 per cent respectively are observed. As can be seen in Figure 9.2, both West Yorkshire and the UK exhibited greater fluctuations of stock and subsequent retrenchment one year later than Leeds.

Figures 9.2 and 9.3 illustrate the two components of changes in stock, business registration and de-registration. Registrations in Leeds reached their annual peak in 1989; by 1993 the rate had fallen to below the 1982 level of 2,074. This figure is substantially lower than that of the UK as a whole, suggesting less buoyancy in small business start-ups. As far as de-registration is concerned, Leeds shows a steady growth to a peak of 2,542 in 1992 with subsequent decline in 1993. This figure compares favourable with the UK where the volatility of de-registration has been greater.

Within these overall trends, there are notable variations between individual sectors. The finance sector for example increased its total stock by 243 per cent over the period, reflecting the particular sectoral specialism developing in the Leeds economy. This growth in stock however hides the internal dynamic of the sector in which there were 2,675 new registrations and 1,525

159

de-registrations over the same period. The production sector on the other hand showed a small decline over the period from 1,850 businesses in 1979 to 1,800 in 1993, a fall of three per cent. As with the finance sector, considerable change within the period is disguised within this overall fall. In this case, the production sector experienced significant volatility; 3,220 businesses were registered and 3,270 were deregistered.

These figures, although subject to margins of error and problems of collection and definition, do raise important issues for small business support in Leeds. First, we can confirm that there is a significant stock of small and medium sized businesses presenting a ready market for business information and advice services. Most important is the significance of micro businesses, namely those businesses employing four employees or less. Such businesses, however, have little or no spare management capacity to engage in searches for assistance or advice (Gibb, 1993). Most can best be regarded as family units in which day-to-day business in concerned with survival rather than growth or expansion. Their needs may not be great, but have to be met in specific ways, notably using outreach approaches.

We have noted significant differences in the dynamics of the sectors in the local economy of Leeds. These variations must inform the approaches to market segmentation and targeting. The numbers suggest that there is a large market who may benefit from receiving information and advice (Stanworth and Gray, 1991). The internal dynamics of each sector suggests that different groups are at different stages in the life cycle. To offer positive support we need to understand these dynamics. In the production sector, so beloved of politicians for its wealth creation and export potential, why are so many businesses being created, only to fail only a few years later?

**Enterprise support structures: some trends in Leeds since 1979**

As the above review shows, there are approximately 16,500 businesses in Leeds, of which 87 per cent have less than 25 employees. Like many other cities throughout the UK, Leeds has witnessed a resurgence in its small business sector since the early 1980s. In response to this growing market, a multiplicity of agencies offering assistance and support to the small business sector has been established over the last 15 years. In terms of Leeds, a comprehensive picture of enterprise support structures, up to the late 1980s, has been provided by Green and Cruttenden (1990) and this offers a useful starting point for considering changes in enterprise support since the mid-1980s. The study identified 48 agencies involved in support delivery and concluded that in general, small businesses in Leeds were well provided for, in terms of enterprise support. The main findings were that:

- The large number of organisations and agencies created confusion within the small business population.
- A large degree of overlap and duplication of services exists within the network.
- There were major gaps in provision such as start-up training and marketing support.
- The majority of agencies were reactive rather than proactive in nature.
- Whilst enterprise support agencies suggested that they referred clients to other organisations within the network, the view of agencies when discussing other agencies tended to contradict this view.
- Many agencies within the network did not know what the other agencies did within the network.
- A large majority of agencies, such as central government agencies, were founded with only short-term security, in terms of funding regimes.
- There was a tendency for agencies to be concentrated in the city centre.

The picture which emerged from this study was that of a variety of local actors targeting a variety of schemes towards the small business sector creating a degree of confusion within the client market. Accordingly, Green and Cruttenden suggested that there was a need for greater co-ordination of support structures in Leeds, and many other cities. Subsequently, the Government addressed this issue when it announced its intention to introduce a national network of one-stop shops, now named Business Link. However, as Curran and Blackburn (1994) suggest, such a picture may take on different forms in different areas depending on the local configuration of institutions and how wider structures and generative mechanisms interact with these local institutions. The rest of the chapter extends the Green and Cruttenden (1990) study by examining the trends in enterprise support in Leeds since the late 1980s.

*Changes in enterprise support: the experience of Leeds*

As Figure 9.4 shows, there are a variety of actors within the present small business policy community of Leeds. At the centre of the policy community are the TEC, the local authority and the Chamber of Commerce. These are the three main agencies in the proposed Business Link for Leeds, whilst the TEC and the local authority have been handed the lead in terms of organising bids for the SRB, a number of which contain elements of support for small businesses. In addition to these three agencies, there are a number of other groups of actors which influence the form of enterprise support within the city. These include the professionals such as the banks, accountants and solicitors, private consultants and training providers, semi-

**Figure 9.4 The small business policy community in Leeds**

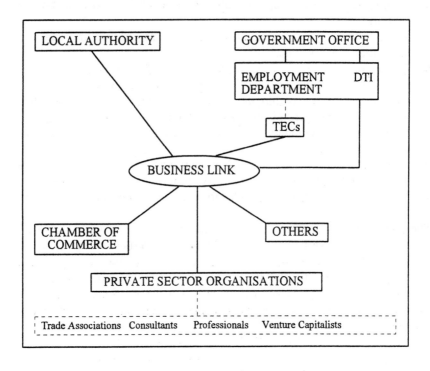

public agencies such as British Coal Enterprise (BCE), Livewire, Princes Youth Business Trust, managed workspaces such as Chapeltown and Harehills Enterprise Limited (CHEL) and Chapeltown Business Centre (CBC) and so on. The spatial scale at which these organisations operate, however, varies enormously. Whereas some agencies target their programmes of support to the city of Leeds, such as the TEC, or even sub-city areas, such as CBC, others agencies offer services which are available to businesses throughout the county or the region, such as West Yorkshire Small Firms Fund and BCE, respectively.

Figure 9.5 shows that the numbers of providers targeting their services to the city of Leeds has increased over-time. During the last 15 years, nearly two-thirds of the support agencies were established between 1984 and 1992. In terms of the geographical remit of the support agencies, 50 per cent of the local providers were formed between 1988 and 1992 and a further 22 per cent were formed between 1984 and 1987. Only 12 per cent of the local

162

organisations were established before 1979. In comparison, only 11 per cent of the region-wide agencies and 16 per cent of the county-wide organisations were established between 1988 and 1992. Such findings support the claims of several commentators that there has been a localisation of support over the last 15 years. Therefore, since the Green and Cruttenden study, the focus of enterprise support in Leeds has become increasingly targeted towards the city or local areas such as Chapeltown.

**Figure 9.5 Increases to stock of SME support agencies in Leeds**

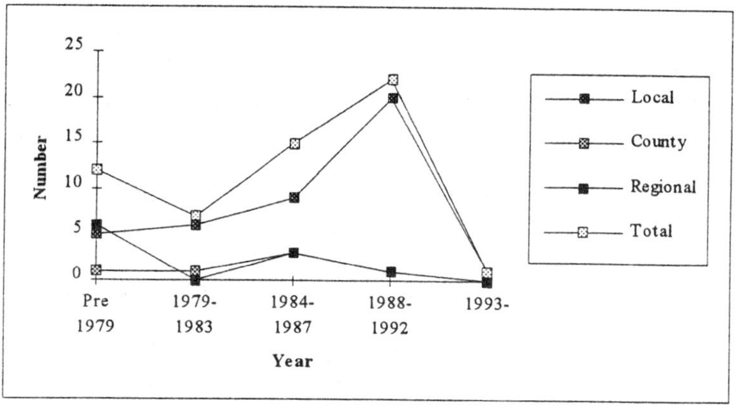

Since the publication of the Green and Cruttenden (1990) report, there has been an increase in the number of support agencies, the majority of which target their activities to the city of Leeds. As alluded to above, Green and Cruttenden noted that businesses were confused as to who to consult for assistance. The further localisation of support since the late 1980s has only served to heighten such confusion, both within the business community and policy community itself. A number of agencies felt that there needed to be greater co-ordination of business support structures. One service provider commented that

> people out in the street are bamboozled by the range of agencies and advice and expertise available. The number of people who confuse us with Leeds City Council and Leeds TEC and vice-versa... your average small business person doesn't appreciate the difference between the TEC, the council and us... people get baffled by the variety of names that are bandied about. They just want help (Service provider).

This proliferation in the number of agencies, largely stemming from the boom of the mid to late 1980s, as Figure 9.5 shows, would not be that important if the majority of agencies, within the small business policy community displayed a greater degree of awareness what other agencies offered in terms of support. Although a majority of the agencies stated that they did refer clients to other organisations within the network, the extent to which this process occurred varied greatly. Again, this situation is not dissimilar to the one reported by Green and Cruttenden (1990). Basically, private sector agencies appeared less likely than public agencies to refer clients on to other organisations. This largely reflected an attitude that, "when we get them we like to try to keep hold of them" (Service provider). Within public and semi-public agencies, a problem emerged when referring cold call clients on to other agencies. Several small business owner-managers complained that the referral process discouraged them from seeking and pursuing further types of assistance. One small business owner-manager commented that

> On occasions I have enquired about training and taking people on through schemes like the YTS but in enquiring, I have been pushed from one person to another. Once I phoned the council, I was then pushed onto someone at another place. But, you get fed up and give up.

These criticisms concerning confusion are inexorably linked to the predominant organisational focus of the agencies within the small business policy community, namely the majority are reactive rather than proactive in nature. Accordingly, the agencies relied on the small business owner-manager approaching them, either directly or indirectly via a referral from another organisation. The agencies offered two reasons for being reactive. First, the majority of the agencies lacked the resources to approach small businesses and obtain work through door to door selling. Second, one provider commented that only certain types of support lend themselves to a proactive approach, "we could not approach a business then not offer it finance" (Service provider). However, improved agency profile could result from more proactive marketing (Green and Cruttenden, 1990).

In terms of the marketing activities of the agencies within the policy community, several agencies had either limited publicity budgets or little staff time to devote to promoting their services. Accordingly, several agencies relied on word of mouth for business

> For us, word of mouth is the best and cheapest form of advertising. If you are providing a good service to a particular client, then hopefully, they will pass that fact on to their business associates and we would

hope to get some referral work from that source (Service provider).

In comparison, other agencies reported that they had quite considerable resources to devote to marketing. One organisation reported that their marketing budget for 1993/1994 was approximately £1.2 million. These agencies tended to be central government agencies, although the intended market group for this literature, namely the small business owner-managers, were largely unimpressed by the marketing literature of this group of agencies

I receive a lot of information through the post, from all different organisations. It must cost a lot of money to set up these organisations and pay the people, the printing and the training. I wish I had the TEC's printing contract (Owner-manager).

The latest development within enterprise support, namely Business Link (see also Chapter 5), intends to adopt a more subtle approach in terms of marketing, in order not to generate more enquiries than it could cope with. In comparison to other initiatives, such as the Enterprise Initiative[5], the DTI has been very careful not to over-publicise Business Link, nationally, until the network has been completed. However, in Leeds, the low publicity profile may stem from another concern, namely that of reducing further competition between the main support providers.

*The emergence of Business Link* Business Link continues the localisation trend within enterprise support, which appears to have started in Leeds after 1986 and peaked in 1990, coinciding with the establishment of the TEC. As noted above, within Business Link, the emphasis is on meeting needs at the local level, reflecting a feeling that local agencies will be more responsive to such needs and will be able to tailor assistance accordingly. More importantly, Business Link aims to bring enterprise support under one roof in attempt to remove confusion within the small business sector, in terms of where businesses can go for assistance. Like the TECs, however, it is emerging that different local areas are reading this national Business Link 'script' in different ways (Peck, 1995) and within Leeds, the establishment of Business Link has involved conflict, struggle and compromise, which has altered the national Business Link script.

Although not yet operational, Leeds Business Link has somewhat of a troubled history. It is planned to open in November 1995, some six months behind schedule. Within the original One Stop Shop prospectus (DTI, 1992), the TECs were directed, by the DTI, to co-ordinate the Business Link bid within their area. Within Leeds, this fuelled suspicions that the TEC would be the lead player rather than a partner within Business Link, with one service provider claiming that this meant that "the Business Link is a loaded partnership."

Further problems emerged in constructing the bid which was required by the DTI. Within Leeds, the three main partners are the TEC, the local authority and the Chamber of Commerce, but attempting to reconcile the interests of each of these agencies delayed the submission of the bid. As one service provider commented

Business Link is a government-driven agenda to resolve political problems in the area... they expect people to have a cosy partnership but it is difficult for three bodies [local authority, TEC and Chamber of Commerce] to get together. We would like to co-operate, but to get into a legal bed is not the solution.

The bid covers every aspect of the proposed model, such as organisational structures, market research, funding regimes and so on. In terms of funding regimes, nationally, Business Links have varied in terms of how they envisage generating funds so that they can ensure their survival after DTI support is gradually withdrawn. One route that has been favoured is requesting that businesses become a member of Business Link. In Leeds, however, certain organisations view this as a source of unfair competition,

We were quite keen on a membership scheme for Business Link; other [organisations] have them. But this was a non-starter from the start. So, one of the objectives of Business Link now is to expand the membership of the Chamber (Policy maker).

The organisational structure of Business Link Leeds has also been shaped by local struggles. In Leeds, Business Link is based on using information technology, so that staff do not need to co-locate. One policy maker stated that, "Business Link is based on the idea that people will be on the node of an IT system, pick up a phone and say, 'Business Link, can I help you'. So, the office will only have a core number of staff." This model is in contrast to the model developed within other areas, such as Hertfordshire and Hereford and Worcester, which are based on a hub and spoke model, and Birmingham which is based on a true one-stop shop model, i.e. one office in the High street. This difference reflects the different institutional structures within these three areas and how the different partners have been brought into the partnership. In Leeds, one service provider commented that it was "being pressed into Business Link by the Government but our members do not want Business Link." In comparison, another support agency reported that "In Leeds, the unease is not from [the organisation], mainly because we don't deliver [programmes]."

The effectiveness of the partnership between the TEC, the local authority and the Chamber of Commerce will be critical to the success of Business Link. Many agencies within the small business policy community expressed doubts concerning the strength of this partnership, as one service provider suggested "it will be a cosmetic partnership." More importantly, several agencies questioned how these agencies, from different cultures, could actually form an effective partnership. This issue has permeated the majority of attempts to assist the small business sector in Leeds since the mid 1980s.


## Conclusion

This chapter has investigated enterprise support structures in Leeds. More importantly, its has explored the form that national trends, such as a localisation of enterprise support, have taken in Leeds. By reviewing the picture in 1995 against a picture of the late 1980s (Green and Cruttenden, 1990), it is clear that many of the earlier findings still hold. For example, Green and Cruttenden noted that the multiplicity of agencies within the small business policy community created confusion within the target market, in terms of where to go for assistance. This confusion still pervades the small business population in 1995. Like many other cities within the United Kingdom, Leeds has witnessed a systems failure in enterprise support (Bennett et al., 1994).

In response to this systems failure, the Government has introduced the Business Link initiative. It is designed to co-ordinate enterprise support under one-roof and, like the TEC model, is based on the idea of meeting needs at the local level within a quasi-market framework of contractual arrangements. However, Leeds has experienced a number of problems in implementing this national script. The explanation for such problems lies in the local configuration of institutions within Leeds and the ways wider structures and mechanisms have interacted with these institutions. The proposed physical form of Business Link illustrates such a point. A model based on an information technology network has been developed to accommodate the needs and resources that the individual partners were willing to devote to Business Link. It is the effectiveness of the partnership between the three main actors, namely the TEC, the local authority and the Chamber of Commerce, that will determine the success of Business Link. At the moment, Business Link looks like it will struggle

I think most organisations treat the idea of a Business Link, even if they are involved with it, with suspicion... I really do not think that Business Link will work. I think that it is just going to add confusion to everything (Service provider).

Yet another centrally imposed solution, insensitive to local conditions and needs, has limped into being, and the early omens for it making a major contribution to agency coordination in Leeds remain none too promising.

## Notes

1. 82 Training and Enterprise Councils (TECs) were launched between 1990 and 1991 to deliver a variety of government training and enterprise development initiatives, although they were given a specific local initiatives fund to develop local projects. Peck (1995) notes, however, that interesting geographical variations have developed in the TEC model, thus suggesting that there are local readings of a national TEC script.

2. Business Links was launched in 1992 to radically alter business support in England (Baker, 1994). There are now 27 Business Links but a network of some 200 outlets, offering businesses a 'one-stop shop' for all types of business support, is planned. Each Business Link is an independent company, run by a partnership of local service providers.

3. The preliminary findings of this research project are summarised in Sear (1995).

4. Wright (1988, p.606) defines a policy community as, '...all those who share a common interest or an identity with a policy focus (which can be defined in terms of products, services, technologies or firm sizes)'. Therefore, the concept specifies all those who wish to play a part in determining public policy.

5. The Enterprise Initiative was introduced in 1988, by the DTI, in an attempt to increase the usage of consultants by small businesses. The Enterprise Initiative offered subsidised consultancy; the DTI would pay half of the costs within Assisted Areas and one-third of the costs outside Assisted Areas. The scheme was withdrawn in 1994 but is currently being re packaged and introduced through the Business Link network.

# References

Baker, N. (1994), 'Making The Links For Businesses', *Employment Gazette,* 102 (7), p. 234.

Bartlett, W. (1991), 'Privatisation and Quasi-Markets', Paper presented at EACES First Trento Workshop, University of Trento.

Beesley, W. and Wilson, P.E.B. (1984), 'Public Policy and Small Firms' in Levicki, C (ed.), *Small Business Theory and Policy,* Croom Helm, London.

Bennett, R. and McCoshan, A. (1993), *Enterprise and Human Resource Development: Local Capacity Building,* Paul Chapman Publishing Ltd., London.

Bennett, R., Wicks, P. and McCoshan, A. (1994), *Local Empowerment and Business Services: Britain's Experiment With Training and Enterprise Councils,* UCL Press Ltd., London.

Birch, D. (1979), *The Job Generation Process,* MIT, Massachusetts.

Clement, B. (1994), 'TECs to be given economic role', *The Independent,* 18th May.

Curran, J. and Blackburn, R. (1994), *Small Firms and Local Economic Networks: the death Of the local economy,* Paul Chapman Publishing Ltd., London.

Daly, J. (1990), 'The 1980s: a decade of growth in enterprise,' *Employment Gazette,* November.

Daly, J. and McCann, A. (1992), 'How many small firms?' *Employment Gazette,* February, 47-51.

Dicken, P. (1992), *Global Shift: Changes In A Turbulent World,* Paul Chapman Press, London.

DTI (1992), *A Prospectus For One Stop Shops For Businesses,* DTI, London.

Gibb, A.A. (1993), 'Key factors in the design of policy support for the SME development process: an overview,' *Entrepreneurship and Regional Development,* 5, 1-24.

Green, H. and Cruttenden, M. (1990), *Enterprise Support Agencies In Leeds: analysis of current patterns. A Report For Leeds TEC,* CUDEM, Leeds Polytechnic.

Green, H. and Johnson, S. (1992), 'Localisation and quasi-markets and enterprise support: implications for TECs,' Paper presented to the 15th National Small Firms Policy and Research Conference, Southampton, November.

Haughton, G. (1993), 'The local provision of small and medium enterprise advice services', *Regional Studies,* 27 (8) 835-842.

Jessop, B., Bonnett, K., Bromley, S. and Ling, T. (eds.) (1988),

*Thatcherism: A Tale Of Two Nations,* Polity Press, Cambridge.

Johnson, S. (1990), 'Small firms policies: an agenda for the 1990s,' Paper presented to the 13th National Small Firms and Research Conference, Harrogate, November.

Mason, C.M. (1987), 'The Small Firm Sector' in Lever, W.F. (ed.) *Industrial Change In The UK*, Longman, London.

Peck, J. (1995), 'Geographies of governance: TECs and the remaking of community interests', Paper presented to the Annual Conference of the Institute Of British Geographers, University of Northumbria at Newcastle, Newcastle.

Piore, M. and Sabel, C. (1984), *The Second Industrial Divide,* Basic Books, New York.

Sayer, A. (1992), *Method In Social Science: a realist approach,* Routledge, London.

Sear, L. (1995), 'Spatial differences in the uptake of external assistance: the experience of small manufacturing businesses within Yorkshire and Humberside,' paper presented to the 'Small firms and business development: new policy perspectives' seminar, Leeds Business School, Leeds, June.

Shiner, P. and Nevin, B. (1994), 'Moving out of the inner city,' *Municipal Journal,* 18, 22-26.

Stanworth, J. and Gray, C. (1991), *Bolton 20 Years On: the small firm in the 1990s,* Paul Chapman Publishing Ltd., London.

Storey, D.J. (1994a), *Understanding The Small Business Sector*, Routledge, London.

Storey, D.J. (1994b), 'Studies savage state aid policies for small firms,' *The Guardian,* 21st June.

Wright, M. (1988), 'Policy community, policy network and comparative industrial policies,' *Political Studies,* 36, 593-612.

# 10 Paid informal work in the Leeds hospitality industry: Unregulated or regulated work?

*Colin C. Williams and Rhodri Thomas*

### Introduction

This chapter examines an aspect of the contemporary city which is often overlooked. Beyond the realm of paid employment, hidden from and ignored by many, is a large and growing sphere of economic activity, often referred to as the informal sector. It is in this twilight world in the metaphorical interstices of the formal city (Laguerre, 1994), that an increasing proportion of the population find themselves snared as they struggle to get-by in these difficult times.

This informal sector is composed of many diverse component parts: domestic work, which is unpaid work undertaken by household members for themselves or for other members of the household; community work which is a variation of domestic work in which work is exchanged not only between household members, but within the extended family and social or neighbourhood networks; voluntary work which is unpaid work undertaken within an organisation in the service of the wider community; and paid informal work, or what in less politically correct terms, has been traditionally called black market work or the black economy (in contrast to the legal 'white' economy). This is paid work that is unregistered by the state for tax, social security or labour law purposes but which is legal in all other respects (Williams and Windebank, 1995).

In this chapter, we shall confine our analysis of the informal sector to the study of paid informal work. It should be noted, however, that our definition of paid informal work, similar to Thomas (1992), includes those activities in which the goods and services produced are legal but their production and distribution involves some illegality, but excludes criminal activities whose goods and services themselves are illegal, such as drug trafficking. This is similar to most definitions of the paid informal sector.

Where we differ from other writers, however, is on the question of whether paid informal work is 'unregulated' (Sassen-Koob, 1984; Sassen, 1991; Portes, Castells and Benton, 1989). Portes and Castells (1989, p.15), for example, define such work as "the unregulated production of otherwise licit goods and services." Here, we challenge such a view. First, therefore, this chapter will critically evaluate the notion that paid informal work is unregulated by revealing a range of economic, social, institutional and environmental conditions which define the nature and level of such activity in any locality. Following this, a case study will be undertaken of the Leeds hospitality industry so as to reinforce how paid informal work is indeed regulated.

Before commencing, it is necessary to distinguish between two types of informal work. First, there is 'organised' informal work, which is work undertaken as an employee for a business which is either wholly underground or conducts part of its business in such a manner. This can take two forms. On the one hand, such work can be characterised by employment in small firms that are usually traditional and labour-intensive, utilising old technology and producing cheap products and services for local markets and export. The firms tend to possess low levels of capitalization and profit and are often dependent upon larger firms for their contracts. The employees tend to be poorly paid, may be more likely to be women, children, the unemployed or immigrants, working under exploitative conditions with little opportunity for promotion. On the other hand, organised informal work can also be more autonomous in orientation, in small firms which are more modern and that use high technology to produce higher-priced goods and services. These firms are more capitalised with higher profits and are independent companies, not dependent upon large firms (Benton, 1990). They can often be linked together through dense small firm networks (Amin, 1994). The employees are more likely to be men and are well paid, use higher skills and have more autonomy and control over their work, with relations between employers and employees based more upon cooperation than domination (Warren, 1994).

Second, there is 'individual' informal work, which ranges from activity conducted by somebody on a self-employed basis and may involve a large proportion, if not all, of their earnings, to casual one-off jobs undertaken on a cash-in-hand basis, such as for a neighbour or an acquaintance. Of course, all such informal economic activity can be placed on a continuum ranging from highly exploitative to highly autonomous at the polar opposites, with the relatively exploitative organised informal work and the relatively autonomous individual informal work at the two ends of the spectrum and

172

the more autonomous organised kind being somewhere in the middle. In addition, there is some limited overlap and interaction between the various kinds of informal work. For example, the employer of exploited informal employees may her/himself be engaged in well-paid individual autonomous informal work.

### The paid informal sector: unregulated or regulated work?

To identify the instruments which regulate paid informal work, the multiplicity of one-off locality studies which have been conducted throughout the European Union (EU) have been reviewed elsewhere (see Williams and Windebank, 1993, 1994, 1995 for a more detailed analysis of these locality studies). This has resulted in the recognition of a range of institutional, economic, social and environmental regulators of paid informal work. Each is now briefly outlined.

*Institutional regulators*

As shown above, many believe that the informal sector is unregulated in the sense of not being controlled by the state. This section reveals, however, not only that the nature and extent of the informal sector is very much a product of the state rules and regulations prevalent at any time and place but also that the state plays an active role in shaping its form and magnitude.

*Labour law* By definition, paid informal work is a product of the state, especially labour law, in the sense that it is "created by government rules and regulations" (Guttman, 1977,p.26). In some nations, for example, industrial homeworking is legal whilst in others it is illegal and thus, by definition, paid informal work. Nevertheless, labour laws, although creating the informal sector, are alone insufficient to explain its varying nature and extent amongst different populations.

*Welfare benefit regulations* Universal access to permanent state benefits reduces the participation of the unemployed in paid informal work compared to populations with poor access to permanent benefits. This is because the unemployed in these latter populations have little or nothing to lose if caught. Hence, welfare benefit regulations are an important regulator of paid informal work, especially amongst the unemployed (Wenig, 1990).

*State interpretation of laws and regulations* It is not only the institutional regulations themselves which influence the nature and extent of paid informal work but also the way in which such regulations are interpreted by implementing agencies. Some turn a blind eye to some or all paid informal work in their area in a bid either to help local businesses to compete in the global market-place or to help people unable to otherwise get-by (Warren, 1994). In addition, different sub-sectors of paid informal work are targeted in different areas in a bid to clamp down on such activity (van Geuns et al., 1987).

*Corporatist agreements* Paid informal work is not only regulated by the state, but also by industry, company and individual agreements. These can limit individuals' rights to take on additional work, undertake overtime and so on. Such work can be used to attempt to circumvent these rules and such corporatist agreements thus become a factor in regulating the nature and level of paid informal work.

*Economic regulators*

*Level of unemployment* In general, the higher the unemployment rate in the area, the lower the level of paid informal work and that which is undertaken is more likely to be of the low-paid exploitative kind (Williams and Windebank, 1995). Nevertheless, there are exceptions. Studies of West Belfast (Leonard, 1994) and Brussels (Kesteloot and Meert, 1994) reveal that it is the unemployed who conduct informal work and that in areas of high unemployment, such work is rife. These studies uncover contrasting findings to other studies because the unemployment rate is not the sole regulatory mechanism.

*Industrial structure* Localities dominated by a few large enterprises generally have relatively little informal work (Barthelemy, 1991; Van Geuns et al., 1987; Howe, 1988), which is usually attributed to the fact that large companies tend to use less organised informal work than their smaller counterparts, whilst the skills acquired in such industries are less often transferable to individual informal work than those obtained in other types of employment. In local economies composed of a large number of small firms (Barthelemy, 1991; Cappechi, 1989), in contrast, there is more organised paid informal work. This is because in small firms, trade unions are less active and thus there is greater opportunity for such work to occur either directly or through sub-contracting arrangements so that costs can be reduced and they can compete more effectively with larger companies.

*Sub-contracting* In some areas, sub-contracting has often weakened the workers' bargaining position and frequently led to a decrease in wages, a reduction in the standard of working conditions and a loss of state benefits (Benton, 1990). Sometimes, however, the outcome is a thriving informal sector of small businesses that have adapted to shifting market demands for specialised products whilst retaining relatively high wages and good working conditions (Cappechi, 1989; Warren, 1994). The result depends upon the local economy, the skills base of the local labour market and local political circumstances as well as national level factors.

*Tax and social contribution levels* Some have argued that this alone determines the nature and extent of the informal sector (Klovland, 1980; Geeroms and Mont, 1987; Matthews, 1982). However, it is simply one regulatory condition in a 'cocktail' of mechanisms which combine to shape the character and magnitude of paid informal work. As these costs rise, the incentive to undertake such work increases. Of course, this does not mean that all firms and self-employed people automatically undertake a greater proportion of their work 'off-the-books'. Neither does it mean that all consumers switch to paid informal work to get their work done. It depends upon the alternatives open to them. Some consumers may turn to self-provisioning. Furthermore, where taxation is raised more through employers' contributions, there is more likelihood of organised paid informal work, whilst when these contributions are raised more through income taxes, individual informal work will be more likely (Williams and Windebank, 1995).

*Social regulators*

*The nature of social networks* Populations with dense social networks undertake a greater proportion of the total work using informal work than areas with sparse or dissipated social networks, who use relatively more formal sector purchases (Legrain, 1982; van Geuns et al, 1987; Morris, 1988). Dense social networks, therefore, are strong regulators of paid informal work but the manner in which they regulate such work is dependent upon how they co-exist with a number of other factors.

*Socio-economic mix* When a population combines 'time starved but income rich' people with 'time rich but cash starved' people, then a relatively high proportion of the total workload may be undertaken using informal work and a higher amount of such work overall may take place (De Klerk and Vijgen, 1985; Pestieau, 1984; Renooy, 1984; Terhorst and Van de Ven, 1985).

*Local cultural traditions* In some areas, paid informal work is more acceptable than in others because a feeling of resentment and of being let

175

down by the state is more intense (Legrain, 1982; Leonard, 1994; Kroft et al, 1989; Weber, 1989) or due to such work being undertaken more for social than for economic reasons (Cornuel and Duriez, 1985; Barthelemy, 1991). For instance, the formal welfare state has meant a move away from self-provisioning, with money from rates, taxes and national insurance being passed, along with responsibility, to government agencies. Unfortunately, it is now seen to be the duty of the state, or indeed society as a whole, to provide people with what they need, thus engendering a 'dependency culture.' For some, the belief is that if society is breaking its side of the bargain, by not offering jobs for instance, then they have a right to contravene their side of the bargain. This can take the form of criminal activity, but also paid informal work.

*Education levels* The more educated the population, the more likely they are to supply paid informal work (Renooy, 1990). Such work is generally more autonomous and well-paid in character than that typically undertaken by those who are lesser educated and/or with fewer years in education, who tend to be engaged in informal work more of a exploitative and low-paid kind (Bloeme and Van Geuns, 1987; Hellberger and Schwarze, 1987; Renooy, 1990).

*Environmental regulators*

*Size and type of area* Although little is known about how urban settlement size shapes the nature and extent of paid informal work, rural areas are known to conduct more informal work than urban areas (Legrain, 1982; Jessen et al, 1987; Hadjimichalis and Vaiou, 1989).

*Type and availability of housing* Populations with high levels of privately owned households conduct a wider range of informal work than areas dominated by rented accommodation. In addition, a larger living space, especially the availability of garden space, offers greater possibilities for participation in individual paid informal work (Van Geuns et al., 1987). Owner occupiers are also more likely to use employment and paid informal work to get a job done and tenants more likely to use unpaid work (Mogensen, 1985; Renooy, 1990). However, the degree to which tenure regulates the level and nature of informal work is, in part, a function of the institutional context. In situations where tenants are not allowed to partake in alterations, maintenance and/or repairs to their dwellings, less informal work is likely than in situations where such activities are allowed. It might be expected, for example, that the shifts in housing policy in Britain over the last fifteen years away from a 'dependency culture' towards greater autonomy will have facilitated a growth in informal work.

In summary, and as argued elsewhere (Williams and Windebank, 1995), it is not necessarily the case that the existence of a particular condition in an area, such as high unemployment, will have a straightforward effect on paid informal work in that locality. Rather, it depends upon the other factors present and how these inter-relate. Put another way, the nature and extent of paid informal work in any locality will be the outcome of a 'cocktail' of factors, composed of a range of economic, institutional, social and environmental regulators, which combine in multifarious ways in different localities to produce particular local outcomes. With this understanding of the paid informal sector as a form of regulated work in hand, attention now turns towards an examination of the paid informal sector in Leeds. To do this, an investigation is undertaken of the Leeds hospitality industry. The aim, in so doing, is to reveal how the regulatory conditions discussed above are in operation and are shaping this supposedly 'unregulated' sphere of the Leeds economy.

## Paid informal work in the Leeds hospitality industry

The empirical research into the paid informal sector in the Leeds hospitality industry on which this section is based, involved interviews with officers at the Low Pay Unit, Benefits Agency fraud investigators, personnel managers and head housekeepers from six city centre hotels, two contract cleaners and eight workers from the hotel and catering industry (see Thomas and Thomas, 1994). Those interviewed were not exclusively from Leeds Metropolitan District nor did the information which was provided give any more than a partial indication of the nature and extent of paid informal work in the Leeds hospitality industry. Nevertheless, the empirical data presented does provide evidence of the existence of paid informal work in this sector and of the manner in which it is regulated.

In Leeds, the economy has increasingly diversified away from its manufacturing origins, resulting not only in a tertiarisation of the economic base but also an industrial structure founded upon a large and growing number of small firms (Thomas and Thomas, 1994; see also Chapters 5 and 9). Studies of the informal sector suggest that in localities with large numbers of small firms, paid informal work will be likely to be higher and of the organised variety, because in such firms trade unions are less active and there is greater scope for organised informal work either directly or through sub-contracting arrangements so as to reduce costs. This is precisely what appears to be happening in the Leeds hospitality industry. The growth of smaller firms and sub-contracting is resulting in a rise in organised paid informal work. These firms conduct either the whole or part of their work 'off-the-books' and this is undertaken for low wages under exploitative conditions with little chance of promotion or advancement for the workers.

For instance, several interviewees highlighted the high and growing level of paid informal work in commercial cleaning, much centred around the small firms which have emerged as a result of the sub-contracting of this function. One striking illustration concerned a cleaning contract for a large mail order catalogue company which had previously employed its own cleaning staff at £3.50 per hour but had then decided to sub-contract part of this work to a cleaning firm which paid less than half that amount but guaranteed anonymity to its workers. Presumably, this was so as to enable such workers to claim state benefit without declaring their earnings or not pay tax. Nevertheless, paid informal work is not exclusive to small firms taking on sub-contracted work. At least two separate sources identified instances of large firms engaging people outside the constraints of state regulation in a bid to reduce costs. Whether it is small or large firms using paid informal workers, however, most of the work appears to be poorly paid and exploitative so far as the Leeds hospitality industry is concerned.

Two of the six city centre hotels questioned had sub-contracted their night cleaning so as to overcome recruitment difficulties. Both firms which serviced these hotels were small operators, one relying to a large extent on family labour, the other was slightly larger and had won contracts with breweries, a local authority and a factory. The workers employed by this company earned two-thirds of what they would have been paid had they been directly employed by the hotel. The suggestion is that they continued to work for such wages because their income was not declared. One of the housekeepers, moreover, was disgruntled at the number of cold calls received from cleaning operators who wanted to tender (at lower prices) for their cleaning work.

Similarly, an interviewee noted that some well-known high street retailers used small local cleaning firms for periodic cleaning at much lower than general market rates. Although there was no definitive evidence that the lower rates depended on informal labour, it is a plausible speculation, and is consistent with the arguments developed above, that small businesses offer greater scope and appear to have more propensity for paid informal work. It is also noteworthy that this respondent, the manager of a large contract cleaning company, had also acted in a similar way herself. In circumstances where the fulfilment of a contract was difficult to achieve, she had sub-contracted the work quite legitimately to an individual for a fixed fee. It was obvious that casual staff would be employed with no reference whatsoever to formal documentation.

In this case study, some of the recently privatised utilities did not appear, *prima facie* at least, to operate on the basis outlined above. At least one respondent insisted that all sub-contractors pay a particular rate and make information available, such as names of employees and hours of work, for inspection by the contracting firm. The extent to which there may be a difference between theory and practice was not clear.

The organisation of casual labour was tackled in a number of ways by the hotels. Some used agencies, though most organised their own pool of staff where possible, based on students. Not surprisingly, these large companies paid their employees with due regard to state regulations but recognised opportunities for, and the likelihood of, informalisation when they sub-contracted part of their work to small companies.

The workers interviewed offered confirmation of this impression, suggesting that informalisation was endemic in small hotels, restaurants, pubs and cleaning firms. These findings were not surprising in the light of the literature referred to earlier in this chapter. Two brief case studies serve as an illustration of what was seen as common practice in this sector. One worker was registered with several employment agencies as a cook, waiter and bar person. These organisations operated quite legitimately, receiving payment from firms, passing on a proportion to the worker and apparently abiding by appropriate employment regulations. Frequently, however, this worker's placement by an agency into a job represented simply an introduction to the firm. The firm then requested longer hours for payment in cash (with no records) and/or contacted the person directly for additional days. The respondent who admitted to this was clear regarding the benefits to himself and to his new (periodic) employers arising from these arrangements. Another worker interviewed was employed on a part-time basis in a bar (as well as working full-time for a manufacturing company) and was paid in cash with no employment records kept in his name. He felt that this type of small hotel and catering outlet was heavily dependent upon workers like himself.

The nature and extent of paid informal work in Leeds in general, and the local hospitality industry more particularly, is thus a function of the economic, social, institutional and environmental conditions in the locality. This brief and rather anecdotal picture of the Leeds hospitality industry has only looked at ' organised' paid informal work, rather than the full range of such work which is taking place in Leeds. Nevertheless, it does reveal that the character and magnitude of organised paid informal work in the Leeds hospitality industry is regulated. It is regulated not only by national level conditions such as labour law, welfare benefits regulations and the level and type of tax and social contributions, but also by local conditions such as the level of unemployment, the industrial structure, level of sub-contracting, socio-economic mix in the locality and the local cultural traditions vis-a-vis paid informal work.

Given this identification of the regulatory conditions which shape the nature and extent of paid informal work, the challenge over the next few years will be to distinguish the key factors that generate paid informal work, especially of the organised exploitative variety. Once this is understood, we will be able to explore how intervention could occur to either harness or eradicate such work. Our preliminary research in the Leeds hospitality industry leads us to the very tentative conclusion that sub-contracting is a key factor in creating high levels of organised paid informal work of the exploitative variety. In this sense, our study of this sector of the Leeds economy reinforces the findings in many southern European nations about the influence of sub-contracting on the paid informal sector (Benton, 1990; Cappechi, 1989; Warren, 1994). Further research is required, however, of the ways in which other national and local level conditions interact with sub-contracting to produce particular configurations of paid informal work both in this locality and others. At present, this is poorly understood.

## Conclusions

This chapter has revealed that Leeds has an informal city existing behind the facade of the formal city. Many take part in it but few speak loudly of its existence. However, the work which takes place in this informal city is not unregulated. Rather, it is regulated work in the sense that it's nature and extent is shaped by the prevalent economic, social, institutional and environmental conditions. The importance of this finding that paid informal work is regulated is that it means that such work is not beyond the scope of adjustment. Instead, and similar to other forms of work, the possibility exists to regulate it by controlling those economic, social, institutional and environmental conditions which determine its character and magnitude. As such, some aspects of paid informal work are well within the reach of state intervention both by local and national government. The challenge for the future will be to decide what is to be done and how to do it.

## Acknowledgements

The authors would like to express their gratitude to both Huw Thomas and Jan Windebank for their assistance in helping us to formulate our ideas on the paid informal sector. Nevertheless, any faults or omissions are, of course, the sole responsibility of the authors.

# References

Amin, A. (1994), 'The difficult transition from informal economy to Marshallian industrial district,' *Area,* 26 (1), 13-24.

Barthelemy, P. (1991), 'La croissance de l'economie souterraine dans les pays occidentaux: un essai d'interpretation,' in Lespes, J-L (ed) *Les pratiques juridiques, economiques et sociales informelles,* PUF, Paris.

Benton, L. (1990), *Invisible Factories : the informal economy and industrial development in Spain.* State University of New York Press, New York.

Bloeme, L. and van Geuns, R.C. (1987), *Ongeregeld Ondernemen: eeen onderzoek naar informele bedrijvigheid,* (irregular enterprising: research into informal industry). Ministerie van Sociale Zaken en Werkgelegenheid (Ministry for Social Affairs and Employment), The Hague.

Capecchi, V. (1989), 'The informal economy and the development of flexible specialisation in Emilia-Romagna,' in Portes, A., Castells, M. and Benton, L.A. (eds) *The Informal Economy: studies in advanced and less developed countries,* John Hopkins University Press, Baltimore

Cornuel, D. and Duriez, B. (1985), 'Local exchange and state intervention,' in Redclift, N. and Mingione, E. (eds) *Beyond Employment,* Basil Blackwell, Oxford.

Geeroms, H. and Mont, J. (1987), 'Evaluation de l'importance de l'economie souterraine en Belgique: application de la methode monetaire,' in Ginsburgh, V. and Pestieau, P. (eds) *L'Economie Informelle,* editions labor, Bruxelles.

Geuns Van, R., Mevissen, J. and Renooy, P. (1987), 'The spatial and sectoral diversity of the informal economy,' *Tijdschrift voor econ. en soc. geografie,* 78 (5), 389-398.

Guttmann, P.M. (1977), 'The subterranean economy,' *Financial Analysts Journal,* 34 (Nov-Dec), 26-7.

Hadjimichalis, C. and Vaiou, N. (1989), 'Whose flexibility? : the politics of informalisation in Southern Europe,' Paper presented to the IAAD/SCG Study Groups of the IBG Conference on Industrial Restructuring and Social Change: the dawning of a new era of flexible accumulation?, Durham.

Hellberger, C. and Schwarze, J. (1987), 'Nebenerwerbstatigkeit: ein indikator fur arbeitsmarkt-flexibilitat oder schattenwirtschaft,' *Wirtschaftsdienst,* 2, 83-90.

Howe, L. (1988), 'Unemployment, doing the double and local labour markets in Belfast,' in Cartin, C. and Wilson, T. (eds) *Ireland From Below: social change and local communities in modern Ireland,* Gill and Macmillan, Dublin.

Jessen, J., Siebel, W., Siebel-Rebell, C., Walther, U. and Weyrather, I.

(1987), 'The informal work of industrial workers,' Paper presented at *6th Urban Change and Conflict Conference,* University of Kent at Canterbury, September.

Kesteleoot, C. and Meert, H. (1994), 'Les fonctions soci-economiques de l'economie informelle et son implantation spatiale dans les villes belges,' paper presented at Conference on *Cities, Enterprise and Society at the Eve of the 21st Century,* Lille.

Klerk de, L. and Vijgen, J. (1985), 'Cities in post-industrial perspective : new economics, new lifestyles - new chances?' *Grote Steden: verval of innovatie,* Reader ASVS, Lustrum Congress.

Klovland, J.T. (1980), *In Search of the Hidden Economy: tax evasion and the demand for currency in Norway and Sweden,* Norwegian School of Economics and Business Administration, Bergen.

Kroft, H.G., Engbersen, G., Schuyt, K. and van Waarden, F. (1989), *Een Tijd Zonder Werk. Een onderzoek naar de levenswereld van langdurig werklozen* (A time without employment: a study into the way of life of long term unemployed), Leiden.

Laguerre, M.S. (1994), *The Informal City,* Macmillan, London.

Legrain, C. (1982), 'L'economie informelle a Grand Failly,' *Cahiers de l'OCS,* no. 7, CNRS, Paris.

Leonard, M. (1994), *Informal Economic Activity in Belfast,* Avebury, Aldershot.

Matthews, K.G.P. (1982), 'Demand for currency and the black economy in the UK,' *Journal of Economic Studies,* 9.

Mogensen, G.V. (1985), *Sort arbejde i Danmark,* Institut for Nationalokonomi, Copenhagen.

Morris, L. (1988), 'Employment, the household and social networks,' in Gallie, D. (ed) *Employment in Britain,* Basil Blackwell, Oxford.

Pestieau, P. (1984), 'Belgium's irregular economy,' Paper Colloque IV, Economie Parallele, ULB, Brussels.

Portes, A. and M. Castells (1989), 'World underneath: the origin, dynamics and effects of the informal economy', in Portes, A., Castells, M. and Benton, L. (1989) (eds) *The Informal Economy: studies in advanced and less developed countries,* John Hopkins University, Baltimore.

Portes, A., M. Castells and L. Benton (1989) (eds), *The Informal Economy: studies in advanced and less developed countries,* John Hopkins University, Baltimore.

Renooy, P.H. (1984), *De Schemerzone: 'werplaats' tussen vrije tijd en arbeid* (The twilight zone: 'workshop' between leisure and labour), Ministry of Social Affairs and Employment, The Hague.

Renooy, P. (1990), *The Informal Economy: meaning, measurement and social significance,* Netherlands geographical studies no. 115, Amsterdam.

Sassen-Koob, S. (1984), 'The new labour demand in global cities,' in Smith, M.P. (ed) *Cities in Transformation,* Beverley Hills.

Sassen, S. (1991), *The Global City,* Princeton University Press, Princeton.

Terhorst, P. and Van de Ven, J. (1985), *Zwarte Persoonlijke Dienstverlening en het Stedelijk Milieu* (Black personal services and the urban environment), Social Geografisch Instituut, Amsterdam.

Thomas, R. and Thomas, H. (1994), 'The informal economy and local economic development policy,' *Local Government Studies,* 20 (3), 486-501.

Thomas, J.J. (1992), *Informal Economic Activity,* Harvester Wheatsheaf, Hemel Hempstead.

Warren, M.R. (1994), 'Exploitation or cooperation? the political basis of regional variation in the Italian informal economy,' *Politics and Society,* 22 (1), 89-115.

Weber, F. (1989), *Le Travail a Cote: etude d'ethnographie ouvriere,* Institut national de la recherche agronomique, Paris.

Wenig, A. (1990), 'The shadow economy in the Federal Republic of Germany,' in *Underground Economy and Irregular Forms of Employment,* Final Synthesis Report, Office for Official Publications of the European Communities, Brussels.

Williams, C.C. and Windebank, J.E. (1993), 'Social and spatial inequalities in the informal economy: some evidence from the European Community,' *Area,* 25 (4), 358-364.

Williams, C.C. and Windebank, J. (1994), 'Spatial variations in the informal sector: a review of evidence from the European Union,' *Regional Studies,* 28 (8), 819-825.

Williams, C.C. and Windebank, J. (1995), 'Black market work in the European Community: peripheral work for peripheral localities?' *International Journal of Urban and Regional Research,* 19 (1), 22-39.

# III
# THE ENVIRONMENTAL CHALLENGE: CORPORATE AND COMMUNITY RESPONSES

# 11 Greening the Leeds economy: The Leeds Business Environment Forum

*Peter Roberts*

## Introduction

Sustainable development is the latest manifestation of a deeply-rooted concern amongst planners and policy-makers to achieve a balance between the requirements of economic development and the capacity of the environment. Most recent treatments of this subject tend to emphasise either the individual and sectoral considerations of economic activities, or they focus their attention upon the broad sweep of environmental and socio-economic issues that comprise the sustainable development agenda. Both of these approaches fail to place sufficient emphasis upon the spatial implications of the nature and content of the discourse between business and the environment. There are exceptions to this general rule in the academic literature, for example, Gibbs (1993), Welford and Gouldson (1993), Roberts (1995), Blowers et al. (1993) and Ravetz et al. (1995), and there are also a growing number of contributions by practitioners including the work of Hams et al (1994), Bartone et al. (1994), Wood (1994) and the classic contribution of Winter (1988). However, with these few exceptions, the majority of contributions to the debate on the greening of local and regional economic development tend either to treat the problems encountered at the economy: environment interface as an issue that can be resolved solely by public policy, or they deal with these difficult policy issues at a national or global level.

This chapter aims to rectify some of the deficiencies apparent in the current literature and to illustrate the means of achieving a solution by reference to the case of a single city-region. Much of the material used to construct this examination is drawn from the author's experience as a

187

participant-observer in the formation and operation of the Leeds Environment City Initiative and, in particular, as Chair of the Leeds Environmental Business Forum. Despite this emphasis, and because it provides a number of important lessons that may be of assistance elsewhere, the chapter also considers a wider set of issues that represent the parameters within which a local response to the economy: environment debate can be constructed.

The following section of the chapter outlines the foundation for this examination of the links between economy, environment and place; this is followed by a brief discussion of the key features of the relationship between the economy and the environment, and the major factors that should be taken into account in constructing a local or regional strategy for sustainable economic development. The penultimate section of the chapter offers a case study of the Leeds city-region, and from this, together with the messages that can be gleaned from preceding sections, a number of conclusions are presented.

**Economy, environment and place**

Even in a world where multinational businesses exert considerable power and influence, many companies still value their association with a particular regional or local area. Indeed many of these companies, some of which were once locally-owned independent businesses before being absorbed into larger transnational enterprises, operate at higher levels of environmental performance than smaller indigenous companies. This is the case in the Leeds economy, with companies, such as Sandoz and Du Pont, operating at corporate standards which reflect the requirements of stricter legislation that is in force elsewhere and which are already at a higher level than those required by their host government. However, the majority of business organisations remain as independent enterprises, and such organisations range in size from micro-firms employing a handful of workers, to large regional, national or international actors.

Irrespective of their size, sector of activity, or pattern of ownership, the majority of businesses are influenced by the economic and environmental conditions obtaining in a locality. These sources of influence vary from place-to-place and from company-to-company, but, in general, they reflect the traditions of a local business peer group and wider sectoral pressures, the strength of local and national legislation and its enforcement, supply chain requirements, the awareness of management with regard to consumer demands and internal employee pressures, and the extent to which a business wishes to operate at the leading edge of both environmental and economic practice. Other local and regional environmental factors can also influence the behaviour of a business: the presence or absence of a green-minded local authority, the availability of recycling and secondary transformation facilities, and the availability of help and advice for the local or regional business community, can assist or hinder an individual enterprise in its search for improved environmental performance.

The links between business, the environment and place represent an expression of the deep-rooted sense of attachment that people have to the places where they work, live and seek recreation. This relationship, which is a central component of sustainable development, has been the subject of academic and practice discourse for much of the past century and only the ill-informed would deny the merits of learning from previous attempts to translate theory into practice (Roberts, 1994).

A helpful starting point in the search for concepts and models of practice that can assist in the operationalisation of sustainable economic development can be found in the work of the Garden City movement and the scintillating vision of Patrick Geddes. Inspired by the pioneering experiments of philanthropists such as Owen, Salt, Cadbury and Lever - they appreciated the benefit for both the environment and productivity of combining the essential elements of sustainable development - Ebenezer Howard (1902) generalised the idea of combining working and living in a healthy environment. The result was the Social City, a new form of settlement that combined the virtues of town and country, and this concept was later translated into practice with the establishment of Letchworth in 1903.

This civic activism on the part of Howard coincided with the wider analysis presented by Geddes. Drawing upon the work of de la Blache and Le Play, Geddes (1915) considered that an appreciation of the links between folk, work and place, was fundamental to understanding the origins and operation of local and regional economic systems in relation to the constraints imposed by the environment.

Travelling across the Atlantic and moving forward in time, these ideas provided the stimulus for the work of Lewis Mumford and his colleagues in the Regional Planning Association of America (RPAA). Mumford was all too aware of the dangers inherent in a model of urbanisation that sacrificed environment for the scale of economic growth. This diagnosis was informed by observation:

The industrial city did not represent the creative values in civilization: it stood for a new form of human barbarism. In the coal towns of Pennsylvania, the steel towns of Ohio, and the factory towns of Long Island Sound... was an environment much more harsh, antagonistic and brutal than anything the pioneers had encountered (Mumford, 1922).

Mumford's prognosis, allied to the work of his colleagues in the RPAA, led to the emergence of a doctrine that sought to identify and implement a mode of urban and regional development which "involves the development of cities and countrysides, industries and national resources, as part of the regional whole" (MacKaye and Mumford, 1929). This doctrine, based upon the idea that cities could only survive in organic balance with the totality of their regional environment, represented a practical expression of the call made by Geddes for the generation of a synoptic vision (a holistic view) from which individual actions could proceed. Other elements of the Geddes doctrine will be familiar to modern readers, including his advocacy of the precautionary principle and his support of the need to think and plan long-term.

Britain had its counterparts of Mumford's harsh, antagonistic and brutal environment. Leeds was described by Sir George Head in 1835 in the following terms:

There is no manufacturing town in England, I should imagine, where more coal is consumed in proportion to its extent than Leeds. The sun himself is obscured by smoke as by a natural mist (Sigsworth, 1967).

Although environmental conditions had improved by the twentieth century, the legacy of industrialisation, and the attitudes that went with it, survived for far longer. Despite the analytical and practical efforts of Howard and Geddes, and notwithstanding the unintended improvements in environmental conditions that have accompanied the decline of heavy industry, the gulf between the economic imperative and needs of the environment has continued to widen during the present century.

This brief review of previous attempts to introduce a more measured approach to the relationship between the economy and the environment provides a frame of reference within which current attempts to implant the notion of balanced development can be tested and elaborated. The selective cultivation of seedlings from the intellectual arboretum of the past can help to accelerate the recolonization of the sterile territory that has been created by the muck and brass attitudes of previous eras of industrialisation. A realisation that this is not the first attempt to promote sustainable development is of immense assistance in avoiding the mistakes of the past and this, as we shall see later, is the model that has helped to guide the Leeds Environment City Initiative.

## Strategies and tactics for sustainable economic development

Having outlined the origins and experience of previous attempts to achieve sustainable economic development, this section of the chapter attempts to isolate the key features from this experience and to identify some principles upon which future policy can be based. Although it is likely that a number of difficulties will be experienced in mapping from past experience to the present - substantial differences can be observed both in terms of the socio-political context within which past policies were constructed, and in the structure, ownership, organisation and location of economic activities - there are also numerous points of similarity. The lessons that can be distilled from other experience, both in the past and from different places, can prove to be of considerable assistance in the development of local and regional policy through the provision of proven elements that can be grafted onto the stock of a self-generated local initiative. This concept of providing local exemplars has guided the ACBE programme (1993).

Key issues that have to be addressed in the generation of a sustainable economic development policy for a city-region include: the standard elements of sustainable development (environment, futurity, participation and equity); issues related to the structure and functioning of the economy; the desirability of encouraging local and regional self-sufficiency; and the need to ensure that a high degree of territorial integration is provided in order to link together the various elements of policy. Examining each of these issues in more detail and applying them to the generation of policy:

- Environment should be defined so as to include both the immediate and the remote environments that are affected by economic activities; defining both the visible and the "shadow ecology" (MacNeill et al., 1991) of a city-region is an essential step in ensuring that any problems are tackled in situ and not simply transferred elsewhere; this implies preventing problems at source.

- Futurity concerns the need to consider the effects upon future generations of actions taken by the present generation and, for example, it argues against the excessive use of natural resources, advocates the avoidance of environmental damage, and warns against taking irreversible actions; futurity is also known as inter-generational equity.

- Participation indicates the importance of establishing and maintaining consensus with regard to the goals of sustainable economic development and of ensuring the fullest participation of all stakeholders in the process of policy-making and implementation.

191

- Equity implies the promotion of greater distributional justice and a concern for social welfare; a sustainable economic development policy would encourage the creation of employment, the avoidance of exploitative labour practices in both the locality and elsewhere, and the redistribution of wealth; this principle is also known as intra-generational equity.

- Economic structures, forms of ownership and the patterns of production evident in a local or regional economy help to determine the extent to which economic activities can be adjusted in order, for example, to create joint ventures at local or regional level that are concerned with the processing of waste materials, to take advantage of a new market opportunity that requires collaboration between two or more companies in order to pool knowledge, skills and capital, or to provide leadership and advice to other companies located in a city-region.

- Self-sufficiency is an important element in the generation of a sustainable economic development strategy - despite the fact that its achievement is both unlikely and, in many cases, undesirable - because it highlights the many resource-inefficient and costly transfers that currently take place and which can be eliminated without any significant damage to overall economic efficiency.

- The promotion of territorial integration, which places emphasis upon the integration of environment and socio-economic systems within a territory, is an essential component in generating a sustainable economy; territorial (or spatial) coherence and integration add value to the sum of the individual components of policy and allows for the rooting of policy in the conditions of place, as Gibbs (1991) observes "people's activities cannot be divorced from their relationship with the environment".

Although it will be necessary to identify detailed aims and objectives for each individual local or regional area, the general guidelines presented above provide a broad indication of the institutional and procedural tools that are necessary in order to generate a strategy for sustainable economic development. The application of these ideas to the Leeds city-region will be considered in the following section, however, at a more general level it is helpful to highlight a number of the more important tactical and operational implications that flow from these guidelines.

The first of these implications is the need to establish a broadly-based forum that represents and reflects the view of the stakeholders present in the city-region. By creating a capacity for stakeholders to participate in the process of strategic decision-making, and by involving them in a form of partnership that seeks to operate in a transactive manner, it is possible to create a procedural model within which it is possible to reach agreement on matters such as strategy, modes of operation, budgeting and other resource contributions, and the elements and chronology of an implementation schedule. This form of consensus-seeking behaviour "implies the adoption of a shared agenda for change and the pooling of financial and other resources in the pursuit of common goals" (Roberts 1995).

A second implication is the need to agree and implement 'general rules' for the tactical elaboration and adjustment of strategy. It may prove necessary, for example, to develop a particular form of reprocessing facility not envisaged in the initial strategy, such variations should be possible and procedures should exist to ensure that they are evaluated and either accommodated within the approved strategy, agreed but delayed until a later point in time, or rejected. Other forms of tactical elaboration may include agreements on local purchasing, sectoral inter-trading, training and awareness programmes, initiatives to encourage the sharing of scientific and technical knowledge, access to ethical funds, and the application of common methods of environmental review, audit and management. An additional reason for establishing such 'ground rules' is to encourage the adoption and integration of a sustainable economic development perspective in all other relevant forms of policy and decision-making in the city-region. As the International Institute for Sustainable Development (1992) observe it is "essential for multinational, national and local agencies and governments to integrate and harmonize economic and environmental policies".

Two remaining issues can be considered together. There is a need to agree upon performance criteria, methods of monitoring and strategy review; and it is vital to develop effective methods of communication and for the dissemination of the progress with the strategy and best practice. Such steps are essential in order to define and identify progress towards addressing Gray's (1993) questions: "whose problem is it?" and "which problem are we addressing?"

Having determined strategy and tactics, a programme for sustainable economic development can proceed to deal with the operational matters that form the substance of policy. Davis (1991) has outlined the fields of action that form the basis for a schedule of implementation:

- discriminating development - economic activities should be discriminating in their use of resources in order to minimise waste and prevent environmental damage;

- conserving resources - preference should be given to the use of renewable resources and local resources should be used where possible;

- maximise the 4Rs - repair, reconditioning, reuse and recycling should be given priority;

- creative work - work should be organised in such a way as to make the fullest use of human abilities and job creation possibilities should be identified:

- maximisation of non-material growth - priority should be given to activities and forms of employment which do not consume excessive amounts of resources;

- self-directed personal investment - opportunities should be identified and supported which will encourage sustainability and serve the needs of individuals and communities.

There are many concrete ways in which this schedule can be translated into specific policies and projects. Amongst a range of measures are the examples identified by Gibbs (1991):

- develop environmental technology parks;
- audit local companies involved in "green" products and processes;
- invest pension funds in sustainable economic activities;
- direct financial assistance towards environmentally friendly companies;
- develop projects that combine local environmental action with job creation; and
- establish environmental business forums.

As a footnote to this section it is important to emphasise that changing course will take time. Achieving the goals of a sustainable economic development strategy is a long-term affair; some projects will accelerate ahead of the pack, others will falter and fail, whilst some may take a different pathway to that initially envisaged in order to achieve success. The following section reports the progress made by the Leeds city-region in moving towards a more sustainable economic future.

## Policy in action: the case of Leeds

Implementing sustainable economic development in practice is a difficult and complex task, and it is made more so by the onset of recession. Companies lack the financial resources necessary in order to act philanthropically, local authorities do not have the powers of direction to be able to impose change, even if they wanted to, and local communities and voluntary groups face a range of other more immediate problems. No individual groups holds the key that will unlock a solution and no single action will bring about a transformation of the environmental condition of the local economy.

In such a situation the only productive way forward is one that is based upon the development and implementation of a strategy that seeks to establish consensus and to create a mode of working in which belonging is more important than leading. This is the philosophy that underpins the efforts made in Leeds during recent years to tackle the problems that have been outlined earlier in this chapter.

The Leeds Green Strategy (Leeds City Council, 1991) places sustainable economic development at the forefront of its agenda for change. This strategy provides an overall context for sustainable development and, most importantly, it aims to ensure that environmental considerations are entrenched within the full range of policies. On the question of the economy-environment relationship, whilst it concentrates upon exerting influence through the land use planning system over the type, design, location and performance of economic activities, it also offers guidance on matters related to purchasing, raising awareness, transport, and waste and recycling.

Moving forward from this strategy, and working within the consensus-seeking model provided by the already well-established Leeds Initiative, a new partnership venture on business and the environment was formed in late 1991. Support for this organisation, the Leeds Environmental Business Forum, was provided by the Chamber of Commerce, the City Council, the higher education establishments in Leeds, and a number of local businesses. Following initial meetings in late 1991 and early 1992, the Forum was launched in May 1992.

As has already been noted, the Forum represents an attempt to generate and implement a model of balanced development, rooted in the realities of the local economy and the environment, that can assist in the stimulation of enhanced business practices. It seeks to achieve this objective through:

- raising the awareness of the business community with regard to environmental issues;
- acting as a focal point for the collection, dissemination and exchange of information and actions relating to best practice;
- providing an interface with organisations and agencies responsible for environmental regulation;
- sharing and distributing expertise and resources and channelling advice

which will enable positive environmental action to occur;
- developing a programme of environmental projects;
- publicising the achievements of the Leeds business community in the environmental field.

The development of the Forum, and of a range of projects and activities hosted by local businesses and public agencies, was given further impetus through its selection as one of the eleven pilot projects funded by the Advisory Committee on Business and the Environment (ACBE). As an ACBE pilot project the Forum is now a major player in a regional and national network of environmental business organisations, and its services have been expanded in order to assist other localities and regions in their search for enhanced business performance in the environmental field.

In parallel with this development, the Forum was one of the three major partners involved in the preparation of a bid to achieve for Leeds the status of an Environment City (Leeds Environment City Bid Team, 1992). This bid was successful and, working within the structure of the Leeds Environment City Initiative, the Forum now functions as one of the three focal points of environmental action within the City. It participates in a number of specialist working groups alongside its partner organisations, including groups that focus on economy and work, transport, waste and recycling, energy, and the built environment.

The Forum has promoted a number of specific projects, some of which have achieved national recognition, and also participates in a variety of regional and sub-regional networks that share resources and expertise. Of particular note amongst the projects promoted by the Forum are the preparation of the Good Environmental Business Practice Handbook (a mechanism for disseminating examples of good practice and providing local advice for other companies), the provision of an Initial Environmental Review Service, the publication of the Leeds Waste Manual, and the organisation of a series of briefing meetings and seminars which offer specialist advice. Above and beyond these specific services, the Forum has assisted in the creation of a large and growing local peer group that is willing to assist companies in their search for environmental improvement and to encourage the faint hearted.

It is possibly too early to offer an authoritative judgement on the long-term success of the Forum, but, when taken together with the work of individual companies, the City Council (especially through its own economic development initiative on the environment), the local TEC, utility organisations, and the voluntary sector, the achievements represent a major step towards the goal of establishing a lasting programme of sustainable economic development in Leeds.

## Sustained effort for a sustainable economy

Returning to the theme introduced earlier in this chapter, there is now an accumulating body of evidence which suggests that it is essential to ensure that a programme for sustainable economic development is based upon a realistic assessment of the conditions evident in both the local economy and the local environment. The folk, work, place relationship holds true, and whilst the oft-quoted maxim "think globally, act locally" expresses the need to consider sustainable development within the context of subsidiarity, it is also important to "think locally, act locally".

The messages of past and present practice, which have been reported in this chapter, demonstrate the importance of ensuring the entrenchment of the sustainable development debate within both the public and private policy systems. Local action at the level of an individual city-region has the opportunity to work towards a higher degree of territorial integration than can be achieved at either national or international levels. This advantage, when allied with a well-formulated and properly-resourced programme of action, offers the possibility of achieving a significant and lasting change in both attitudes and behaviour.

As is the case in certain other aspects of public and private policy in Leeds, the Leeds Environment City Initiative and the Leeds Environmental Business Forum are seeking to push forward the limits of current understanding and practice. Building upon local projects, increasingly refined organisational arrangements, the demonstrated success achieved by those companies which have adjusted their practices in order to incorporate environmental values, and the influence that can be exerted by a local business peer group in order to influence the behaviour of companies, this locally rooted model demonstrates the synergies that can be harnessed in order to bring about change. It is hard work to create sustainable economic development, but it is well worth the effort.

## References

Advisory Committee on Business and the Environment (1993), *The Environment: a business guide,* Department of Trade and Industry, London.

Bartone, C., Bernstein, J., Leitmann, J. and Eigen, J. (1994), *Toward Environmental Strategies for Cities,* The World Bank, Washington D.C., USA.

Blowers, A. (ed) (1993), *Planning for a Sustainable Environment,* Earthscan, London.

Davis, J. (1991), *Greening Business,* Basil Blackwell, Oxford.

Geddes, P. (1915), *Cities in Evolution,* Williams and Norgate, London.

Gibbs, D.C. (1991), 'Greening the local economy,' *Local Economy,* 6 (3), 224-239.

Gibbs, D. C. (1993), *The Green Local Economy,* Centre for Local Economic Strategies, Manchester.

Gray, R., Bebbington, J. and Walters, D. (1993), *Accounting for the Environment,* Paul Chapman Publishing, London.

Harris, T., Jacobs, M., Levett, R., Lusser, H., Morphet, J. and Taylor, D. (1994), *Greening Your Local Authority,* Longman, London.

Howard, E. (1902), *Garden Cities of Tomorrow (3rd Edition),* Swan Sonnenschein, London.

International Institute for Sustainable Development (1992), *Business Strategy for Sustainable Development,* IISD, Winnipeg, Manitoba.

Leeds City Council (1991), *Leeds Green Strategy,* Leeds City Council, Leeds.

Leeds Environment City Bid Team (1992), *Leeds BT Environment City Bid,* Leeds Environment City Bid Team, Leeds.

MacKaye, B. and Mumford, L. (1929), 'Regional Planning,' *Encyclopedia Britannica (14th Edition),* Vol 19.

MacNeill, J., Winsemius, P. and Yakushiji, T. (1991), *Beyond Interdependence,* Oxford University Press, New York.

Mumford, L. (1922), 'The City,' in H. Stearns (ed) *Civilization in the United States,* Harcourt Brace, New York.

Ravetz, J., Carter, G., Fox, J., Roberts, P., Rookwood, R., Servante, D., Winter, P. and Young, S. (1995), *Manchester 2020: Sustainable Development in the City Region,* Town and Country Planning Association, London.

Roberts, P. (1994), Sustainable regional planning, *Regional Studies,* 25 (8), 781-787.

Roberts, P. (1995), *Environmentally Sustainable Business: a local and regional perspective,* Paul Chapman Publishing, London.

Sigsworth, E. M. (1967), 'The Industrial Revolution,' in M.W. Beresford and G.R.J. Jones (eds) *Leeds and its Region,* British Association for the Advancement of Science, Leeds.

Welford, R. and Gouldson, A. (1993), *Environmental Management and Business Strategy,* Pitman Publishing, London.

Winter, G. (1988), *Business and the Environment,* McGraw-Hill, Hamburg.

Wood, C. (1994), *Painting by Numbers,* BT Environment City-Royal Society for Nature Conservation, Lincoln.

# 12 Inventing a better place: Urban design in Leeds in the post-war era

*Lindsay Smales and David Whitney*

## Introduction

This chapter examines recent attitudes towards the planning and design of Leeds' central area; its buildings, places and spaces. The main focus is upon developments that have taken place since the Second World War. We begin by examining the period between 1945 and 1980, with the latter part of the chapter concentrating on the past 15 years. This division is based on the fact that by the late Seventies the city had begun yet another process of re-assessment and renewal. It was a time when the impact and effectiveness of previous initiatives aimed at improving Leeds' physical and social fabric were being reviewed and when the city was on the threshold of a new era of relative economic vitality.

While Leeds may not provide clear-cut or well-defined examples of specific approaches to urban design, it is true to say that there are a small number of the city's design initiatives which have been both innovative and influential. By placing these design initiatives in a wider context it should be possible to arrive at a meaningful appreciation of the qualities and characteristics that have contributed to the Leeds environment in the latter half of the twentieth century.

As well as drawing upon articles in the local, national and professional press, we have interviewed some of the key players from the period under scrutiny. The unique perspectives of recent events offered by these individuals have been added to our own insights, as interested observers who have variously lived, worked and studied in the city, in order to form a critique of some of the more important design and development projects in this fascinating, yet frustrating place.

One of the admirable aspects of the city of Leeds is that it has rarely succumbed to complacency. This is a necessary trait in a settlement that aims to be at the forefront of modernity and a leading contender in the increasingly tough game of inter-urban competitiveness. But it is also a facet which has occasionally resulted in the city being too open to the temptation to re-model and re-make itself.

If there is a theme running through the range of schemes described and analyzed in this chapter, it is therefore the story of how the city has recently endeavoured to gain control of inevitable urban change by re-inventing itself. This is a process based upon the simple belief that Leeds could always be a better place than it is at the present time. As such, it is a principle we are happy to share and endorse.

## Post-war blue-prints

Perhaps the earliest post-1945 expression given to design in and of the city was made in 1951 when the first Leeds Development Plan was submitted to the Ministry of Housing and Local Government; (Leeds City Council, 1951). Wartime conditions had interrupted the clearance and rebuilding of the city's unfit housing, with the result that there was a substantial backlog of much-needed environmental improvements. As well as these long-standing weaknesses in the structure and layout of housing environments, the second world war had delayed and offset plans to replenish the city's stock of civic buildings, following on from Blomfield's example of re-planning the Headrow in the 1930s.

The most dramatic response to renewal needs was made within the city centre. Leeds City Council proposed the comprehensive redevelopment of up to a dozen major blocks of properties. In keeping with all local authorities at this time, the Council was afforded increased powers of compulsory purchase for comprehensive redevelopment, backed up by central government monies (Burt and Grady, 1994).

The wording of the 1951 Development Plan Written Analysis is revealing. Key streets were to be enlarged and a roundabout provided in order to make a 'wide processional way' leading to the Town Hall from Wellington Street. It was also deemed necessary for these plans to project a suitably 'worthy and dignified approach' to redevelopment; this was partly due to the desire to add to and improve upon previous attempts at displaying civic pride (Nuttgens, 1979). The 1951 Plan also provided for a diverse assortment of public buildings in close proximity to the Town and Civic Halls, including a new Law Courts, Museum and Main Library. Elsewhere, the city centre was to accommodate a newly improved bus station, fire station, exhibition hall, police HQ, multi-storey car parks and yet further covered markets.

In reality, little of this visionary statement was implemented. Office development permits were not lifted until 1953 and the majority of urban development projects of this period had to focus upon the repair of war-damaged properties and minor infill schemes such as Headrow House and the College of Technology. Nor was the important proposal for a northern inner ring road implemented.

Given the extensive programme of unfit housing clearance and new residential development which the city council had been undertaking in the City in the period before the Second World War - it being noteworthy that the city celebrated the 21st anniversary of the founding of its Housing Committee as early as 1954 - there was a very real sense in which the powerful City Architects Department and its Committee were the de facto civic designers of the time. The 1957 Housing Act greatly strengthened the powers of local authorities such as Leeds to pursue further their efforts to address long-standing inadequacies in the city's housing stock. The succession of architectural styles, the large numbers of units built and the geographical extent of Leeds' outer council estates bear witness to the practical influence and avowed technical distinction of more than one Chief Architect of this period.

Interestingly, throughout the 1950s, town planners formed only a small adjunct within the equally influential City Engineers Department - working closely with both engineers and architects as development opportunities grew within the city's expanding economic climate.

**Catering for the car**

If architects acted as the key arbiters of civic design at this time, it was the civil engineers who really began to have a massive and lasting impact upon the face of the city. Increasingly, the job of rebuilding became preoccupied with accommodating the needs of motor traffic. In 1959 the council appointed Geoffrey Thirwall as Deputy Chief Engineer and he was able to marshall resources for the construction of a new inner ring road and was responsible for ensuring that links were made between the city and the national motorway network. He was also effective in planning for the comprehensive redevelopment of large areas of the city centre and inner city housing, including Brunswick and Harehills, in ways which provided for the accommodation of road and motorway building.

By 1961 a fresh and informal City Centre Plan was produced (Leeds City Council, 1961). Prepared 'in house', without the benefit or indeed burden of public consultation, this was significant as a fundamental and lasting framework for development control and developer negotiation. Not surprisingly, it incorporated many of the civil engineers' ideas and themes. The Plan envisaged comprehensive redevelopment as being the way to handle estimated traffic growth and put forward proposals for extensive new road and motorway construction and the creation of segregated pedestrian ways. It was also the first publication to refer to an innovative system of elevated deck access routes for pedestrians, whereby new buildings in the central area would be linked at or above first floor-level by a series of concrete pathways.

The fact that this City Centre Plan and its design ideas survived as the key planning instrument up until the introduction of the Development Plan Review (1967) and the publication entitled 'The Leeds Approach' (1969) - see below - can partly be accounted for by the educational experiences of many of the city's senior officials. These people often studied locally and had frequently trained together. Many would have been taught to believe in the primacy of modernist architectural and planning principles of the type put forward by Le Corbusier and his followers. Like their contemporaries elsewhere in the country, this would have entailed exposure to the important urban design ideas of the time, including: the separation of people and vehicles, weather-protected environments, radical and comprehensive housing solutions and the value of visionary professionals in addressing the social and environmental issues facing the twentieth century city. Reading through the 1961 Plan more than thirty years after its introduction, it is clear that its authors saw a chance to put into practice some of these notions and that they were convinced the city and its council could solve many of its urban problems through rational planning and functional design.

The urban motorways surrounding the centre, together with their complementary multi-storey car parks, also introduced somewhat grim, brutalist concrete structures into Leeds which, together with extensive hard and soft landscaping, had the unhappy effect of isolating surrounding residential areas from the city's core. This created real problems of accessibility to services and facilities for the populations of adjacent inner housing areas, places once easily linked by foot to the central area.


**Principles for redevelopment**

Nationally, concern about traffic congestion continued to mount and in 1960 the then Transport Minister, Ernest Marples, commissioned Colin Buchanan to report on possible solutions (Smithers, 1993). Published in 1963 and entitled 'Traffic in Towns', this influential project took Leeds as one of its case studies (Buchanan, 1963; see also Chapter 14). It was recommended that even to accommodate restricted car use, nearly half of the existing city centre should be comprehensively redeveloped, providing for the separation of vehicles and pedestrians. It was within this climate of concern for the impact of the car that Thirwall was promoted to Chief Engineer in 1964. He was immediately responsible for setting up a new redevelopment team within his own department, the aim of which was to provide a detailed planning and design context for the rapidly changing city centre. Working through the mechanism of Comprehensive Development Areas (CDAs), the team came to determine the future shape and form of the city centre.

Thirwall was also primarily responsible for the passing in 1966 of the Leeds Corporation Act giving local powers to remove traffic from city streets and the opportunity for the council to work with developers on traffic exclusion schemes. Using these powers, a number of the city's main thoroughfares were closed to traffic and came to form the basis of a later initiative aimed at the widespread pedestrianisation of much of the retail core. Redevelopment also exploited the ground levels within the city centre, which sloped from north to south and divided about the central spine of Park Row. These changes in level enabled redevelopment schemes for retail and office use to be designed to provide for the previously-mentioned continuous pedestrian walkway system. In reality, public sector resource constraints, together with a lack of enthusiasm from the private sector, did not permit this system to be completed in its entirety and awkward or truncated connections today bear witness to the difficulties of realising this bold, if somewhat misplaced, idea for improved civic design. As Burt and Grady have noted:

While the pedestrian shopping precincts were to prove immensely successful, the high level walkway was a white elephant. A section was constructed from Bond Street Centre across Park Row into the pedestrianised Bond Court. Other sections were never completed, and as a result important new buildings such as the Bank of England on York Place have the embarrassment and disfigurement of concrete walkways at first floor level which have never been used (Burt and Grady, 1994, p.234).

What other urban design principles guided development in the city centre during the 1960s? In the first instance, plot ratio control was employed to achieve the desirable height and massing of new buildings. In addition, to ensure the city's streets and car parks could absorb the additional capacity generated by increased activity, it was deemed necessary to have some form of limitation upon building densities. This was also to secure a reasonable spread of development across the central area, avoiding over-provision in any one part and possible disincentives in others. The maximum limit on density varied from 3.5 to 1 in the main retail area, to 2.0 to 1 on the fringe of the city centre. Secondly, consideration was given to special building heights and shapes and the impact proposed new development would have upon the existing skyline. An extract from the Development Plan Review (1967) illustrates the townscape-derived philosophy underpinning this type of preoccupation:

A pleasing ever-changing aspect varying from the small square enclosed by buildings to extensive open areas with sweeping vistas of tall groups of buildings (will be sought)... Particular care is exercised in the siting and design of tall buildings, their visual impact and the closing of vistas (Leeds City Council, 1967).

Despite these fine sounding words, this is a policy whose positive impact is hard to perceive when surveying the city's urban landscape some three decades later.

**The Leeds approach**

Critical of the resource implications of the Buchanan Report, but fundamentally influenced by its arguments, Leeds City Council co-operated with national government in 1965 in a further study aimed at once more tackling the city's traffic problems. The recommendations were published in 1969 in a document entitled 'The Leeds Approach' (Leeds City Council, 1969). Proposed changes in the road system were more modest than those envisaged by Buchanan, and road alignment was urged to have less impact upon the existing built fabric (Judge, 1983). Improvements in public transport allied to restrictions upon all-day commuter parking were seen as key solutions to the traffic conundrum. In essence, the 'Leeds Approach' recommended a fully integrated transport model entailing long and short-stay parking controls, limited new road construction, better public transport provision and management, extensive separation of traffic and pedestrians and a network of traffic-free precincts, arcades and walkways. Once again, and perhaps not surprisingly given the fate of earlier ambitious plans and designs, the resulting implementation of these ideas was only partial, due to increasing constraints upon resources.

The Leeds Development Plan Review was published in 1967, foreshadowing the principles set out comprehensively in the later 'Leeds Approach', and indeed noting the unsatisfactory planning conditions which the later, more radical document attempted to tackle. It affirmed - even after an extensive period of comprehensive renewal in the 1960s - that "the whole pattern of the town centre is inadequate" and proposed that the city centre master plan should proceed according to the guiding principles of improving the functionality of existing streets, yet further pedestrian segregation, controlling the density of development, ensuring an 'open form' of development and attending to the grouping and massing of buildings to create integrated, three-dimensional designs and an attractive skyline. For the first time, the Review called for attention to be given to the conservation and improvement of the built fabric of the city centre - a proposal facilitated by the powers afforded under the 1967 Civic Amenities Act.

## The image of the city

The urban or civic design strategies put into place from the late 1950s onwards were predicated on the belief that, with one or two exceptions, the majority of Leeds' buildings, roads and spaces did not meet the needs of the contemporary city. The logical conclusion to be derived from this perspective was therefore to sweep aside, wherever possible, that which was deemed inadequate and replace it with a more functional and better planned alternative. This was a philosophy of urban change that, up until the early 1970s seemed to be shared equally between the city's politicians and their officers, if not necessarily its residents and visitors.

The city therefore continued to 'bulldoze' the 'Byelaw' terraces of its Victorian past well into the 1960s, when, in the face of mounting opposition, the policy of comprehensive redevelopment was put on hold and gradually phased out. At the same time, the council was attempting to advance the image of Leeds as 'Motorway City of the Seventies'- a slogan to be found on the council's own postal frank - by creating the South East Urban Motorway, linking the M1 and the northern Inner Ring Road Motorway Distributor.

In addition, an alliance of the most senior officials and local politicians promoted Leeds as a dynamic city rapidly gaining new roles, functions and overall image. An initiative supported jointly by the city council and the Chamber of Commerce was put into place to facilitate this process and given the title 'Project Leeds'.

A study produced at this time by the City Development Officer for the newly elected council leader (1971) illustrates the proactivity of this department, which was by then responsible for co-ordinating the city's design-based strategies and charged with modifying its image. The Report recommended a 'co-ordinated impact programme of environmental work' to 'involve the entire city population' in multiple aspects of the city's image.

As an attempt to consciously 'talk-up' the virtues of the city and adopt a deliberate marketing approach to selling Leeds it managed to provide the foundations for later efforts to improve the city's image.

By the early 1970s, however, the context for planning and design in the city was shifting, partly in response to growing criticism of the cost of extensive change to the physical fabric of towns and cities and partly as the result of a deterioration in the national economic situation. The 1974 reorganisation of local government also prompted the city council to re-shape its structures and responsibilities and bring in new thinking. But by this time, many of the once cherished features of the city's skyline were lost (Powell, 1986; Burt and Grady, 1994). The public were becoming conscious of the fact that some of the more recent developments in the central area were insensitive to the existing townscape and were of dubious quality, while, like elsewhere in the country, some inner city communities had experienced ruthless housing clearance programmes and their poorly built replacements.

In 1974 for the first time the council established a Department of Planning, separate from the City Engineers Department, enabling planning and civic design to be considered side by side with civil engineering issues. Indeed from the outset, a separate Environmental Design Group was created as a specialist body within the Planning Department to give urban design-related advice. Work was also instituted on an extensive series of planning design briefs for site or area redevelopment. A renewal programme of conservation was implemented, with a marked increase in the designation of Conservation Areas. Work also started on a new series of Local Plans under the 1972 Planning Act powers, with the Central Business District Plan the first to be prepared (Leeds City Council 1976). Increased attention was also given to new areas of focus within the city centre, including the urban waterfront and the south central zone towards the M1 'Gateway' to the city.

The newly established Planning Department carried on the momentum of the later 1960s/early 1970s in extending the pedestrianisation of the retail core. Priority was also given to linking up pedestrian routes, promoting the remaining development opportunities such as the St Johns project, and in general much more serious attention was given to urban design considerations in planning schemes and development applications. The demolition of the Quarry Hill flats was itself evidence of a change of heart as regards urban form, urban scale and the imposed blueprint solution to urban questions.

# The 'Leeds Look'

Unlike many UK cities during the 1960s and 1970s, Leeds was perhaps fortunate not to provide a resting place for a massive, inward-looking shopping development of the type exemplified by Manchester's Arndale Centre or Newcastle's Eldon Square. Its heart therefore remained relatively intact, despite the intrusion of a wide range of modernist office schemes and the best efforts of the highway engineers. We have seen that by the 1970s, a substantial part of Buchanan's grand designs for the city's motorway network were in place, while its central retail area had become one of the country's first fully pedestrianised precincts.

The northern section of the Inner Ring Road left in its wake a landscape of car parks, pedestrian subways and isolated grassed areas, one of which came to provide the location for what can now be seen as the quintessential building of the city's revived economic fortunes of the Eighties. Westgate Point is situated on an elliptical roundabout at the western end of the Headrow, where Leeds' foremost piece of 1930s urban design meets the 1970s Ring Road. On this prominent site, 'a gateway to the city,' the developers erected a speculative office scheme of 45,000 square feet, some seven storeys in height and consisting of a red brick and stone facade with a steep overhanging slate roof.

Although a relatively undistinguished piece of post-modern architecture, this building has come to be seen as the prime example of the so-called 'Leeds Look'. Like many other office developments in the city during this period, Westgate Point is occupied by a firm of accountants and supposedly "takes its style from Leeds' Victorian heritage" (Leeds City Council, 1988). So prevalent was this approach to the design of new building in the city that, although not constituting an architectural movement in itself, it became a central concern of a number of articles in both the local and professional press (Powell, 1989; Thompson, 1990. 1991; Parkyn, 1993).

The city has become almost infamous for insisting that new schemes reinterpret the style of its riverside warehouses. This approach to development control was first highlighted by the critic Ken Powell. It consists of the planning authority requesting that developers and their architects follow a set of unwritten design principles based upon a desire not to repeat the aesthetic failings of the immediate past, whilst using the more distant past as the model for the future. In an article in the *Architect's Journal,* Powell argued that "this style has been imposed with monotonous thoroughness and a marked dearth of imagination" (Powell, 1989).

Perhaps the least inspiring building design associated with the 'Leeds Look' is the Holiday Inn on Wellington Street. This 122-bedroom facility was described by Ray Beery of Abbey Hanson Rowe, one of the city's leading architectural practices, as being a 'missed opportunity' (Thompson, 1990). To us, the hotel represents a bland exercise in facadism, complete with badly proportioned towers, archways and pediments, supposedly based upon earlier brick warehouses, architecture whose structural integrity it manages to both mimic and mock.

What the 'Leeds Look' does serve to highlight is the way in which the local authority currently intervenes in the development process. The Planning Committee does not discourage the development of buildings in the central area, quite the opposite, but tinkers with those elements of design it is able to influence within the confines of government planning guidance and regulations. The net result is a form of building that reflects their limited scope and abilities. For instance, there is precious little debate about the urban context, or the extent to which a building contributes towards creating a vibrant and exciting street life, and instead much discussion on the use of materials and styles of fenestration. The impression given is that the Committee and their officers are of the view that a bad building can be improved through a change of external appearance and a poor design enhanced merely by the addition of a pitched roof.

The chair of the city's Planning Committee at this time was perhaps correct in saying that the city had yet to see a really exciting and innovative planning application, but was partly responsible for creating a climate within which such a building would not be accepted - even were it recognised as such. Thus we see in Leeds a heightened version of events taking place elsewhere in the country, whereby aesthetic conservatism has replaced bold, top-down planning.

**European aspirations**

Of all the city's stated objectives, there is one aim that is highlighted in most of its planning and economic development publicity material and which features in the growing number of press articles extolling Leeds' virtues (Nicholson, 1991; Williams, 1994). This is to be "one of the principal, progressive European cities of Europe" (Leeds City Council, 1994a). For the observer trying to discern trends and patterns in the city's current evolution, this ambition provides a recurring theme in a broad range of design initiatives.

It has been noted elsewhere that major urban centres within the European Community are now engaged in a struggle to maximize the opportunities provided by their nation's membership (Smales, 1994). They therefore strive to demonstrate the characteristics which mark them out as 'growth poles,' centres of international communication and transport, or merely the most

208

attractive place for the footloose European tourist to spend a weekend break. Leeds is no different in this regard.

Some of the initiatives developed in the city in order to attain this heady Euro-ambition include: a '24-hour city scheme', the establishment of an internationally recognised Museum, an innovative landscaping project based around sculptural street furniture, and investment in a more integrated public transport strategy. Taken either collectively or on their own, these projects are laudable and an integral part of the city council's approach to the physical Europeanisation of the city. The problem is that they seem to be based upon a limited understanding of the characteristics that make any city truly 'European'. This theme is also a central thrust of policy-making which singularly fails to be supported by any in-depth analysis or detailed appreciation of the factors which contribute to the difference between a cold, wet product of the Industrial Revolution and its continental counterparts.

The 24-hour city initiative encompasses the liberalising of the city's licensing regulations and an attempt to foster a 'cafe culture' whereby the city's streets are once more peopled out of regular office hours (Leeds City Council, 1994b). Working from the premise that "it's arse-end upwards, this country's attitude to entertainment," the council has taken on board its Deputy Mayor's typically blunt assessment and can now boast a number of the country's leading nightclubs and a vibrant youth culture (Wainwright, 1995). However, there is very much more to creating a viable and secure nighttime economy than encouraging local magistrates to be more broad-minded.

Yet another attempt at 'Europeanisation' and a scheme that can also be seen to be a missed opportunity, albeit one admired by other cities, is the so called 'Landmark Leeds' project. This is the redevelopment of the pedestrian retail core first established in the late Sixties and encompasses decorative paving, planting, new street furniture, lighting and a series of 'gateways' planned to act as focal points and shelters for vendors and shoppers (Wainwright, 1992). Designed by Newcastle-based architects Faulkner Brown, the scheme deliberately attempts to introduce innovative sculptural elements into the city's streets - most of which are copies or versions of urban furniture to be found along Barcelona's famous Ramblas.

Coming in for criticism from Ken Powell, as being 'out of place', 'meretricious'; and 'a disgrace in a city full of fine Victorian craftsmanship' (Powell, 1992), this £3.6 million scheme was very much the brainchild of the city council's leadership. The Leeds Civic Trust has also been critical of the 'Landmark' project from the very start and is concerned that the development was not a product of 'the normal process of public consultation' (Leeds Civic Trust, 1994). To its credit, the City Council has used this early scheme as a springboard towards a more modest, and environmentally successful programme of traffic calming and street furniture design; going on to produce its own design guide for streets and spaces within the central area (Leeds City Council, 1995).

There is still much more work to be done, for instance, in improving the pedestrian's first impression of the city en route from the Railway Station, and it may be the case that the politicians and officers responsible for this key part of the urban area have indeed learnt from the failures of the Landmark scheme. This is despite the fact that, at the time of writing, Leeds still has no clearly articulated policy towards the use and development of public art within the city.

If there is one clear omission from these attempts to improve the quality of public space along European lines, it is the marked absence of meaningful and relevant public art and sculpture in the city. Apart from a few bits of statuary remaining from previous exercises in civic pride, the only noteworthy examples of modern sculpture are to be found outside the City Art Gallery, where one might expect to come across such a work, a large black horse at the entrance to a bank, and the statue of a brewer's drayman in Dortmund Square, a piece that was not even generated at home - being a gift from Leeds' German twin city. This may account for the architects of the Landmark scheme's apparent desire to overcompensate with their post-modernist I-beams, purple metal grids and flashing red lights. But it is a grave oversight in a place that aspires to shake off the clinging provincialism of the past in favour of a more sophisticated image. And one that is surprising given Birmingham's well-publicised efforts in this area and the abundance of such works in the European streets, spaces and places the city professes to admire.


## Quarry Hill: lost in space

The Quarry Hill site in Leeds has a long and infamous pedigree. Formerly the location for one of the city's worst Victorian slums, this large area to the south east of the city centre was swept aside in the 1930s and replaced by the massive modernist housing scheme that was to share its name for the next forty years (Ravetz, 1974). The city was left with what can be perceived as either a dilemma or an opportunity when the flats finally succumbed to the bulldozer in the mid-1970s.

A small part of the site, opposite the city's local Bus Station was chosen as the location for the new West Yorkshire Playhouse. This uninspiring building - described by Parkyn as having the aesthetic characteristics of a 'retail park' (Parkyn, 1993) - was to remain the sole occupant of the area for a number of years and came to be surrounded by a large and unwieldy

210

version of the British land-use phenomenon known as 'the surface car park.'

In the late 1980s the Government was looking to decentralise some of Whitehall's major departments and chose Leeds, and latterly Quarry Hill, as the location for a purpose-built office for the Departments of Health and Social Security. This was something of a coup for the City Council, the owners of the site, who were afraid the Government would opt to develop within the boundaries of the Urban Development Corporation area, and thereby deprive them of the chance to use the proposed facility as a catalyst for regenerating the southern part of the city centre.

Having secured the new headquarters building for Quarry Hill, the Council commissioned the urban design practice of Terry Farrell to produce a Masterplan for the area. This envisaged the 'Quarry House' headquarters as the centrepiece of the scheme, and as a landmark structure closing off the vista created by Blomfield's 1930s redevelopment of the Headrow. The plan also put forward a 'mixed use', speculative development incorporating a new hotel, shopping facilities, car parking and a total of 68,000 square metres of office space. These were all to be grouped around the front of the new government building and a series of landscaped open spaces, with the existing Playhouse sitting somewhat awkwardly to one side. Echoing the ambitions of the developers of Canary Wharf in London, the whole scheme was also conceived as 'the new business heart of the city' (Leeds City Council, 1990).

When it opened in 1993, Quarry House became the workplace of approximately 2,200 people, about 1,000 of whom were former London-based civil servants enticed to the city by favourable relocation packages. It also had the questionable distinction of being the largest building ever built in the city. However, the structure has not received a good press. It has been described by *The Architectural Review* as an 'Outrage'; and an 'appropriately naff crowning building' for a city that has 'some of the most dreary architectural design in Europe' (*The Architectural Review, 1993*). A front page investigation by the *Daily Mirror* into the design and build contract for the development's construction was headed 'Virginia's Deathtrap' and purported to reveal serious safety failures in the building's fire protection equipment (The Daily Mirror, 1994). The *Yorkshire Evening Post* has variously referred to the building as 'The Beast' and 'The Kremlin' (Marsh, 1993) and Kevin Grady, Director of Leeds Civic Trust has described how he and his members find it 'massive and brooding' and regard the edifice as an example of 'fascist architecture' (Barrick, 1990).

Some six years on from the original plan, the great majority of the Quarry Hill site remains undeveloped. Apart from the Government office and the theatre, there has been no other development to date. The proposed linkage with the rest of the central area has not come about. The existing business district in the city continues to remain unchallenged and the council is left with a poorly executed monster of a building, an isolated and uninviting regional theatre and a half-hearted piece of urban landscaping.

The reasons for the apparent failure of the Quarry Hill scheme are to be found in the reluctance of the private sector to invest in this location. Since being surrounded by urban motorways in the 1970s - ranging from the relatively small scale four-lane junction between Headrow and Eastgate, to the elevated section of the York Road - the site has been physically cut off from the rest of the city. It is an island. For the pedestrian, office worker and property investment manager it is therefore less enticing than cheaper, and arguably more accessible sites on the city's southern fringe. Leeds also has something of an abundance of potential office sites, particularly along the river frontage - many of which are within easier reach of the railway station and retail core. The Masterplan maintains that it is providing a 'mixed-use' environment, when in reality the range of uses is very limited and does not include the vital ingredient essential to the stimulation of sustainable out-of-hours activity, namely housing. It may be that developers will eventually come to build as envisaged. But the claims of the city and its consultants that Quarry Hill will provide Leeds with a first class business environment are beginning to ring hollow.

In many ways, the story of recent attempts to, once again, revitalise Quarry Hill are indicative of contemporary approaches to urban design and planning within the city as a whole. Having been 'given' the new HQ of two of the nation's foremost ministries, the city was not in a position to either dictate or influence in any meaningful way the shape, form and nature of the final building. This is a lack of local power over key development decisions that has direct parallels with the designation, some would say imposition, of an Urban Development Corporation as the planning authority for other important parts of the city. Yet, in this instance, the city and its elected representatives were happy to embrace the prospect of local employment that came with the new building, even if it was the brainchild of their political opponents. So if it turns out to be an insensitive monster that sits like a beached ocean liner in the heart of the city, then this is of little consequence relative to perceived economic benefits.

Once it had welcomed this urban giant into its midst, the city then embarked upon a process of capitalising upon its good fortune, and spurred on by their consultants, attempted to use it to attract the attention and investment of the private sector. Having had a good track record in encouraging speculative development to the city during the late Eighties, this appeared to be a fairly logical way to proceed. However, the net effect of both these means of facilitating urban change - public sector or government intervention in the form of buildings or subsidised development, and wholly private sector-led schemes - is that neither tend to result in urban environments of quality. Without the benefit of a true and equal partnership, both approaches come vested with priorities that are self-centred and focused upon their own site and building-specific needs. The result is a failure to adopt the wider perspective concomitant with a responsibility to place and 'placemaking'.

**Fifty years of civic design**

Through necessity, the immediate post-1945 era in Leeds was a time of renewal, when the tools of modern architecture and planning were the means by which environments created by previous generations were re-shaped in order to conform with contemporary requirements and standards. Even the most cursory reading of the plans and design ideas generated within Leeds in the Fifties, Sixties and Seventies gives the impression that their political and technocratic authors were profoundly dissatisfied with the physical, and through this the social fabric of the city. In the name of progress and as a way of addressing very real and substantial urban problems, they envisaged a future that was to be better planned, better designed.

It is quite difficult for today's professionals to comprehend the visionary outlook of their predecessors. It is perhaps equally hard for them to imagine the sort of self-belief and righteousness that could justify utopian policies of comprehensive development - or the circumstances in which an established neighbourhood could be destroyed because a senior engineer sitting in Headrow House had convinced his political masters that it was in the way of a highway which would meet the city's traffic needs.

There is also another theme running through the design strategies of this time. This was the notion that commercial development in the city's central area was to be welcomed, yet tamed through the application of contemporary thinking. The key difference between the stance adopted thirty years ago and today is that architects and planners were then very confident they could design their way into a better city and seemingly more capable of persuading civic leaders and the general public to share these certainties. Later generations, on the other hand, are more used to the schemes and ideas of the architect and planner becoming unstuck, failing to meet expectations, or creating buildings and spaces which, at their worst, are the antithesis of the humane.

Design experimentation was also an integral part of this earlier professional climate. If there was a conflict between pedestrians and vehicles, the answer was to try a new technical solution. They could put 'streets in the sky' because people saw this might create superior conditions for those on foot and lead to the smoother flow of the city's traffic. If Leeds' road network was out of date, the rational way forward was to start again. If its stock of office accommodation failed to meet contemporary requirements then they must remove the old and build anew. In this way, the general feeling of the times that technology and its masters would lead us to a brighter future, was applied to Leeds and its needs.

One of the arguments that is often put forward by the architects, planners and urban designers of this and other periods to suggest why a scheme or development was not as successful as it should have been, is that it was only partially implemented. They maintain their ideas would have worked better but for a lack of commitment from those in power and a correspondingly meagre allocation of the necessary resources; and not because the fundamental principles upon which they were premised were wrong or inappropriate. It may be, therefore, that a full implementation of Buchanan's and Thirwall's road schemes for the city would have resulted in a lessening of current traffic problems. Shopping and working in the city might also have been a more pleasant experience if only the high-level pedestrian walkways had been built according to plan. Instead, we are left with partly completed visions; facilities that are often unfinished versions of once bold and innovative plans.

This is a heritage of inadequacy and failure that has led to a distrust of modern architecture and urban design, a lack of confidence in the ability of the planner and urban designer to create better places, and scepticism about the power of the highway engineer to improve anything other than the share price of large construction firms. With the benefit of hindsight, it is easy to say that such ideas were misplaced and to feel that we now know better. For Leeds, the days of the sweeping strategy, the grand gesture, the Bible-like civic plan and the all-powerful Chief Officer have been relegated to the city's past.

Like most other large cities, the Leeds of the 1980s and 1990s has come to live with the power and influence of market forces and the role of the private sector in the development process. Visitors to the city during these decades have often been struck by the fact that cranes are still to be found towering over the urban horizon, at a time when the vibrant places of the 1960s and 1970s, such as Reading or Croydon, are relatively inactive. But the thought of following good urban design practice and creating a set of development guidelines in the context of the prevailing political and economic climate does not come easy - especially when central Government has so long endorsed a policy of non-intervention in matters of design.

Powell's fear that the city could degenerate into a northern version of the Isle of Dogs reflects the reality of a place where local planners, designers, politicians and architects have more recently become used to the idea that the private developer sets the civic agenda, and that their role is to limit the potential for disaster and excess. Leeds' attempts to replicate or mimic the qualities its politicians admire in other European centres is an acknowledgement that their own in-house professionals have failed them and partly a desire to prove that they, the peoples' representatives, are in-tune with contemporary urban trends. Yet no amount of sculptural furniture or street cafes can turn the city into what it is not and perhaps never will be.

Although the city claims to have embraced concepts of environmental sustainability, Leeds is not about to become a haven of green thinking and action. Leeds is wedded to commerce in a manner that is different to the cities of the South. It owes its very existence to the type of entrepreneurial attitude that fostered the likes of Montague Burton and Marks & Spencer. Couple this umbilical relationship with enterprise to what can be seen as a traditional, 'Old Labour Party' approach to local politics and it is not surprising that the city's leaders have yet to embrace the sort of radical 'green' intervention necessary to achieve dramatic environmental change.

A place that only recently called itself 'Motorway City' is bound to find it difficult to re-assess the physical and social implications of the type of development that enabled this title to be embraced in the first instance. Nor can the recent mistakes of Quarry Hill and a legacy of mediocre buildings and unco-ordinated planning be made good overnight. As the city edges towards the millennium, there is at least the perception that from now on things must be done differently; with or without the help of the professionals.

Planners always suggest we need more planning and architects more architecture. In this respect, urban designers are no different. Each discipline is premised on the principle that they can help create better environments, buildings or places; if only they were given a free reign and their potential contribution was truly acknowledged by decision makers. Although urban designers have been involved in projects spread across Leeds, including the retail core, the Rail Station and some of the key sites on the waterfront, there has not been any attempt to produce an overview of the city's built fabric similar to that undertaken in Birmingham. The result is that the city has pockets of good or 'better' design, but no overall, co-ordinated structure within which these appear to fit or operate.

Hence the redevelopment of Boar Lane may work well within the confines of contemporary approaches to commercial space, but the quality of the pedestrian thoroughfares leading to the scheme from the main retail area is still poor. Similarly, the city has a wealth of surface car parks. These no doubt generate a great deal of money for their owners or tenants and fulfil an obvious parking need. But areas of crushed building rubble sit very uneasily within the urban environment, like sad and sorry cavities in a mouth full of otherwise healthy teeth. The linkage between the inner city and the central area also continues to suffer from the spatial blight created by the city's network of urban motorways, resulting in environments across and through which it is unpleasant to even cycle, let alone walk (see Chapter 17).

## Conclusions

In summary, Leeds presently has a more realistic if limited approach to urban design than that which prevailed in the first thirty years after the Second World War. The city and its people have a more considered attitude towards the ability of professionals to plan or design their way out of urban problems, and now use them as surgeons specialising in different parts of the body, rather than practitioners whose prescriptions and remedies will lead to miraculous cures and a rapid improvement in general health. If anything, this cynicism has perhaps gone too far and it is partly the fault of the professions concerned for having failed to demonstrate their ability to help a city such as Leeds make the most of its opportunities and become more itself.

It is never too late for an urban design-based evaluation of the existing characteristics of Leeds' physical environment - its pathways, streets and spaces - and an analysis of how these elements combine, interrelate and work with or against one another relative to human use and satisfaction. This in turn could be used as the starting point for a set of flexible, yet creative principles aimed at guiding future development. In this way, urban design might yet become a catalyst for enhancing any existing sense of place and for facilitating this elusive quality when it is absent or in danger of being eroded. Leeds would then be in possession of a greater understanding of those factors that make it different to other cities and have the basis for a finer appreciation of where it and its residents would like to head in the future. Without such a strategy, the city will continue to stagger from one good idea to the next, putting into place this scheme, to be followed by that project, which is in turn matched by yet another of the latest ideas aimed at making it more competitive, European, vibrant, greener or visitor-friendly.

## References

The Architectural Review (1993), 'Outrage: poor Leeds,' *The Architectural Review,* May.
Barrick, A (1990), 'Civic Trust slams d & b proposals for government hq,'

216

*Building Design,* 5th Oct.

Buchanan C. et al. (1963), *Traffic in Towns,* HMSO, London.

Burt S, and Grady K. (1994), *The Illustrated History of Leeds,* Breedon Books, Derby.

*The Daily Mirror* (1994), 'Virginia's deathtrap: scandal that will shock Britain,' *The Daily Mirror,* 10th June.

Judge E. (1983), 'Leeds since Buchanan 1963-1983,' *Built Environment,* 9 (2).

Leeds City Council (1951), *Development Plan Written Analysis* (approved 1955), Leeds City Council, Leeds.

Leeds City Council (1961), 'City Centre Plan,' Leeds City Council, Leeds.

Leeds City Council (1967), *Development Plan Review (Written Analysis),* Leeds City Council, Leeds.

Leeds City Council, M.O.T., M.H.L.G. (1969), 'Planning and Transport. The Leeds approach,' HMSO, London.

Leeds City Council (1971), 'Impact 71 July,' Leeds City Council, Leeds.

Leeds City Council (1976), *Central Business Area District Plan. Report of survey,* Leeds City Council, Leeds.

Leeds City Council (1988), 'City centre developments,' publicity brochure, Leeds City Council, Leeds.

Leeds City Council (1990), 'Quarry Hill: summary of masterplan,' Leeds City Council, Leeds.

Leeds City Council (1994a), *The Leeds Initiative: annual report 1993-4,* Leeds City Council, Leeds.

Leeds City Council (1994b) 'Twenty-four hour city,' Leeds City Council, Leeds.

Leeds City Council (1995), 'City centre street style: design guide for streets and spaces,' Leeds City Council, Leeds.

Leeds Civic Trust (1994), 'Landmark Leeds - an appraisal,' Leeds Civic Trust, Leeds.

Marsh, D. (1993), 'Beauties and the beast: city turns to past for a bright future,' *The Yorkshire Evening Post,* 6th May.

Nicholson, L. (1991), 'A monument to brass and the good old days,' *The Observer,* No. 10.

Nuttgens, P. (1979), *Leeds: the back to front inside out upside down city,* Stile Publications

Parkyn, N. (1993), 'Parkyn's progress: Leeds,' *Building Magazine,* 21 May.

Powell, K. (1986), *Leeds - a lost opportunity?* SAVE Britain's Heritage, London.

Powell, K. (1989), 'The offence of the inoffensive,' *The Architect's Journal,* 3rd May.

Powell, K. (1990), 'Leeds' latest,' *The Architect's Journal,* 25 April.

Powell, K. (1992), 'What have they done to our cities?,' *The Daily Telegraph,* 11th April.

Ravetz, A. (1974), *Model Estate: planned housing at Quarry Hill, Leeds,* Croom Helm, London.

Smales, L. (1994), 'Desperate pragmatism or shrewd optimism?: the image and selling of West Yorkshire, in Haughton, G. and Whitney, D. (eds) *Reinventing a Region: Restructuring in West Yorkshire,* Aldershot: Avebury Press.

Smithers, R. (1993), 'Radical roads report that ended in a blind alley,' *The Guardian,* Nov. 27th.

Thompson, A. (1990), 'The Leeds Look,' *The Yorkshire Evening Post*, Oct 24th.

Thompson, A. (1991), 'A hard look at a 'dull' city of the 80s,' *The Yorkshire Evening Post,* 4th March.

Wainwright, M. (1992), 'Society sees red at purple and pink,' *The Guardian,* 28th Nov.

Wainwright, M. (1995), 'Open All Hours,' *The Guardian,* 7th June.

Williams, G. (1994), 'New decor for Cafe du North,' *The Guardian,* March 5th.

# 13 Conflicts over open space in Leeds

*Claire Freeman and Derek Senior*

## Introduction

When William Pitt the Elder suggested that "Parks are the lungs of London" he was affirming one of the widest needs of an urban population - access to public open space. Now as then, however, development pressures and economic considerations bedevil attempts to protect and conserve open space in the major UK cities.

This chapter examines the development of policies for open space provision in the city of Leeds, beginning with an examination of the provision made during the nineteenth and early twentieth century by the city's civic leaders, followed by an analysis of the evolving role of the local planning system. The final sections of the chapter focus on policy developments over the past ten years.

In developing an open space policy for the future, Leeds starts from a position of strength. The city benefits greatly from its close proximity to the Yorkshire countryside, a wealth of parks dating back to the early twentieth century when Leeds was known as 'the city of public parks' (Burt and Grady, 1994), and significant tracts of open land within the urban fabric. In planning terms, Leeds has recently been highly active in providing a series of interlocking strategies and support mechanisms, which together have set the foundations from which a progressive long-term open space policy framework can develop. These policies include the Leeds Green Strategy, the Leeds Nature Conservation Strategy, and most recently a Countryside Strategy; the city is even developing its own forestry programme. The Unitary Development Plan (see below) also includes a number of positive open space protection and enhancement policies.

219

## Historical development of open space provision in Leeds

Northern cities such as Leeds have long struggled to prove to outsiders that they have been transformed from their heavily polluted industrial past, to provide an increasingly pleasant urban environment, not least in respect of open space provision. For too long, the external image of the dark satanic mill town and endless rows of back-to-back housing has remained dominant. Certainly in the case of Leeds, the image is now ill-deserved. And indeed, Leeds has a long history of open space provision, as this section illustrates, whilst the more recent development of supportive planning policies has meant that today 140 square miles (65 per cent) of the city's land area is protected from inappropriate development by Green Belt designation. In this chapter, our primary concern is with the provision of green open space within the built-up areas of Leeds, close to where the majority of people live.

The provision of open space in the form of major parks has been a particular success of the locally elected members of Leeds since the nineteenth century. Reflecting the city's economic buoyancy, in the 1850s, at the same time as Cuthbert Brodrick's monumental Town Hall was being built, the town council also purchased the 63 acres of Woodhouse Moor. This was to become the first municipal park in Leeds.

Prior to this purchase, the main public open space provision in the city had been the small Georgian squares, of which Park and Queens Squares still remain in the centre of the city. Numerous purchases of land for open space soon followed the Woodhouse Moor acquisition. An early development (1864) was the Lemon Street playground, adjoining St. Peter's Square, in a poor area of the city, close to the present West Yorkshire Playhouse, but now gone. The last third of the nineteenth century proved to be a period of continuous park provision: Bramley, Roundhay, Holbeck, Hunslet and Armley Recreation in the 1870s; Crossflatts, East End, New Wortley, Farnley in the 1880s; North Street, Armley Park, Stanningley, Chapel Allerton and Burley in the 1890s. Harehills, Potter Newton and Lower Wortley were purchased in the early years of the twentieth century. These are all celebrated in Allsop's Handbook of 1906. In many respects, the incremental provision of new parks reflected the outward growth of the city in various directions. Additionally, Kirkstall Abbey and its grounds were donated by a private benefactor.

Not all forays into land purchases were popular at the time. In retrospect the purchase of Roundhay Park in 1873, an acquisition of over 600 acres, was a superb example of municipal vision, but it was not without its contemporary critics, one of whom labelled it "a criminal waste" (Broadhead, 1990). Roundhay was inaccessible to most Leeds residents for over a decade, located three miles to the north of the then city. It became accessible with the electric trams in the 1890s, and has since remained one of the city's best loved and most heavily used parks.

Evidence of the relatively generous provision of open space in Leeds can be seen from a late Victorian survey which found that Leeds fared very well indeed in terms of open space provision per resident relative to Manchester, Birmingham, Liverpool, Glasgow and Bradford (Dolman, 1895). The earlier purchase of Roundhay was dwarfed by activity in the 1920s when the City purchased over 300 acres at Middleton Park to the south of the city, and followed this with over 900 acres around Temple Newsam house on the eastern edge of the city in 1923, and incorporated into the city in 1927. By the time of its 1939 submission to the Barlow Commission on the location of industry, the city council was justly able to claim that it "possesses within its boundaries beautiful parks, green open spaces and playing fields which are unrivalled in any large city." Further extension came in 1968 when the Lotherton Estate was given to the City Council, an estate and historic house some eight miles to the east of the then city boundary. This site was encompassed within the expanded Leeds Metropolitan District in 1974.

By the late twentieth century the city council controlled over 220 sites for open space, in total covering 4,800 acres, more than an eighth of the area of the old county Borough of Leeds. A major study of open space in British cities (Whittaker and Brown, 1971) showed that Leeds County Borough had nine acres of open space for each thousand of its inhabitants. This compared well once again with the figures for Glasgow (3.95 acres), Manchester (3.8 acres) and Belfast (2 acres), and was superior to the very low figures for many Inner London authorities.

## Planning for open space

Since the early acquisitions of open space, the control and usage of such sites has changed dramatically. The introduction of a regulatory town planning system since 1947 has allowed the City Council to produce a series of plans to promote and protect the recreational needs of its citizens. At the same time the needs of the citizens have changed, as lifestyles, leisure time and personal mobility (especially with increases in personal transport) have changed dramatically. Similarly, the development of a widespread interest in the natural environment and its protection has introduced concepts of wildlife and nature conservation into the urban open space issue which were not much contemplated by the Victorian civic leaders of Leeds. The new challenges of shifting towards creating sustainable cities, of generating less traffic movement, of possible higher densities, of possible town cramming, also have important implications for the development of contemporary open space policies.

The City of Leeds suggested the first Green Belt outside London in 1944 (Burt and Grady, 1994). This was eventually incorporated within the first City Development Plan, which followed the introduction of a comprehensive planning system in 1947. Since then, there have been a number of policies and proposals put forward for the County Borough of Leeds, and from 1974 for the enlarged Leeds Metropolitan District.

*Early plans*

The early plans, such as the written statement of the 1951 City Development plan, clearly reflect a functional approach to open space. There is an emphasis on the provision of open space to meet identified needs, with the focus being almost entirely on formal open space provision. Clear targets were set out for such provision, the primary aim being to provide a total of ten acres of public open space per 1000 population by 1971, including within this four acres of playing fields. There is little discussion of developing any broad open space policy, virtually no reference to informal open space, and the bulk of the material constitutes a detailed inventory of identified open space types. These included playing fields, children's playgrounds, parks, allotments and golf courses.

Similar plans were drawn up at the same time for those towns within Leeds District which before 1974 were within the West Riding County Planning area, such as Morley, Pudsey, Otley, Rothwell, Horsforth, Garforth and Wetherby.

The review of the Leeds Development Plan in 1967 made tentative steps towards broadening the open space agenda, and reference is made to woodlands, common lands, and nature conservation. This identified areas with recognised and significant natural interest. Similarly tentative steps were taken towards a broader term of reference for the importance of open space, as indicated in the proposal to initiate "a separate programme... of environmental improvement of residential areas which include layout of incidental open spaces" (Normington, 1971). This represented a clear move to recognise the role of less formal open space in city life, especially at local level.

*Local plans, 1974-1986*

The enlarged Leeds Metropolitan District produced over a dozen local plans, following the preparation of the County Structure Plan for West Yorkshire, of which Leeds was a part. The most important themes for open space,

222

which emerged from these Plans, were the issue of local authority resources, and local authority provision of open space. A number of these local plans identified local shortages of both formal and informal open space, and also playing fields (Garforth in 1983, Pudsey in 1985, Morley in 1985). In each of these Local Plans, the City Council pointed out that little finance was available for such uses from the public purse, and stressed difficulties in identifying suitable sites.

These plans do, however, identify the wider aspects of recreation, with references to countryside close to towns, footpaths, woodlands and riverside walks. Significantly, the North Leeds local plan introduced the concept of recreational and open spaces corridors linking town and country.

*Leeds Unitary Development Plan, 1986-*

Following the abolition of the metropolitan county of West Yorkshire in 1986, the city council assumed new powers in developing a strategic planning framework for the city. The Unitary Development Plan (UDP) for Leeds which has been developed in recent years follows a number of the earlier themes for recreation and open space, but in an altered context. In consultation with the local authorities, central government set out strategic guidance for all plan production in West Yorkshire in 1989. This highlighted the problem facing a city like Leeds: to meet the development needs of the city, which were seen to be quite extensive, whilst protecting green and open space in its many guises.

The Leeds Unitary Development plan of 1993 includes a green strategy, as well as a nature conservation strategy. This is developed into specific policies for the protection of existing urban green space, the provision of new green space, playing fields, and urban green corridors. Whilst management and improvements in the green corridors are suggested in the UDP, the main planning power will remain the control of development. Wider concepts of recreation, leisure and even tourism are also introduced in the UDP, reflecting the increased mobility and changed lifestyles of local people: by 1991 two-thirds of households had access to a car, and over 18% have access to two or more. The plan thus begins to reflect and respond to changing recreational perceptions and demands, and to the increasing breadth of open space concerns that must of necessity be considered and provided for in meeting the needs of Leeds' residents in the twenty-first century.

The city plan also acknowledges that problems of future open space provision remain. Under current financial restraints, today's city council leaders can no longer expect to emulate the purchases of their predecessors. In consequence, the provision of future green space is a key area where planning obligations will be sought from prospective developers, and a central fund for public provision is suggested in some cases. In addition, working in partnership with other agencies the city council is seeking to improve the quantity and quality of green space.

## Towards the twenty-first century

This section provides a more detailed examination of the physical opportunities for green space development, including the priorities, concerns and obstacles in developing green space policies. It reviews examples of good practice locally which can provide important lessons in planning for the future in Leeds, and suggests some steps which can be taken to consolidate and enhance Leeds' green space legacy.

### Planning context

The late 1980s and 1990s have seen considerable activity within the whole field of environmental planning. At international level, the Earth Summit in Rio focused attention on planetary environmental concern. The Local Agenda 21 process has been encouraged as the vehicle for translating the global concerns and initiatives at the Earth Summit into local action. Leeds, in common with most local authorities, has engaged in producing a Local Agenda 21, which will set out the city's environmental agenda. Green space policy will form a central consideration within this.

At European level, and particularly significant for Leeds City Council in light of its desire to promote Leeds as a European city, has been the work of the Council of Europe Committee of Ministers on Urban Open Space. The Council of Europe (1986, p.2) stresses the significance of open space in urban areas encouraging local authorities to "take steps to ensure that the securing, provision, and management of open space are an integral part of urban development." This emphasis is seen to be important since:

> the significance, value, and role of open space, particularly of an informal or small-scale nature, have often been neglected and its contribution to the well-being of a community ignored... the enjoyment of open space contributes to the legitimate aspirations of urban inhabitants for an improvement in their quality of life (ibid, p.3).

Support for green space has also been forthcoming at national level. In 1990 the Department of the Environment (DOE) produced the White Paper *This Common Inheritance,* which set out the government's environmental programme. The White Paper has been followed by a range of government-led initiatives and publications designed to encourage positive integration of environmental considerations in the land use planning process. Those that have been of particular significance in green space planning include *Environmental Appraisal of Development Plans* (Department of Environment, 1993); *Development Plans and Regional Planning Guidance: Policy Planning Guidance Note 12* (Department of Environment, 1992); *Nature Conservation: Planning Policy Guidance Note 9* (Department of Environment, 1994); *Sport and Recreation: Planning Policy Guidance Note 17* (Department of Environment, 1991). The last of these provides useful guidance for local authorities such as Leeds which are looking to develop and enhance their open space provision. The PPG supports the adoption of a broader approach to open space provision which includes a wide spectrum of provision, from regional parks to small local parks and open spaces. It similarly advises on a broad range of open space issues, such as the setting of open space standards, accessibility, children's use of open space, planning agreements and the role of the countryside. In preparing open space policies local authorities have access to a much greater level of advice, theoretical support, and local environmental data than has hitherto been the case. However, the situation is not all rosy in that this wealth of national development policies and strategies, together with growing public awareness, has increased demands on local authorities, without a corresponding increase in the resources being made available to them for meeting these demands.

**Policy considerations**

The provision of open space in Leeds incorporates elements of opportunistic and in some cases far-sighted acquisitions by the council. Planned provision, as with parks, playing fields and land that is sometimes disparagingly referred to as SLOAP (space left over after planning), must all be taken into account and planned for. In developing an open space planning strategy three key elements require particular consideration: the protection of open space from development; the type of open space provision; and the need for forward strategic planning. The development of an effective open space strategy that will see Leeds into the twenty-first century demands a clear understanding of key problem areas and a clear vision of what type of open space outcomes are sought.

*Open space under attack: development versus protection*

The issue of reconciling the economic development needs of the city whilst protecting its open space remains the focus of much debate within Leeds. The Strategic Planning Guidance issued by central government (Department of Environment, 1989) directed that in addition to meeting the requirements for industrial development, the preservation of its open character and other demands, the Leeds UDP "should provide land for the completion of 28,500 dwellings in the period between 1986 and 2001."

Such diverse and often conflicting open space and development requirements have been a recurrent theme in the planning and development history of Leeds. In 1858 one of Leeds earliest parks, Clapham's Zoological and Botanical Gardens in Headingley was taken over for building plots. The enterprising Clapham then opened the Royal Park and Horticultural Gardens at Woodhouse Moor, which in turn were closed in 1890 to be sold as building land to accommodate the expanding town.

In the 1990s the arguments for supporting development at the expense of green space are being repeated with a vengeance in Leeds, currently focusing around the need to prioritise economic development and the need for major road developments. The respite offered by the economic recession of the late 1980s has been by no means universal, with some important open space areas still the focus of development proposals. Some of the most intractable conflicts have concerned the development of 'valued' open space. Even Temple Newsam, one of the city's most revered and valued open spaces is not immune to the development threat, with the A1-M1 link road scheduled to be routed through part of the estate. Fortunately the loss of parkland to development is unusual; more typical is the development of informal open space. Protection measures for informal open space are limited in that even where land is protected, for instance as a site of special scientific interest designation (SSSI), it is not necessarily immune from development. The granting of permission to develop part of the Leeds-Liverpool Canal SSSI as a Marina in 1994 is a case in point.

Loss of green space to building continues to attract often vociferous opposition. Hawthorn Farm in East Leeds and Kirkstall Valley in the west are just two examples where proposals to develop valued local green space are vigorously opposed by local residents. Hawthorn Farm, comprising meadows, superb hedgerows and ponds, is an area of remnant agricultural land encapsulated within the urban fabric. Its position within the urban area has protected it from the fate of nearby farmland which has suffered from intensive agricultural development with the loss of much of its habitat diversity and related wildlife interest. Leeds City Council owns the site and has in recent years attempted to sell it off for industrial development. The sale has been delayed by the energetic opposition of local residents who have formed the Hawthorn Farm Action group.

Kirkstall Valley is a much larger and more diverse area bordering the

River Aire and located some two miles from the city centre. The valley is a mixed area, comprising derelict land, allotments, market gardens, sports grounds, some industry, a railway, canal, river and a variety of natural areas. In the late 1980s the area came under the planning control of the Leeds Development Corporation (LDC), which inherited a much despised major redevelopment scheme for the valley. Local residents banded together to oppose these proposals and the Kirkstall Valley Campaign was formed. Since its inception the Kirkstall Valley Campaign, has strongly, and in part successfully, opposed the various proposals for the wholesale development of the valley. This has certainly influenced the LDC, which after various consultation exercises has gradually shifted away from large scale commercial redevelopment, and helped fund major environmental works. Most importantly, residents have engaged in a Planning for Real exercise, and put forward their own proposals for development of the area, in the process gaining national recognition for their efforts. The future of both these areas of informal green space remains uncertain, though part of the Kirkstall Valley does now benefit from the designation of a nature reserve.

It is not only the larger open spaces that are under threat, though development of these may be more noticeable, but also small local open spaces, which face an insidious process of in-fill development. Overlooked and unnoticed, the process of development is gradually removing the network of green spaces that form an integral part of local neighbourhoods. Unless there is a radical reappraisal of the process of land valuation and the implementation of stronger protection policies, at both national and local level, green space will remain at the tender mercies of developers and cash-strapped local authorities who stand to benefit from the sale of open space for development.

*Reappraising the nature of open space provision*

The most significant change in open space policy in recent years has been the growing recognition of the contribution of informal and natural landscapes to the total green space resource. Heaton and Bramhill (1993, p.13) forcefully put forward the argument that:

> Urban greenery is appreciated equally whether it appears in urban parks, private landscaping, streets or housing amenity land. Recent research has shown that people do not differentiate between types of 'open space' in the way that planners do... greenery is most valuable if it is introduced into the right place, which need not necessarily be a defined or functional open space. In fact, that space may have no defined public function at all.

In Leeds the shift towards recognising the value of natural open space, has had positive repercussions. Green corridors such as the Meanwood Valley, parts of the Aire Valley, and other large areas of previously un-designated open space such as encapsulated farmland, natural flood plains, cemeteries, local wildlife havens, and areas with other types of valued landscapes are now covered by green space protection policies. However, some of these protection policies are weak and several of the city's best natural areas remain under threat from development. In mitigation it has to be said that this is often due to the fact that such areas are covered by development permissions or zonings which pre-date the recognition of the value of natural landscapes.

Chris Baines, arguably the country's best known proponent of natural landscapes (1986) attacks what he refers to as the 'repressing of nature' and the creation of a landscape of mown chemically retarded grass (Elkin et al., 1991). Not only can naturalistic landscapes be aesthetically more pleasing than swathes of mown grass with the odd tree but they can also be cheaper (see Elkin et al., 1991, p.24 for illustrative costings). This is not to say that naturalistic planting should replace formal planting (Leeds benefits from a wealth of formal gardens such as Canal Gardens in Roundhay that are held in high esteem), but that naturalistic and formal landscaping should form part of an integrated landscaping policy.

Just as the value of naturalistic landscaping is being recognised, so too do we need to acknowledge specifically urban landscapes rather than just focusing on encapsulated countryside (Gilbert, 1989). In a multi-ethnic city such as Leeds it is essential that the desire to promote native species is tempered by a recognition of the potential value of exotics and not treat all exotics as noxious invaders that need wiping out, as has been the case with Japanese Knotweed. Not only should the role of naturalistic landscapes and culturally valued natural features be recognised, but equally importantly recognition should be given to the totality of urban greenery (Heaton and Bramhill, 1993).

Leeds has developed elements of an overall greening strategy, through strategic green planting, usually undertaken in partnership with Groundwork Trust and other organisations, on major roads leading into the city. Other projects include extensive hanging basket schemes and one scheme, best viewed from the top of a double decker, the growing of flowers in gro-bags on the flat tops of city bus shelters. Urban greening should not be seen in narrow terms whereby it is a purely site-based activity but can be a process that has a much broader impact upon the city. The green heritage of a city, lies in its diversity; any open space and greening policy has to reflect the totality of the city's green character.

## Strategic approach

The development of a strategic approach to open space is the third of the key elements to be explored in preparing an open space strategy. In her assessment of the planning and management of parks and open spaces, Morgan found that "in most urban areas the pattern of open space is a result of opportunistic provision, it does not reflect current population densities nor provide equitable distribution of a variety of landscapes and facilities" (1991, p.12). In Leeds there have been some undoubted benefits of opportunistic provision, as in the purchase of Roundhay Park, but the corollary is a lack of overall strategic open space planning. The absence of a strategic overview is evident in the uneven distribution of open space provision in Leeds. There is a disparity between the generally well-endowed north Leeds suburbs and the considerably less well-provided for inner city residential areas, the inner city wards of Harehills and Headingley being the least well provided for. Provision in the inner areas is characteristically that of Victorian parks which serve high density residential areas and suffer from problems relating to accessibility, and misuse, with the parks being particularly susceptible to the effects of local authority financial constraints. If the type of open space provision is examined, the situation in these inner areas gives particular cause for concern. There is, for example, a significant deficit of any sizeable natural open space. In central Leeds, green space is conspicuous by its almost total absence: the provision of a city centre park must be a priority for any future city centre plans.

Whilst there is an identifiable deficit of open space provision in the inner city wards generally, there is not a clear outer suburb-inner suburb divide. Several of the outer suburbs such as Garforth and Swillington, Pudsey, Wetherby and Whinmoor, have relatively low levels of open space provision, a shortage identified in the 1985 local plans. This is surprising as several of these wards are perceived as 'desirable' residential areas, and are located close to the green belt. The explanation for the lack of open space appears to lie in the fact that these areas experienced large scale residential development in the 1960s and 1970s, when provision of open space was not a priority issue. In addition, their location close to the green belt may have led to the perception that the proximity of large areas of countryside mitigated against prioritising the need to provide open space within these newly developed areas. In current residential developments, developers are expected to identify, and if necessary provide, public open space as part of the total development scheme.

**Planning for the future**

Open space is continually evolving: the nature of its habitat changes, its function changes, and its place in the consciousness of society changes. There have, for example, been massive changes in the nature of formal recreational activities since the formation of many of Leeds' parks early this century. There is a danger that the "creation and upkeep of urban landscapes are largely seen as a static endeavour; where once created the objective is to maintain the status quo. The dynamics of natural communities follow quite different laws that change and evolve in response to natural forces" (Hough, 1989, p.19). Leeds, in common with other UK cities, has begun to address and respond to the changing function and role of its open space, and develop policies and practices designed to meet the needs of the city in the years to come. The city has developed a number of initiatives which reflect new and innovative ways of working to enhance the city's open space. Areas where progress are being made include:

- *Open space standards:* Leeds has started to respond to the need to develop open space standards, which are lacking at both national and local levels. "In Leeds the aim is to provide 1.8ha of amenity open space and 1.2 ha of playing fields for every 1000 people in addition to the provision of major parks and gardens" (Metropolitan Planning Officers Society, 1992, p.16), but there is no overall open space standard, with informal open space being conspicuously absent. Any standard has to be introduced with care, so that major showpiece initiatives do not overshadow the need for neighbourhood level open space provision, with the Liverpool Garden Festival site a classic example of this happening.
- *Strategies and Plans:* Leeds has been actively developing open space strategies such as the Countryside and Nature Conservation strategies which provide a useful base on which to develop comprehensive open space strategies. In the process of preparing its Unitary Development Plan (UDP), open space and the conflict over development has already proved to be a critical and controversial issue. Two of the three main topics of concern to those responding to the UDP were loss of Green Belt and loss of open space. It is essential that the protection and enhancement policies proposed in strategies and plans are implemented and supported in practice.
- *Leeds Environment City Initiative:* Leeds is one of four Environment Cities in England. The initiative acts to co-ordinate and promote environmental developments in the city (see Chapter 11). The presence of the Environment City and its associated groups, such as the Environmental Action Forum for Voluntary Groups, provides a positive

atmosphere in which ideas and knowledge can be shared, and progress in greening the city encouraged.

- *Partnerships:* The Lower Aire Valley Strategy provides an example of a partnership initiative which involves a range of bodies with an interest in the protection and use of open space. It aims to put forward a long-term plan for the development of the Lower Aire Valley, which has a history of mining activity (predominantly open cast), but also contains valuable areas for nature conservation and attractive agricultural landscapes. The strategy is the product of a partnership between Leeds City Council, British Coal and the Countryside Commission, with input from local residents and voluntary groups being widely encouraged. The strategy shows how partnerships can provide a way forward in enhancing the city's open space resource in one of Leeds most degraded industrial areas. The city needs to develop similar co-operative working methods for all major open space areas, particularly where the potential for conflict exists.

This assessment of open space provision in Leeds has so far been largely positive, recognising the wealth of high quality green space both within and adjacent to the city. It is imperative though that this relatively good provision of open space does not lead to complacency, or obscure the very real obstacles facing the city in developing an equitable and effective open space distribution. The current distribution in the city is manifestly unequal, the areas of highest population density often having the least access to open space, and too much of what is provided is of a relatively poor quality. Leeds in common with other authorities suffers from a lack of resources (particularly capital and revenue finance); a lack of practical government advice on broad open space provision standards and methods; a lack of data; and a constrained planning system where it can be required to pursue developments (e.g. the A1-M1 road link) that in themselves mitigate against the protection and enhancement of open space. However, even given these constraints, there are steps that the city can and should take:

- Develop a comprehensive open space database (the council has recently made progress on collecting basic open space data).
- Preparation of an open space policy and strategy for the city.
- Recognise the value of a diversity of open space types, particularly small informal open space.
- Develop open space standards for the city covering all types of open space.
- Incorporate and strengthen open space policies in all development plans and other local authority plans and strategies.

- Press for a presumption against development of green space at national level, and refuse planning permission for such developments at local level.
- Utilise the knowledge and skills within the authority, and from the private and voluntary sectors.
- Actively support local community initiatives.
- Respond positively to opportunities to develop the open space resource e.g. restoration of derelict land.
- Develop a flexible open space policy which can respond to the changing requirements of the users of open space.

## Conclusion

The local authority is likely to remain the key player in determining the future of open space in Leeds for the foreseeable future. But, if it is to respond effectively to the growing demands being placed on open space, in terms of amenity use, to the economic pressures on open space and to the diversity of the open space resource, particularly the informal resource, the local authority cannot act in isolation. It will need to mobilise resources from the private and voluntary sector and harness public support for open space, not alienate it as is too often the case at present. A priority for the city is the development of a city-wide open space action programme, which identifies the strength and deficits of the open space resource, and is integrated into the city's overall environment programme. The city needs to develop and commit itself to a clear vision of the future not rest on its laurels, whilst developers, and the various commercial leisure interests compete to denude and estrange Leeds' green heritage.

## References

Allsop, A.J. (1906), *Official Handbook of Public Parks in Leeds,* Leeds.

Baines, C. (1986), *Wild Side of Town,* BBC Publications, London.

Broadhead, I. (1990), *Leeds,* Smith Settle, Ilkley.

Burt, S. and Grady, K. (1994), *The Illustrated History of Leeds,* Breedon Books, Derby.

Council of Europe, Committee of Ministers (1986), *Recommendation No.R (86) 11 of the Committee of Ministers to Member States on Urban Open Space,* European Committee of Ministers.

Department of the Environment (1989), *Strategic Guidance for West Yorkshire: Regional Planning Guidance 2,* HMSO London.

Department of the Environment (1990), *This Common Inheritance,* HMSO, London.

Department of the Environment (1991), *Sport and Recreation: Planning Policy Guidance Note 17,* HMSO, London.

Department of the Environment (1992), *Development Plans and Regional Planning Guidance: Planning Policy Guidance Note 12,* HMSO, London.

Department of the Environment (1993), *Environmental Appraisal of Development Plans A Good Practice Guide,* HMSO, London.

Department of Environment (1994), *Nature Conservation: Planning Policy Guidance Note 9,* HMSO, London.

Dolman, F. (1895), *Municipalities at Work, Social Questions of Today,* London.

Elkin, T. McLaren, D. and Hillman, M. (1991), *Reviving the City Towards Sustainable Development,* Friends of the Earth, London.

Gilbert, O. (1989), *The Ecology of Urban Habitats,* Chapman and Hall, London.

Heaton, P and Bramhill, P. (1993), A green grid for the Local Plan, *Town and Country Planning,* January/February, pp. 13 - 16.

Hough, M. (1989), *City Form and Natural Process: Towards a New Urban Vernacular,* Routledge.

Leeds City Council (1966), *City Handbook,* Leeds City Council, Leeds.

Leeds City Council (1991a), *Leeds Nature Conservation Strategy,* Leeds City Council, Leeds.

Leeds City Council (1991b), *The Leeds Green Strategy,* Leeds City Council, Leeds City Council, Leeds.

Leeds City Council (1993a), *Lower Aire Valley Environmental Improvement Strategy,* Leeds City Council, Leeds.

Leeds City Council (1993b), *Leeds Unitary Development Plan Revised Draft June 1993,* Department of Planning, Leeds City Council.

Leeds City Council (1993c), *Leeds Draft Countryside Strategy,* Leeds City Council, Leeds.

Llewelyn-Davies, (1995), *Planning for Open Space: Open Space Planning in London. Findings of Research,* Llewelyn-Davies, London.

Metropolitan Planning Officers Society, (1992) *Urban Greenspace,* Metropolitan Planning Officers Society.

Morgan, G. (1991), *A Strategic Approach to the Planning and Management of Parks and Open Spaces,* Institute for Leisure and Amenity Management, Berkshire.

Normington, R. (1971), *City and County Borough of Leeds Town and Country Planning Act 1971, First Review of City Development Plan Written Statement,* Leeds City Council, Leeds.

Open Spaces Society (1990), *Spaces Between Community Action for*

*Urban Open Space,* National Council for Voluntary Organisations, London.

Thirlwall, C.G. (1967), *City and County Borough of Leeds Town and Country Planning Act, 1962, First Review of the City Development Plan, Draft Report of Survey Written Analysis,* Leeds City Council, Leeds.

Whittaker, B and Brown, K. (1971), *Parks for People,* Seeley, London.

# 14 Transport and personal accessibility in Leeds

*Eamon Judge and David Hick*

## Introduction

The transport system of a city plays a central role in determining the efficiency of its economic and social life. The relative effectiveness of the road and public transport systems affects the choices which people make about how, when and where they will travel, or indeed, whether they have any choice in the matter. Effectiveness impacts differentially depending on access to car, the cost and quality of public transport, the activity being undertaken, the area lived in, and sex, age, ethnic background and disability (if any). The combination of all these factors will determine for any person or household the access to a range of opportunities, and, indeed, be a crucial factor in determining overall quality of life. Personal accessibility is the term used here to indicate an individual's position in relation to the transport system. It is important to note that personal accessibility is not just a function of the efficiency of the transport system, but also depends on the juxtaposition of land uses. For instance, a person's personal accessibility may be made worse without any change in the transport system if the land uses s/he want to access move further away, or disappear altogether.

Whatever the personal circumstances of any individual, a crucial factor in personal accessibility is the success or otherwise of the authorities and agencies responsible not only for the transport system, but also for locational decisions in other activity sectors, such as education, health, and leisure. While this chapter will focus on the role of the transport system in the personal accessibility situation of the people of Leeds, these other actors cannot be ignored. The last fifteen to twenty years have been ones of great change in the transport system of Leeds, and in the way it has impacted on individuals and affected their personal accessibility. But what happens in any ten to twenty year period is not independent of what happened in the previous twenty years. Though this chapter will focus more on recent years rather than distant decades, it attempts to assess how the fortunes of different groups in the community have been shaped over time by their relationship to the city's changing transport system.

While the development of transport policy in Leeds in general terms can be outlined easily, the impacts of policy are less easily identified. Aside from broad analyses of the respective fortunes of road and public transport users, there has been little research done on the losers and gainers. The method adopted here is to map out the key phases in the development of the transport experience of Leeds, and to evaluate each phase, as far as possible, in relation to the experiences of different groups in the community, public transport user to road user, worker to shopper, the young, old, rich, poor, inner/suburban dweller, and so on. The extent to which we can comment on each of these categories inevitably varies according to the information available for each period.

The first period in the modern era is that leading up to the Buchanan study (HMSO, 1963), and its aftermath, up to the creation of West Yorkshire County Council in 1974. We refer to this here as The Defining Period, since it laid the foundations of much that the succeeding periods had to deal with. The second period is that of the life of West Yorkshire County Council, from 1974 to 1985, an era of co-ordination and integration which saw the first systematic consideration of what is the central concern of this chapter: personal accessibility, the way in which it is experienced by different groups in the community, the desirable levels of personal accessibility, and the sorts of policy measures to be instituted to achieve these. We call this The Metropolitan Period. The third period, which we refer to as From Deregulation to Integration, was short and turbulent. Starting in 1985, it encompasses both the re-emergence of Leeds as a transport planning authority, but also the deregulation of urban bus transport from 1986, up to the launching of the Leeds Transport Strategy in 1991, based around a claimed city-wide consensus. The fourth period brings us up to the present day, with the implementation of parts of the strategy, and continuing debate over others. We call this period "The Period of Consensus".

## The Defining Period: 1945-1974

As a more detailed critique of accessibility in this period has been previously provided (Judge, 1983), this section concentrates on setting a more general context for the development of transport policy in Leeds. In 1945 Leeds was a fairly self-contained city of about half a million people which emerged relatively unscathed from the war. It had a markedly radial road system focusing on the central area plus the large industrial area forming a belt immediately to the south of the city centre. This core area provided employment for half the working population of the city, generating heavy peak flows. Combined with a road configuration producing significant through-traffic, these features were to have important effects on the development of traffic and transport policy.

In the immediate post-1945 period of low car ownership, high public transport availability, and small scale localised facilities, it appears that the levels of personal accessibility available to much of the population of Leeds was quite acceptable in terms of the expectations of the time. Moreover, these levels did not differ grossly between different types of traveller and different areas of the city. But the emerging post-war planning framework would contain the first signs of change in this relatively egalitarian situation. The Development Plan (Leeds City Council, 1953) assumed a relatively low population growth, though the need to replace poor housing near the centre meant that there would be substantial peripheral developments. These would provide increased demand for public transport and road use, assuming employment location remained predominantly centrally oriented. While the Plan said nothing about public transport, it recognised that, even with optimistically low traffic growth forecasts, there would be a need for improved radial roads, and outer, intermediate, and inner ring roads. All this was to be completed by 1979.

This relatively moderate pace of expected change was overtaken by the accelerating economic and car ownership growth of the 1950s. Concern with how Britain's cities were to cope with mass car ownership culminated in the Buchanan Report (HMSO, 1963). This report included Leeds as one of four case studies to illustrate the changes that would be necessary to accommodate the perceived public demand for unrestricted car use. The detail of this study is not overly pertinent to this discussion, save to say that it is remembered for some good ideas which have carried through to today, and for others which thankfully were never implemented. The good points relate to proposals to deal with the car's environmental threat by creating car-free areas (which in Leeds finds their expression in the central pedestrian zone), and the recognition that the inability to cope with car demands would require public transport subsidies (less perfectly expressed in Leeds). The bad points relate to the fact that the corollary of car-free areas was new roads, which in Leeds would have required the clearance of half the current central area: this was not implemented (save for the Inner Ring Road).

In fact, despite the prominence given to it, the Buchanan Leeds Study was not a plan for the city as such, more an examination of possibilities, and some might say it made little difference to what actually happened. More influential in practice were the study entitled *The Leeds Approach* (HMSO, 1969) and the First Development Plan Review (Leeds City Council, 1969). These linked the development of transport proposals to the requirements of urban renewal within and around the city centre (like Buchanan), but planned only for a 20 year period (not 50 as Buchanan). Also, they did not envisage significant job decentralisation from the central area and forecast only moderate population increase. The major objective was to cater for peak hour demand, that is, the work journey. Road network proposals were more limited in scope and much more concerned to minimise costs and disruption in the city, though still including the Inner Ring Motorway of Buchanan. Car-driver restraint consisted largely of comprehensive parking controls combined with traffic management measures. The parking allocations of the 1951 Development Plan were almost doubled. More importantly, long stay parking would be in car parks on the edge of the central area periphery, avoiding the need to enter it. There would be better and subsidised public transport, and only 20 per cent of commuters would travel by car (40 per cent was envisaged by Buchanan), and 66 per cent by public road transport. Within the central area, the removal of traffic to the primary network would allow pedestrianisation and environmental improvements to take place.

Even at the outset, problems could be foreseen. Using existing radial roads to carry increased road traffic implied environmental deterioration for local communities, and reduced their usefulness as bus routes. Parking restraint would not stop through traffic. Furthermore, the absence of a decentralisation strategy meant that coping with work accessibility problems by land use change was not possible. The increase in central area employment and its greater service orientation meant that the peak was further accentuated, compounding the problems of public transport. Lastly, the plans proposed were very expensive at a time of resource scarcity.

In the next five years parts of the plan were implemented. Some of the above problems were pointed out by critics in this period (Houghton Evans, 1975). By the July 1973 review (Leeds City Council, 1973) only about a third of the new road network proposals had been completed. However, there had been extensive pedestrianisation in the central area, some new bus services, and a start on building the peripheral car-parks (i.e. one, the current one on Woodhouse Lane). The transitional problems of introducing the new road circulation system had been far more severe than anticipated, and congestion in the central area at peak hours was considered acute. Combined with inadequate public transport, this meant that the expected switch to public transport did not occur. These problems were passed on to the new West Yorkshire Metropolitan County Council (WYMCC) in 1974.

## The Metropolitan Period, 1974-1985

After the formation of the WYMCC, transport planning in the enlarged area of Leeds City Council became a county responsibility. The major component of this was the Structure Plan, and an associated Public Transport Plan, backed up in 1975 by a major Transportation Study. This was the first time that transport problems in Leeds, and the County as a whole, had been studied in real depth. The draft Structure Plan (WYMCC, 1977) saw the role of transport strategy as not an end in itself, but as a means to the achievement of its more general social and economic objectives. These were: maximisation of the use of existing infrastructure, the improvement of the local economy, and the assistance of deprived groups. The transport policies from the Transportation Study (WYTCONSULT, 1977) to meet these objectives may be summed up in the issues of accessibility, safety and environment. Accessibility was an important issue as, in some ways, it underlined the approach of the Structure Plan and its associated studies. Travel demands were viewed as a function of the juxtaposition of land uses, and, for instance, the provision of road space was only one way of meeting peak demands, if, indeed, it was felt necessary to meet them at all. Hence, peak hour road congestion was a problem only in so far as it created more general accessibility, environmental, or safety problems.

Underlying this view was a new approach to the analysis of personal accessibility. This de-emphasised transport facilities and their efficiency per se, and emphasised the role of transport facilities in helping people undertake personal, social, and economic activities. Accessibility defined the degree of opportunity people had to undertake these activities. It is determined not only by an individual's mobility level (e.g. as reflected in a person's income, personal abilities/characteristics, etc), but also by the spatial distribution of land uses, and by the form and operating characteristics of the transport system (Cooper, Daly, and Headicar, 1979). Accessibility is not necessarily coincident with an individual's actual amount of travel (more may be necessary because of low accessibility), nor with congested traffic conditions (accessibility may still not fall below an acceptable threshold). Equally, personal accessibility may be poor even when the transport system is operating efficiently. Conventional transport models are not good at representing accessibility in this sense, producing aggregate measures such as traffic speeds and flows. Thus, they are not good at providing indicators of the extent to which the land-use/transport system meets peoples' activity needs, nor of which sections of the population have transport-related problems, and which sections actually benefit from improvements.

The Transportation Study developed an approach to measuring personal accessibility by defining acceptable accessibility standards for different types of individual to different types of facility (WYTCONSULT, 1977a; WYTCONSULT, 1977b). The actual accessibility from each zone for each category was then measured, and any shortfall from the defined standard would be situations which, potentially, transport proposals would attempt to alleviate. The Main Report (WYTCONSULT, 1977c) gives a summarised account of the accessibility results. For work journeys, it identifies only three areas of Leeds (within its new metropolitan boundaries) as having personal accessibility problems: Garforth, Wetherby and, to an extent, Otley. For shopping, significant accessibility problems were identified in locations largely on or outside the northern Outer Ring Road, in some locations in south Leeds, and in the Garforth/Kippax area. In a similar way, accessibility problems for school, health and welfare journeys are identified. These statements are what can be gleaned from a series of maps (detailed zonal data are unavailable). However, what is of significance is not the detailed data, nor even so much the broad descriptions just given, but more the simple conceptualisation of the issues. The accessibility results usefully combined land use and transport dimensions, whilst highlighting the experience of people in different areas.

The Transportation Study (WYTCONSULT, 1977) faced several severe problems during its execution, especially in the progressive decline in likely resource availability (Martin and Daly, 1978). Overall, it was forecast that travel demand would severely overload both the public transport and highway systems in peak periods, and would require considerable action by the transport authorities even to yield a workable transport system. In particular, the public transport operators would experience the demands which the road and parking systems could not cope with. It was also observed that the main problem in Leeds concerned access to work, especially at peak times (Coombe, 1979). The strategy included: central area parking controls to restrain car use; limited physical improvements to the highway network; bus priority measures; low-cost traffic and environmental measures; urban traffic control; bus service improvements, especially to routing; limited rail infrastructure investment; bus-rail co-ordination; significantly higher public transport fare levels than 1975; car-pooling programmes; staggering of work and school hours; and safe-guarding of routes for a possible light rail transit system. Despite the overall tenor of the Structure Plan, and notwithstanding the extended range of policy measures and strategies outlined above, it would seem that as far as Leeds was concerned the primary problem was the same before: how to cope with the peak. Notably absent from the above list was any mention of long-term workplace decentralisation, a bone of some contention between the County Council and Leeds City Council (Leeds City Council, 1981).

240

The 1970s had been a depressing sequence of receding horizons and diminishing expectations in transport terms. As the end of the existence of WYMCC approached this trend intensified and the achievements became correspondingly stunted. The public transport deficits became particularly severe in 1981, and worsened up to the abolition of WYMCC. While there had been welcome increases in local rail service patronage, there had been substantial reductions in bus patronage combined with substantial increases in real fare levels, representing a major departure from Structure Plan assumptions (WYMCC, 1981). Initiatives aimed at car sharing or staggering of work hours had had minimal effects. Overall traffic growth had been much greater than assumed in the Structure Plan too. But with the progressive completion of major road schemes and the area traffic control scheme, so far as could be measured, traffic congestion did not increase, and indeed diminished in many areas. Within the Area Traffic Control zone, journey times decreased by 16 per cent. In effect then, relative to public transport users, private car accessibility conditions improved, despite the increased level of traffic.

At a time when, in spite of all the financial constraints, there was progress to show in dealing with problems of personal accessibility in Leeds, the plans of the Government to abolish the Metropolitan Counties were gathering pace. Arguably these plans were generated by the activities of some of these counties in attempting to improve personal accessibility in their areas!

## From deregulation to integration, 1985-91

The return of transport planning responsibilities to Leeds City Council was followed by the deregulation of public transport. In two moves a significant part of the flexibility of the local authority to plan strategically for both private and public transport was removed. The previous Transportation Study had already forecast that the personal accessibility of public transport dependent individuals in many areas would get worse. This was without the effects of public transport deregulation from 26th October, 1986. Also, road traffic and congestion increased rapidly as the decade progressed. Deregulation was forecast by the government to reduce fares, increase ridership, and reduce subsidies (it did the latter, but not the former two). While the City Council was still a highway authority, and the West Yorkshire Passenger Transport Executive still existed, the combination of growing traffic congestion and the first results of deregulation (Whitehouse, 1986) influenced the City Council to look for further avenues of transport development. The West Yorkshire Transportation Study had proposed reserving routes for a light rail system. The possibility of developing this started to look very attractive to councillors. The schemes examined by the PTE and the City Council created such a furore when discussed publicly (Whitehouse, 1988) that it became apparent that such radical innovations in city transport could only be instituted after a deeper appraisal of transport needs and possibilities in the new situation. The possibility of the city losing out to the schemes being developed in Manchester and Sheffield was an additional worry.

This was the catalyst for bringing together all political parties to support a transport strategy study to form the basis for the analysis of transport issues in the city, and for the production of new proposals for innovative transport systems. Commissioned in April 1990, the Study report was published in February 1991 (Leeds City Council et al., 1991a). By comparison with previous transportation studies, it was a very short exercise. A key feature was the large public consultation exercise that started in September 1990. Prior to this an opinion survey was carried out in July/August 1990 of a sample of 760 individuals in 30 randomly selected polling districts. This provides a 1990 'snapshot' of the views of residents' relationship to the transport system, and the opportunities available to them. The results were published as part of the overall public participation findings (Viewpoint, 1990). The work was carried out by the Policy Research Unit at Leeds Metropolitan University, and further analysis of the data was carried out for this chapter.

As an overall impression, two-thirds of the sample found Leeds "Easy to travel around". When broken down by area of the city (central, outer and peripheral Leeds), there was virtually no change in this proportion. On the other hand, 54 per cent thought that Leeds had "Good public transport", but this proportion declined from 56 per cent at the centre, to 52 per cent at the periphery. Moreover, only 29 per cent thought that Leeds had good roads, though this proportion rose from 28 per cent at the centre to 31 per cent at the periphery. Respondents were asked what had been the major factors in the improvement or deterioration in their quality of life in the last ten years (51 per cent had said quality had improved, 29 per cent said it had got worse, 18 per cent said it had not changed, and 2 per cent did not know). Those who said quality had improved mentioned better transport facilities and services as the seventh most frequent factor (out of nine factors, mentioned by five per cent). But for those recording a deterioration, transport problems were the first most frequently mentioned factor (out of eight, mentioned by 16 per cent).

Along with the other elements of the public consultation process, three priorities clearly emerged: "An effective and amenable public transport service," "Safety on the roads, and in the streets," and "A clean, friendly environment" (Viewpoint, 1990, p.9). These priorities were carried forward into the detailed work of the technical studies. The published strategy (Leeds City Council et al., 1991a) identified a number of key issues for the transport strategy to resolve, one of which was "the achievement of genuine equality of access to transport for all members of the community" (p.8). In its evaluation of current problems and future trends, apart from some consideration of provision for people with mobility problems, the study follows fairly conventional lines. That is to say, it considers traffic problems at various scales, parking problems, road accidents and safety, and public transport issues. The available information about people in particular places, of particular types, doing particular things is limited.

Equally, the forward look that the study takes deals with aggregates of demographic trends, car ownership growth, and traffic growth. Projections are expressed in the familiar aggregates of worsening congestion and conditions in general and in different parts of the city. Whilst it is argued (p.28) that "Accessibility to the city centre for those with a car available is projected to decrease by 31 per cent (and by 15 per cent for those dependent on public transport)" (p.28), no definition of accessibility is given. The not surprising conclusion from the transport model is that the transport system by 2010 will not be able to cope with predicted growth in car trips. What this implies for future personal accessibility has to be estimated as the Study report gives only broad indications.

Responses to the identified problems in terms of five possible strategies were evaluated, each based on a primary policy theme. These were: highway investment/major road construction; restraint of car use (road pricing); traffic management measures; improving existing public transport (bus and rail), and developing new forms of public transport (guided bus, light rapid transit, automatic guided transit (AGT)). The chosen strategy included aspects of all five alternatives (AGT was ruled out), and was developed in terms of four main elements: new roads, better public transport, management of traffic, and city centre initiatives. A clear commitment was made to particular groups and types of users: "The Strategy also attaches high priority to making improvements in access to transport for those without a car (mainly women) and for disabled and elderly people" ( Leeds City Council et al., 1991b).

The Strategy adopts significant changes from previous car-dominated approaches, explicitly attempting "to continue the movement away from the policies of the 1950s and 1960s that made pedestrians and environment subservient to the needs of the car" (Leeds City Council et al., 1991c). The same document points out that 40 per cent of people do not have regular access to a car, while 30 per cent of public transport users have mobility problems, restricting choice and opportunity. The strategy provides an

243

overall framework within which policies can be developed to cater for the non-car user and for the needs of specific groups.

## The Period of Consensus, 1991-96

The Transport Strategy was a considerable step forward from some of the uncertainties and dead ends that transport planning in the city got into in the late 1980s, and achieved ostensibly a broad social and political consensus. While up to the present the Strategy still appears sound and feasible, and capable of adapting to changing circumstances and priorities, it has not been without its critics. Thus, Tight and May (1991) point out that despite the Strategy's emphasis on encouraging people to shift to public transport, other parts of it place great emphasis on catering for an increasing level of mobility, rather than on managing travel demand. Hence, little is done to actively discourage car use, and indeed some parts of the Strategy would make car use easier. Perhaps a more fundamental criticism is that despite the emphasis on developing a vision of the city, this does not extend to consideration of urban form or lifestyles (ibid). In an era emphasising ever more the link between transport and land use, this is a significant criticism.

Nonetheless, the Transport Strategy can legitimately be seen as a watershed in terms of recent transport policy. As well as setting out new policies and proposals, it also incorporates many earlier measures and projects. These include new roads and improvement schemes, traffic management, pedestrian and bus priorities, improved public transport and specific access measures. In terms of improving access for particular groups and types of user to public transport, the role of the Passenger Transport Authority continues to be of particular importance. Three distinct policy areas are involved: reduced off-peak fares, concessionary fares for specific groups and special services to meet particular needs. The first two of these were well established before the Transport Strategy, which has promoted further development of special services as part of its policies, most notably Access Bus, Nightline, and Shopmobility.

Since the Strategy was adopted several significant changes have taken place in Government thinking and policy. These include the package approach for TPPs, Planning Policy Guidelines - Transport (PPG13) (Department of Environment and Department of Transport, 1994), and two important reports (Royal Commission on Environmental Pollution, 1994; Standing Committee on Trunk Road Assessment (SACTRA), 1994). All of these have a bearing on the Strategy and its development and are taken into account in later plans and programmes e.g. the Unitary Development Plan (UDP) and annual TPP submissions. In addition, revision of the Roads

Programme has resulted in the Department of Transport abandoning major projects which formed part of the 'New Roads' element of the Strategy. As such, it has proved necessary to modify aspects of the Strategy and adapt to changing external circumstances.

The starting point for considering the four main elements of the Strategy must be the wording of the Strategy documents, which clearly defines intentions and sets priorities for new roads, public transport, traffic management and city centre initiatives.

New Roads - not to cater for extra traffic into the Centre, but to help remove though traffic, improve the environment or support economic development... Better Public Transport - not only to raise the quality for existing users, but to cater for growing travel demands and provide an attractive alternative to the car... Bus and rail will remain the mainstay of transport in Leeds and their improvement is a key element... A new form of public transport is proposed - the 'Leeds Supertram' a high quality, environment-friendly electric system, running generally on ground level tracks between City Centre and suburbs, accessible to all... Traffic management - to protect the local environment and improve safety... City Centre Initiatives - to make the heart of Leeds more attractive and accessible (Leeds City Council et al., 1991c).

From such statements it is possible to identify the current major policies and priorities in terms of types of traffic, users and other groups. The intention that new roads will not cater for extra traffic into the centre means low priority in future for the car-borne commuter. Removal of through traffic can potentially bring benefits to almost any group. The latest version of this statement also indicates that this means "improvement of orbital rather than radial routes for through traffic avoiding the City Centre" (Leeds City Council et al., 1994).

Better public transport satisfies two main requirements, reflected in two different sets of priorities and proposals. Improved services are required to retain existing bus and rail users, maintaining and improving their access, while the proposed new Supertram service appears necessary to attract car users back to public transport. Taken together both new and improved provision afford priority to public transport users, among whom various groups can be identified as being disadvantaged in physical and economic terms. To suggest that all bus users are relatively poor or come from households without cars is too simplistic, but some general characteristics can be identified. A large proportion of bus users qualify for concessionary fares, while many bus routes serve inner city areas and council estates, which cannot be served by rail. Supertram will link the City Centre with some outer suburbs and beyond via Park and Ride sites on the fringe of the built-up area. However, from the outset it was intended that "the new system will serve local people and not simply provide fast transport for the long distance commuter or visitor" (Leeds City Council et al., 1991b). Bus users are, and will be, by far the largest group, so that major investment in Supertram and electrified rail services may appear illogical or discriminatory. But this is very strongly influenced by the extent to which the relevant authorities can act directly, given deregulated bus services and the impending rail privatisation.

Traffic Management is a means to achieve various objectives and priorities in the Strategy and will also be used to improve traffic flow and establish priorities. Specific objectives of safety and environment should mean a reduction in the adverse effects of traffic on individuals and communities. Traffic calming will reduce hazard and nuisance and improve safe access within the local area for pedestrians and cyclists. So it is reasonable to argue that such schemes will assist those who were disadvantaged by the previous emphasis on car transport improvements, provided appropriate criteria are used in selecting priority areas within Road Safety and Environmental Improvement programmes.

City Centre Initiatives can be seen in terms of the priorities given to access and movement in the city centre for pedestrians, public transport, and internal traffic, and provision for these in terms of policies and physical measures. Particularly important is the principle of a hierarchy of access for different groups and types of user, based on a roughly concentric layout. At the heart of the area is the Pedestrian Core, which is bounded by the "Public Transport Box." Outside this is a one-way City Centre Loop Road, acting as a distributor road which runs around the main central area, between the Inner Ring Road and the Public Transport Box.

Most of this Pedestrian Core already exists in the form of pedestrian priority areas, linked to arcades and shopping centres, but in future vehicles will be more severely restricted and the quality of the environment enhanced. Using existing main streets the Public Transport Box frames the Pedestrian Core and provides access to the main shopping areas. Users of public transport will be set down and picked up at more central locations than most car users (some multi-storey car parks lie within the Box). This priority applies initially to bus passengers, and in due course will apply to Supertram passengers. The City Centre Loop road will concentrate local traffic onto streets have been redesigned to provide adequate capacity, though it is not intended to cater for through traffic, which will use the Inner Ring Road to by-pass the city centre. Parking policies and provision also form part of the strategy for city centre traffic. The main emphasis is on more short-term parking for shoppers and other users of facilities, and not for car-borne commuters. Overall, two points should be stressed. Firstly, the measures are inter-dependent and will not work well if any one is lacking, or ineffective. Secondly, the main priorities for access to the city centre are, in order: pedestrians, public transport users, and car users.

To understand the wider context of current and future access and transport policies, one must consider the UDP (Leeds City Council, 1994). The scope of this is generally much wider than the Transport Strategy. Transport is one of several strategies which fits into the UDP, with others including the Economic, Countryside and Green Strategies. Transport policies and measures are covered in no less than forty statements falling into five groups: a package of general policies mostly derived from the Transport Strategy plus sets of more specific statements relating to public transport, highway proposals and car parking, plus statements on "Access for All". This might appear to be the key to how policies will affect particular groups, but is in fact confined to a very general statements that all people should have access to services and opportunities (e.g. health, education and employment), and to very specific matters (e.g. detailed aspects of planning for disabled people). An opportunity to 'bridge the gap' with relevant policies for other disadvantaged groups and access for those without a car was missed. Another contentious matter is the emphasis on provision for short-term parking in the City Centre. Coupled with tighter standards for parking related to new development, this has provoked comment from business interests that this would 'kill off the city centre.'

**Beyond 1996**

It is appropriate to say more about progress on implementing the Strategy, looking into the future, and considering what we can glean for the theme of this chapter. We shall consider first a scheme in the pipeline (Supertram), then some schemes taking place on the ground, and, finally, a further scheme in the pipeline (Inner Ring Road Stages 6 and 7). Supertram is a modern tram system which will operate mostly on existing streets, in corridors between the city centre and outer suburbs, with park and ride facilities at their outer termini. Three lines are proposed: Line 1, to the south is now at the point where tenders have been invited from consortia to produce private sector funding and determine who will operate the line. Line 2, to the north west has been through two stages of design and consultation. Line 3, to the north east is still in the earlier stages of design and consultation (see Figure 14.1). Each line is routed to serve a mix of residential areas and major traffic generators, before meeting in the centre.

## Figure 14.1 Leeds Transport Strategy, 1994

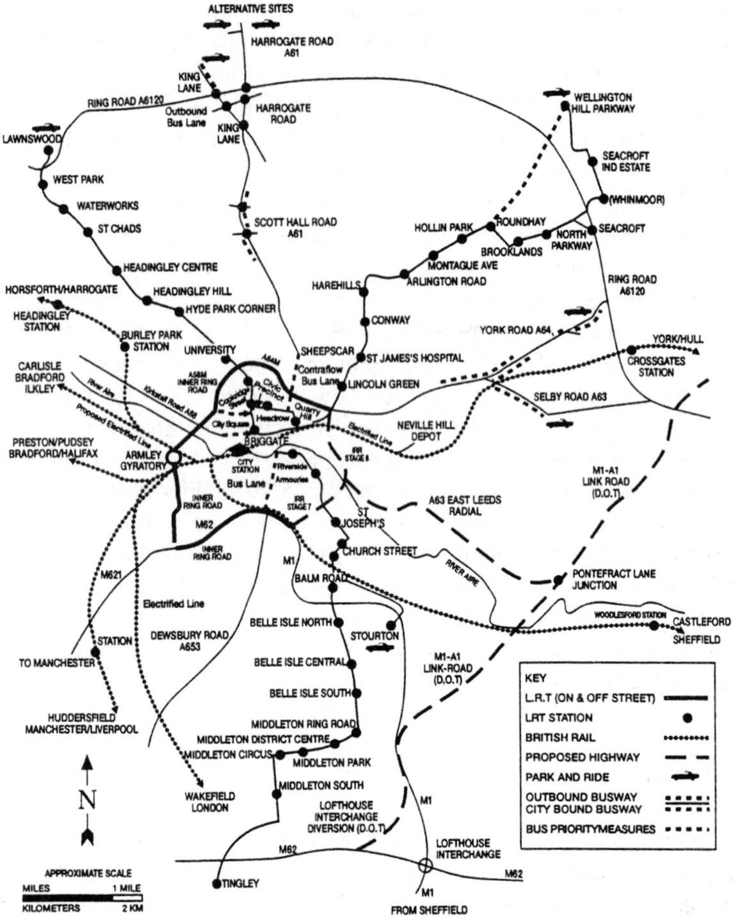

Reactions to these proposals vary. Little opposition was apparent with Line 1, probably reflecting the general support for the Transport Strategy and the priority given to a line serving areas with a large population dependent on public transport. Line 2 has met with considerable opposition and scepticism, particularly from those in the Headingley area. Well-established, organised and articulate residents and community groups have questioned most aspects: the route, stations, effects on other traffic and whether Supertram is good value for money. But more moderate opinion is concerned that Supertram is primarily for longer distance travellers, notably commuters using Park and Ride, and not for the local community.

Unlike the situation in Sheffield and Manchester, the Leeds Supertram has yet to become a reality. However, progress on the ground can now be seen, for instance the Guided Bus, the City Centre Loop, and modified streets (Briggate and Vicar Lane). The Guided Bus is being developed to serve at least two corridors, complementing rail and Supertram, and including park and ride. As an exclusive busway, suitably equipped buses run using guide wheels within the segregated track, but also operating as normal buses on other roads. So far construction has started on one route (Scott Hall Road) whilst another (York Road) is at an advanced stage of planning, with a possible third route in Kirkstall Valley. There has been strong opposition in some areas to the siting of park and ride. Compared with Supertram, Guided Bus is relatively cheap and has been introduced quickly. It should prove beneficial to existing bus users and for park and ride journeys (Pope, 1994).

The City Centre Loop Road is expected to be completed by 1998. Whilst it could create a barrier to pedestrian movement between the inner and outer parts of the city centre, the scheme does include more and better pedestrian crossings so that with the use of the existing Urban Traffic Control System, both drivers and pedestrians should experience little delay. The scheme has produced some adverse reactions. Some believe that the Loop concedes too much to the car driver and impairs safe access on foot or cycle, while others object to the design features intended to guide the motorist through a fairly complex system. As emphasised earlier, the City Centre Initiatives are inter-related, so that the Loop is essential to improved access for all users. Finally, as regards Pedestrian and Bus Priority Streets, works have been carried out to refurbish two main streets, Briggate and Vicar Lane. Briggate will eventually be fully pedestrianised, whilst Vicar Lane will form part of the (two way) Public Transport Box.

Also worthy of mention are Special Needs Services and Access Measures. Two specific services are aimed at particular groups and needs: Shopmobility and Nightlink. These provide examples of where the ideas and intentions of the Strategy have been implemented and monitored so that benefits to current users can be demonstrated. Shopmobility is a service whereby disabled people can hire an electric wheelchair for use in the city centre. Set up in 1992, evaluation research has confirmed that the service is much appreciated (Hick and Whitehead, 1993). Nightlink provides a get-home-safely service in the evening. Operating on similar lines to a taxi services, over 300 journeys per week are now made, and monitoring shows the service is working well. Both of these services demonstrate the way in which ideas from the Strategy have been developed to serve particular groups.

The Inner Ring Road Stages 6 and 7 is perhaps the best example of a major project in the pipeline which shows how the City Council's intentions set out in the Transport Strategy are being developed and applied (see Cooke, 1995; Wallis, 1995). The scheme is the largest single item in the

New Roads element of the Strategy and creates a link from the eastern end of the existing Inner Ring Road to the M1. It will also link up via the East Leeds Radial Road to the M1-A1 Motorway, making areas of East Leeds highly accessible to and from the national motorway network. Also, it will help city centre initiatives, remove through traffic, improve access to areas designated for employment growth in the UDP, and strengthen bids for Single Regeneration Budget funding. Particularly important in terms of the Transport Strategy is the impact on the city centre and enabling various initiatives to be fully implemented. Completion of Stages 6 and 7 should remove about 30 per cent of existing through traffic from the city centre. Once this is done then the Pedestrian Core can be fully established, general traffic removed from the Public Transport Box and the Loop road completed. The overall impression is that the City Council had given much more attention to non-car user effects than hitherto, following the intentions and principles of the Transport Strategy.

**Conclusions**

Transport is an aspect of the life and structure of Leeds where in the last six or seven years the City Council has sought to establish a large measure of unanimity amongst the various sectors of the social and business communities for what it has been attempting to do. At one level it seems to have been remarkably successful in this. The Transport Strategy emerged from an overall attempt to assess and mould together the disparate and often conflicting views of different parts of the community. Clearly, many parts of the Strategy are coming together and the results are visible on the ground, especially in the urban core. Other parts, such as the Supertram await funding, and failure to go ahead here would have knock on effects elsewhere. What is impressive in Leeds is that an innovative strategy has been introduced with considerable support from a broad cross-section of interested parties, in a situation where considerably more opposition might have been expected. This is testimony to the scale of problems facing Leeds and the widespread recognition of this, and also to the process of consultation led by the city council, and the general improvement over time of working relationships between the major stakeholders of the city in terms of developing an overall transport strategy.

## Acknowledgements

Useful discussions were held with the following individuals during the writing of this chapter: John Carr, Ray Heywood, Tim Larson, and Adrian Pope. The usual disclaimer applies. The authors are grateful to Emma Barraclough for research assistance, and to Philippa Boyce for graphics.

## References

Cooke, P.R. (1995), 'Leeds Inner Ring Road Stages 6 and 7: proof of evidence,' Leeds City Council, Public Local Inquiry, 14th February.

Coombe, R.D. (1979), 'West Yorkshire Transportation Studies, 4. Application of the approach and techniques to Leeds,' *Traffic Engineering and Control,* 20 (3), 111-116.

Cooper, J.S.L., Daly, P.N., and Headicar, P.G. (1979), 'West Yorkshire Transportation Studies, 2. Accessibility analysis,' *Traffic Engineering and Control,* 20 (1), 27-31.

Department of Environment and Department of Transport (1994), *Planning Policy Guidance - Transport,* (PPG13), HMSO, London.

Hick, D. and Whitehead, P. (1993), *Shopmobility: Survey and Review,* Report to Leeds City Council, Leeds Metropolitan University, mimeo.

H.M.S.O. (1963), *Traffic in Towns* (Buchanan Report), HMSO, London.

H.M.S.O. (1969), *Planning and Transport: The Leeds Approach,* HMSO, London.

Houghton-Evans, W. (1972), 'Leeds - Model or Muddle?,' *Official Architecture and Planning,* 35 (2), 92-96.

Judge, E.J. (1983), 'Leeds Since Buchanan, 1963-1983,' *Built Environment,* 9 (2), 113-121.

Leeds City Council (1951), *Development Plan,* LCC, Leeds.

Leeds City Council (1967), *First Review of City Development Plan*, August, 1967, approved 1972.

Leeds City Council (1973) *Leeds, Public Transport & the Environment,* LCC, Leeds.

Leeds City Council (1981), *Central Business Area District Plan: Written Statement,* in draft 1978, certified 1981. LCC, Leeds.

Leeds City Council (1993), *Unitary Development Plan,* (Revised draft, June 1993), LCC, Leeds.

Leeds City Council and West Yorkshire PTA (1991a), *Leeds Transport Strategy,* February, LCC, Leeds.

Leeds City Council and West Yorkshire PTA (1991b), *Transport Leeds: to the 21st Century,* February, 1991, LCC, Leeds.

Leeds City Council and West Yorkshire PTA (1991c), *Transport Leeds: a summary of the city's transport strategy,* LCC, Leeds.

Leeds City Council and West Yorkshire PTA (1994), *Leeds Transport Package, 1994/95,* LCC, Leeds.

Martin, B.V. and Daly, P.N. (1978), 'West Yorkshire Transportation Studies 1. The Analytical Approach,' *Traffic Engineering & Control,* 19 (12), 536-540.

Pope, A. (1994), 'Speeding up the Journey - Leeds Guided Bus,' ATCO Conference, 23rd June.

Royal Commission on Environmental Pollution (1994), *Transport and the Environment* (Eighteenth Report) Cm. 2674, HMSO, London.

SACTRA (1994), *Trunk Roads and the Generation of Traffic,* Standing Advisory Committee on Trunk Road Appraisal, Department of Transport, HMSO, London.

Tight, M. and May, A. (1991), 'Transport in Leeds: city strategy with a mobility focus,' *Town & Country Planning,* November, p.316.

Viewpoint (1990), 'Leeds Talks Transport', 3 December, 1990.

Wallis, J. (1995), 'Leeds Inner Ring Road Stages 6 and 7: Proof of Evidence,' Leeds City Council, Public Local Inquiry', 14th February.

West Yorkshire Metropolitan County Council (1980), *West Yorkshire County Structure Plan,* in draft October, 1977, approved July, 1980. WYMCC, Wakefield.

West Yorkshire Passenger Transport Executive (1979), *Public Transport Plan for West Yorkshire,* WYMCC, Wakefield.

West Yorkshire Metropolitan County Council (1974), *Transport Policies and Programme* (and annually from 1974), WYMCC, Wakefield.

West Yorkshire Metropolitan County Council (1981) *A Review of Trends Affecting Transport in West Yorkshire,* WYMCC, Wakefield.

Whitehouse, A. (1986), 'Transport of no delight,' *Yorkshire Post,* December 22nd, p.10.

Whitehouse, A. (1988), 'Missing the point,' *Yorkshire Post,* December 15th, 1988, p.10.

Whitehouse, A. (1991), '£800m transport scheme for city,' *Yorkshire Post,* February 22nd, p.14.

WYTCONSULT (1977a), *West Yorkshire Transportation Studies. The analysis of personal accessibility,* Document 407, WYMCC, Wakefield.

WYTCONSULT (1977b), *West Yorkshire Transportation Studies. The analysis of personal accessibility in the freestanding towns,* Document 431. WYMCC, Wakefield.

WYTCONSULT (1977c), *West Yorkshire Transportation Studies - Final Report,* (Vols. 1-4), October, 1977. Vol. 1 The Extent and Impact of Travel in 1975). WYMCC, Wakefield.

# IV
# LOCAL CAPACITY AND CHALLENGES TO SOCIAL SEGREGATION

# 15  Tackling female exclusion in the labour market: An evaluation of the Opportunity 2000 programme in Leeds

*Jane Kettle*

## Introduction

This chapter examines the situation of working women in Leeds within the context of feminist appraisals of gender inequality at work, and assesses the nature of attempts to redress disadvantage made by Leeds City Council. In contemporary British society, women, on average earn much less than men. They generally advance less well than men in their careers, they hold inferior paid jobs and often carry a double burden of paid and unpaid work. Women are subject to sexual harassment at work; trade unions remain dominated by men, and women rarely achieve positions of real power. How can this be overcome?

There is little doubt that despite such gloomy facts on women's economic position, attempts are being made to mitigate, if partially, these disadvantages. Gender equality in employment, along with the wider political and social implications of equality of opportunity, is receiving renewed attention from policy makers and employer organisations alike. This partly derives from recent developments both in Europe and the UK which have served to protect women's employment rights, and partly by demographic factors and changing patterns of work .

*Leeds: the context*

Leeds City Council, in common with other local authorities, has declared a commitment to the continuing development of equal opportunities practices and procedures, and has taken measures to attempt to reduce the perpetuation of disadvantage. Its approach has been to encourage diversity in the workforce, especially through partnership initiatives with the private sector. One particularly prominent project has been the Opp2K initiative which seeks to promote and enhance women's employment prospects and conditions.

The aim of this chapter is to evaluate critically the underpinning philosophy and rationale of this specific initiative, Opp2K, launched by Leeds City Council. It attempts to understand how, if at all, Leeds sets a precedent among UK cities with its focus on public/private partnerships as opposed to purely public sector solutions for problems of gender inequality, and conversely, how the incorporation of a social affairs dimension into mainstream local economic development policies might be approached.

Opp2K merits attention for a number of reasons. First, it is an important development in the city and it highlights an aspect of Leeds as a 'corporate city.' Second, Opp2K is unique in the United Kingdom. As a local initiative concerned with gender inequality, it is notable as a partnership between the public and private sectors. Third, it is unusual in that the situation involves the public sector charging the private sector to join an initiative on the basis that there may be future financial advantage in so doing. Fourth, this approach combines (with a degree of effectiveness that is still to be assessed) two key concerns of the European Commission. Equality for women is central to current thinking in terms of the restoration of the European Union's competitiveness in the world economy, together with the need for greater involvement of the private sector. This is contexualised as "the progressive decline in the importance of traditional households (husband, wife and children) as the main economic unit in society, and the increasing participation of women in the labour market" (CEC, 1993, p.128).

*Leadership and partnership*

The European White Paper *Growth, Competitiveness, Employment* (CEC, 1993) acknowledges the general shift in political and public preferences from the public provision of goods and services, and asserts that this has increased the pace of change needed to maintain a competitive economic performance. One of the central implications of this is that there must be considerable changes in international labour forces, both in the way work is organised and in the development and provision of supporting activities.

Leeds City Council has grasped the underlying philosophy of this approach and has attempted to implement it at both a regional and international level. The local authority certainly retains its focus on advancing women in a rapidly changing climate, where the local government role is seen increasingly as one of strategic enabler (LGMB, 1993). That local government is undergoing a sea change due to national policy, the significance of the European Union and changing local needs is indisputable. A role of community leadership is therefore essential in that it "looks outwards rather than inwards... leads from alongside rather than in front... orchestrates rather than provides... [community leadership is crucial] if new players are to be brought into those arenas in order to provide real choices and opportunities to the communities that are served by local government" (LGMB, 1993, p.2).

However the extent to which the local authority can influence by example and persuasion must be assessed with caution, particularly in an environment where business interests and predominantly patriarchal notions about the world of work override concerns for social justice. In order to address these concerns, this chapter will examine the gender inequalities in the labour market at a national and local level; it will offer an overview of the main feminist analyses of this form of disadvantage in contrast with mainstream approaches and will relate this to the local authority context. It will then consider the ideological tensions between equality and business interests, using the Opp2K initiative as a case study. Finally it will offer an assessment of the potential effectiveness of this initiative.

### Women and the labour market: national and local

*Structural inequality*

It is indisputable that on average, across the range of occupations and professions, men earn more than women, substantially so; and that this situation has not changed significantly since the Equal Pay Act was finally implemented in 1975. This can be partly explained by occupational sex segregation and has not been demonstrably challenged by the equal pay for equal value amendment to the Equal Pay Act. The gender pay differential is wider for non-manual workers than for manual workers. Indeed the differential for the former is now greater than it was 20 years ago (EOC, 1991).

There have been recent empirical studies on both the position of women in management (Rosener, 1990) and women's career patterns and training and development trends (White et al., 1992). These illustrate the continuing problem of women remaining under-represented in senior positions throughout the country (Alimo, Metcalfe and Wedderburn Tate, 1993). This phenomenon of limited career opportunities for women has been described as the 'glass ceiling': an invisible but impenetrable block to promotion beyond a certain level. Many of those occupations which are high status and demand high qualifications for entry show gender imbalance and it is likely that policies and incentives to attract women into these male dominated sectors have had limited success (Corti et al., 1995). This 'professional' sector of employment is growing, however, and Department of Employment forecasts (1992) suggest that it is women who will represent over half the increase in higher level employment (managers, professional, para-professionals and technicians).

In Britain, the proportion of the workforce that is female is the second highest in the European Union, behind only Denmark, yet the earnings gap is up to 10 per cent higher than across the rest of Europe. In March 1994, women constituted 46 per cent of the UK civilian workforce; 25 per cent of all self-employed people were women; and 47 per cent of all women employees were engaged on a part-time basis. On average, women's hourly wage was 80 per cent that of men's (Chwarau Teg 1994). Women will continue to play an increasingly prominent role in the British workforce: forecasting for the medium and long term, the Department for Employment (1993) argues that women will account for over 85 per cent of growth in the late 1990s. The social as well as economic implications of this should not be underestimated.

*The regional perspective*

Evidence from Yorkshire and Humberside suggests that women's employment patterns are broadly similar to the national situation in terms of the percentage of women employed, and the proportion of those women who are in full-time work (Kelly and Sanderson, 1994). An increasing number of women are economically active, although these activities are still considerably lower than for men. Recent research shows that the gender segregation of the subject preference base in schools is closely linked to subsequent occupational distribution: once in employment there is an uneven distribution of training and development activities undertaken by women in different occupations and industries (Knight and Pritchard, 1994).

Women working in the region are concentrated in the service sector and make up the majority of workers in the health, education, distribution, hotels and catering and banking and financial services sector. It has been these areas of work that have seen the greatest increase in women's participation, whereas the manufacturing sector has declined sharply as an employer of women. The growth of the numbers of women in employment over the last decade has coincided with the growth of the service sector: this has nationally always been a traditional employer of women, but it is likely that the continued decline of the predominantly male employment opportunities may result in increased competition for job opportunities in this area.

258

Around 23 per cent of all jobs in the region are part-time, that is 30 hours or fewer. Women hold 85 per cent of these posts: over the last decade, part-time employment has increased by 100,000, while the numbers in full-time employment have decreased by 20,000. This rapid and extensive growth in part time working has been greater in the Yorkshire and Humberside region than in Britain as a whole (Policy Research Unit, 1994).

In the region, average weekly full time pay is lower for women than for men across the full range of occupations, but the largest differential occurs in management and administration, where women on average earn £150 per week less than men. For example, women managers can expect to earn just 65.2 per cent of their male colleagues salary; for professionals this rises to 84.3 per cent, but still represents considerable disparity (New Earnings Survey, 1993).

It must be stressed that increased participation is in no way an indication that policies to enhance equality of opportunity have been implemented successfully. Leigh, Stillwell and Tickell (1994) have discussed the rapid increase in women's employment rates during the 1980s and comment how this increase has been partially informed by the shifting economic structure of the regional economy, and by an increased emphasis on flexible (i.e. cheap) labour. While women's earnings have risen at a faster rate than men's, this apparent feminisation of the labour force has not generally improved women's economic status. Indeed, the continuing growth of marginal and part-time working arrangements documented by Kelly and Sanderson have, in effect, decreased women's participation when assessed by Full Time Equivalent standards. Women are more likely to follow what is euphemistically referred to as a 'portfolio career' of poorly paid, part-time jobs, with high levels of double job holding (Kelly and Sanderson, 1994, p.10)

Many explanations about why women have remained disadvantaged at work have been offered during the second half of the 20th century, and an examination of prevailing theories of gender and work helps illuminate actions and initiatives.

## Explaining gender inequality: feminist perspectives and mainstream approaches

Much consideration has been given by feminist theorists to gender relations in employment (Witz and Savage, 1992; Cockburn, 1991) and a consideration of these feminist perspectives can offer insights into the causes and effects of structural inequality. The particular features that have typically attracted attention are: why do women normally earn less than men? Why do women engage in less paid work than men? Why do women do different jobs from men (Walby, 1990)? These analyses differ strongly from conventional approaches, which offer only superficial consideration of gender difference and make sexist assumptions about sex roles in society generally.

*Mainstream approaches*

Mainstream approaches include economic and sociological functionalism, which asserts that women's roles as carers prevent them from acquiring the necessary skills, qualifications and experience to compete on an equal footing with men for the jobs and benefits that are on offer (Becker, 1981; Mincer, 1962). An alternative perspective, the conventional liberal approach, is informed by role theory and focuses on the processes (including dual roles, cultural pressures and organisational features) which result in a differentiation between men and women's positions at work. The cumulative effect of these features is to prevent women achieving professional success (Kanter, 1977). In effect, this perspective (which has underpinned anti-discrimination legislation in the UK) sees unjustified disadvantage as a distortion of free competition which "embodies an individualistic and meritocratic emphasis on the need to unshackle personal talent and ability without regard to irrelevant group characteristics such as sex" (Collinson et al., 1990, p.11).

It is this focus on the need to maximise personal talent and to draw on the widest range of human resources which is a central tenet of current initiatives to enhance the employment prospects of women. Such an approach, however, ignores or devalues the causes and processes that lead to gender inequality: for this reason a consideration of feminist theories is essential to develop the context for this chapter.

*Feminist perspectives*

While the liberal and liberal feminist approaches have been highly influential, other theoretical approaches have also impacted substantially on feminist epistemology. For example, marxist feminist accounts stress that it is capitalism and the capital-labour relation that underpin women's employment patterns. Hence, gender relations are accommodated within class relations. Commentators have used Marx's original, non-gendered account of the reserve army of labour and have applied this to women (Beechey, 1987). Dual systems theorists, or socialist feminists (those who attempt to combine class analysis with gender analysis, through an exploration of the differential but equal impacts of both capitalism and

260

patriarchy), have considered the exclusion of women by men by way of job segregation: that is, barring women from the better kinds of work by closure or exclusion. Hartmann (1981) asserts that the gendered nature of the structure of employment cannot be understood in terms of capitalism and the domestic division of labour alone, and identifies a vicious circle in which women's forced absence from the best kinds of jobs leads to them taking on disproportionate domestic responsibilities.

Radical feminists, because of their empirical focus on sexuality and violence, have devoted far less time to a consideration of paid employment, although they have made an important contribution to the study of sexual harassment, and the unequal relations bound up within this practice. Sexual harassment in the workplace is a crucial and topical issue: the fact that women at work may be defined by men according to unspecified notions of femininity is disadvantageous, and clearly a way in which access and progress can be blocked. Most recently, Hearn and Parkin (1987) have examined the place of sexuality within ideology, and have asserted that, within the context of organisations and places of employment, this is overwhelmingly patriarchal, manifested by particular managerialist assumptions, organisational sub-cultures, the presence of sexual harassment and heterosexist language and joking. Current feminist debate has challenged all the theories outlines above, however, and has raised many questions about the existence of a feminist praxis in the 1990s.

*Feminism for the 1990s?*

Attempts to establish agreement or consensus on gender issues have been challenged most recently by post-feminists who see integrated theories as problematic if not impossible. This is because women as individuals experience such difference in their lives, on account of their class, race and cultural backgrounds (Tong, 1989). Rather, they proclaim the advantage of women's 'otherness' (De Beauvoir, 1949), viewing this as a way of thinking and being that "allows for openness, plurality diversity and difference" (Tong, 1989, p.219). Certainly echoes of these sentiments may be perceived in contemporary accounts of women and work.

The Employment Department suggests, for example, that increasing participation stems from changing economic and social attitudes, and from the increased availability of part-time work and better child care facilities, asserting that "self-employment and part-time work provide useful flexibility allowing many women to combine work with domestic commitments" (Department of Employment 1992, p.30). This statement reflects particular prevailing assumptions about the gendered nature of the division of labour and maintenance of family life in millennium Britain which would be challenged by many feminist commentators. However, the development of women's employment patterns must be set in the context of British society generally: For example, Collinson et al. (1990) note how the conventional divisions of labour along gender lines within the home are often considered to be the root cause of the routine legitimising of practices in access to employment which directly disadvantage women. They assert that a key factor which would constitute a significant impact towards organisational and attitudinal change would be the introduction of childcare facilities, in order to break down traditional perspectives and structures, while generating the level of flexibility in the workforce that is deemed to be essential to meet employers future demands. Clearly there are difficulties faced by working women at all levels: some of these are structural, some are attitudinal. According to Asplund (1987), a childless woman can expect to take three or four years longer to progress up the career ladder than her male colleague, while the woman who chooses to have children can expect to add another two or three years for each pregnancy.

Whichever theory of gender inequality one most ascribes to, it can be argued that the labour market is more significant (relative to the family/household) in determining women's participation rates than has previously been conceded, and that it is material constraints rather than choice or cultural values that affect women's employment patterns. The current focus on flexible working as a means of reconciling family responsibilities and work for women under-stresses the negative implications for women, particularly in terms of low-pay, reduced access to training and development, and the assumption of dual responsibilities for work and home-life. It also ignores many unresolved issues including the assumption of the *masculine* pattern of work as normal, with alternatives viewed as concessions, and notions of the male as the prime breadwinner. At the same time no real redetermination of social values is offered. These issues have been addressed by policy makers in some local authorities, however, and equal opportunities for women (and other disadvantaged groups) has been a significant aspect of the local authority agenda.

## Equal opportunities for women: the local authority context

Gender equality and equal opportunities are often perceived to be interchangeable terms. Equal opportunities as a term has its origins in British legal history in the context of post-war legislation to enhance the opportunities afforded to disabled ex-servicemen and women to obtain employment (Cheung-Judge and Henley, 1994). With specific reference to women, legislation was enacted in the 1970s (Equal Pay Act 1970, amended in 1983), and the Sex Discrimination Act 1975 (amended in 1986), together with the establishment of the Equal Opportunities Commission. This followed the Government White Paper *Equality for Women* which argued forcefully for practical solutions to change the status quo. This then paved the way for the establishment of local authority initiatives, which in retrospect can be most closely associated with the Labour-controlled Greater London Council (GLC), which was elected in 1980. Certainly the GLC took a lead in furthering vigorously the causes of disadvantaged and oppressed groups particularly in terms of combating inequalities in access to employment and other services. In 1982, the GLC became the first elected authority to establish a committee to promote the interests and welfare of women: by 1986 there were 30 such committees nation-wide. These initiatives can also be related to the first wave of British feminist action.

With many controversial methods the GLC certainly achieved a change in general attitudes towards equality of opportunity: many public and some private sector organisations became stated equal opportunities employers, and "within less than a decade the idea of equal opportunities changed from a sleepy ideological abstraction to a controversial and high profile fact of life" (Cheung Judge and Henley, 1994, p 3).

*Leeds: the regional perspective*

Leeds City Council has certainly not been labelled 'loony left' in the same way as the GLC and some of the London Boroughs, but it has been active in the development of policies and procedures to impact on and improve the life of women. Local authorities such as Leeds must be seen as key players in the equal opportunities arena, partly because the growth in their importance as employers of women has, over the last 20 years, far outstripped that of the economy as a whole (Stone, 1988), and partly because of their profile in terms of service delivery and enabling. Leeds City Council is a major employer of local women, but those in senior positions are in a minority (see Table 15.1)

While generally it remains the case that key decision-making about the way local authorities are administered and managed is in the control of men (Leeds is not atypical in that it has a 'pyramid' structure within its officer profile), Leeds as a region has a history of feminist action (Rowbotham, Segal and Wainwright 1979), and Leeds City Council has had a women's committee for over a decade. The present (1995) Chair of the Women's Committee attributes its present strength to successful outreach work and an incrementalist approach from a small base. This has avoided major restructuring and shedding of resources which has been a feature of several of the pioneering London Boroughs.

## Table 15.1 Employment profile by gender, Leeds City Council

| | |
|---|---|
| Percentage of women employed in all departments | 75.5 |
| Percentage of those on posts graded PO1 and above | 33.8 |
| Percentage of women employed in the Direct Services Organisation | 56.8 |
| Percentage of those on posts graded PO1 and above | 11.2 |

Note: PO = Principal Officer

*Source: LCC payroll March 1994, cited in Women's Committee Report 13.9.94*


### Equality and business: an ideological collision?

Evidence of the actual location of women in the workforce of the Leeds region would suggest that there is a gap between theory and practice in terms of equal opportunities. There is reason to assert that for many employers, equal opportunities remains an issue of marginal concern. The actuality of employment indicates that women's disadvantaged position in the work force is informed by both structural and attitudinal barriers. That is, established ways of working conflict with women's needs and out of work responsibilities, and in the work-place women are hampered by prevailing conceptions about the appropriateness of their participation, or an unawareness of inequality. A consideration of ideology is effective in that it provides a vehicle for an examination of how particular behaviours and attitudes are adopted to establish a power position which is then perceived as natural or ideal, and that it illustrates how culturally sexist behaviour or attitudes are part of this ideology. Connell (1987) describes how, in contemporary theory, there is a strong tendency to make ideology the site of sexual politics, and he agrees that it is in studies of the workplace that the interplay of situation and ideology is clearest. For example, he describes how the ideology of the "natural" weakness of women and their unsuitability for work as compositors in the printing industry effectively expelled women from this sector of work. Similarly Collinson et al. (1990) discuss how ideological rationalisation for discriminatory action by managers in an insurance company occurred not as excuses, but as the articulation of the validity of the explanation: their actions were normal and natural.

Recent commentaries on the economic strength and future potential of Leeds and the surrounding region have adopted a largely gender blind approach. Indeed Ian Green, writing in the *Investors Chronicle* (24.11.94) refers to the "men of the building societies" and attributes the region's successes in part to the "tenacity... and natural bluntness of the Yorkshireman." Is this a manifestation of a particular form of (patriarchal) ideology? Certainly the populist image of this blunt Yorkshireman is one which lends itself to witticisms and jokes. "But this is Yorkshire, not Islington" was the attention grabbing bullet point used by Michael Bichard, Director of the Benefits Agency, when he delivered a presentation to Opp2K members on 'Implementing an Equal Opportunities in a Traditional Hierarchical Organisation' on 23rd March 1994. His good humoured, if flippant suggestion that the region projected a less than progressive attitude is not without its serious side. One of the few women Chief Executives of a local authority, describing her 14 year sojourn in Leeds during the last decade, including her employment experience at a very senior level, offers a precise impression of a pervasive ideology within her world of work. It led her to believe that the women here were really up against it.

That's where you see the most crude outcome of that male dominated, intensely secretive culture that grows up around power and influence... it was a closed society where women were not supposed to participate They sold the last woman into marriage in the market place at Barnoldswick, Lancashire in 1926. Women are regarded as chattels. They are allowed to work but men are supposed to run society (Coote and Patullo, 1990, p.49)

It should be stressed that such attitudes and cultures are not exclusive to the region, but recent research does indicate a continuing lack of awareness, or acceptance of unhelpful practices.

*Equality strategies in Leeds*

As part of a recent research project on women and the Leeds economy which was undertaken by the Policy Research Unit on behalf of Leeds City Council and the Leeds TEC, quantitative and qualitative information was collated on the implementation (or lack of) equality initiatives for women by a range of companies and local organisations. A total of 254 companies supplied information during a telephone survey. More substantial details about the issues surrounding positive action measures to enhance women's participation at work on a more balanced footing were elicited during 30 personal follow-up interviews with selected companies, as well as four with key local organisations (Kelly and Sanderson, 1994). The nature of women's participation rates across the sample (women constituted almost half the employees, were six times more likely to be employed part time and half as likely to be full time) led the authors to consider that the survey data, being broadly in line with national trends (New Earnings Survey 1993), was an accurate baseline by which future trends and progress could be measured. For the purposes of that research, measures to enhance the position of women were defined as family-friendly policies, that is:

> not only those arrangements which concentrate on the reconciliation of family responsibilities with employment requirements, but also practices which cover training, development, support and equality considerations which benefit employees irrespective of gender, or whether or not they have family responsibilities (Kelly and Sanderson, 1994, p.35)

The responses gave an accurate indication of the levels of attention that had been directed towards gender equality. A key feature was the perceived correlation by employers between so-called family/employee-friendly working practices and cost effectiveness, with this economic criterion being a driving force behind the implementation. The business advantages to employers of adopting this family friendly approach was seen to offer more flexibility, to facilitate a reduction in costs, to optimise human resources (sometimes by 'down-sizing') and to improve public image. It has also been suggested, however, that increased flexibility correlates with increased casualisation, fewer legal entitlements and slower career progression for individuals, together with a weakening of trade union activity (Mouriki, 1994). The link between increased business opportunity and more equality of opportunity does seem tenuous: two-thirds of the sample group had equal opportunities policies but the incidence varied according to the nature of the organisation: for example 80% of public sector organisations had developed them compared with only half of companies involved in the retailing trade. The fact that only 60% of all organisations with an equal opportunities policy have determined an action plan, through which to transform policy into practice indicates that a substantial number of these statements have a merely cosmetic value. Indeed the report considers that it is concern for the company's image which is by far the most important consideration in the development of an equal opportunities policy.

*Actions speak louder than words*

The qualitative response element of the research impacts most strongly. Only

266

a minority of organisations with an explicit policy statement had actually used strategic planning or positive action as a central plank of policy: there was generally a strategic vacuum as to how gender equality might relate to the wider aspects of human resource management. Nevertheless, the majority of responding organisations genuinely believed that their organisations offered equality of opportunity for women. A benchmark system for comparison is the Department for Employment's (1992) 10 point plan for employers, a voluntarist, incrementalist strategy designed to provide guidelines for the development of fair and equitable practices. The Department has issued a package to elaborate on its basic tenets for achieving a more equal workplace (see Table 15.2). The message being conveyed is that, while inequality and discrimination is morally reprehensible it is equally bad business sense, for equal opportunities is really a natural and integral ingredient of good management practice, which will ultimately benefit the organisation as much as redress individual wrongs.

While there is little that is radical or costly contained within these proposals, only one per cent of Kelly and Sanderson's sample had implemented points 1-9 of the plan and 33 per cent had implemented one or no points. Despite their apparent belief in their own reputation as being impervious to promoting or merely perpetuating practices and procedures that do not enhance gender equality, employers were making little or no concerted attempt to engage in a tangible process to monitor and reflect.

Although evidence from British Social Attitudes suggests that attitudes to gender equality have changed over the last 20 years and that the principle of equality of opportunity appears to be broadly accepted (Jowell et al., 1993), in 1995 it is likely that many people have not yet disentangled the political and emotional legacies of equal opportunities and are ambivalent or confused about what the significance may be for business organisations. It remains associated with political extremism, particularly the "loony left." By the same token, attitudes towards the concept of feminism indicate a tendency to dissociate and disregard (Siann and Wilkinson, 1995).

### Equality or diversity: which one prevails?

Politics and the state are important in the structuring of the sexual division of labour (Walby 1990) and for this reason there must be a concerted effort by employing organisations with public endorsement to challenge this status quo. That there is a strong business case for expanding the role of women in the workforce is a most voguish concept. Current emphasis is placed on the economic rationale for the promotion of diversity (that is non-traditional

## Table 15.2 Equal opportunities ten point plan for employers

1. Develop an equal opportunities policy, embracing recruitment, promotion and training
2. Set an action plan including targets, so that you and your staff have a clear idea of what can be achieved and by when.
3. Provide training for all, to help people, including management, throughout your organisation to understand the importance of equal opportunities, and provide additional training for staff who recruit, select and train your employees.
4. Monitor the present position to establish your starting point, and monitor progress in achieving objectives to identify successes and shortfalls.
5. Review recruitment, selection, promotion and training procedures regularly to ensure that good intentions are being put into practice.
6. Draw up clear and justifiable job criteria and ensure these are objective and job related.
7. Offer pre-employment training, where appropriate, to prepare potential job applicants for selection tests and interviews and positive action training to help under-represented groups.
8. Consider your organisation's image; do you encourage applicants from under-represented groups and feature women, ethnic minority staff and people with disabilities in recruitment literature, or could you be seen as an employer who marginalises these groups?
9. Consider flexible working, career breaks, provision of childcare facilities etc. to help women in particular meet domestic responsibilities and pursue their occupations: and the provision of special equipment and assistance to help people with disabilities.
10. Develop links with local community groups, organisations and schools, and so reach out to a wider pool of potential recruits.

*Source: Department for Employment 1992*

structures) in the workforce. There is certainly a business case for this revived interest in gender issues, but should this, together with the quest for competitiveness and total quality, override moral considerations of equity and justice?

Joanna Foster, the then Chair of the Equal Opportunities Commission, stressed this business case in 1991 when she stated that equal opportunities in the 1990s was about economic efficiency and social justice, in that order. The forceful message is that wasting women's abilities is bad management practice. As Taylor asserts, "keeping an open mind about who can do what will mean a more efficient business" (Taylor, 1994, p.3).

This suggests that, while employers might take a particular stance on women's work issues on the grounds of social justice, there are stronger business arguments for redressing the imbalances and injustices that are still manifest in most aspects of working life, and it is those arguments that carry most weight with employers who wish and need to maintain a competitive edge.

*National initiatives*

The most significant recent national initiative to redress structural gender inequality in the workforce was launched by John Major, the Prime Minister, on October 28th, 1991. Opportunity 2000 is a business-led campaign which is independent of the Government, and is aiming to promote the business case of equalising opportunities at a national and local level. That is to say, it presents a voluntarist case for creating a balanced workforce. Opportunity 2000 requires that its members set their own targets for increasing the representation of women throughout their organisation, by means of establishing individual ways by which they can achieve a balanced workforce with men and women at all levels by the end of the century.

*The role and effectiveness of Leeds City Council*

Many local authorities have taken the decision to become members of Opportunity 2000. Indeed, there are a significant number of employers in the Leeds area who believe that it is a worthwhile and beneficial arrangement. Leeds City Council, however, has chosen not to make a formal association with the initiative, but has opted to plough a parallel but separate and distinct furrow. In Leeds, 'Opp2K' was launched at the Marriott Hotel on 16th November 1993, by the Right Hon. David Hunt MP, Secretary of State for Employment. Opp2K operates within the auspices of the Leeds Initiative, a partnership established in 1990 and made up of a variety of public and private sector organisations. One of the original objectives of the Leeds Initiative was to "ensure the economic vitality of the city" (Leeds City Council, 1993). Part of this project then involves improving women's participation in the workforce and part of this thrust has included the establishment of Opp2K.

The local venture, which has broadly similar aims and objectives and shares common goals, but is independent from the national programme, was launched to facilitate a local collaborative venture to redress inequalities in the workplace. The focus of the initiative, therefore, is to disseminate information on how an equalising process will bring advantages to everyone: men; women; employers and employees. This is pertinent in the context of the present and future role of the local authority. In the 1990s, many local authority functions are being subjected to a blurring of boundaries: the relationships with the private sector and the voluntary sector are rapidly changing and the promotion of business principles is being applied throughout the institutional world. Indeed the Local Government Management Board sees the future role of the local authority as "using its overview and knowledge of local patterns of provision to inform and promote good practice" (LGMB, 1993, p.2).

*The specific aims and objectives of Opp2K*

Opp2K aims "to enrich the future of Leeds by drawing to the full on the currently untapped or undervalued contribution of all its women" and to "work in partnership with the appropriate agencies to support and encourage Leeds employers to achieve a more balanced workforce by creating more opportunities for all women through recruitment, retention, development and promotion" (Siddall et al., 1994, p.27).

While Opp2K is sponsored by the Leeds Initiative, it is financed by its members and relies heavily on partnership. Opp2K draws its membership from a variety of organisations with current emphasis lying in the private sector. Local education institutions are participating alongside Leeds City Council, the Chamber of Commerce and major local employers including Asda, Yorkshire Water, Barclays Bank, Marks and Spencer and the British Library. These are joined by a number of smaller but influential organisations including solicitors' practices and media/marketing agencies. A steering committee directs the focus for action and is using commissioned research as a basis for focusing on all women who work in Leeds.

Three main strands have been identified: the retail and distribution trades; the clothing industry, and banking and finance. This has informed a decision to target certain business areas with a strategy of capturing major influencers with a view to achieving a trickle-down effect to the smaller companies. The co-ordinator advocates a persuasive approach with an emphasis on promoting the benefits of membership in terms discussed below, while at the same time offering a support service, acting as a source of information to facilitate interested organisations, and offering a less traditional, more accessible networking opportunity (interview with Carolyn Collier, co-ordinator of Opp2K, July 1994).

Opp2K is therefore a broad-based initiative relying on partnership which seeks to enhance the job and career opportunities of women in Leeds, and in so doing, enrich the future of Leeds itself by releasing so much untapped or undervalued potential. Opp2K differs from the national Opportunity 2000 initiative in that it has not set hard targets which will be measured against specific performance indicators. Rather it seeks, by the year 2000, to "achieve a measurable increase in the number and position of women in the Leeds workforce and in activities which will help shape the economic, social, political and cultural future of the city" (Opp2K information pack for launch, 16.11.93).

Its general approach is one of persuasion and co-operation, with an emphasis on the range of benefits opened up to employers participating in the scheme. Such benefits identified include: the achievement of market advantage, by reflecting the range of the customer/client base; the achievement of organisational advantage by being able to draw on a wider variety of managerial styles and developing a more flexible structure that is responsive to the dynamics of change; attaining a strategic advantage by pre-empting demographic trends and maximising the potential of the workforce; and achieving a human resource advantage by selecting the most appropriate applicants for situations, whilst also fostering loyalty and commitment amongst staff.

*Cascading good practice*

A linked but independent project. has recently been launched by the Leeds Initiative. Leeds City Council successfully proposed the Women's Labour Market Integration Programme through the European "exchange of ideas programme" (a forum for the consideration of urban regeneration). Five cities are involved and Leeds, being the lead authority, has overall responsibility for co-ordination and financial control. Leipzig and Lisbon, Glasgow and Munich are the other participants. Local issues obviously vary in their relative immediacy: in Leipzig for example, a particular cause for concern is the high unemployment rates for women following reunification, whereas the Leeds focus is less on the quantity of jobs but rather their quality (with particular reference to homeworking in the textile/clothing and printing sectors). This project is therefore unique in that it has tapped into a pot of money which has hitherto been used for traditional urban regeneration work, such as tourism. Crucially, the economic development strategy, which adopts a sector approach (Chapter 5), also focuses on issues which cut across all sectors, and one of these is the role and potential of women in the economy. This project thus offers a prime opportunity to publicise and promote Opp2K as an exemplar, as a local initiative which is unique both in the UK and the European Community.

## Is Opp2K working?

One of the reasons for the apparent success of Opp2K in attracting members is that it stresses the economic case for gender equality rather then any particular theory of social equity or feminism. That is to say, it totally avoids association with concepts or movements that attract controversy or conflict. For example, consider the work done by Opp2K on drawing organisations' attention to sexual harassment in the workplace. Sexual harassment is now recognised as constituting unlawful sex discrimination (Kirby, 1990). However, both definitions of the nature of harassment and procedures for eliminating it have drawn very mixed reactions.

Opp2K's approach has been to highlight the major and practical disincentives involved in failing to tackle harassment. These include the recent removal of the ceilings for compensation and the bad publicity associated with cases, as well as the possibility of European sanctions (individuals being subjected to imprisonment), rather than any notion of "political correctness." Indeed, there is a tendency to dissociate from identification with feminism. This rather suggests that despite the thorough feminist epistemologies outlined earlier, measures to promote gender equality are less informed by any form of women's movement than has been the case in the past, and that feminist praxis is bearing increasingly little relevance to contemporary public life. This is partially illustrated by the apparent distance between Opp2K and the Women's Committee of Leeds City Council. In a conversation on 2nd February 1995, Cllr. Lowe outlined her perceptions of Opp2K and the work it has achieved so far. It is certainly seen by the women's committee as an important and significant initiative but must be set into a particular context where the local authority has other urgent and pressing concerns, including aspects of service delivery, recruitment and selection issues and specific duties towards constituents. That there are benefits in looking holistically at women's lives is indisputable, but Opp2K does not replace the more traditional approaches favoured by Labour local authorities. Many women, particularly those limited in their access to secure employment, are marginalised or excluded from the benefits of the initiative.

### Drawbacks and merits

A major flaw in this type of partnership is that it is voluntary and progress can be slow: reliance on goodwill is a fault of the partnership structure in that either the public or the private sector, working independently, may achieve faster results. The nature of the structure also encourages the development of a growing bureaucracy to fulfil the complex administration needed by this type of organisation. When participation in steering groups and committees is voluntary, there is a heavy reliance on individual commitment which is difficult to sustain when there are competing and conflicting demands on time.

That Leeds has chosen not to be a part of the national initiative has both merits and drawbacks. The reasons for not associating with Opportunity 2000 are unclear, but it is likely that they are politically motivated. On the one hand this leads to confusion between the two and a lack of clarity in identifying the different rationales underpinning the initiatives. Some observers appear to believe that the schemes are inter-changeable and this is clearly not the case. There has been a considered decision to establish an independent initiative - Opportunity 2000 does appear to be dominated by larger companies and Leeds City Council did want to emphasise the importance and the relevance of input by smaller companies. While during the first six months large organisations were targeted, because income generation was a priority, small and medium companies are perceived to be crucial to the success of the initiative (interview with Steering Group member, Christine Atkinson, 10th March 1995). This reflects European Commission thinking that it is the small and medium enterprise sector that will be the main generator of new jobs and where the best uses and development of women's work may be made (CEC White Paper, 1993).

**Conclusions**

The key issues considered in this chapter have been whether the basic tenets of equal opportunities are being addressed by Opp2K, the extent to which Opp2K is informed by a feminist agenda, and the potential impact of the initiative. In the absence of legislative measures to promote positive action (and these are unlikely to be forthcoming), this chapter has revealed that there are clearly benefits in the pragmatic approach which focuses on family friendly policies and stresses the business case for enhancing women's participation in the workforce. This appeals to a wide range of organisations and any underlying messages concerning social justice can obviously be disseminated. Meanwhile, such an initiative does not attempt to redress the basic sexist structures of society and there could be a moral dilemma for some in pandering to the white male agenda. Certainly there appears to be a level of cynicism in the attitude of those self-defined working class women who see Opp2K's key players as 'pandering.' However, given the overall gap between words and deeds in the development of equal opportunities policies across the employers of Leeds, the Opp2K approach is probably the most appropriate, given current antipathy to notions of feminism that have been noted.

An incremental approach can certainly lead to a situation where trailblazing women are in a position to ameliorate the situation for others, and there is a real need in Leeds for some alternative role models. A lot of what Opp2K is about though, is networking, and transferring information by word of mouth, and it is most likely that there are areas of sexism and racism that will be untouched by the culture of Opp2K. However, it could well be that an incrementalist approach based on co-operation may be most appropriate given prevailing attitudes to gender equality in the area, and Leeds City Council has certainly grasped that pragmatism, ultimately, is a more convincing approach than coercion. It would appear that any feminist agenda is subsumed within the culture of competition and business. This implies that Leeds City Council has grasped the need to stress particular advantages in this partnership situation and, while liberal feminist strategies may underpin specific action, they are by no means explicit. The potential impact of Opp2K has yet to be assessed. It is unique, and its very existence ultimately reflects a far sighted and sophisticated approach to public/private partnerships which is both a national and international example of good practice.

## References

Alimo Metcalfe, B., Wedderburn Tate, C. (1993), 'Women in Business in the UK,' Davidson, M.J. and Cooper, C.L. (eds) *European Women in Business and Management,* Paul Chapman Publishing, London.

Asplund, G. (1988), *Women Managers: changing organisational cultures,* Wiley, Chichester.

Becker, G.S., (1981), *A Treatise on the Family,* Harvard University Press, Cambridge Mass.

Beechey, V. (1987), *Unequal Work,* Verso, London.

CEC (1993), *Growth, Competitiveness, Employment,* CEC, Brussels.

Cheung-Judge, M. & Henley, A. (1994), *Equality in Action: introducing equal opportunities in voluntary organisations,* NCVO, London.

Chwarae Teg (1994), *Fair Play for Women,* Employment Department/EOC, London.

Cockburn C. (1991), *In the Way of Women: men's resistance to sex equality in organisations,* MacMillan, London.

Collinson, D.L., Knights, D. and Collinson, M. (1990), *Managing to Discriminate,* Routledge, London.

Connell, R.W. (1987), *Gender and Power: society, the person and sexual politics,* Polity Press, London

Corti, L. and Dex, S. (1995), 'Highly qualified women,' *Employment Gazette*, March 1995.

Dale, A. (1987), 'Occupational inequality, gender and life cycle,' *Work, Employment and Society,* 1 (3), 326-351.

De Beauvoir, S., (1949), *Le Deuxieme Sexe*, Gallimard, Paris.

Department for Employment (1992), *Equal Opportunities Ten Point Plan for Employers*, Employment Department Group, London.

Employment Gazette (1993), 'Women in the labour market,' *Employment Gazette,* Department for Employment, London

Equal Opportunities Commission (1991), *Women and Men in Britain,* HMSO, London.

Foreman A., Kelly, M. and Percy-Smith J., (1995), 'Fair Play for Women in Yorkshire and Humberside: a study for the Government Office for Yorkshire and Humberside,' Policy Research Unit, Leeds.

Hartmann, H. (1981), 'The unhappy marriage of marxism and feminism: towards a more progressive union,' in Sargent, L. (ed), *Women and Revolution,* Pluto, London.

Hearn, J. and Parkin, W. (1987), *Sex at Work: the power and paradox of organisation sexuality*, Wheatsheaf, London.

Jowell, R. et al. (1993), *British Social Attitudes*, Gower, London.

Kanter, R.M. (1977), *Men and Women of the Corporation*, Basic Books, New York.

Kelly, M. and Sanderson, I., (1994), 'Women and the Leeds Economy: a Sector Study,' (Draft), Policy Research Unit, Leeds.

Kirby, R. (1990), 'Sexual harassment at work,' IRLI Bulletin No. 398, April 1990.

Knight, J. and Pritchard, S. (1994), 'Women's development programmes: no, we're not colour consultants!' in Tanton, M. (ed) *Women in Management: a Developing Presence*, Routledge, London.

Leeds City Council, (1994), *The Leeds Initiative Annual Report 1994-1994*, LCC, Leeds.

Leigh, C., Stillwell, J. and Tickell, A. (1994), 'The West Yorkshire economy: breaking with tradition,' in Haughton, G. and Whitney, D., *Reinventing a Region: restructuring in West Yorkshire,* Avebury, Aldershot.

Local Government Management Board (1993), *Local Government Community Leadership: the strategic role of the local authority,* LGMB Luton.

Mincer, J. (1962), "Labour force participation of married women: a study of labour supply" in National Bureau of Economic Research, *Aspects of Labour Economics*, Princeton University Press, Princeton.

Mouriki, A. (1994), 'Flexible Working: towards further degradation of work, or escaping from stereotypes?' *Warwick Papers in Industrial Relations,* No. 49, Industrial Relations Research Unit, University of Warwick, Coventry.

New Earnings Survey (1993), *New Earnings Survey,* HMSO, London.

Policy Research Unit (1994), 'Women in the Yorkshire and Humberside economy: a study for the Employment Department's Yorkshire and Humberside Regional Office,' Leeds Metropolitan University, Leeds.

Rosener, J. (1990), 'Ways women lead,' *Harvard Business Review,* 68, 119-25.

Rowbotham S., Segal, L., and Wainwright, H. (1979), *Beyond the Fragments: feminism and the making of socialism,* Merlin Press, London

Siann, G., Wilkinson, H. (1995), *Gender, Feminism and the Future,* DEMOS, London.

Siddall, K., King, H., Coleman, T., and Cotton, B. (1994), 'Working for women working in Leeds,' *Executive Development,* 7 (3), 27-29.

Stone, I. (1988), *Equal Opportunities in Local Authorities: developing effective strategies for the implementation of policies for women,* HMSO, London.

Taylor, G. (1994), *Equal Opportunities: a practical handbook,* Industrial Society, London.

Tong, R. (1989), *Feminist Thought: a comprehensive introduction,* Routledge, London.

Walby, S. (1990), *Theorizing Patriarchy,* Blackwell, Oxford.

White, B., Cox, C., and Cooper, C. (1992), *Women's Career Development: a Study of High Flyers,* Blackwell, Oxford.

Witz, A. and Savage, M. (eds) (1992), *Gender and Bureaucracy,* Blackwell, Oxford.

# 16 Social inequalities, housing needs and the targeting of housing investment in Leeds

*Celia Moran*

## Introduction

This chapter examines housing and housing investment in Leeds, with a particular emphasis on the targeting of public sector housing investment and the so-called inner city problem. The analysis begins with an examination of urban decline within the city, focusing on social and housing inequalities. The case for targeted housing intervention in dealing with stress areas is reviewed, and its application to Leeds is discussed as part of an assessment of the changing pattern of public housing investment in the city. Over time, the geographical focus of spending has shifted away from the traditional inner city areas, in part relating to changes in identified areas of housing stress, and in part relating to the funding constraints imposed by central government, which increasingly have privileged new build over rehabilitation work. As part of this theme, the analysis focuses on the work of Leeds Partnership Homes, a social housing partnership between the Leeds City Council and five housing associations. In conclusion, the likely impact of recent and future developments in housing policy and practice are considered.

## Urban decline in Leeds

As Chapter 4 has already illustrated, the main socio-economic indicators in Leeds reveals a distinctive pattern of spatial segregation, with the inner areas generally least favoured. A similar story emerges in terms of housing tenure and quality patterns, where again there is a marked polarisation between the inner city and outer areas. The inner city of Leeds, consisting of twelve of the city's thirty-two electoral wards, contains large areas of poor housing in both public and private sectors and a concentration of households experiencing multiple social and economic deprivation. This area of Leeds has suffered serious losses in industrial employment, particularly in textiles and clothing and in mechanical engineering (Leeds City Council, 1993a, p.3), and high levels of unemployment (Chapter 3). Of particular concern are the high rates of long-term unemployment, male unemployment and unemployment amongst young people and ethnic minorities; the concentration of unskilled and partly skilled workers; and, the limited residential and labour market mobility of many residents. Moreover, recent research has found that incomes in the inner city wards were 66.8 per cent of the EU average and that full and partial benefit dependency were 139.6 per cent and 146.8 per cent respectively of the EU average (reported in Leeds City Council, 1993a, p.12).

## Housing tenure and condition in Leeds

Housing provision in Leeds has been influenced and shaped by a wide variety of factors, including general economic change, central government policy and finance, and also local determinants, such as key influential city leaders (see Gibson and Langstaff, 1982). In broad terms, the geography of housing in Leeds is similar to that of most similar-sized, older UK cities, with its oldest areas of inner city terraced housing closest to the urban core, large areas of post-second world war council housing around the periphery (but still largely within what is accepted as the inner city boundary), and better quality owner-occupied property in the suburbs and satellite villages.

Of the 296,100 dwellings in the city, approximately 70 per cent are privately-owned (owner-occupied or privately-rented), 27 per cent are local authority-owned, and 3.5 per cent are housing association-owned. Compared to national figures, there is a slight skew in favour of council housing at the expense of the private sector, with housing associations representing a similar proportion to the national average.

Whilst there is no fully comprehensive data about the locational characteristics and conditions of housing in Leeds, information from the 1991 Census (Airaud, 1993) and from local authority documents (Leeds City Council, 1990, 1992a, 1992b), together provide strong indicative evidence of the major patterns. Geographically, Leeds retains a distinctive urban core which includes much of the city's stock of poor-condition private housing, mainly pre-1919 terraced housing, including more than 17,700 back-to-back houses. These are usually low grade, privately-rented and low income

278

owner-occupation houses, with a high incidence of unfitness and disrepair. Four of the inner wards (Harehills, Chapel Allerton, Headingley and University) also contain the highest proportion of ethnic minority households, with Harehills also having the greatest incidence of over-crowding (Airaud, 1993).

Many of the 80,000 council houses are concentrated within the inner city wards of Burmantofts and Seacroft, and to a slightly lesser extent within University, Richmond Hill, Hunslet and Middleton, and the outer wards of Bramley and Whinmoor. Much of this housing is situated on large medium- and low-rise post-war estates on the edge of the older urban core, with particular stock quality problems concentrated in Richmond Hill, Harehills, Seacroft, Hunslet, Middleton and Bramley, with only the latter falling outside the inner city boundary. Although some of these are high- or medium-rise flats and maisonettes, the city council's flirtation with the larger deck access developments, which are still such a burden for many large cities, ended with the demolition of Hunslet Grange in the mid-1980s. Within these areas are clearly identifiable neighbourhoods which display the typical social, economic and physical characteristics of multiple deprivation: poverty, high unemployment, racial tension, crime and vandalism, as well as unsatisfactory housing and a poor environment.

In Leeds as elsewhere, poor housing cuts across all tenures, although the problems associated with each type can vary considerably (cf Forrest and Murie, 1980, p.35). In the social-rented sector, continued residualisation of council housing means that deprived families are often to be found in unpopular local authority estates, in houses or flats which suffer from design faults and inadequate repair and maintenance (English, 1979). Recent research has warned that this pattern could now be repeating itself with respect to new housing association schemes (Page, 1993). Areas of older private housing, especially in the inner city, also demonstrate problems of decay brought about by a lack of investment: this can be attributed in part to high levels of private renting and to marginal home ownership (Mason, 1979), and in part to trends in housing renewal policy and activity.

What emerges from this analysis is that housing problems in Leeds are most closely associated with two broad types of area. The first is the traditional inner city area of older (pre-1919) poor quality terraced housing which forms the bottom end of the owner-occupied and private rented sectors. The second is the low-grade peripheral, post-war council estate, frequently high-rise, but in the case of Leeds, predominantly medium- or low-rise, and frequently suffering physical neglect. Whilst declining housing quality is associated with wider economic and social change, poor conditions overall (in particular large council estates), are often more the result of public sector decision-making (Maclennan et al., 1990, p.69).

## Urban policy and targeted housing investment

Housing intervention has rarely been effective in the battle against inner city or urban decay. In the past, as Forrest and Murie (1980, p.82) point out, it has mainly consisted of 'bending' mainstream capital programmes towards priority areas. However, there are those who criticise such an area-based approach, partly because of the differential rates of growth and decay inherent within a capitalist system, and partly because in simple numerical terms many deprived people and unsatisfactory houses can be found outside of identified priority areas (Holterman, 1978; Kearns, 1990). Therefore, effective housing policy must also tackle broader aspects of deprivation, in particular the economic prospects of residents. Much of the available evidence indicates that past area-based intervention has been largely ineffective. Paris and Blackaby (1979) argue, for example, that the rehabilitation programmes of the 1970s produced little improvement: indeed there is now a general consensus that many Housing Action Areas and General Improvement Areas did little more than to slow the rate of deterioration in the targeted areas.

Notwithstanding these arguments, the benefits of targeted housing action are also well documented. Maclennan (1985), in his study of housing association rehabilitation in Glasgow, criticises past analyses for failing to consider the wider economic impacts of housing policies on neighbourhood, urban and regional scales, and attempts to measure these 'spillover' benefits to support the case for continued investment. Investment in construction, for example, has a significant multiplier effect in creating employment in the local economy, an effect which is usually greater in areas where land prices are low (Regional Equity Group, 1992). Carley (1990, pp.28-29) concludes that although neighbourhoods are part of a world capitalist system, meaning that action at the local level is inevitably constrained in what it can achieve, nonetheless "change at local level is both possible and desirable. Indeed, the neighbourhood is a good level of social interaction and change, and neighbourhoods (like cities) may be able to shift themselves from the economic and social periphery back towards the mainstream of capitalist culture."

Concentrated housing deprivation is not simply a function of housing market processes, to be dealt with by a compartmentalised housing policy. Although recent initiatives, such as Estate Action, City Challenge, Renewal Areas and the Single Regeneration Budget (SRB), increasingly acknowledge that this is the case and advocate a comprehensive and co-ordinated strategy aimed at addressing all aspects of social and economic deprivation, it must also be recognised that the immediate possibilities are constrained by short-term political and economic considerations. It remains incumbent upon local authorities and other agencies, therefore, to operate within the legal and administrative framework, and with the resources and partners available to them, in a positive and imaginative way to make whatever contribution they can to meeting housing need and ameliorating disadvantage.

## The strategic context

Set within the 'new right' agenda of the Thatcher and Major administrations, urban policy since 1979 has been based on the view that direct intervention in the past has contributed to, rather than alleviated inner city decline by restricting private enterprise. Drawing upon this analysis, recent policy interventions have sought to encourage the private sector and to facilitate the market rather than displace it (Lawless, 1989). Within this context, local authorities are charged with "taking a strategic approach to housing needs and acting as enablers to secure the effective development and use of all tenures" (Department of Environment, 1995, p.11). Allocation of mainstream funding for the local authority capital programme and housing association development, plus supplementary funding for initiatives such as Estate Action, Single Regeneration Budget and City Challenge, are all determined on the basis of competitive bidding. Judgement is based on: the local authority's effectiveness in identifying housing need and the nature of the problems; and, the extent to which the local authority has embraced an enabling role. The enabling role involves setting a local strategic framework, exploring new partnerships and initiatives, levering in private finance, and achieving housing provision and renewal through other agencies. The city council in Leeds is, therefore, pivotal to housing activity across the city, and sets the tone for investment through partnership and participation amongst other agencies and the local community.

There are in essence two key dimensions to the strategic context as set by the local authority. Firstly, the Unitary Development Plan (UDP), produced by the planning authority, gives an overall assessment of housing need and planned provision for a ten year period. Secondly, there are the more detailed priorities and proposals of the housing authority, most notably the Housing Investment Programme, which constitutes the annual bid for credit approval from the Department of the Environment. However, the matter is further complicated by the growing importance of the Housing Corporation in allocating and distributing resources to housing associations, whose policies and priorities need to be superimposed upon, and reconciled with, those of the local authority.

The housing authority, then, has the key role, but cannot set the context without due consideration and collaboration with the planning authority, the

Department of the Environment, the Housing Corporation and local housing associations. Partnership is clearly the key to an appropriate and workable strategic framework. Given that the main purpose of this co-operation is to secure public resources for the city and to attract private investment, the approach in Leeds is unashamedly top-down. What is also apparent, however, when considering the nature of partnerships, and the forces which determine public sector housing investment, is that decisions are led by a thinly veiled pragmatism which is ostensibly about finding innovative and effective solutions to housing problems, but in reality is concerned primarily with securing maximum resources. As a result, the local authority has no alternative but to grapple with a range of inherent tensions concerned with establishing and meeting priorities and need, providing the right environment in which housing associations and the private sector can operate, and satisfying the demands of both the Department of the Environment and the Housing Corporation.

There is considerable evidence within the strategic documentation produced by Leeds City Council, that the benefits of concentrating resources are recognised. The planning authority expresses concern about the extent of housing disrepair and unfitness within the city and recognises that the burden of maintenance that this represents is beyond the resources of the local authority alone (Leeds City Council, 1992b). It supports a strategy which seeks to continue the targeting of funding for private sector renewal into priority areas within the inner city. Similarly, for public sector housing there is support for the concentration of resources through the Estate Action programme: "Priority will be given to the improvement of the quality of the housing stock within the defined urban renewal areas, and within those council estates subject to the council's Estate Action Programme" (p.75). It is notable that, whilst in the past this has tended to focus upon programmes concentrated within the inner city, future policies and programmes will apply to "pockets and problems" within "identifiable neighbourhoods and localities" across the entire district (p.116).

In line with Government policy, the housing authority has sought to concentrate its own diminishing resources upon the repair and modernisation of its own stock, especially through the Estate Action Programme at Belle Isle North, Gipton South, Halton Moor and Ebor Gardens, and also upon assistance with the improvement of private housing. At the same time, housing association development through the Leeds Partnership Homes (LPH) initiative (see below) has become the main vehicle for the provision of new low cost homes for rent and sale. The locational distribution of such development is determined primarily by the availability of council-owned land, but is also guided by the Council's Housing Association Strategy (Leeds City Council, 1993b). It is interesting to note that the earlier version

282

of this strategy expressed in very general terms a desire to redress the trend for housing association development to take place away from the city centre, and to ensure that finances for regeneration "are spent wisely as part of a targeted approach" (Leeds City Council, 1992c, p.24). However, following the appointment of a Research Officer funded jointly by Leeds City Council and LPH and the establishment of a Strategy Group, the document for 1994/95 plots in detail the distribution of housing needs across the city and outlines plans to undertake a stock condition survey across all tenures, which taken together should facilitate effective targeting of resources in the future (Leeds City Council, 1993b).

Given this strategic framework, the next section examines the targeting of public sector housing resources in Leeds and considers the factors which determine the pattern of investment.

## Housing investment in Leeds

Public sector housing investment is directed firstly through the Department of the Environment to the local authority capital programme, and secondly through the Housing Corporation to housing associations. The local authority capital programme includes all capital investment in council-owned stock, incorporating any funding allocated under Estate Action, as well as private sector urban renewal. There are, therefore, potentially three dimensions to the targeting of resources within the city: local authority capital expenditure on council-owned stock; local authority expenditure on private sector renewal activity, and housing association development.

*Local authority capital programme*

An examination of local authority capital spending on housing in Leeds in 1987/88 as compared to 1993/94 demonstrates a dramatic shift away from new build towards the rehabilitation of the local authorities own stock, particularly under the Estate Action Initiative. In 1987/88 new build accounted for £6.5m or 20 per cent of spending; by 1993/94 this had fallen to £66,900, or less than one per cent. Over the same period, Estate Action investment rose dramatically from £917,000 (three per cent) to £8.15m (21 per cent). These figures bear witness to the strength of Government policy at local level, in particular the pressure on local authorities to concentrate upon planned maintenance and the regeneration of run-down estates. What is perhaps more disturbing, however, is the decline in spending on local authority miscellaneous properties, mainly older terraced housing in inner city areas, from £2.3m (seven per cent) to £1.02m (three per cent). This has occurred despite a stated commitment to urban renewal at the local level, providing one of a range of factors indicative of reduced activity in traditional inner city renewal.

Analysis of local authority capital investment by location in 1987/88 and 1993/4, reveals that the distribution of resources in both corresponds largely to the pattern of existing council housing within the city. However, a much greater degree of targeting is apparent in 1993/4 relative to 1987/88. Local authority capital expenditure in 1987/88 was much more dispersed, covering a large area of the city, with slightly higher levels of spending in three high stress areas and one area of redevelopment following the clearance of defective council dwellings. By 1993/94 the targeted programmes were almost entirely focused within the inner city, and those outside were just adjacent to the boundary. In particular, a much greater level of investment than elsewhere was targeted on just three wards, namely Hunslet, Richmond Hill and Burmantofts.

*Private sector housing renewal*

Leeds has a long history of area-based urban renewal activity, having declared 23 GIAs and 22 HAAs containing 9,000 properties, in the twenty years between Housing Act 1969 and the Local Government and Housing Act 1989 (Leeds City Council, 1990). In 1985 the council implemented its first Urban Renewal Area Strategy, providing a mechanism for targeting resources upon spatially concentrated housing need, predominantly within the inner city. This local initiative was non-statutory and carried no extra subsidy, but represented a relatively early strategic and enabling approach to urban renewal, using a range of tools to facilitate inner city regeneration. The selected areas benefited from specific local authority housing activity, such as targeted discretionary grants, private sector enforcement action, and miscellaneous property improvement. This was supplemented by new build and rehabilitation by housing associations, environmental improvement secured using Urban Programme funds and the resources of other local authority departments, and Urban Programme support for Commercial Improvement Areas located within or adjacent to areas of housing activity.

Private sector housing renewal is a constituent part of the overall local authority capital programme, the relevant legal and administrative framework being provided by the Local Government and Housing Act 1989. Enacted within the context of the local authority enabling role, and embracing the pervading ethos of individual responsibility and private sector involvement, this legislation introduced a new fitness standard as a trigger to intervention, most notably mandatory grants, and established Renewal Areas as a comprehensive and co-ordinated approach to housing renewal.

Initially, this revised renewal policy received a positive response; it was suggested that it provided a more holistic approach to urban problems in which agencies could come together, and with stable funding and genuine partnerships, it could have made a significant contribution to turning round some of the worst inner city areas (Carley, 1990).

The reality, however, has been very different, as a shortage of funding, inherent contradictions and implementation difficulties, exemplified by the Leeds experience, have served to undermine the effectiveness of the new regime. In a revised strategy for 1991/92 onwards, the City Council acknowledged the high levels of unfitness remaining amongst the pre-1919 stock in the existing inner city priority areas, and the need to complete and protect the work already started. It reaffirmed its commitment to an area-based approach, but made the decision not to declare any statutory Renewal Areas, partly because of uncertainties regarding future funding. This decision has since been reconsidered with the declaration of a Renewal Area in Burley in June 1995.

Despite this strategy, the proportion of renovation grant expenditure targeted towards the inner city stress areas declined from 98 per cent in 1987/88 when, under the 'old' grant regime there was a greater degree of local discretion, to 63 per cent in 1993/4 under the new arrangements outlined above. Furthermore, it is worthy of note that in 1993/94 fewer properties were renovated for an increased level of expenditure. While this demonstrates a greater degree of targeting on individual properties, there is little control over their geographical distribution. This is because, paradoxically, although resources are constrained, along with other areas of local authority housing expenditure, the grant regime is highly demand-led, with 90 per cent of expenditure nationally being spent on mandatory grants (Walton, 1993). This has had the effect of squeezing out discretionary grants, as mandatory grants linked to unfitness, created a scatter-gun approach to investment, rather than a more strategic, programmed and cost-effective approach.

*Investment by housing associations*

Housing Corporation allocations to housing association schemes in Leeds in the years 1987/88 and 1993/94, provide an indication of the type of schemes prioritised and the locational distribution of resources. During this period there was an increase in the overall Housing Corporation programme from £9.9m to £17.1m, an indication of the enhanced status given to housing associations as social housing providers. A second marked difference was the dramatic shift from traditional rehabilitation to new build. In 1987/88, 55 per cent of the allocation was spent on traditional rehabilitation in the older inner city areas as compared to only eight per cent in 1993/94. At the same time new house building increased from 45 per cent to 84 per cent of the programme. In addition, housing association rehabilitation on ex-local authority estates emerged to take up a proportion of the allocation, again apparently at the expense of traditional rehabilitation schemes.

In 1987/88, all housing association new house building was contained within the inner city boundary, being focused upon just four wards, two of which have particularly high levels of unemployment and high proportions of ethnic minority households. Within the context of an enhanced level of spending and new financial arrangements in 1993/94, the pattern of investment changed in two ways. Firstly, there was an overall geographical dispersion of schemes, with new developments in twelve of the city's wards, six of which were outside the inner city boundary. At the same time there was more intensive activity in some wards, for example Burmantofts, which corresponds with the focus of local authority attention, particularly under Estate Action.

It has already been noted that there has been an overall reduction in traditional rehabilitation by housing associations since 1987/88. In 1987/88 there was a focus of activity in Chapel Allerton, for example, a ward with one of the highest concentrations of ethnic minority households in Leeds and higher than average unemployment. There was also investment in this type of work in six other inner city wards and two wards just outside the boundary. In 1993/94, in contrast, there was a much lower overall level of rehabilitation work, with a notable shift in favour of ex-local authority stock rehabilitation, linked to Estate Action on run-down ex-council property, as opposed to the traditional rehabilitation of older terraced housing previously associated with housing associations.

When considering total Housing Corporation inputs, the entire programme in 1987/88 was focused upon the inner city with the exception of some limited activity in Weetwood and Beeston, just outside the inner city boundary. The most concentrated effort in 1987/88 was targeted towards the Headingley, Chapel Allerton and University wards, where the greatest concentration of ethnic minority households are found. The picture is somewhat different in 1993/94 with a much more dispersed programme generally, albeit with pockets of more intense activity in a number of key inner city wards.

Given the local authority's repeated preference for targeted investment, the most obvious explanation for these more recent dispersed patterns of development lies with the new funding regime under which housing associations operate. Specifically, legislation has sought to: increase the amount of housing which could be provided for a given amount of public money by introducing mixed public/private funding; improve the efficiency of housing associations by exposing them to development risk; and, introduce assured tenancies at economic rents which would allow them to repay private loans (Cope, 1990). At the same time, the Housing Corporation's value-for-money policy now requires housing associations to compete for funding on the basis of selecting the most economical schemes (in terms of location, built form and procurement method) which address identified housing need. The overall effect is, therefore, to coerce housing associations into cheaper, less risky development opportunities, particularly new build on out-of-town green field sites, rather than riskier, more expensive inner city rehabilitation.

## Leeds Partnership Homes (LPH)

Much of the housing association investment discussed above has, since 1991, been channelled through Leeds Partnership Homes (LPH) Ltd, a three year partnership between Leeds City Council and five local housing associations. The scheme was conceived in 1988, as a response to growing competition for the allocation of both local authority and housing association resources, and intensifying housing need due to the deterioration of existing stock and demand for new homes. It took three years of protracted negotiations to develop, emerging as one of the largest, and most innovative social housing initiatives in the country.

Fundamental to the scheme was the transfer of council-owned land worth approximately £33m, which was either to be used by housing associations to develop affordable social housing, or, in the case of higher value sites, sold to raise development profit which is then reinvested in social housing. This land value was matched by £33m of Housing Association Grant committed by the Housing Corporation, which when supplemented by private finance gave rise to a total programme worth approximately £100m. The original proposal was to build 1,800 homes to rent and 300 low cost homes for sale, and included a five year local authority nomination and rental agreement. For the city council, the partnership provided a mechanism whereby it could use its existing land assets to secure much needed low cost rented accommodation.

LPH represented the manifestation of the enabling approach in a highly ambitious and direct form. The three year legal and political negotiations are testimony to the dilemma it presented to Ministers. On the one hand, Leeds City Council was taking on board its enabling role in a most imaginative and entrepreneurial way. On the other, its total commitment and direct input required the relaxation of legal provisions and debt redemption rules which would allow it to use 100 per cent of the value of its land on social housing

287

projects in the city. In the event, therefore, whilst much of the initial impetus came from the senior local authority and housing association officers in developing proposals, the fact that there was all-party support among councillors and local MPs, who were able to provide the requisite political input, probably secured the initiative.

Whilst housing partnerships are by no means unique, particularly in the 1990s, Leeds Partnership Homes is notable for its relatively long-term and holistic approach, and the scale of investment it has generated. These features have helped to secure a housing programme which otherwise would not have been possible. By March 1995, a total of 3,933 rent and low cost homes for sale were either completed, on-site or planned. LPH has attracted additional Housing Corporation funding for the city and provided some continuity in the development programmes of the housing associations involved, as well as giving rise to other, perhaps more intangible benefits associated with collaborative working.

The pattern of housing association development in Leeds, facilitated through this partnership, has already been discussed. However, the influence of the partnership scheme in this respect cannot be ignored. Since the LPH initiative is based primarily on land and property gifted by the local authority, the location of these assets must inevitably have influenced the nature and distribution of development activity undertaken. Although the choice between social housing development and subsidy raising through sale to private developers could be made entirely on the basis of identified need, there was also clearly a financial appraisal to be made with respect to each site. There was, therefore, the potential here for LPH to engineer particular patterns of investment and indeed there were cases of low cost home ownership or speculative building on some sites where this had previously not been considered. However, given that the most valuable sites are most likely to be those in areas of least need, there seems unlikely to have been any tension between the need to develop social housing and the desire to sell for profit.

Notwithstanding the benefits and achievements of LPH, the scheme has not been without its problems. Firstly, because the package has been dependent on economic variables, most notably the value of land and the state of the construction industry, there has been an element of risk involved. In this respect LPH has operated in a favourable period in terms of building costs, but conversely, the early 1990s have been a time of falling land prices, and for this reason, some of the profit-raising sites have not raised the level of funds originally anticipated. By March 1995, land to the value of £27.06m had been acquired from the city council, of which £16.76m worth had been transferred to housing associations for development and £10.3m worth had been used to raise subsidy.

Secondly, although the partnership was able to facilitate a relatively secure three year programme for the five housing associations within the partnership, and had advantages to the additional 'beneficiary associations,' it was based on a very specific achievement model of financial and legal contractual arrangements. In consequence there have been other housing associations which effectively became excluded from development in Leeds because of the way the Housing Corporation's development programme for the city was tied to the partnership. There has also been only one scheme completed with Leeds Development Corporation, perhaps a reflection of local political tensions (see Chapter 2). There has, however, been a greater degree of flexibility with respect to private sector partners, where LPH has worked with a whole range of firms, chosen on a project-by-project basis. What is notable about the nature of the partnerships is that they have been entirely 'top-down,' and although individual housing associations involve tenants to a greater or lesser extent, there has been apparently very little community involvement in the major decisions about housing investment patterns. Finally, there is the danger that as a result of the very formal and legal basis of LPH, that in the longer term innovation and further development could be stifled. Having completed its originally intended three year life, the door is now open for the city to re-examine the political and economic environment in which it has to meet housing need, to explore new initiatives and funding opportunities, such as community care and SRB and perhaps find new, more flexible arrangements for the future.

## Conclusions

This chapter has examined the pattern of public sector housing investment in Leeds in relation to patterns of housing and social inequality, in the context of changing local and national policy agendas. The emergence of an enabling role for the city council is clearly demonstrated, most evident through the Leeds Partnership Homes Initiative, but also by the current emphasis upon strategic planning exemplified in the Urban Renewal (1990) and Housing Association (1993) strategies. Whilst collaborative working in Leeds has given rise to tangible benefits in terms of housing investment, there are continuing difficulties imposed by inherent contradictions between financially-led development requirements and the desire to focus on areas of greatest housing need. In consequence, investment decisions are not based on the pursuit of a single, common goal, but on a variety of goals, reflecting different administrative frameworks and the ever-changing criteria for securing funding.

With respect to local authority capital investment, an increased emphasis on estate-based regeneration has emerged in Leeds, reflecting the national trend. Nevertheless, the scale of the maintenance problem means that a large proportion of the budget is still allocated to programmes which are not based upon concerted area-based action. There are still many areas within the city which cannot be prioritised but which, in a climate of more readily available resources, would benefit from a comprehensive and concentrated regeneration effort.

The Leeds experience illustrates the current problems associated with private sector renewal. Competing demands have prevented the local authority from declaring any Renewal Areas and are undermining efforts to target renovation grants into inner city priority areas. The legislative framework has forced the 'pepper-potting' of grants to deal with individual unfit properties at the expense of area based approaches. This situation has now been acknowledged by the Government and new proposals in the 1995 White Paper (Department of Environment, 1995) will make grants to remedy and unfitness and disrepair discretionary, thereby allowing the council more scope for making better use of resources through targeting on area-based renewal.

Private sector renewal in Leeds has also been jeopardised by the reduction of housing association activity on this type of scheme. As in other cities, housing associations have recently concentrated primarily on new build, combined with an emerging involvement in ex-local authority estate regeneration, and are now carrying out very little traditional rehabilitation. However, the tide now seems to be about to turn here as well. The 1995 White Paper places regeneration firmly back on the agenda, looking in particular for much better use of urban land: "The Government will challenge private developers, public bodies and housing associations to bring forward development proposals on major brownfield sites in key urban areas" (Department of Environment, 1995). Indeed, the Housing Corporation has made explicit its policy to prioritise schemes contributing to urban renewal and rehabilitation, with over 70 per cent of the allocation in the North East Region being devoted to such projects in 1995/96 (Mason, 1995, p.32). However, this does not mean, apparently, that there will be a return to the traditional forms of rehabilitation to individual properties, but rather a further move to a more holistic partnership approach which mixes renovation with new build on cleared sites, either on SRB-supported council estates or in areas which are covered by a local authority strategy for upgrading poor condition private sector housing (Mason, 1995).

The Leeds Partnership Homes initiative demonstrates the commitment of the city council and key housing agencies to find imaginative and effective solutions to housing need and urban deprivation. As the three year programme has now reached its conclusion, this allows the opportunity to explore new funding opportunities and forge new partnerships. Whilst the Single Regeneration Budget recognises the need to deal with complex social and economic problems within a comprehensive approach, there is a fear that the role of housing in urban regeneration will once again be marginalised, and therefore the importance of developing partnerships with non-housing agencies cannot be over-emphasised. Similarly, the continued expansion of community care affords new opportunities to work collaboratively with Social Services, Health Trusts and voluntary agencies, as well as the private sector. Finally, although there has been some attempt to involve residents in the management and development of their estates, the level and nature of participation varies considerably throughout the city and key investment decisions have tended to be predominantly 'top-down.' Whilst the level and nature of involvement desired by tenants will vary and should reflect what they themselves want, there are potential benefits which need to be recognised. Meaningful participation in a regeneration strategy invariably helps in the identification of both problems and solutions, whilst facilitating a process of building communities from within.

## References

Airaud, M. (1993), 'Analyse Sur L'Efficacit De La Politique Des Villes En Matiere De Lodgements: Une Etude de Cas Leeds,' University of Bordeaux in association with the University of Leeds.

Carley, M. (1990), *Housing and Neighbourhood Renewal,* PSI, London.

DoE. (1987), *Finance for Housing Associations. The Government's Proposals,* HMSO, London, cited by Cope, H. (1990), *Housing Associations: policy and practice,* Macmillan, London.

Department of Environment (1995), *Our Future Homes,* HMSO, London.

English, J. (1979), 'Access and deprivation in local authority housing,' in Jones, C. (ed) *Urban Deprivation and the Inner City,* Croom Helm, London.

Forrest, R. and Murie, A. (1980), 'Housing Market Processes and the Inner City,' SSRC, London.

Gibson, M. and Langstaff, M. (1982), *An Introduction to Urban Renewal,* Hutchinson, London.

Holterman, S. (1978), 'The welfare economics of priority area policies,' *Journal of Social Policy,* 7 (1), 23-40.

Kearns, A. (1990), 'Housing policy, deprivation and space: the case for stress areas,' *Policy and Politics,* 18 (2), 119-134.

Lawless, P, (1989), *Britain's Inner Cities,* Paul Chapman, London.

Leeds City Council (1990), 'Housing Investment Programme 1991/92

Submission: Supplementary Report II: Urban Renewal,' Department of Housing Services, Leeds.

Leeds City Council (1992a), 'Housing Investment Programme 1993/4,' Department of Housing Services, Leeds.

Leeds City Council, (1992b), *Leeds Unitary Development Plan: Draft Plan, Vol. 1,* Department of Planning, Leeds.

Leeds City Council (1992c), 'Housing Association Strategy,' Department 6 Housing Services, Leeds.

Leeds City Council (1993a), 'Leeds European Action Plan: the case for Leeds' Inner City to qualify as an Objective 2 Area,' Leeds City Council, Leeds.

Leeds City Council (1993b), 'Housing Association Strategy 1994/95,' Department of Housing Services, Leeds.

Maclennan, D. (1985), 'Urban housing rehabilitation: an encouraging British example,' *Policy and Politics,* 13 (4), 413-429.

Maclennan, D., Gibb, K., and More, A. (1990) *Paying for Britain's Housing,* Joseph Rowntree Foundation, York.

Mason, P. (1995), 'Green shoots from brownfields,' *Housing,* 3 (4), May.

Mason, T. (1979), 'Politics and planning of urban renewal in the private sector,' in Jones, C. (ed) *Urban Deprivation and the Inner City,* Croom Helm, London.

Page, D. (1993), *Building For Communities,* Joseph Rowntree Foundation, York.

Paris, C. and Blackaby, R. (1979), *Not Much Improvement,* Heinemann, London.

Regional Equity Group of Housing Associations (1992), *Regional Equity? Policy for the Effective Regeneration of the North's Housing,* University of Newcastle Upon Tyne on behalf of the Regional Equity Group of Housing Associations, Newcastle.

Sharples, S. (1995), 'Power to the People,' *Housing,* 31 (5), June.

Walton, P. (1993), 'The future grant system,' unpublished paper, Institute of Housing Conference, Harrogate.

# 17 Black communities and processes of exclusion

*Max Farrar*

## Introduction

This chapter focuses on the inner area of Leeds popularly known as Chapeltown, the neighbourhood inhabited by the majority of Leeds' black citizens. It addresses one of the key themes of the book, the 'invisible divides' in the city; in particular the partition that still exists between black people, and their principal area of settlement, and 'white' Leeds. It traces the physical and social construction of this area as an excluded site of the Other, a 'zone apart' from the rest of Leeds from the post 1918-period onwards. It argues the paradoxical view that, simultaneously with their injection of significant amounts of material and political capital into the area from the 1970s onwards, the city council and the government have, perhaps unwittingly, continued the process of excluding the black communities who live in this area from the mainstream of city life. The explanation of this paradox is sought in an analysis of the physical and ideological construction of social space, in political decisions about the built environment, and in the impact of global processes of economic re-structuring on the material and social lives of the black peoples of Chapeltown.

## Theorising inclusion/exclusion

First, let me make clear what I mean by 'inclusion' (and its opposite). Inclusion and exclusion are social practices which may be undertaken by individuals or groups of all types (from tenants associations to council departments). Like all social processes, they have both material and cognitive dimensions. In the 1990s, in an English city like Leeds, the material context in which these activities are situated is one of global economic and social transformation. The elements of the practice of inclusion and exclusion which I have referred to as cognitive are best understood by reference to the concept of discourse. Only those actors with a specific intellectual training will offer a fully worked out theory to justify their practices; most people will employ more or less consistent sets of ideas, which they might present as common sense, to explain why they engage in inclusionary or exclusionary action, if, indeed, they are even aware that they are doing so. Enlarging slightly on the definition offered in O'Sullivan et al. (1994, pp.92-4), I use the concept of discourse as a shorthand for articulation of these more or less consistent sets of ideas that people use to make sense of the world as they see it. When discourses express the values of particular social, political or economic interest groups, they are referred to as ideologies. As Eagleton (1991, p.9) points out: "You could not decide whether a statement was ideological or not by inspecting it in isolation from its discursive context."

Discourses which focus on the interaction between social groups can often be analyzed in terms of their underlying references to an opposition between a 'positively defined Self' and the 'negatively defined Other'. English history is littered with hostile representations of other cultures (Miles, 1989, pp.11-40). Anti-racist discourse, at its best, contains explicit efforts to subvert this formulation of the Self/Other division. Anti-racists recognise that the discursively constructed 'positively defined Self' - the "true-born Englishman/woman" - for most white people in post-colonial England is historically structured by imperialist domination of Others, and that the negatively defined Other is embedded in racist discourse.

Social policies arise sometimes from academically elaborated theory, with its cloak of objectivity, but more often they arise from discourses which openly express political ideologies. I regard as 'inclusionary' those policies which emerge from theories or discourses which challenge the Self/Other divide that has historically structured the thinking of most of the white, Christian people of England. These will usually ally themselves with ideologies of the left. Inclusionary discourses, further, are underpinned by the theory that inclusion is restricted in circumstances of social subordination, that inclusion is only fully possible when subordinate groups develop real, independent social authority. Thus, inclusionary policies are those which enhance the social, economic and political power of groups in subordinate positions in society; in short, they promote the autonomy of the marginal groups. These policies ensure that people cross social boundaries, and that groups symbolically defined as negative/Other shed the hostile representations that surround them and enter the mainstream of society as equals. In contrast, exclusionary discourses and policies are those that, whatever their stated intentions, maintain the Self/Other distinctions inherited from imperial history, circumscribe the development of the autonomy of subordinate groups, inhibit social equality and preserve social boundaries.

This chapter investigates, in turn, the discursive and symbolic aspects of exclusion in Leeds, the social and political policies (particularly those of the city council) which have been generated alongside these discourses, and the global economic context in which these practices have taken place.


## Producing the space and constructing the Other

An understanding of the social production of space, in both material and ideological terms, is the basis for understanding the modes in which the inhabitants of an area of a city - in this case, the black residents of Chapeltown - are denied access to important features of the social, cultural and economic life of a city. Henri Lefebvre has argued that:

> Space has been shaped and molded from historical and natural elements, but this has been a political process. Space is political and ideological. It is a product literally filled with ideologies (Lefebvre, 1976, p.31).

While Sayer is right to criticise Lefebvre for using the word 'space' here when the word 'territory' is more apt (Sayer, 1985, p.60), the construction of Chapeltown is usefully understood within Lefebvre's theoretical framework. This land, a few square miles situated just to the north of the city centre, was acquired, from the sixteenth century onwards, by families whose heads became Lord Mexborough and Earl Cowper, and sold by them in the latter quarter of the nineteenth century. The third substantial landowner, a Mr Brown, also sold his territory in this period, and it was rapidly developed into large, terraced (and some detached) houses fit for the burgeoning Leeds bourgeoisie (Treen, 1982). This activity was political in the narrow sense of the word. Cowper and Mexborough had initially intended to reserve their land for the rich, and to make the richest pickings, by attempting, earlier in the nineteenth century to sell in ten acre plots. No purchasers could at that time be found, but from 1875 onwards surburbanisation proceeded with the sale of plots large enough for exclusive middle class housing to be erected. Ford and Warren, Brown's agents, were assiduous in their efforts to ensure that the lower orders kept their distance. In correspondence to another Brown agent, they bemoan the failure to control every aspect of the building in the area. One decision, they complain, "removes all line of demarcation between the better houses and the cheaper ones which is most necessary if we are to sell our land to best advantage" (WYAS, BEP, 3rd January 1896).

If relationships of social class were inscribed on the landscape in this way in the earliest construction of the built environment, ethnic relationships are equally strongly marked in the post-1918 changes in the physical use of the territory. These are evidenced by a close reading of an obscure novel written about the area now known as Chapeltown, but then called 'Button Hill'. In a chapter headed 'The First World War and the Decline of Button Hill', the author writes:

Industry, overflowing the confines of Lambswell and Tannersdale [Sheepscar, an area once crowded with small tailoring manufacturers, in which a leather factory still operates, just to the south of Chapeltown] has begun to invade the lower reaches of Bathwater Road [Chapeltown Road]. Not openly, with honest, unashamed factories and warehouses that look like factories and warehouses; but stealthily, insidiously. Three of the larger detached houses on the main road have been converted into makeshift premises for firms of ready-made clothing manufacturers, wooden sheds being erected indiscriminately over lawns and flower-beds. Another house has become a new telephone exchange, and another a Jewish maternity home (Stowell, 1929, pp.373-4).

Judging by the meticulous detail of the novel, Stowell appears to have been a resident of the area throughout much of the period he describes, and can be assumed to be writing here in the voice of that section of middle class opinion which resented these developments. Note that this voice does not oppose 'industry' as such; it is particular in its hostility to 'stealthy,' 'insidious' industry with its 'makeshift' and 'indiscriminate' fabrications. These are coded references to *Jewish* factories, as most Leeds readers would know. Readers who lack that special knowledge learn that a '*Jewish* maternity home' [my italics] is another of the regrettable transformations of the neighbourhood's buildings.

Here we have a hint of what Lefebvre, in the quote above, meant by space being "literally filled with ideologies." By the mid 1950s, Chapeltown is described in the Leeds newspaper as 'a little Israel in full working order,' with Kosher shops, representative organisations, clubs and 'at least six major synagogues' (Stott, 1956). The process of coding the response of gentile Leeds to this presence has become far more sophisticated. The ideological stance of the writer, Ronald Stott, is carefully obscured. A superficial reading of this article reveals a sympathetic portrait of the 'transplanted' Leeds Jewish community as necessarily close-knit because of its status as an 'exiled minority' with a 'saga of suffering.' There is a gesture towards the cultural 'Otherness' of this community, to use the concept developed by Frantz Fanon (Bhabha, 1988) and applied by Miles (1989). But then Stott goes on to make it quite explicit that Jews are 'not like us':

> Leeds Jewry, while often giving service to the city, remains an outpost of an ancient civilisation, loyal to the age-old doctrines, precepts, customs and beliefs of the race (Stott, 1956).

'They' often give service to the city, we are told, but the implication is inescapable that 'they' do not *always* put the city's interests first, because 'their' 'ancient' loyalties lie elsewhere. Stott goes so far as to subscribe to the biologically absurd notion of Jews being a 'race.' We infer that the reader is a gentile who is to understand Chapeltown as a foreign place, a zone of the city inhabited by the Other.

Although the changes in the built environment of Chapeltown in this period were not radical in structural terms, symbolically the transformation was huge. Jewish names appeared on many shops and small businesses, the material culture of the shops changed drastically, and the erection of synagogues on major roads - combined with the keeping of Saturday as the Sabbath - made a dramatic impact on the way that Leeds people imagined this neighbourhood and its people. Perhaps the most vivid indicator of this demarcation of Chapeltown as a place of the Other was the prominent part that fascists played in Leeds politics - gaining, even in 1940, the first year of the war against Germany's Nazis, 722 votes at a Parliamentary by-election in the Leeds North East constituency (of which Chapeltown is a part) (Benewick, 1972 p.292).

There is no hint of overt racism in Stott's depiction of Jewish Chapeltown, because it is impossible, after the Holocaust, for a respectable English newspaper to offer anything but a seemingly sympathetic account of Jewish migration and settlement. But I want to link Stott's clear demarcation of Chapeltown's Jews as 'not us' to Zygmunt Bauman's analysis of the representation of Jews in European society. He writes:

> Christianity... endowed the Jews with a powerful and sinister fascination they would otherwise hardly possess... The conceptual Jew was... slimy (in Mary Douglas's terms) - an image construed as compromising and defying the order of things... he visualised the horrifying consequences of boundary-transgression... of any conduct short of unconditional loyalty... he was the prototype and arch-pattern of all nonconformity, heterodoxy, anomaly and abberation (Bauman, 1989, pp.38-9).

297

Stott depicted the Jews as not loyal to 'us'; he contributed to the process of drawing a boundary around Chapeltown, the place of abberation.

When black people from the Caribbean began to reach Leeds in the mid 1950s they appear to have settled in Chapeltown because the first migrants had purchased one or two large houses there and made rooms available for rent. No-one from the Caribbean now settled in Leeds has ever suggested to me that there was any particular affinity between themselves and the Jewish residents; so far as I can gather, there was no overt recognition of their common status in Leeds as Other. Nevertheless, over the next fifteen years, small but significant numbers of people from Caribbean, and then from the northern parts of the Indian sub-continent, moved into this area as Jewish people moved steadily northwards towards the outer suburbs of Leeds. The 1971 census recorded 3,820 people from India, 2,525 from Pakistan and 4,540 from the Caribbean, the majority of whom had settled in Chapeltown (although the Indian Hindu population had begun to settle in the Burley/Headingley area of Leeds) (King, 1974). Despite the number of black people in Leeds being a tiny proportion of the whole population (2.2 per cent), within a short period of time, this area was stamped in the popular imagination with the marks of 'race' and sexuality, confirming its inherited status as a ghetto, but, in contrast to Stott's view of the Jews "often giving service to the city," there is no record of any expectation that these new migrants were bringing any benefit to the city.

The work of Rob Shields is helpful in analysing the reconstruction of Chapeltown as a zone in which the black population is substituted for the Jews as pariah, an object onto which the projected fantasies of white Leeds can be latched. Shields is concerned with 'the logic of common spatial perceptions accepted in a culture... the recodings of geographic spaces [in which] sites become associated with particular values, historical events and feelings' (Shields, 1991, p.29). He argues that sites become symbols of good and evil and states of mind: 'zones of the social imaginary' (p.30). For Chapeltown, this process starts with the irrevocable mark of its colour. For example, successive newspaper reports in 1973 ensure that no-one doubts that Chapeltown is to be understood as a 'coloured,' or 'black,' 'colony within':

### Coloured parents in school rumpus
Emotions ran high as black parents demonstrated today outside Earl Cowper Middle School, Chapeltown, Leeds, where 90 per cent of the children are black (*Evening Post,* 25.6.73).

### The Colony Within
What is happening in Chapeltown, Leeds, melting pot for immigrants

298

from many lands for many years? Black children demonstrate outside their school, and fears of discrimination are voiced at the annual meeting of the Yorkshire Committee for Community Relations (*Evening Post*, 27.6.73).

The quotation above is part of the header for a feature article titled 'A quiet unrest that could lead to black revolution.' 'The Colony Within' header is repeated the following day, with the same graphic of a black parent and child, above the second feature article, which is headed 'You can't legislate against the heart.'

Given England's imperial history and the anti-colonial revolts of the 1950s (in particular the Mau Mau insurrection in Kenya) 'black' is a symbolically negative colour for whites; black protest is terrifying, potentially revolutionary. Even a youth club report is read through the prism of white racial consciousness:

### Beauty shop plan ends in swinging club for black and white
The end of Mr Alvin Ducasse's dream of opening a beauty shop in Roundhay Road was a great day for the young people of Chapeltown (*Evening Post*, 21.8.73).

The report informs us that Mr Ducasse is a Jamaican businessman, and the accompanying photograph contains four black people and one white.

But this neighbourhood is not simply to be understood in terms of black protest and youth clubs. It is portrayed as a zone of sexual licence. In 1974, for instance, the local newspaper ran a 'Mecca of Vice' headline over a photograph of a street in the heart of Chapeltown, and a resident said that there are sometimes as many as 50 'young lasses' working the local streets (Smith, 1974). Having lived within a short walk of these streets ever since 1970, I can testify that this figure is a product of a fertile imagination, but there is little doubt that the report fitted the fantasy of the majority of the white citizens of Leeds who live outside Chapeltown. It should not be thought that this process was confined to the local press or to the 1970s. If anything, the representation of the neighbourhood in symbols of evil becomes even more firmly, and widely, established, aided no doubt, by repeated reports of murders or attempted murders, between 1975 and 1977, of six women living in this area carried out by the so-called 'Yorkshire Ripper' (Yallop, 1981). In 1986, the *Times* sent a reporter to Chapeltown, who informed his readers of the precise locations in which (he claims) the "rapings, muggings and stabbings" take place, and where you can "pick up just about any drug you want" (Franks, 1986). In 1994, a *Guardian* reporter took us inside "The other side of hell." The strap lines read: "Chapeltown, a small triangular district of Leeds, is the worst district for crime in West

Yorkshire. On the frontline, the drug dealers are busy and mobs of youths look for victims." Just as the Leeds newspaper sometimes provides positive images of the area with its reports on the Carnival and other activities, the *Guardian*'s sub-editor writer continues: "But there is another side: a strong sense of multicultural community, and many people trying desperately hard to make something of their lives" (*Guardian*, 1.11.94). (For a full examination of this particular characterisation of the area, see Farrar, 1995.) Nevertheless, the metaphor of Chapeltown as hell is the one that is most firmly established in the minds of the vast majority of Leeds' residents. And hell is the place of ultimate exclusion.

The foregoing discussion is intended to establish the view that the territory called Chapeltown should be understood as a built environment whose black inhabitants have been represented in discourse as a negatively defined 'Other' - slimy people, black people, sexually unlicensed people. While it is not suggested that the Jewish and the black populations in Leeds are to be easily equated, it has been argued that, in moving into the formerly Jewish area of the city, black people were taking over a territory which was already symbolically loaded with 'alien' meanings and which was already surrounded by an invisible boundary, demarcating it from the rest of Leeds. Foucault has argued that discourses are vehicles for social power (Foucault, 1980, p.113) and this analysis has been developed by Goldberg:

Racist discourse has for the most part dominated the definition of otherness, and furnished the material power for the forceful exclusion of the different (Goldberg, 1990, p.305).

It is not my intention, however, to argue that the newspaper reports quoted above are written by people who intentionally promote racial discrimination. Their aims might often be the precise opposite. My point is that the sub-text of these reports is exclusionary, and that they contribute to a discourse which has, at its (often hidden) root, the notion that Chapeltown's black peoples are to be held at bay. This, I argue, is the dominant discourse in Leeds, and it has, no doubt despite their best intentions, influenced much of the policy developed by the Leeds city council.


## The politics of Chapeltown's built environment

Policy makers in Leeds have, since the 1970s, consistently argued that they are promoting the welfare of Chapeltown's inhabitants. To 'prove' that they are attempting to include, rather than exclude, their black citizens they can provide an impressive list of improvements to the physical fabric of the area

300

as evidence of their commitment to amelioration of the social problems which are seen as the inevitable result of persistently high unemployment levels throughout the 1970s, 1980s and 1990s. These physical improvements, funded by the city council with government support, are listed in Table 17.1.

While Leeds' council estates, such as Belle Isle and Ebor Gardens, have had sums of the order of £20 million invested in their housing, infinitely more than the total invested in Chapeltown, Table 13.1 shows that the council, with the support of the government's urban programmes, has made extensive efforts to improve the infrastructure of this area. In addition, the government's Chapeltown and Harehills Task Force initiative spent £6.6 million between February 1986 and October 1991 on projects designed to assist employment generation, although only 37 per cent of this reached the actual residents of the area (Department of the Environment, 1992, p.54). Given this investment, it may be argued that it defies the 'facts' to suggest that exclusion is the narrative that underlies the development of this part of the city. To substantiate my case, I will examine the political processes in which these investment decisions emerged over the past twenty years, and discuss the social meaning of the buildings and facilities that resulted.

In an earlier article (Farrar, 1988) I have presented an analysis of the perspectives which underlay policy development in Chapeltown during the 1970s and 1980s. I argued that policy making was largely reactive to the political mobilisations of black people in the area, starting with protests over education in the early 1970s, developing in England's first urban rebellion by black youth in November 1975, coming to a head in the uprising in July 1981, and continuing with community-based campaigns over specific issues in 1986 and 1987. I identified two distinct policy approaches within the city council. The first, starting in 1981 immediately after the July uprising, led by the Labour Leader of the council, was to co-opt black community leaders into a council-lead Liaison Committee and to provide several jobs in new equal opportunity posts within the council. The second, led by the council's Community Education department, was to nurture and employ as youth workers a group of young black men and women, with organic connections to the neighbourhood. Combining these two policy initiators with the role of community-based political protest, we see that Hill's summary of the process by which social policy is formed is relevant to Chapeltown:

Policy-making outcomes may be determined by the interaction of three forces: political input (ideological politics), organisational considerations within departments (administrative politics) and external pressures (bargaining politics) (Hill, 1988 p.64).

**Table 17.1 Provision of facilities in Chapeltown, 1973-1993**

*1   Education/Youth*

Roseville Adult Education Centre
Chapeltown Adventure Playground
Boys Club/Mandela Youth Centre
Prince Philip Adult Education Centre

Bankside Street School
Palace Youth Project
Potternewton Park Play Area

*2   Ethnic/Community Centres*

United Caribbean Association House
Barbados Overseas Association office
Chapeltown Community Centre
Pakistani Muslim Mosque and Hall
Ramgarhia Sikh Centre
West Indian Centre

Bangladeshi Mosque
Jamaica House
Vietnamese Centre
Sikh Centre
Namdari Sikh Centre

*3   Business/Training Centres*

Pakistani Community/Training Centre
Bangladeshi Community/Training Centre
Chapeltown Business Centre
Chapeltown and Harehills Enterprise Ltd
Dr B's, Bernardos Training Restaurant

East Leeds Women's Workshops
Technorth Training Centre
Rutland Lodge Training Centre

*4   Health/Advice:*

Harehills and Chapeltown Law Centre
Chapeltown Citizens Advice Bureau

Harehills Housing Aid Centre
Spencer Place Health Centre

*5   Traffic:*

Highway construction, Sheepscar interchange
Traffic calming: Spencer Place, Bankside Street and little Sholebrokes

*6   Housing:*

Leopold Street new houses
Cowper Street new houses
Gathornes/Gantons new houses

Louis Street new houses
Reginald Terrace new houses

Sholebroke Avenue new Housing Association flats
Enveloping programmes in Gathorne Terrace and little Sholebrokes
Extensive Housing Association refurbishment schemes.

The problem with Hill's formulation, however, is that, in claiming that council departments are engaged merely in administrative politics, it neglects the relevance of the ideological stances taken by senior officers in these departments. Further, the meaning of the concept of ideology in this context must be clarified. By ideology Hill appears to mean 'party political beliefs.' In my analysis, however, stress is laid upon value commitments which are wider than those encompassed in political programmes. To understand the developments in Chapeltown's built environment the value positions of the key actors, both those actors with overt political positions such as councillors, and those such as departmental officers whose position is supposedly ideologically neutral, are crucial.

Let me illustrate this by reference to the process by which Chapeltown's built and social environment was changed in the 1970s and 1980s. For most of the 1970s, the Conservatives controlled the Leeds city council, including the wards which covered Chapeltown, and the overtly political interest in the area was muted. The Conservative chair of the Education Committee, Cllr. Paddy Crotty, however, was well-known for his positive attitude towards the black communities. Crotty provided the political backing for the initiatives of Stanley Menzies who, during the 1970s, headed the section of the Education Department with responsibility for adult education and youth and community work in Chapeltown. Menzies' values dictated a 'bottom-up' approach to the development of services. He consistently appointed locally-based teachers to the adult education provision at the Roseville Centre and he supported the appointment of locally born (usually black) people to the youth and community services at the Chapeltown Community Centre and the Adventure Playground. In the 1980s, in a more senior position in the Community Education Department, he continued to support a grass roots approach to community development with his intervention in taking over the Boys Club and creating the Mandela Centre. Menzies' policies, based on his values, were designed to enhance the self-development of local people, through education and community organisation. I would characterise his approach as 'inclusionary', in the sense that he deliberately stepped over the boundary around Chapeltown, engaged with black people in a way which did not treat them as Other, and supported their efforts to establish a power base from which they might begin to define a relationship with the city in their own terms.

Labour took control of the council in 1979, and George Mudie became Leader of the council. It was under his leadership that the built environment changed most dramatically. Symbolically, however, the most important development at this time might have been the huge new roadworks at the south edge of Chapeltown, the Sheepscar interchange. By the 1970s most of the back-to-back houses and shops in this area had been cleared and the old road system was a bottleneck for cars commuting from the affluent suburbs into their city centre offices. The provision in 1982 of six new lanes and a sophisticated system of traffic lights made a huge improvement to travel-to-work times. Simultaneously, it put tarmac and control lights between Chapeltown and the city. It seems as though the lights are always on red. Only the most intrepid would continue to walk from Chapeltown to the city centre. Instead of a steady change in the built environment from city shops to edge of city businesses, to the dilapidated buildings at the south side of Chapeltown, the commuter or the resident now experiences a vast, fast open space between the city and the neighbourhood, hardly noticing the recent cluster of new offices nestling uncomfortably between two of the three pairs of lanes. After reading reports of so-called car-jacking on Chapeltown Road in the 1990s, many commuters either lock their doors on entry to the area, or use the adjacent dual carriageway to by-pass it altogether. This road system seems to confirm Chapeltown's discursive status as a forbidding zone.

The city council recognised the so-called riots of July 1981 as a sign that black youth in Chapeltown were seriously disaffected. (It appears to have ignored the participation of large numbers of white youths from outside Chapeltown in these events.) The Leader put his considerable weight behind the formation of the Harehills and Chapeltown Liaison Committee, which met consistently from 1981 to 1992, and provided a mechanism by which officers from all council departments met with local residents to discuss services in both Chapeltown and the neighbouring area of Harehills. The strategy appears to have been to enter into dialogue with local black people, to consult them about their needs and respond to their grievances. Accepting this at face value, it can be seen as a step towards a process of inclusion. Certainly, the subsequent appointment of several local people to salaried posts in the newly formed equal opportunity units within the council during the 1980s, adds substance an 'inclusionary' claim.

I want to offer an interpretation of the working of the Liaison Committee which modifies that claim. I argue that the council's approach to policy formation and implementation was not driven so much by principled values as by the considerations of party politics. While there was a genuine commitment to racial justice, a desire to ameliorate social problems and forestall further disruption, the Labour Party was strongly focused on removing the possibility of Conservative or Liberal candidates ever re-capturing the inner city and suburban wards which include the Chapeltown area. The Liaison Committee was not intended to enhance the social power of the many local organisations who were initially represented at its meetings; it was constituted as a vehicle for the expression of grievance and the formalities of consultation. In terms of simple notions of proportional representation, the Committee was hardly inclusive. Only at its earliest, post-uprising meetings, were so-called 'frontline' youths represented, but even when the Leisure and Youth sub-group was formed, these young people did not attend, and no real efforts were made to encourage their presence. While there was a good case for not linking participation in the Committee's work to membership of a local organisation, the absence of representation from several important groups (notably some of the churches and the Bangladeshis) lessened the claim to inclusive consultation. Even at its most active stage, in the mid-1980s, the Liaison Committee's full meeting only attracted between 20 and 30 local residents. While this may seem a significant number compared to attendance at similar meetings in other areas, it has to be compared with the ability of all sorts of Chapeltown organisations to muster hundreds of people to issue-based meetings (Farrar, 1988, 1992).

Not only was the Liaison Committee hardly representative in the formal sense, it never took on the role of building independent community power. In a leaflet produced towards the end of the 1980s the Committee made it clear that it saw its aims as being: "to act as a consultative body... to help resolve issues arising out of aspects of Council services to the Community... to focus on all aspects of community development... to help provide employment, training and job experience... to develop community spirit and improve the environment." Community development theory and practice has been developed by both radicals and neo-conservatives (Martin, 1987) and there is nothing in the Liaison Committee's leaflet, or its practice, that suggests it would adopt a radical approach to its work; the emphasis is placed on consultation, with a clear implication that 'the community' is a consumer of council services, rather than an initiator of policy. The Liaison Committee was entirely divorced from the community campaigns of 1986 and 1987 (Farrar, 1988).

Finally, and perhaps most significantly, the Liaison Committee can be characterised as exclusionary because of the way that it reinforced the sense of the Otherness of the local residents of Chapeltown. At the start of its career, the Committee was visibly polarised between a set of formally dressed white people, the councillors and officials, and casually dressed black (and some white) people, the local residents. Frequently, the polarisation was audible, as local people, sometimes raising their voices, articulated their views in accents quite different from those of the councillors and officials. The social gulf between the two groups was striking. Many of the whites, perhaps influenced by the negative media representations of Chapeltown discussed above, exhibited the body language of discomfort felt in the presence of a threat. By the latter part of the 1980s, with significant numbers of black officials and one or two black councillors, and with a much more routinised style of meeting, the earlier form of the division was less obvious. While the black officers appear to have become included within the discursive frameworks and procedures of the council, the absence of 'ordinary' people at the meetings meant that the council-Chapeltown boundary had only partially been breached.

But the failure of the Liaison Committee lay not only in its symbolism and its inadequate policies on community development. It became a forum in which sectarianism within the black populations of Chapeltown and Harehills could not only find a voice, but could mobilise itself for the appropriation of material resources for special interests. The most palpable result of the council-Chapeltown liaison was a series of buildings to be controlled and run by the leadership of organisations based on ethnic and religious divisions. It resulted in three separate buildings for factions within the Sikh community, separate buildings for Pakistani muslims and Bangladeshi muslims, separate buildings for Jamaicans, Barbadians, the United Caribbean Association and 'West Indians,' and a separate building for the Vietnamese. Mudie's final act as Leader of the council was to fund (with some Task Force support) two separate training/community centres for Pakistanis and Bangladeshis. There is no dispute here about the legitimacy of the argument that groups whose cultures (linguistic, material and religious) are radically different require support for institutions which maintain and develop those cultures. Nor am I making any particular comment on the view widely expressed that these ventures were supported because they bought votes for the Labour Party. My critique lies in the meanings that are attached to these buildings both by their users and by members of other cultural groups in the neighbourhood. These buildings, from the day they opened, became the virtually exclusive province of the members of the group whose leaders had secured the funding. They contained and expressed the systems of meaning germane to that particular culture. This is not to suggest that members of these groups are hostile to non-members. On many occasions individuals will take friends from other cultures into social events; in some education and training classes members of other cultural groupings will be present; and open days will occasionally be organised in which outsiders are made welcome. All this, however, takes place as an act of goodwill. These acts have the momentary function of countering the sense of internal exclusion that is now to be found in Chapeltown.

The strategic approach to community development evidenced in the 1970s and early 1980s by the provision of generic adult education, a Community Centre and youth clubs open to all, and by the voluntary organisation that established the Harehills and Chapeltown Law Centre and the Citizens Advice Bureau, all of which saw their role as providing forums in which the

306

disparate cultures of the area could come together, evaporated during the life of the Liaison Committee. These places, in the 1970s and early 1980s, had varying degrees of success in bringing separate cultures together, but they presented themselves in a way which made that outcome possible. From the late 1980s no initiatives which sought to investigate and develop common interests among the various cultural groups were forthcoming from Labour councillors, their officers or members of any of the other agencies whose funds contributed to these buildings. Ethnically-based institutions serve essential needs of intra-cultural consolidation, but they simultaneously reinforce cultural separatism. They may contribute to the development of the power of a specific cultural group, but in reinforcing essentialist notions of the uniqueness of that culture, they re-instate the negative aspects of the self/other division which I have identified as the basis for exclusionary practice.

## Exclusionary impacts of global forces

Many contemporary sociologists accept the view that 'globalization' is currently taking place. Waters defines this as:

A social process in which the constraints of geography on social and cultural arrangements recede and in which people become increasingly aware that they are receding (Waters 1995, p.3).

He suggests that there are three elements to this process: the economic, the polity (power arrangements) and the cultural (the symbolic) (1995, pp.7-8). The first section of this chapter analyzed one aspect of the symbolic dimension of global processes, and the second section analyzed the local deployment of power in Chapeltown. This section concentrates on the impact of global shifts in economic and cultural arrangements on the social life of the people of Chapeltown. My argument is that, as influences on Chapeltown's social life that were once geographically rooted - such as those exerted by the local authority and the national state - decline in significance, there is a contradictory effect on the lives of local people which allows for both inclusionary and exclusionary processes to develop. To the extent that people become critically reflexive about these processes, and pro-active (in a politically progressive manner) upon them, inclusionary effects are strengthened.

It is clear that the influence of global shifts in patterns of production of manufactured goods of which Leeds was once a successful producer (mainly in engineering and garments) has had a detrimental effect on the availability

307

of work (and therefore living income) to the residents of Chapeltown. An enumeration district analysis of 1991 census returns for the area shows an overall unemployment rate of 32 per cent for men (36 per cent for black men, 32 per cent for Asian men and 29 per cent for white men) at a time when the rate for Leeds as a whole was 11 per cent. Exclusion from waged work is perhaps the most fundamental of all exclusions. It is important to acknowledge that the differential impact on black people of economic recession is nothing new to Chapeltown. In 1974, when the current recession was only just beginning, a specially commissioned city council survey of Chapeltown established a 12.6 per cent unemployment rate at a time when the national rate was less than three per cent (Leeds City Council, 1974). But it can be argued that between the 1981 and 1991 censuses, the exclusionary effects of unemployment declined slightly. The 1981 census showed rates between 30 per cent and 47 per cent for individual enumeration districts within the area; no Chapeltown enumeration district in 1991 reached the highest rate of 1981. The important point is that, for the past fifteen to twenty years, around one-third of Chapeltown's men have been shut out of the economy.

This has had a heightened symbolic effect at a time when Leeds is seen (at a national level) as being an economically successful city. In early 1993 the *Financial Times* noted that unemployment for the city as a whole was down to nine per cent and gave its opinion that "Leeds has weathered the recession better than most large cities in Britain. Now the economy is stirring and the recovery may have begun" (Fazey, 1993). Lash and Urry (1994, p.152) include Leeds among a group described as "restructured cities [which]... have effected a successful transition to a post-industrial city." This restructuring, as Leigh, Stillwell and Tickell (1994) point out, is based upon a reorientation of employment from manufacturing to services, particularly the financial sector. Between 1981 and 1991, Leeds lost 28 per cent of its employees in the production of metal goods, and 27 per cent of those in 'other manufactured goods', which includes garment-making (Leigh, Stillwell and Tickell, 1994, p.76). This followed huge declines in the garment factories in previous decades - over 24,000 jobs had been lost in clothing between 1951 and 1973, but even in 1976, the Burtons factory still had 2,850 workers. Today it produces nothing. Engineering, on the other hand, had lost few jobs between 1951 and 1971, but between 1971 and 1975 around 4,700 workers were made redundant (Wiener, 1976a, 1976b).

The impact on Chapeltown's black population of the decimation of manufacturing in Leeds has not been sufficiently stressed. Black men worked in large numbers in engineering and black women in clothing throughout the 1960s and early 1970s. While the shift to service based work has provided some part-time employment opportunities for older black women, older black men have hardly found any work at all. Where younger black people have managed to find work, a 1990 survey showed that they are severely over-represented in low status jobs, and under-represented in higher positions: 38 per cent of white employed people in Leeds were classified as 'operatives', while almost 56 per cent of black employees are in this category. Only one per cent of managerial posts in Leeds are held by black people, even though they represent about 5 per cent of the Leeds' population (Law, 1990). The move to service sector industries is sometimes thought to have benefited women, and a crude examination of the statistics for Chapeltown bears this out, in the sense that unemployment among women of African descent is much lower than that for men of the same origin. But, at 17 per cent, this is still about twice the current rate of unemployment in Leeds, and those that are in work tend to be employed part-time, on low-wages in unfulfilling work. The unemployment rate among south Asian women is 25 per cent, only marginally 'better' than the rate for men, and the same caveats apply about the nature of their work. In general, however, employment statistics for women are hardly comparable to those for men, since gender-related exclusion from waged work (through patriarchally defined arrangements for domestic labour) operates strongly for all women, and Asian women in particular.

There are clear indicators of the disparities in life-styles between those who live in Chapeltown and the rest of Leeds which result from this economic discrimination. On most counts, Chapeltown is worse off than Leeds taken as a whole. The private rented occupation is twice that for Leeds, and this is the most disadvantaged form of tenure. (Figures for the whole of Leeds' black population show that "12% of black and ethnic minority households were living in overcrowded conditions in comparison to a city average of 1.9% and to 1.5% of white households and at least 38% of black and ethnic minority households were either sharing or lacking facilities or were without adequate heating" [punctuation as in original] (Leeds City Council, 1994, p.26). But the statistics do not always present such a negative picture. Despite the highly disproportionate level of overcrowding for black people in the city as a whole, the situation for black people resident in Chapeltown is not so bad. Chapeltown's households are only slightly more overcrowded than Leeds' (two per cent of households, compared to 0.3 per cent), and only a very small proportion do not have exclusive use of basic facilities for personal hygiene (three per cent compared to one per cent). Housing Associations have refurbished Chapeltown's properties to high standards, and to rent from an Association is no major indignity. Council property is not so well maintained, but the situation in Chapeltown is probably no worse than the rest of Leeds.

Other figures from the census seem to indicate that Chapeltown is not as disadvantaged compared with the rest of Leeds as is sometimes believed. Around 47 per cent of Chapeltown's households which include children are headed by a single parent, while the figure for Leeds as a whole stands at 34 per cent. Leaving aside the debate about the emotional effects of single parenthood, if income is acknowledged as a key variable in the household's success, we can see that Chapeltown's single parents do better than those of the rest of Leeds. In 18 per cent of households with children in Chapeltown, the single adult is employed, compared to 12 per cent for Leeds as a whole. In 8 per cent of such households, the single adult is registered as economically active - i.e. as seeking work - whereas the figure for Leeds is 2 per cent. Of households with children in Chapeltown, 8 per cent contain two or more adults who are seeking work and none who are in work, compared to 12 per cent for Leeds (figures derived from Table 36 of the 1991 census). None of this is to suggest that Chapeltown is prosperous, but it is intended to show that, within an economically disadvantaged inner city area, there are indicators that some people in the area are in a better position, compared to the rest of Leeds, than is usually depicted. (It should be noted in passing that statistics about Leeds are most often generated by those who have a vested interest in 'proving' deprivation, since they are usually developing the statistics as justifications for grants for projects designed to ameliorate hardship.)

One aspect of the impact of global forces on the deployment of social power in Chapeltown should be mentioned because it links with the economic dimension. The effects of long-term unemployment in the area, the ability of large scale supermarkets to wipe out small shops, and the increase in size of the service sector has resulted, for Chapeltown, in what has been called 'an emptying out of economic space of many institutions' (Lash and Urry, 1994, p.18). The decline of both Chapeltown Road and Roundhay Road as places in which local people, in the daily patterns of social intercourse that carry on alongside shopping for food and other goods, reassert the meanings embedded in their relationships with their family, neighbours and friends, might have had the effect of diminishing the cultural integrity of the area. But Lash and Urry go further than this. They argue that the emptying out of economic space results in a 'deficit of institutional regulation' (Lash and Urry, 1994, p.19). By this they imply that there is a decline in those inter-subjective aspects of power which are consequential from economic transactions and which pattern and control daily social life. They argue that this deficit, in black American inner-city areas, is not effectively replaced by 'market regulation' or 'state governance', with 'tragic' consequences (1994, p.19, pp.146-156). For Chapeltown, I would argue, the situation is somewhat different. As we have seen, although the area experienced high levels of political intervention by the city council in the 1980s - which is analyzed here as an assertion of regulatory power and governance by the local state - the absence of this kind of regulation is marked in the 1990s. But one form of regulation - the governance of the market - has dramatically increased in the past ten years as the small scale 'shopping' economy has declined. The burgeoning of banks, offices for building societies, solicitors, council housing department and housing associations, particularly on Roundhay Road, in place of small, single proprietor shops, has brought with it a new set of power relations, in which those who control local people's money or tenancies, and who have ready access to the courts, are able to exert formidable control over daily life. It should not be thought, however, that these power relations will always result in the exclusion of black people from their rightful place in the social economy of Leeds. Council and housing association offices are increasingly staffed by black people with local roots, and even when resources do not permit them to meet tenants' precise needs, their personal aims are usually inclusionary. Some local solicitors are well known for their commitment to providing the best legal services to the neighbourhood. It has already been noted that Housing Association properties are well maintained; their staff and procedures are usually held in high regard by their tenants. On the other hand, black customers no doubt sense exclusion in the absence of black staff in the banks, and complaints that the managers discriminate in their decisions about loans requested by potential black businesses surface from time to time.

**Conclusion**

This chapter set out to explain the historic process of the creation of a space in Leeds called Chapeltown in which the black populations have been symbolically, and in many respects practically, excluded from the mainstream of the city's life. But it is not intended to convey an impression of a space which has been 'emptied out' either materially or socially. If the overall impression is one of exclusion, two countervailing forces are noted. Firstly, in response to the serious material problems facing the inhabitants of Chapeltown (black and white), there is evidence of some positive government and council-funded interventions, and these, combined with some aspects of global economic changes make for the inclusion of the black populations. Second, the long history of independent political action by Chapeltown's black organisations (Farrar, 1988, 1992) indicate the high resolve of black people to maintain the momentum for inclusion.

# References

Bauman, Z. (1989), *Modernity and the Holocaust,* Polity Press, Cambridge.

Benewick, R. (1972), *The Fascist Movement in Britain,* Allen Lane, London.

Bhabha, H.K. (1988), 'Interrogating identity: the postcolonial imperative,' in Goldberg, D.T. (ed) (1990) *Anatomy of Racism,* University of Minnesota Press, Minneapolis.

Department of the Environment (1992) *An Evaluation of the Government's Inner Cities Task Force Initiative, Volume 2,* Prepared by P A Cambridge Economic Consultants, Department of the Environment, London.

Eagleton, T. (1991), *Ideology,* Verso, London.

Farrar, M. (1988), 'The politics of black youth workers in Leeds,' *Critical Social Policy,* Issue 23, Autumn 1988.

Farrar, M, (1992), 'Racism, education and black self-organisation,' *Critical Social Policy,* Issue 36, Winter 1992-3.

Farrar, M. (1995) 'Re-presenting the inner city,' *Regenerating Cities,* No. 7.

Foucault, M. (1980), *Power/Knowledge,* (Colin Gordon (ed)) Harvester Wheatsheaf, Hemel Hempstead.

Franks, Alan (1986), 'Where trouble waits on the corner' *The Times,* 1.4.86

Goldberg, D.T. (1990), 'The social formation of racist discourse' in Goldberg, D.T. (ed) (1990), *Anatomy of Racism,* University of Minnesota Press, Minneapolis.

Hill, M. (1988), *Understanding Social Policy,* (Third Edition) Basil Blackwell, Oxford.

King, J.R. (1974), 'Immigrants in Leeds,' *Working Paper 58,* Department of Geography, University of Leeds, Leeds.

Lash, S. and Urry, J. (1994), *Economies of Signs and Space,* Sage Publications, London.

Law, I. (1990), *A Study of the Pattern of Black Employment in Leeds,* Equality Services, Leeds City Council, Leeds.

Leeds City Council Finance and Housing Departments (1974) *Chapeltown Residents Opinion Survey,* Leeds City Council, Leeds.

Leeds City Council Department of Housing Services (1994), *Housing Strategy 1993-4,* Leeds City Council, Leeds.

Lefebvre, H. (1976), 'Reflections on the politics of space,' *Antipode,* 8 (2) May 1976) (translated by Michael J Enders from the French journal *Espaces et Societies,* No. 1, 1970).

Leigh, C., Stillwell, J. and Tickell, A. (1994), 'The West Yorkshire economy: breaking with tradition' in Haughton, G. and Whitney, D. (eds) *Reinventing a Region: Restructuring in West Yorkshire,* Avebury,

Aldershot.

Martin, I. (1987). 'Community education: towards a theoretical analysis,' in Allen, G., Bastiani, J., Martin, I. and Richards, J.K. (eds) *Community Education: an Agenda for Educational Reform*, Open University Press, Milton Keynes.

Miles, R. (1989), *Racism*, Routledge, London.

O'Sullivan, T., Hartley, J., Saunders, D., Montgomery, M. and Fiske, J. (1994), *Key Concepts in Communication and Cultural Studies*, Second Edition, Routledge, London

Sayer, A. (1985), 'The·difference that space makes,' in Gregory, D and Urry, J (eds) (1985) *Social Relations and Spatial Structures*, Macmillan, Basingstoke.

Shields, Rob (1991) *Places on the Margin: alternative geographies of modernity*, Routledge, London

Stott, Ronald (1956) 'There's Really No Such Place As Chapeltown' *Yorkshire Evening News*, January 1956

Stowell, Gordon (1929) *The Story of Button Hill*, Victor Gollancz, London.

Treen, C. (1982), 'The process of suburban development in north Leeds, 1870-1914,' in Thompson, F.M.L. (ed) *The Rise of Suburbia*, Leicester UP, Leicester.

Waters, M. (1995), *Globalization*, Routledge, London.

Wiener, R. (n.d., 1976a), *The Economic Base of Leeds* Workers Education Association, Leeds, citing Allen and Campbell *Economic Performance and the Structure of Industry in Leeds 1948-73*, Leeds Polytechnic.

Wiener, R. (1976b), *The Engineering Industry in Leeds*, Workers Education Association, Leeds.

WYAS: West Yorkshire Archive Service. Documents as numbered in their files.

Yallop, D.A. (1981), *Deliver Us From Evil*, Macdonald Futura, London.